# an introduction to
# SYSTEMATIC REVIEWS

an introduction to

# SYSTEMATIC REVIEWS

**DAVID GOUGH   SANDY OLIVER   JAMES THOMAS**

Los Angeles | London | New Delhi
Singapore | Washington DC

Foreword © Ann Oakley 2012
Chapter 1 © David Gough, Sandy Oliver and James Thomas 2012
Chapter 2 © Rebecca Rees and Sandy Oliver 2012
Chapter 3 © David Gough and James Thomas 2012
Chapter 4 © Sandy Oliver, Kelly Dickson, and Mark Newman 2012
Chapter 5 © Jeff Brunton and James Thomas 2012
Chapter 6 © Ginny Brunton, Claire Stansfield and James Thomas 2012
Chapter 7 © Sandy Oliver and Katy Sutcliffe 2012
Chapter 8 © Angela Harden and David Gough 2012
Chapter 9 © James Thomas, Angela Harden, Mark Newman 2012
Chapter 10 © Ruth Stewart and Sandy Oliver 2012
Chapter 11 © David Gough, Sandy Oliver and James Thomas 2012
Glossary © David Gough, Sandy Oliver and James Thomas 2012

First published 2012

SAGE Publications Ltd
1 Oliver's Yard
55 City Road
London EC1Y 1SP

SAGE Publications Inc.
2455 Teller Road
Thousand Oaks, California 91320

SAGE Publications India Pvt Ltd
B 1/I 1 Mohan Cooperative Industrial Area
Mathura Road
New Delhi 110 044

SAGE Publications Asia-Pacific Pte Ltd
3 Church Street
#10-04 Samsung Hub
Singapore 049483

**Library of Congress Control Number: 2011936634**

**British Library Cataloguing in Publication data**

A catalogue record for this book is available from the British Library

ISBN 978-1-84920-180-3
ISBN 978-1-84920-181-0

Typeset by C&M Digitals (P) Ltd, Chennai, India
Printed and bound by CPI Group (UK) Ltd, Croydon, CR0 4YY
Printed on paper from sustainable resources

# Contents

# Foreword

This book is a gateway and a guide to an extremely important but often ignored area of research: the art and science of collecting and pooling information from primary research studies. The aim of research synthesis, or systematic reviewing – the terminology varies – is to arrive at a more comprehensive and trustworthy picture of the topic being studied than is possible from individual pieces of research. Systematic reviews are now carried out in and across many academic, scientific and policy domains both in the UK and internationally. They contribute to a view of knowledge which is both practical and conceptual: one that insists on the central rationale of research as being the promotion of human welfare in the real social world; and one that requires knowledge to be cumulative – we should undertake research in such a way that what we know is capable of being updated as circumstances, time and contexts change, and as new studies are done.

*An Introduction to Systematic Reviews* is a team effort. Its 12 authors work together at the Evidence for Policy and Practice Information and co-ordinating Centre, which is based in the Social Science Research Unit at the Institute of Education in London. The EPPI-Centre has its roots in my own induction into research synthesis when I worked as a member of the enterprise where the Cochrane Collaboration – an international network of people and organisations committed to systematic reviews of health care – first began. While the reasons for thorough reviews of research and for pooling data from different studies may appear most urgent in the health care field, the logic of systematic reviewing and synthesis applies equally in all those fields which are drawn on as examples in this book: crime and justice; education; employment; health promotion; social welfare; and transport and the environment. We certainly would not wish to die because a doctor has prescribed a drug whose sometimes fatal side-effects would have been known had a systematic review of all studies of the drug been carried out; but neither would we want our children and grandchildren to be affected by educational policies which inhibit learning and motivation; and we would prefer to avoid watching anti-social behaviour escalate because no one has taken a careful look at strategies capable of reducing it. The lives of many people are touched by what policy-makers decide to do to promote health, education and welfare. It is therefore essential that policy decisions and strategies are founded on the best evidence, not only about what works, but also about what people want and what they consider to be appropriate. At its heart, systematic reviewing is a tool of democracy. It exposes the policy-making process and the work of professionals and others to the standard of good evidence, and it opens up to public scrutiny the 'academic' business of collecting and analysing research. Whoever does systematic reviews has to be clear about every stage of the process: the question the review is designed to answer; the appropriateness of the methods chosen; where the studies come from and why some are included and others not; how judgements are made about the value of particular studies in answering the review question; and what it all adds up to in terms of lessons learnt for policy and practice.

The story of the EPPI-Centre's evolution has been told in more detail elsewhere (Oakley et al. 2005). It is a key part of my own development as a social scientist, as someone who has used and promoted both 'qualitative' research and the contribution 'quantitative' and experimental research can make to our understanding of social interventions, structures and experiences (Oakley 2000a). This catholic perspective is reflected in the chapters of this book, which tell a story about how the EPPI-Centre's vision and techniques have developed in the 18 years since the early reviews of social research were done. In 1993, the Economic and Social Research Council gave us a grant to establish a database of social interventions, and we subsequently carried out reviews of behavioural interventions for AIDS prevention and of sex education funded by the Medical Research Council and the (then) Health Education Authority; by 1995 we had moved on to a programme of health promotion reviews funded by the Department of Health in England. In 2000 there was also a five-year grant from the (then) Department for Education and Skills to work with educationalists undertaking systematic reviews of theory, policy and practice. In the last decade the range of work and funders has expanded enormously: in 2011, funders included, for example, the Cochrane Collaboration, the Economic and Social Research Council, the Nuffield Foundation, the Wellcome Trust, six government departments and several other research enterprises and non-governmental organisations. What started out as a cottage industry in a basement room in Bloomsbury is now a sophisticated and professional exercise, though I like to think it still benefits from the creative intellectual atmosphere of Bloomsbury. The chapters of this book bear witness to an extraordinarily imaginative and sustained endeavour in honing the tools of systematic reviewing to the task of examining the complex world of social research.

*An Introduction to Systematic Reviews* takes us on a very particular journey through the EPPI-Centre's own approach to systematic reviewing. This will be seen by some as a strength and by others as a weakness. There is no enterprise anywhere in the world like the EPPI-Centre (so far as I know), and it has been impressively successful in developing collaborative ways of working and in encouraging policymakers, practitioners and other academics to use its services. The members of the EPPI-Centre who have written these chapters do not boast about their achievements, but there is much to be proud of in the singularity of their enterprise. First, there is the EPPI-Centre's success in promoting systematic reviews of social research and in providing a 'brand name'. Second, what we have as a result of the EPPI-Centre's work is an armoury of tools and approaches and strategies and devices for conducting research reviews in the messy world of social research. In 1993 very little of this existed. Social researchers who wanted to do systematic reviews really only had the medical model to copy – a model inappropriately based on usually quite specific 'what works' questions and relatively unconcerned with ethical issues about inclusiveness in research. Third, the chapters in this book chart another form of innovation: the development of new approaches to conceptualising, framing and assessing different types of knowledge. It has been a feature of EPPI-Centre reviews from the start that the exercise of doing a particular review has been used to push methodological development further. Questions about obesity prevention, about interventions to reduce crime, or about promoting cultural diversity in education (for example) are always, in part, questions about the best way to get at and represent what we know, and about the most effective ways to transmit these representations to the people whose occupation it is to make decisions about what is done to and for whom and why.

Some of the lessons learnt from all this have been surprising. For instance, from hundreds of reviews we know that the universe of studies that are potentially relevant to answering a single research question is usually vast – much vaster than the reviewer(s) initially thought – and that the diversity of bibliographic databases and their mode of operation makes trawling through these a laborious exercise. We have also had to confront the unhappy finding that a good deal of social research is quite uncommunicative about how it was done, and/or what it tells us about is a research design which is a poor match with the research question (Oakley 2002, 2003; Rees et al. 2007). Too much reliance is placed on our believing what researchers say they found. In a democratic world, we would rather be in a position to decide for ourselves.

When social scientist and policy activist Barbara Wootton carried out one of the first systematic reviews of research on anti-social behaviour in 1959 (Wootton 1959: Chapter 3), she incurred the wrath of many in suggesting that the conclusions of some studies could not be replied upon because these studies were not done or reported soundly enough for policy-makers to have any confidence in them (Oakley 2011). The exclusion or criticism of studies that supported cherished ideas (about, for example, the value of social workers or the adverse effects on children of maternal employment) was particularly liable to evoke outrage. Systematic reviewing is not the best way to make friends. All research, and all research reviews, happen in a social context which both shapes how they are done and contributes to what is done with them. The complicated matter of how to get the policy and practice world to sit up and pay attention to the findings of research is not a unique challenge for systematic reviews, but it is a very important one because the nature of systematic reviewing is to ask targeted policy and practice questions. The EPPI-Centre has found some helpful strategies, for example working closely with commissioners and policy-makers in developing the review process and in deciding the formats in which review results should be written up.

The view of research and knowledge subscribed to by the authors of this book is contested in some circles, where it is held to be based on the misleading idea of a stable external reality. This clash of paradigms is acknowledged and discussed at various points in the text, and it is to the authors' credit that they do not get seduced into a full-blown disputation about the use and meaning of terms such as 'qualitative' and 'quantitative' or 'positivist' and 'realist'. 'Isms' are notoriously unhelpful as aids to communication, since people tend to use them in different ways. What matters is not the label that can be attached to the method, but whether the method is the right one for the question. What matters is the question, and then the answer. The bit in-between the question and the answer is a long and careful process requiring much thought and judgement as well as dedicated tools and approaches. Anyone who wants to know more about this process will reach the end of this book much wiser and better informed and in a much sounder position to contribute their own skills to the undervalued but critical exercise of finding out what we really do know.

Ann Oakley
June 2011

# Acknowledgements

This book draws on the collective learning that has arisen from systematic reviewing at the EPPI-Centre between 1993 and 2011. This learning began with Professor Ann Oakley, whose pioneering work has advanced methods for social science research on both sides of the 'paradigm wars'. She established the EPPI-Centre and inspired a new generation of multidisciplinary researchers with a commitment to accumulating knowledge from rigorous, theoretically grounded research. We are grateful for her continuing contributions to the EPPI-Centre's intellectual endeavours. This book would not have been possible without our funders, not only their financial support, but also their engagement with reviews and review teams over many years to find solutions to the challenges encountered when requiring research to inform policy, and policy to inform research. We are also grateful to all the policy, practitioner, research and voluntary sector partners who have advised individual reviews. By working with you, each review has provided lessons about review methodology and ways of working together. We particularly appreciate contributions to debates each time we have taken our reviewing into new disciplines or new policy sectors; our review methods could not have advanced without learning from these. People coming to the EPPI-Centre for formal training, whether for a Master's degree or short courses, have made us clarify our thinking and our review methods. We have particularly enjoyed and benefited from the methodological discussions with colleagues equally committed to finding justifiable ways of drawing together research findings to inform important policy, practice and personal decisions. The chapter authors are long-standing members of the EPPI-Centre who continue to learn from all these people, and from the ideas and inspiration of colleagues who have joined more recently. We are also grateful to our colleague Dr Alison O'Mara-Eves for her contribution to Chapter 9. The crafting of ideas offered in this book owe much to the thoughtful comments on an earlier version of the manuscript from Professor Ann Oakley, Dr Sophie Hill, Marcello Bertotti and two anonymous peer reviewers. Final responsibility remains with the authors. Lastly, we learnt far more from writing this book than we anticipated, so we are particularly grateful to our publishers for their patience as the book evolved.

# About the authors

David Gough is Professor of Evidence Informed Policy and Practice and Director of SSRU and its EPPI-Centre. Prior to this he was Senior Research Fellow at the University of Glasgow and Professor at Japan Women's University. His early research focused on child welfare policy including roles in the international, British and Japanese societies for the prevention of child abuse and co-editor of *Child Abuse Review*. His interest in the study of research synthesis and research use started in 1988 by developing coding guidelines to systematically describe and assess the child abuse intervention literature. He also studies evidence use including the EIPPEE project for the European Commission and is co-editor of the journal *Evidence & Policy*.

Sandy Oliver is Professor of Public Policy and Deputy Director of SSRU and its EPPI-Centre. Her special interest involves making knowledge more democratic, through public involvement in doing and using research, and synthesising and sharing research literature. Ten years as an advocate of maternity service users was followed by an academic career developing systems to support public involvement in research and policy, nationally and internationally. She is an editor for the Cochrane Consumers and Communication Review Group.

James Thomas is a Reader in Social Policy, Assistant Director of SSRU and Associate Director of the EPPI-Centre  He directs the EPPI-Centre's Reviews Facility for the Department of Health, England, and undertakes systematic reviews across a range of policy areas. He has specialised in developing methods for research synthesis, in particular for qualitative and mixed methods reviews and in using emerging information technologies in research. He leads a module on synthesis and critical appraisal on the EPPI-Centre's MSc in Evidence for Public Policy and Practice and development on the Centre's in-house reviewing software, EPPI-Reviewer.

# Contributors

Ginny Brunton is a research officer, Evidence for Policy and Practice Information and Co-ordinating Centre (EPPI-Centre), experienced in systematic reviewing and research methods, and is also a practicing midwife, with interests in mixed methods synthesis in relation to public health and maternity policy and practice.

Jeff Brunton, Research Officer, Evidence for Policy and Practice Information and Co-ordinating Centre (EPPI-Centre), Social Science Research Unit, Institute of Education, University of London.

Kelly Dickson, Research Officer, Evidence for Policy and Practice Information and Co-ordinating Centre (EPPI-Centre), Social Science Research Unit, Institute of Education, University of London.

Angela Harden, Professor of Community and Family Health, Institute for Health and Human Development, University of East London.

Mark Newman, Reader in Evidence-informed Policy and Practice in Education and Social Policy and Associate Director of its Evidence for Policy and Practice Information and Co-ordinating Centre (EPPI-Centre), Institute of Education, University of London.

Ann Oakley, Professor of Sociology and Social Policy and Founding Director of the Social Science Research Unit and its Evidence for Policy and Practice Information and Co-ordinating Centre (EPPI-Centre), Institute of Education, University of London.

Rebecca Rees, RCUK Academic Fellow, Evidence for Policy and Practice Information and Co-ordinating Centre (EPPI-Centre), Social Science Research Unit, Institute of Education, University of London.

Claire Stansfield, Information Officer, Evidence for Policy and Practice Information and Co-ordinating Centre (EPPI-Centre), Social Science Research Unit, Institute of Education, University of London.

Ruth Stewart is a researcher at the EPPI-Centre with special interests in participatory decision-making and in international development, a research fellow at CLC, University of Johannesburg, South Africa, and a methods advisor to the UK's National Audit Office.

Katy Sutcliffe, Research Officer, Evidence for Policy and Practice Information and Co-ordinating Centre (EPPI-Centre), Social Science Research Unit, Institute of Education, University of London.

# ONE

## Introducing systematic reviews

### David Gough, Sandy Oliver and James Thomas

---

**Aims of chapter**

This chapter:

- Introduces the logic and purpose of systematic reviews
- Explains their value for making decisions
- Considers what 'systematic' means when applied to reviewing literature
- Explains how review methods may vary while being systematic
- Introduces some of the current debates
- Explains to readers what to expect from the rest of the book

---

## The role of research reviews

Research can be understood as systematic investigation to develop theories, establish evidence and solve problems. We can either undertake new research or we can learn from what others have already studied. How, then, do we go about finding out what has already been studied, how it has been studied, and what this research has found out?

A common method is to undertake a review of the research literature or to consult already completed literature reviews. For policy-makers, practitioners and people in general making personal decisions, engaging with mountains of individual research reports, even if they could find them, would be an impossible task. Instead, they rely on researchers to keep abreast of the growing literature, reviewing it and making it available in a more digestible form. This book is an introduction to the range of approaches and methods for undertaking such reviews. These range from reviews of statistical data in order to answer questions about what interventions are effective to reviews of more qualitative research trying to develop new theories and concepts. We define a systematic review as 'a review of research literature using systematic and explicit, accountable methods'.

Reviewing evidence, and synthesising findings, is something that we do all the time when going about our daily lives. For example, consider the range of activities involved in buying a new car. We approach the problem with an overarching question: 'which car shall I buy?' that can be broken down into a series of questions including: 'what cars are available?'; 'what type of car do I need?'; 'which cars can I afford?'; and, if manufacturers' marketing departments are doing their job, 'which car will make me happy?'. We then gather data together to help us make our decision. We buy car magazines, read online reviews, talk to people we know and, when we've narrowed our options down a little, visit car showrooms and take some cars out for a test drive. We critically review the evidence we have gathered (including our personal experience) and identify possible reasons for doubting the veracity of individual claims. If we've decided that we need a small, cheap car, for example, we will understand that the conclusions of a review written by people who like to drive the latest sports cars may be less useful than a review written for the 'thrift supplement' of a weekend newspaper. We may prioritise particular characteristics, such as reliability or boot space, above others, such as fuel economy or safety, and attempt to identify reviews which assess cars with similar requirements to our own.

The example above, while simple compared to the many very complex decisions made in life, introduces us to the purpose of reviews and some of the key issues that we need to grapple with while undertaking a review. Starting our product research by relying first on what other people have written gives us access to a wide range of ideas about how to judge cars, more evidence than we could collect ourselves and more confidence in our conclusions, and leaves us with a smaller task when it comes to visiting showrooms or test driving cars. Our 'decision question' drives what we are doing ('which car shall I buy?') and all the other decisions and judgements we make are based on the need to answer this question. We are faced with many different possible answers (e.g. the make, model and optional extras of our car) and a mass of evidence that purports to answer our question. We need to come to an overall understanding of how this heterogeneous set of data is able to help us come to a decision and, in order to do this, we need to understand why the data are heterogeneous. In the example above, reviews of the same cars come to different conclusions because the people conducting them have different perspectives, priorities and understandings about what they understand the 'best' car to be. In the same way, reviews often depend on judgements, not only about the methodological quality of research (was it well conducted?), but also its relevance to answering the question at hand.

Our experience as reviewers of research is that there are very many excellent studies published in the social science and health research literatures. However, there are also many studies that have obvious methodological or conceptual limitations or do not report adequate detail for their reliability to be assessed. Even where a study is well conceived, executed and reported, it may by chance have found and reported atypical findings and so should not be relied upon alone. For all these reasons, it is wiser to make decisions on the basis of all the relevant – and reliable – research that has been undertaken rather than an individual study or limited groups of studies. If there are variations in the quality or relevance in this previous research, then the review can take this into account when examining its results and drawing conclusions. If there are variations in research participants, settings or conceptualisations of the phenomena under investigation, these also can be taken into account and may add strength to the findings (please also see Chapter 8 for a discussion of these issues).

While primary research is essential for producing much crucial original data and insights, its findings may receive little attention when research publications are read by only a few. Reviews can inform us about what is known, how it is known, how this varies across studies, and thus also what is not known from previous research. It can therefore provide a basis for planning and interpreting new primary research. It may not be a sensible use of resources and in some cases it may be unethical to undertake research without being properly informed about previous research; indeed, without a review of previous research the need for new primary research is unknown. When a need for new primary research has been established, having a comprehensive picture of what is already known can help us to understand its meaning and how it might be used.

In the past, individuals may have been able to keep abreast of all the studies on a topic but this is increasingly difficult and (as we shall see in the next section) expert knowledge of research may produce hidden biases. We therefore need reviews because:

1  Any individual research study may be fallible, either by chance, or because of how it was designed and conducted or reported.
2  Any individual study may have limited relevance because of its scope and context.
3  A review provides a more comprehensive and stronger picture based on many studies and settings rather than a single study.
4  The task of keeping abreast of all previous and new research is usually too large for an individual.
5  Findings from a review provide a context for interpreting the results of a new primary study.
6  Undertaking new primary studies without being informed about previous research may result in unnecessary, inappropriate, irrelevant, or unethical research.

## Systematic, traditional and expert reviews

It has become clear that, when intervening in people's lives, it is possible to do more harm than good (Chalmers 2003) (see Box 1.1). Examining existing research is one way of reducing the chances of doing this. As reviews of such research are increasingly used to inform policy and practice decisions, the reliability of these reviews is critically important. Methodological work on reviewing over the past two decades has built up a formidable empirical basis for reviewing health care evaluations and systematic reviews have therefore become established as a key component in evidence-informed decision-making. So influential has the use of research through systematic reviews become that their development can be considered to be one of the turning points in the history of science:

> This careful analysis of information has revealed huge gaps in our knowledge. It has exposed that so-called 'best practices' were sometimes murderously flawed; and by doing nothing more than sifting methodically through pre-existing data it has saved more lives than you could possibly imagine.[1]

The logic of reviewing is thus twofold: first, that as the opening section discussed, looking at research evidence is a useful thing to do; and second, that as reviews inform decisions that affect people's lives, it is important that they be done well. This book uses the term 'systematic review' to indicate that reviews of research are themselves pieces of research and so need to be undertaken according to some sort of method.

---

### Box 1.1

## Examples: Decisions not informed by research

**Expert advice:** Dr Benjamin Spock's advice to parents was to place infants on their fronts to sleep – advice not supported by research. When this policy was reversed, rates of sudden infant death dropped dramatically (Chalmers 2001).

**Expert panel:** In the BSE (mad cow) crisis in the UK in the late twentieth century where there were many deaths from eating infected meat and '...highly problematic policy decisions were often misrepresented as based on, and only on, sound science' (van Zwanenberg and Millstone 2005).

**Well-intentioned interventions:** In the Scared Straight programme criminals give lectures to 'at risk' youth about the dangers of a life of crime, but this is statistically associated with higher not lower rates of crime in the at-risk youth (Petrosino et al. 2002).

Reviewing research systematically involves three key activities: identifying and describing the relevant research ('mapping' the research), critically appraising research reports in a systematic manner, and bringing together the findings into a coherent statement, known as synthesis (see Box 1.2 for definitions). As with all pieces of research, there is an expectation that the methods will be explained and justified, which is how we reach our definition that a systematic review of research is a review of research literature using systematic and explicit, accountable methods.

Most literature reviews that were carried out a decade or more ago were contributions to academic debates, think pieces, not done in a systematic way. Reviewers did not necessarily attempt to identify all the relevant research, check that it was reliable or write up their results in an accountable manner.

Traditional literature reviews typically present research findings relating to a topic of interest. They summarise what is known on a topic. They tend to provide details on the studies that they consider without explaining the criteria used to identify and include those studies or why certain studies are described and discussed while others are not. Potentially relevant studies may not have been included because the review author was unaware of them or, being aware of them, decided for reasons unspecified not to include them. If the process of identifying and including studies is not explicit, it is not possible to assess the appropriateness of such decisions or whether they were applied in a consistent and rigorous manner. It is thus also not possible to interpret the meaning of the review findings.

---

| Box 1.2 |

## Key definitions

**Systematic:** undertaken according to a fixed plan or system or method

**Review:** a critical appraisal and analysis

**Explicit:** a clear, understandable statement of all the relevant details

**Accountable:** answerable, responsible and justified

**Map (systematic):** a systematic description and analysis of the research field defined by a review question

**Synthesis:** creating something new from separate elements

**Systematic review:** a review of the research literature using systematic and explicit accountable methods

---

[1]BBC Radio 4, *Moments of Genius*: Ben Goldacre on systematic reviews. www.bbc.co.uk/radio4/features/moments-of-genius/ben-goldacre/index.shtml

The aim of reviewing systematically is to have such explicit, rigorous and accountable methods. Just as primary research is expected to report transparent, rigorous methods, the same standards can apply to systematic reviews. Just as primary research is undertaken to answer specific questions, reviews of existing research can be productively focused on answering questions rather than addressing topic areas. The focus on a question drives the choice of the methods to find the answers.

Individual experts or expert panels are often consulted to answer questions about what is known from research. Experts may of course have many specialist skills, including knowledge of research, practical experience of the phenomena being considered and human insight and implicit knowledge that have not been formalised in research. However, there are also dangers from this richness of knowledge not being explicit.

One danger is that the experts' ideological and theoretical perspectives, and thus the conceptual framework determining their assessment of the research, will not be explicit; and as with everyone, these perspectives may be influenced by personal interests in the issues being discussed. Second, the boundaries of the experts' knowledge may not be transparent; that is the boundaries of studies familiar to them and thus the evidence being considered. A third danger is that even if the boundaries of the studies are clear, the expert may know some of the studies within those boundaries better than others so not all of the research will have equal representation in the conclusions they draw. Fourth and fifth dangers are the related problems of how the experts assess the quality and appraise the relevance and then synthesise different pieces of evidence. Sixth, it may not be clear the extent to which the expert draws on other forms of knowledge, such as practice knowledge, in forming their overall conclusions. An expert witness in a court may, for example, provide an opinion that the court believes is based on research, but is in fact based on a mixture of research and practice wisdom. Seventh, the manner in which someone is assessed as being expert on a particular area may not be appropriate. They may not be expert at all on this topic, or they may be expert but their esteem and credibility is based on practice knowledge. A court may, for example, give high credibility to research reports from someone who has high esteem as a practitioner rather than as a researcher.

In many ways an expert review or expert panel is similar to a traditional literature review. There may be great insight and knowledge but with a lack of transparency about what this is or how it is being used. With experts and expert panels there may be a lack of clarity about the:

- perspective and conceptual framework, including ideological and theoretical assumptions and personal interest;
- inclusion criteria for evidence;
- nature of the search for evidence;
- sort of evidence that is thus being considered;
- quality and relevance appraisal of that evidence;

- method of synthesis of evidence;
- use of evidence other than research;
- basis for their expertise: (i) how their expertise is assessed; (ii) how its relevance to the topic in question is assessed; (iii) how its relationship to research skills and knowledge is assessed.

In order to address such issues, systematic reviews often proceed through a number of stages, as shown in Figure 1.1. We shall see in later chapters that these stages are an oversimplification, but they are sufficiently common for them to provide a guide to the part of the review process being discussed in each chapter.

Though the idea of systematic reviews is simple, and their impact profound, they are often difficult to carry out in practice, and precisely how they should be done is the subject of much debate and some empirical research. Identifying the relevant research, checking that it is reliable and understanding how a set of research studies can help us in addressing a policy or practice concern is not a straightforward activity, and there are many ways of going about reviewing the literature systematically. This book takes a careful look at how approaches differ (while still being systematic) and considers the issues involved in choosing between these different approaches.

## Questions, methods and answers

Primary research asks many different questions from a variety of standpoints (Gough et al. 2009), and this richness of questions, approaches and research methods is also reflected in systematic reviews. If, for example, questions are asked about the meaning attached to different situations by different actors in society, then qualitative exploratory methods are likely to be appropriate. To find out how societal attitudes vary across the country, then a survey may be most helpful, whereas knowing how many people receive different state services may be found from routine government administrative data. To investigate whether a particular social intervention has had the required effect, an experimental study may be the most powerful method.

The idea that different research questions may be answered best by different methods and by different types of data also applies to reviews. For instance, systematic reviews addressing questions about the effects of health interventions have widely agreed systematic methods for setting the scope, judging the quality of studies, and presenting the synthesised findings, often using statistical meta-analysis of the results of randomised controlled trials (see, for example, Higgins and Green 2011). However, a systematic question-driven approach to reviews can apply equally to research questions of process or of meaning that are addressed by more qualitative primary research and by review methods that reflect those qualitative research approaches (see, for example, Patterson et al. 2001; Pope et al. 2007; Sandelowski and Barroso 2007).

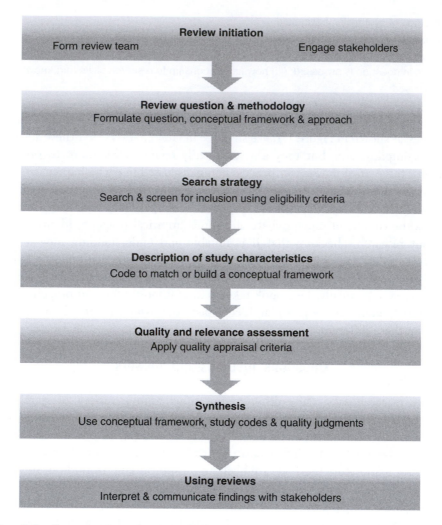

**Figure 1.1** Common stages in a systematic review

Reviews and their findings can vary on many different dimensions and these are discussed in detail in Chapter 3. The diversity of review methods we portray are a spectrum of methods spanning those reviews that aim to *aggregate* or 'add up' findings from multiple, similar studies and those reviews that aim to *configure* or 'organise' findings of studies (Sandelowski et al. 2006, 2011; Voils et al. 2008). Aggregative reviews often answer tightly specified questions using quantitative pre-specified methods to test theory using empirical observations (a deductive method). Reviews that take a configurative approach are more likely to ask more open questions that are answered with qualitative data and more iterative methods that interpret specific examples of things to address questions about experiences and meaning to generate and explore theory (an inductive method). Many reviews include some aggregation and some configuration. Reviews need to specify the questions they are asking and the methods used to address these, and this is often written as a 'protocol' prior to undertaking the review.

---

**Box 1.3**

## Key definitions

**Quantitative research:** the systematic empirical investigation of quantitative properties of phenomena and their relationships. Quantitative research often involves measurement of some kind.

**Qualitative research:** in-depth enquiry in order to understand the meaning of phenomena and their relationships.

**Aggregative reviews:** reviews where the synthesis is predominantly aggregating (adding up) data to answer the review question. Aggregative reviews commonly use quantitative data but qualitative data can also be aggregated.

**Configurative reviews:** reviews where the synthesis is predominantly configuring (organising) data from the included studies to answer the review question. Configurative reviews commonly use qualitative data but quantitative data can also be configured. Aggregation and configuring fall on a continuum and all reviews are likely to be both aggregating and configuring data to some extent.

**Protocol:** a statement of the approach and methods to be used in a review made prior to the review being undertaken.

---

With these complex choices about review methods, it is important for reviewers to have a clear understanding of the 'meaning' of the question. For example, the starting point for a review might be, 'We want to know about the effects of classroom teaching assistants'. Further discussion may clarify that this question could be more precisely framed to indicate the more specific question being asked and then the type of synthesis that would be most appropriate, for example:

- 'Do students in classes where there is a classroom teaching assistant get higher or lower scores on test scores?' The most appropriate synthesis method is probably aggregative quantitative, preferably meta-analysis (if the primary research meets the necessary conditions).
- 'How can we conceptualise the way that the presence of classroom assistants changes relationships between students and teachers and between teachers in class?' The most appropriate synthesis method is probably configurative (if the primary research meets the necessary conditions).

Once the meaning of the question is clear, the appropriate method can be chosen. Although it may seem a simple task to match methods to question types, the reality is more complex. A question may be answered in more than one way. The selection of the appropriate method for a review depends on the type of question to be answered, but also has to consider the use to which the review will be put, and practical issues, such as the experience and perspective of the review team (see Chapter 4). Also, reviews vary in how extensive the review question is (the breadth of question and the depth in which it is examined) and in the time and resources used to undertake it (see Chapter 3).

## Challenges and critiques for systematic reviewing

Systematic reviewing has only recently become a major area of methodological development. Although the idea of being more explicit about reviewing research is not new, it was only in the 1980s that some of the texts on some of the major types of review, such as statistical meta-analysis (Glass et al. 1981) and meta-ethnography (Noblit and Hare 1988), were published (these types of review are explained later in the book, particularly in Chapters 3 and 9). Although reviews of literature have been advocated for very many years (Bohlin, in press; Chalmers et al. 2002), systematic reviewing is still a young and rapidly developing field of study and methods of reviewing have not yet been developed for all areas of science. It is an exciting time yet there are many challenges to be overcome (Oakley et al. 2005).

First, there are many conceptual and methodological challenges. This book discusses a wide range of approaches to reviewing from an equally broad range of different epistemological positions. In it we argue that this range of methods is useful, but we realise that this diversity raises many complex issues, particularly in relation to mixing results from different research traditions. Related to the conceptual challenges are more detailed methodological issues. While there is a strong empirical base underpinning some review methods, many have been designed and developed based on primary research methods and on the logic of systematic reviews, with comparatively little methodological study of the impact of different approaches to particular aspects of reviewing – such as search strategies and data coding. In a sense, the methods of evidence-informed policy and practice are not always evidence informed. We need more empirical data to support the selection of individual review methods.

A second challenge, and related to the methodological issue, is the lack of an agreed terminology to describe, discuss and develop methods (Gough et al., in press). Some of this linguistic confusion arises from fundamental debates about the nature of knowledge and the role of research in this. Some of the confusion is a lack of clarity about widely-used but unclear distinctions, such as quantitative and qualitative research. There are, however, many further problems in the terminology used for reviews of research evidence.

The term 'meta' is one such confusing word. Meta has many meanings and in relation to research it is often used to mean 'about' or 'beyond' and so 'meta-evaluations' are 'evaluations of evaluations'. Such meta-evaluations can be a form of systematic review, but they can also be simply the evaluation of the quality of one or more evaluations (Gough et al. in preparation). The term 'meta-analysis' can mean analysis of analysis and so can be another term for systematic review, but meta-analysis has been used so often to refer to statistical reviews that it has become synonymous with statistical synthesis. A 'meta-review', on the other hand, is a review of ('about') reviews, of which there are several forms (see Chapter 3). Also, many words used in reviewing can give the impression that a particular type of review is being assumed. Words such as 'protocol' (methods of a review) suggest pre-specified methods and even the word 'synthesis' may suggest aggregation to some people and the configuring of findings to others (see Chapter 3 on dimensions of difference in reviews).

---

**Box 1.4**

## Key definitions

**Meta:** about or beyond something.

**Meta-evaluation:** evaluation of evaluations. These can be systematic reviews; alternatively they can be formative or summative evaluations of evaluations, including standards for such evaluations.

**Meta-analysis:** usually 'statistical meta-analysis of data from primary research studies', though the term can refer to all forms of review.

**Review of reviews:** a review of previous reviews. This is in contrast to reviews that only review primary research studies.

---

A third challenge relates to resource constraints. Reviews are major pieces of research and require time and other resources. The resources available will impact on the type of review that can be undertaken. More fundamentally, there is the extent of investment by society in reviews of research. This is not just an issue of overall funding for research, but the balance of investment between primary research and reviews of what is known from that primary research. Currently, the funding of reviews is minimal compared to the funding of primary research.

The most appropriate balance between primary research and reviews is difficult to specify but is likely to vary for different funders, producers and users of research. A research institute closely related to policy or practice decision-makers, for example, would be particularly likely to have a high balance of reviews to primary research. The challenge for all the individuals and organisations involved in research is to consider whether their needs, roles and responsibilities are best met by the current balance they take between primary research and reviews of that research.

A fourth challenge is the capacity constraints in terms of individual and organisational skills and infrastructure to undertake reviews. There are relatively few people with advanced review skills and so even if funding was available, it would take time to build up the necessary capacity.

Fifth are the capacity constraints for using reviews. This not only involves the capacity to read and understand reviews, but also the capacity to interpret and apply reviews in meaningful and useful ways. Reviews of research are only part of the research generation and use cycle. The cycle cannot work effectively without the links between research and the users of research and this may require further intermediary processes and intermediary organisations (Gough et al. 2011; and see Chapter 10). If formal processes are required to be explicit about ideological and theoretical perspectives and methods in the production of knowledge, then maybe more formal processes are required for some of the uses of knowledge.

Sixth are broader political challenges. There are many critics of systematic reviews. One criticism is the mistaken belief that systematic reviews are only concerned with questions of studies of effectiveness and so represent an empiricist (or positivist) research paradigm. In social science there are often strong views about the appropriateness of different research paradigms (Oakley 2000a, 2000b) and some argue that the empiricist paradigm is deficient, making systematic reviews deficient too. However, as has already been explained in this chapter, the logic of reviews can apply to many questions and methods, not only empirical statistical reviews; meta-ethnography, for example, was introduced as a method in the late 1980s (Noblit and Hare 1988). Moreover, we argue that systematic reviews of effectiveness, framed with the help of stakeholders, are not deficient but important contributions to accumulating knowledge.

A related criticism is that the review process is atheoretical and mechanical and ignores meaning. This is another criticism of the empiricist paradigm where (in both primary research and reviews) a pre-specified empiricist strategy is used to test hypotheses such as the effectiveness of interventions. It is a criticism of a particular research paradigm and of the narrowness of some studies within that paradigm rather than of systematic reviews. The preference of one research paradigm over another or the existence of some poor quality primary research studies or systematic reviews is not an argument about the inherent appropriateness or importance of systematic reviews, and this book does not partake in these wars between different research paradigms. Decision-makers at various levels need to have different kinds of research questions addressed in order to inform the formulation of policy or practice and to implement change, and so the authors of this book value a plurality of perspectives, research questions and methods and thus also of review questions and methods (Oakley 2000a, 2000b). We value theory-testing reviews asking questions of effectiveness that aggregate findings and we also value reviews that configure and develop and critique concepts and ideas.

Another criticism is that reviews often only consider relatively few studies and thus are ignoring much relevant research. There are at least two issues here. First, many reviews have narrow review questions and so narrowly define the boundaries (inclusion criteria) of the studies they consider and so their conclusions must be limited to research so defined. This needs to be explicit in the title, introduction and summary of a review to avoid misrepresenting the data on which it was reaching its conclusions. The review needs to state what it is not including and thus what it is not studying. A review that was titled 'the importance of X for Y' which only considered a few aspects of X and Y could rightly be criticised for misrepresentation or bias.

The criteria for the inclusion and exclusion of studies can include such things as the topic focus, the method of primary research and the quality of the research. Researchers, as with different perspectives and working within different research paradigms, will have different views of what constitutes good quality and relevant evidence. This is the nature of academic discourse and occurs just as much in primary research as with research reviews. With reviews the argument is being played out at a meta-level rather than in discussing individual studies. Reviews allow broader discussions with explicit assumptions and leveraging many studies rather than debates about individual studies.

The second issue in relation to the low numbers of studies in some reviews is concerned with the inefficient process of searching for studies on electronic data-bases. Many irrelevant studies have to be sifted through in order to find the few that are on topic. Reports of reviews will include the number of studies found in the search, which may be very many thousands of which only a few may actually be relevant. Critics use those numbers of discarded studies to argue that studies are being ignored. What is being ignored here, however, is that electronic search-ing is imprecise and captures many studies that employ the same terms without sharing the same focus. These extraneous studies need to be excluded after the electronic searching is completed. In sum, there are two related issues: what is the focus of a review and what number of studies will help in addressing that focus?

A broader and potentially more powerful criticism is that systematic reviews appeal to government because they fit with a new managerialism for controlling research. The state can specify what research it wants and how this should be reviewed and thus control the research agenda and the research results. The overt process of setting review questions in discussion with a range of different users safeguards against any such concern. Researchers and research funders are in a very strong position to determine the nature and outcome of research. Involving a broader range of users in defining reviews of what we know, what we don't know and what more we want to know, can give voice to others in society and make research more not less democratic (Gough and Elbourne 2002; Gough 2007a, 2011; and see Chapter 2). Being more explicit about the personal and political in research and increasing the potential for the increased involvement of different sections of society nationally and internationally is an important goal for systematic reviews.

Systematic reviews have an integral role in the production of research knowl-edge and are an essential part of the process of interpreting and applying research findings to benefit society. Systematic reviews play a key part in developing future primary research and in advancing methods that better achieve their purpose – so-called 'fit for purpose' research methods. They provide a potential means by which all voices in society can engage in determining research agendas.

We cannot predict all the possible roles that systematic reviews will fulfil in the future, but some ideas about methodological and societal issues relating to reviews already on the horizon are discussed in Chapter 11.

# The aims of this book

This book provides an introduction to the logic of systematic reviews, to the range of current and developing methods for reviewing, and to the consequences of reviewing systematically for the production and use of research. There are many excellent books available on different types of systematic review. This book differs from most others currently available in examining the nature of the basic components of all reviews driven by any research questions and including any research methods and types of data.

It examines formal, explicit and rigorous methods for undertaking reviews of research knowledge. This idea of gathering research literature together is straightforward; the challenge is that research questions and methods are very diverse and so we need many different types of review addressing different questions using different types of research for different purposes. Understanding the complexities of reviewing research has practical relevance for using the messages that research offers, but its importance is greater than this.

The book has been designed as a resource for four main audiences. First, it is primarily a resource for those undertaking reviews. It does not provide a step-by-step guide for carrying out every stage of every possible type of review. Considering detailed methods of reviewing for all possible types of research question, ranging from measuring the effects of interventions to developing theory to understand how things can be best understood, would be too much for a single volume and sections would quickly become out of date as new insights are being published regularly. Instead, it aims to provide an explanation of the main issues encountered at different stages of different types of systematic reviewing, and thus the thinking behind the many decisions required in any review. As we shall see later in the book, reviews vary considerably in their questions and methods, and in their scope and purpose. An understanding of how the aims of a review can be achieved is the most fundamental requirement for being able to undertake a review or for using review findings appropriately.

Systematic reviews also raise issues about how primary research is undertaken, how different approaches and methods are fit for purpose, and the implications for what more needs to be known and how the gaps can be filled by primary research. The second audience for the book therefore consists of those who fund, plan or undertake primary research. Reviews tell us what we know and don't know in relation to a question, and how we know this. They also raise the issue of what future research might be, what we might know and how we might know it. The review process thus enables a consideration of what would be the appropriate, fit-for-purpose research strategies and methods to achieve specific research objectives. It also provides an opportunity for non-researchers to be involved in such processes; to consider the research to date and to participate in developing future research agendas.

The third audience for the book consists of those who may use reviews to inform decision-making. If decisions are being made on the basis of a review, and yet reviews can vary considerably in terms of focus, question, purpose, method, data and rigour, then an understanding of these characteristics is important for interpreting the quality and relevance of that review for the decision-makers.

The fourth audience for the book will be those who have a wider interest in the production and use of research in society. In being question-driven, systematic reviews raise issues about the purpose of research and thus the drivers producing that research. They raise questions about whose questions are being asked and the methods being used to provide those answers. Reviews of research are driven by the needs of the different people asking these different questions, including all those who may use the research or other stakeholders affected by it. For this reason, reviews and their methods need to be relatively fit for achieving their intended purpose(s). These questions relate to fundamental issues about the funding and use of research and its role in society. They also relate to how reviews can be interpreted and applied in practice, thereby raising a whole range of issues about moving from knowledge to action, described in different ways as knowledge translation, knowledge mobilisation and exchange (see Chapter 10).

The book reflects the development of theory and practice at the EPPI-Centre where all of the authors do or, until recently, did work (Oakley et al. 2005). There is not an EPPI-Centre method for undertaking reviews; rather there are principles that guide our work. These include the following:

1  Both primary research and reviews of research are essential to progress research.
2  There is a wide range of review methods just as there is a wide range of primary research methods.
3  Reviews should follow the research method principles of quality, rigour and accountability that are expected in primary research.
4  Review methods often reflect the methods, epistemological assumptions and methodological challenges found in primary research.
5  Reviews should be driven by questions which may vary in many ways, including an ideological and a theoretical perspective.
6  Those asking questions of research are 'users' of that research, with particular perspectives and priorities that can usefully inform the process of undertaking primary and secondary (reviews of) research.

## Conclusion

The starting point for the book is that research as systematic enquiry is an important form of knowledge and that we should balance the investment of resources and energy in new research with the reviewing of what we know from previous research. Traditionally, reviews have been undertaken without clear, formal, explicit and systematic methods, which undermines their status and usefulness as research, and similar arguments can be made about expert opinion (even if such opinion may have great uses in other circumstances). Systematic reviews have common principles and similar processes, but can vary as much as primary research in terms of their extent, breadth and depth, and in types of question, data and method. Systematic reviews, like any form of research, can be undertaken well and badly, and so need appropriate quality assurance processes to evaluate them. To progress, systematic reviewers need to be aware of the many practical, methodological and political challenges involved in this work and their wider role in the production and use of research in society.

# TWO

# Stakeholder perspectives and participation in reviews

*Rebecca Rees and Sandy Oliver*

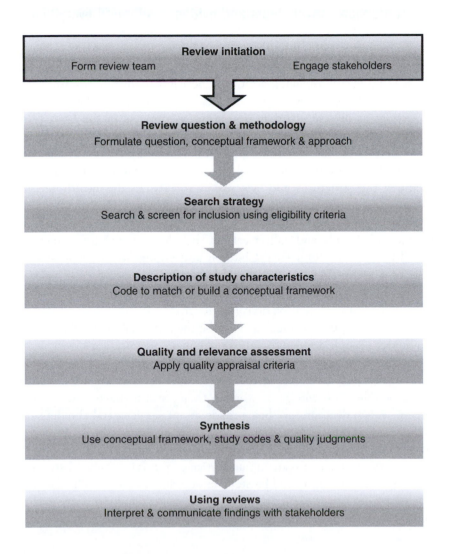

---

**Aims of chapter**

This chapter addreses the initiation stage of a review. It aims to:

- Introduce participative research and practice: where evidence-informed decision-making meets stakeholder involvement
- Describe the different types of knowledge and expertise that come with different perspectives to inform systematic reviews
- Describe stakeholder roles for overseeing and influencing systematic reviews
- Explore different models for this participation
- Consider the practicalities of stakeholder involvement in a review

---

## Introduction: stakeholders and evidence-informed everything

There was a shift in ethical and political thinking in the field of public policy throughout the twentieth century. This saw a move away from the idea that knowledge and decision-making are things best left to authorities, towards more inclusive, shared approaches. Advocates of inclusive approaches have written about settings as diverse as urban development projects in the USA (Arnstein 1969) and participatory research with farmers in rural Africa (Cornwall 1995). It is now widely held that the views of the public in particular, but also those of other people, such as employees, should be taken into account when decisions are made about the structures and systems in society. In the health sector such approaches are endorsed by the long-established World Health Organisation's *Declaration of Alma Ata*, which states, 'The people have the right and duty to participate individually and collectively in the planning and implementation of their health care' (WHO 1978). Children and young people, who stand as an example of a group that is marginalised by society, have had their right to participate in all decision-making that relates to them recognised by all but two member states of the United Nations (UNICEF 2010).

One of the concepts now in use to describe the potential players in a policy area is 'stakeholder'. People are said to hold a stake in an organisation's work when that work can affect them or when they have contributed to it (Phillips 2003). The stakeholders for public services include the people the services are established to serve, the people who manage or work in them, and taxpayers and others who fund them. When decisions are being made about services, stakeholders are seen as having a right to have their opinions considered. For instance, changes to the length of the school day would affect most directly school children, carers, teachers and others involved in planning and managing services related to schooling. These groups can be said to hold a stake in any decision about change. Inclusive approaches to decision-making would allow these stakeholders a say in the decision, either expressing their opinions or sharing the decision-making.

The move to more participatory decision-making has been driven to a great extent by the campaigning of groups seeking to improve their own lives. Where parents were once concerned about the isolation of their children in hospital, they now share the care with greater visiting rights. Where communities objected to the proximity of industrial waste, planning and environmental development now includes public consultations to widen the debate about options for reducing waste, re-using resources, recycling and recovering energy from waste. 'User groups' also exist for transport services, IT services, libraries, housing (as residents associations), and many other public and commercial services. Thus users of specific services and the wider public play a role in any act of public scrutiny if it is their own lives or actions that are under discussion, and a role in developing services and products. They claim rights as citizens and service users, hold authorities accountable and assume responsibilities when acting on behalf of themselves and their peers.

The movement for greater stakeholder involvement has evolved alongside the growth of another movement, one that challenges the idea of professionals as the sole holders of expertise (Bastian 1994; Chalmers 1995; Oliver 1997). This movement is aimed at increasing the use of relevant, rigorous research when policy and professional practice decisions are being made – so-called 'evidence-informed' decision-making (see Chapter 10 for further discussion of the use of research evidence).

---

## Box 2.1

### Key terms and how we use them

- **Collaboration:** an ongoing partnership to work together and share decision-making
- **Consultation:** seeking others' opinions, but not necessarily acting upon them
- **Communicative competence:** the ability to exchange ideas about pertinent issues with other people
- **Stakeholders:** people having some self-interest in a piece of work, either because they might use the findings or because decisions made by others in light of the findings might have an impact on them
- **Participatory research:** undertaking research together in order to generate knowledge and act on that knowledge

---

Gradually, these two movements grew closer together, first by decision-makers drawing on both research evidence and stakeholder opinions, and weighing the two before coming to a conclusion. An example of this is when women accept or decline antenatal screening for Down's Syndrome on the basis of their views on caring for a child with Down's Syndrome, their views on terminating a pregnancy and the research findings estimating the statistical risk of tests prompting a miscarriage. Then, more inclusive approaches allowed stakeholders to weigh the evidence themselves and share the decision-making; for instance, decision aids have been developed to help women navigate the evidence of effects, and consider the value they place on those effects, when considering hormone replacement therapy. More fundamentally still, stakeholders can play an active role in generating the research evidence before decisions are made together; for instance, women's groups choosing outcomes and recruiting their peers for randomised controlled trials.

As the two movements integrated, participatory approaches to generating and using research evidence became established elements of research programmes and the development of evidence-informed guidelines. Many research commissioners require research teams to involve service users and the wider public (Staley and Hanley 2008), and the participation of stakeholders is seen as an indicator of quality for the development of guidelines for practice (Brouwers et al. 2010).

These approaches, where a range of stakeholders play an active role in decision-making for policy, and in the research that can inform policy, are summed up in the phrase 'participatory research and policy'. Participatory research and policy, in general, and participatory systematic reviews in particular, are grounded in the ethical and political arguments touched upon earlier, where reference is made to rights and responsibilities, and the accountability and governance of publicly funded activities (e.g. Bannister et al. 2011; Gough 2007a; Irwin 2001). They are also informed by instrumental arguments, which assert that inclusive approaches lead to more relevant and valid research, and findings that are more readily used (Entwistle et al. 1998). Research to drive change, taking into account the perspectives of disadvantaged groups, has also been described as 'transformative-emancipatory' research (Mertens 2003) (there is more of this in Chapter 4).

While these arguments apply to individual research studies, they perhaps apply even more to systematic reviews, as these are designed to provide a shortcut to evidence and so might have a greater influence over decisions than individual studies.

---

| Box 2.2 |

## MYTHS: Systematic reviews address effectiveness but neglect opinions and values

Archie Cochrane advocated a national health service based on both 'tender, loving care' and 'effective care', the latter being informed by randomised controlled trials (Cochrane 1972/1989). The growth of randomised controlled trials and, subsequently, systematic reviews of randomised controlled trials, prompted concerns that the 'softer' elements of 'tender loving care' might be neglected and that qualitative research, so important for eliciting perspectives and values, would be undermined.

Systematic reviews can address the 'softer' elements of care, and stakeholders' perspectives and values, in more fundamental ways than measuring satisfaction or quality of life:

1  By involving practitioners and service users in setting questions and frameworks that reflect their priorities and ways of seeing in order to systematically review studies in terms of issues important to service users (Rees and Oliver 2007; Stewart et al. 2011);

2 By systematically reviewing evaluations of 'care' interventions such as RCTs of one-to-one support for women during childbirth (Hodnett et al. 2011), or hospital discharge plans (Shepperd et al. 2010);

3 By systematically reviewing evaluations of interventions designed to enhance communication and participation in decision-making (Prictor et al. 2010);

4 By systematically reviewing qualitative research about, for instance, looked-after children and young people's and carers' preferences for the care system (Dickson et al. 2010).

This chapter addresses the first of these issues. Chapter 4 covers the careful framing of complex interventions so as to address the second issue. Reviewing qualitative, as well as quantitative and mixed methods research, is addressed throughout the book.

## The potential impact of perspectives on systematic reviews

Anyone working on a review will always bring their own subjective ways of looking at the world that they are researching, and their own ways of seeing the practice of research itself. These perspectives can include ideas about the issues that are being addressed, for example which research questions it is important to address, and which factors and relationships it is important to consider in an analysis. They can include ideas about how phenomena should be interpreted, which might play out when deciding what an interviewee quoted in a study might mean by a specific statement, or when evaluating the implications of a study's findings. Perspectives can also differ on methodological issues, for example which study designs can provide valid findings for different kinds of research question, or the relative importance to validity of the different methodological components of any given design. A common way in which review teams differ in terms of methodological perspective is in the study designs that they consider most valuable for addressing a given type of review question (see Chapter 3 for a discussion of the choice of research approach within a review).

A study of two systematic reviews focused on preventing obesity illustrates the existence and potential for impact of different perspectives (Doak et al. 2009). At approximately the same time, two systematic review teams set out to find studies of interventions focused on diet or physical activity and to collate findings about the effects of these interventions on physical measures of body size in children (Doak et al. 2006; Summerbell et al. 2005). Here, these reviews will be referred to as Review 1 and Review 2 respectively (see Table 2.1).

The reviewers found the same studies, but presented very different findings as to what they judged to be effective. Review 1 included the findings from 24 studies and judged 17 interventions (71%) to be effective. Review 2 included findings from 22 studies and categorised four interventions (18%) as effective. Only ten of the studies contributed findings to both reviews. The difference in findings between the two reviews arose from eight differences in how the reviews were conducted, all of which related either to different ways of seeing the challenge of obesity, and potential solutions to obesity, or to different ideas about how best to judge an intervention as 'effective'.

Table 2.1 describes a selection of these differences. For example, Review 1 only examined interventions aimed at children in the general population. Review 2 also addressed interventions directed at children at a particularly high risk of obesity, such as those living in low-income communities. The authors of the first review argued that initiatives on a large scale were a priority. Deciding which children to include was an early decision and was built into the review's inclusion criteria (see Chapter 4).

Perspectives can be expected to differ even more substantially between different kinds of stakeholders. Policy-makers, practitioners and others tasked with developing or implementing initiatives, for example, have indicated the value to them of detail about the content of interventions, and detail about factors that influence whether or not an intervention is successfully implemented.

Potential or actual users of services, or the general public more broadly, can again be expected to differ in their perspectives, especially when compared with people with a professional responsibility for providing a service. Several studies have compared service users' and professionals' priorities for research information. They find that service users tend to highlight issues about patients' views, long-term outcomes and social and other kinds of support, whereas professionals tend to focus on technical and economic issues (e.g. Oliver 1997; Oliver et al. 2001a).

**Table 2.1** Comparing two reviews of obesity prevention measures for children: the influence of perspectives on a selection of decisions that differed between the reviews

| Where teams differed in perspective | Impact on the review's scope | | Supporting arguments for restricting scope |
| | Review 1 (Doak et al., 2006) | Review 2 (Summerbell et al., 2005) | |
|---|---|---|---|
| **Assumptions about intervention effectiveness** | Included interventions regardless of their duration | Only included interventions that ran for 12 weeks or more | Short-term interventions are insufficient for lasting behaviour change (Review 2) |
| **Assumptions about intervention applicability** | Included interventions regardless of when they were evaluated | Only included interventions evaluated from 1990 onwards | Older studies are less relevant for current environment and context (Review 2) |
| **Priorities for intervention** | Interventions excluded if they targeted populations at high risk of increased body size | Studies were included regardless of characteristics of participating children | Initiatives are needed:<br>• That can be implemented on a large scale (Review 1 & 2)<br>• For communities at a high risk (Review 2) |
| **Outcomes for judging 'effectiveness'?** | Interventions judged 'effective' only if they reduced size as measured by BMI | Interventions judged 'effective' if they reduced any body size measure | Change in body mass index (BMI) is by far the most useful measure of intervention effects on body size (Review 1) |

In terms of the topic of obesity prevention, we might anticipate that groups representing public interests hold perspectives that focus more on the experience of children and their carers. Some groups campaigning against discrimination on the basis of body size, for example, might want a review to focus on initiatives that emphasise and measure improved physical and mental health more generally. Too much emphasis on body size, and on personal responsibility for this, they argue, can reinforce the social stigma experienced by people who are already overweight, and in turn lead to poorer mental health, less healthy eating and physical activity, and, as a consequence, to weight gain. They might also argue that the behaviour of many people is so severely constrained by factors in their physical and social environments (such as the low pricing of calorie-dense foods or reduced access to outdoor space) that a review should focus on interventions that aim to modify those environments.

Figure 2.1 illustrates the wide range of ways in which subjectivity can act in a systematic review. This starts, but does not end, with the review's question and design. The choice of review question depends on who is prepared to fund a review or reviews, who is prepared to invest their time in conducting a review, and what questions these people see as important. The subjectivity of the review team and any advisory input into the review is then also exercised in the design of the review and the review tools, as this necessarily rests on their substantive knowledge and experience.

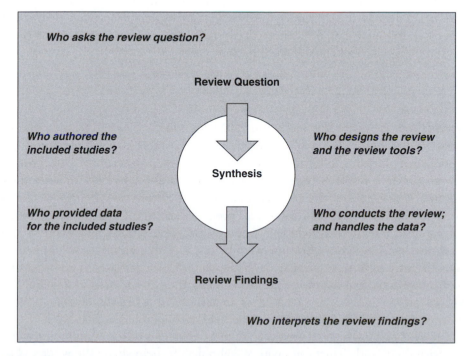

**Figure 2.1**  Points of subjectivity in a systematic review

Sensitivity to the substantive issues covered by the review is another form of subjectivity. This is often seen as an asset in qualitative analysis where the prior experience and expertise of whoever immerses themselves in the data is acknowledged as being likely to influence the research findings (Crotty 1998). The studies included in a review not only offer the subjective views of the study participants, but also frame these with the questions asked and how they are addressed by the studies' authors. Finally, before they can influence decisions, the review findings are interpreted, first by the reviews' authors, and then by readers of their work. Chapter 4 presents more on choosing a focus for a review and on choosing review methods.

Accepting the subjective element of systematic reviews implies a need to draw on a range of perspectives, to produce a rounded piece of work. Through participation, reviewers aim to make use of and account for differences in meaning and context when setting research questions, when scoping the issues that reviews should consider and when interpreting review findings. Examples that illustrate the forms that participatory reviews might take are presented later on in this chapter. First, we need to look in a bit more detail at the full range of attributes that stakeholders can bring with them to the tasks involved in a systematic review.

## What stakeholders bring to systematic reviews

Along with their perspective, a stakeholder can also bring potential to add to the scrutiny of a review, as well as different types of knowledge and expertise. These have been organised here under the headings of oversight and knowledge and expertise, although it is difficult to draw rigid boundaries around any of these ways of classifying stakeholder contributions.

### Oversight

Systematic reviews are frequently funded, at least in part, by the public purse or charities. Members of the public in general, and charitable givers in particular, can expect such activities to be accountable and thus open to scrutiny. This scrutiny can encourage a research team to question the assumptions that underlie their own approaches to a review and can result in these assumptions being articulated more fully in reports of the review. This process also contributes to good governance and accountability, including emphasising expectations for products and timelines. Involvement is also supported by citizenship arguments, where people have a right and duty to participate in the oversight of public services affecting them as service users, citizens or taxpayers. Thus, the participation of stakeholders in decision-making can also be seen as an activity of a healthy democracy, if it helps to ensure that public bodies can be held accountable for their work.

However, systematic reviewers can ask more than this of the people they invite to advise their work. They can invite stakeholders to help shape the work and so produce a review that is more relevant, is reported in more accessible language and formats, and is therefore more likely to spread more widely through stake-holder groups or networks (see Chapter 10). For this they need stakeholders with relevant knowledge and expertise.

## Types of knowledge and expertise

The complementary backgrounds of different stakeholders can also be thought of in terms of different types of expertise. Blackmore (1999) has described three types of expertise:

- specialist knowledge gained through formal study, or
- people's competencies or skills for a task, or
- their capacity to set or solve problems.

In terms of this model, systematic reviews benefit from both the specialist knowl-edge that researchers and others bring from their academic topic knowledge, and from their competencies and skills in systematic review methods. Technical exper-tise is required to formulate research questions, plan the review's methods and manage the project (see Chapter 4). Reviewers can benefit from the input of other experts who have not necessarily undertaken formal study. This expertise may come from knowing a very different job that is, nevertheless, relevant to the topic focus of the systematic review, or from having experience of using a product or a service that is the focus of the review.

Pawson et al. (2003) consider different types of knowledge: knowledge that may be gained about how organisations work by observing them from the inside; by accruing experience through professional practice or by using services; and by having a familiarity with policy issues (see Box 2.3).

---

| Box 2.3 |

## Types of knowledge

Types of knowledge include:

- organisational knowledge – accrued from an organisation's collective experience of governance, regulation and other operations of services;
- practitioner knowledge – based on professional skills, experience and craft knowledge;
- user knowledge – gained from first-hand experience of, and reflection on, services;
- research knowledge – derived from systematic enquiry;
- policy community knowledge – knowledge about the organisation and implemen-tation of services that exists in the broader policy community of ministries, civil service, think tanks and agencies.

Adapted from Pawson et al. (2003)

So, in a systematic review, professional researchers might benefit from the contributions of a variety of stakeholders who bring different kinds of knowledge. Building on the earlier example, a review aimed at supporting the development of school-based interventions to promote children's health could benefit from input from the following:

- Children and young people themselves, who hold insights into their own social worlds, including the likely acceptability of different intervention approaches to them and their peers, and ways of communicating about the issues involved.
- Teachers, clinicians, parents and others who work with or care for children, who can bring, for example, knowledge about the settings (homes, schools, clinics, workplaces, etc.) where the different components of interventions to promote health might be experienced.
- Policy-makers and managers with knowledge of the national or local environments in which policies and plans are made or implemented, as well as relevant legislation and regulations. Important policies might already have been developed, for example, by educational and health authorities, or could already be in place, to promote things like active travel, increased access to healthy food, leisure facilities, etc.
- Others who know about the findings from research and conceptual thinking in this area, for example, bringing awareness of the types of school-based initiative studied by existing empirical work, or theories of change that might be relevant.

Any of these people may also bring problem-solving skills that can help to apply systematic review methodology to the issues seen as being most important by the stakeholders.

Crucially, working together constructively requires the different stakeholders to offer their own expertise and to appreciate each other's expertise, so that there can be mutual learning. This may not always be easy, especially if people are used to thinking in terms of one kind of expertise and tend to overlook the whole range of types (Stewart 2007). Stakeholders need to engage with the issues, but also need to be able to listen to and understand as well as support others so that they can have their say. Having a say can mean either introducing new ideas or commenting on other people's ideas. The skills required for these kinds of interactions have been described as *communicative competence* (Webler 1995, on Habermas 1970).

It is important to note that the classification of stakeholders used above, while it usefully emphasises some similarities that are found within and between groups, tends to simplify the range of experiences that many people have, and underplays the distinctly different experiences seen within groups. Children with experience of being excluded from school, or those with existing health problems, for example, might well offer considerably different insights from children who do not have these experiences.

Reviewers might also want to bear in mind that stakeholders can sometimes have a particularly strong vested interest in the topic under review. Review organisations have provided guidance on dealing with potential conflicts of interest (see Higgins and Green 2011 for the Cochrane Collaboration's guidance). More generally, reviewers can report clearly who was, and was not, involved in a review, and in what way, so as to help readers evaluate potential influences on the review.

## Different models of stakeholder participation in systematic reviews

Stakeholders can be involved at any point in a review, as happened during the conduct of a systematic review about education for looked-after children (see Figure 2.2).

The young people working on this review became involved at an early point. With the assistance of a researcher, they selected the review's question. The review had been funded by a body with a remit for health and social care, but in initial discussions, the young people interpreted this widely, touching on a wide range of issues relevant to the health of looked-after children, including illegal drugs, mental health, bullying, placement moves and offending. Some people in the group felt that you can have a healthy life without an education, but most agreed that a good education is likely to support your health. Reflecting this, they selected a final review question that focused on support for the education of looked-after children in school. This direction for the review was one that had not been considered prior to the young people's involvement.

Different members of the group learned and applied several of the skills used in systematic reviewing. The group also shared its knowledge to improve the quality of the review. For example, at the stage of searching for literature, they identified potentially relevant sources of studies, and terms that might have been used by authors to describe looked-after children and their lives. They also applied their experience of being looked after to the task of judging the relevance of study findings from around the world to the UK context.

Although young people were involved in every stage of this review, participation is sometimes targeted at key stages, in particular, choosing the review question and interpreting the findings. Participation in reviews also differs in terms of how it happens. There is a body of theoretical literature on how participatory approaches to research can vary (see for example, Oliver et al. 2008b). Much of this literature has explored the particular case of involving service users or the public in health research, but it can also be useful for considering the participation of other kinds of stakeholder, and for research that addresses issues other than health.

Although methods of participation may be infinitely varied, there are a number of key distinctions:

- Whether people are involved as individuals, drawing on their personal experience alone, or whether they are involved as members of stakeholder organisations from which they can draw wider perspectives, and/or whose perspectives they may need to represent.
- Whether stakeholders are invited into an existing project, or whether researchers join in with a project initiated by stakeholders.
- Whether stakeholders are only consulted for their opinions, whether they collaborate and share the decision-making, or whether they direct the decision-making.
- The forum where people 'meet': face-to-face or in writing.
- How frequently people meet: only once or repeatedly to allow ideas to develop.
- How people are involved in making decisions: formally or informally.

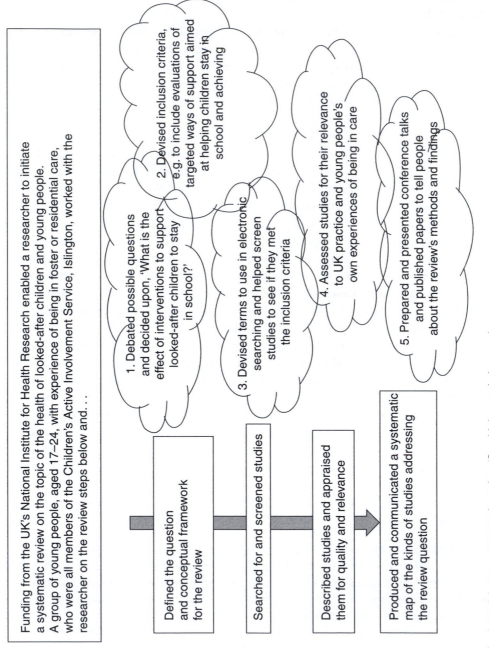

Funding from the UK's National Institute for Health Research enabled a researcher to initiate a systematic review on the topic of the health of looked-after children and young people. A group of young people, aged 17–24, with experience of being in foster or residential care, who were all members of the Children's Active Involvement Service, Islington, worked with the researcher on the review steps below and...

1. Debated possible questions and decided upon, 'What is the effect of interventions to support looked-after children to stay in school?'

2. Devised inclusion criteria, e.g. to include evaluations of targeted ways of support aimed at helping children stay in school and achieving

3. Devised terms to use in electronic searching and helped screen studies to see if they met the inclusion criteria

4. Assessed studies for their relevance to UK practice and young people's own experiences of being in care

5. Prepared and presented conference talks and published papers to tell people about the review's methods and findings

Defined the question and conceptual framework for the review

Searched for and screened studies

Described studies and appraised them for quality and relevance

Produced and communicated a systematic map of the kinds of studies addressing the review question

**Figure 2.2**   A participatory systematic review (See Liabo et al., in press)

These options can be combined in multiple ways. Table 2.2 presents the range of types of participation that result from combining variations of only the first three of the above bullet points. Within each of the cells in the table, further variation could result from a project's selection of how, and how often, people meet, and the formality of the processes for making decisions. Furthermore, research projects can use different types of participation for different components or stages of research.

The range of stakeholder involvement in systematic reviews in Table 2.2 can be simplified further by grouping the types into three key approaches: stakeholders taking control (type H); stakeholders collaborating (types A, C or E); and stakeholders being consulted (types B, D or F). No examples of Type G approaches to systematic reviews are known to the authors. There are a few examples where stakeholders have taken a lead role in directing a review (the Type H involvement shown in Table 2.2). Here researchers are brought into a review by people who hold some other kind of stake in the review topic (see for example, Garcia et al. 2006; Sakala and Mayberry 2006).

Most frequently, stakeholders are consulted individually (Type D). This might be for their comments on draft protocols (see Chapter 1) or reports, which are an extension of the conventional scientific peer review process. An alternative approach to consultation is the use of focus groups or interviews with stakeholders to develop understanding about a topic or to seek comments or suggestions. Examples of this approach are provided by reviews about travel to school and smoking cessation for pregnant women (see Gough et al. 2001; and Oliver et al. 2001b).

More collaborative approaches (A, C or E) require reviewers to work in dialogue with stakeholders at more than one point in the life of a review. As part of 'advisory' or 'steering' groups, stakeholders meet at several points with each other and the review team (face-to-face or virtually), discuss plans and progress, and help determine the direction at key decision-making stages. Work is focused

**Table 2.2** Framework for describing stakeholder involvement in research agenda setting (adapted from Oliver et al. 2004)

| | | Stakeholders' engagement with researchers | | | |
| --- | --- | --- | --- | --- | --- |
| | | Stakeholder control | Collaboration | Consultation | Minimal |
| Researchers' engagement with stakeholders | Inviting organised stakeholders | | Type A | Type B | |
| | Inviting individual stakeholders | | Type C | Type D | |
| | Responding to stakeholders' initiative | | Type E | Type F | Type G |
| | Minor partner or absent | Type H | | | |

around a group so as to promote discussion and debate about the particular review. This collaborative approach, and the various opportunities and challenges that different versions of the approach present, are illustrated by the stories of three different reviews conducted by teams from the EPPI-Centre (see Table 2.3).

The reviews illustrated share some similarities. In all three cases, while the advisory group informed or made important decisions in the review, the ultimate responsibility lay with the research team. All three of the reviews also used a two-stage approach to examining literature, in that initially they all used quite broad research questions to describe what research was available, thereby producing a systematic map (see Chapters 3 and 7). In all three cases, this map was a basis for the discussion by stakeholders prior to making decisions about which narrower question or questions would ultimately be used to synthesise the findings.

In terms of the degree of involvement, all three examples were relatively collaborative in nature. Two of the reviews were commissioned by government departments which had a policy interest in the topic areas (the review of HIV prevention for men who have sex with men – Rees et al. 2004; and the review of incentives for healthy behaviours – Kavanagh et al. 2006), although in both examples, representatives from government handed over decisions about the review's precise scope to a broader group of stakeholders. In the third example (of personal, social and health education (PSHE) – Garcia et al. 2006), the review group received funding to conduct a review in an area of their own choosing.

As for the perspectives involved, all three reviews involved both policy-makers and academics in addition to researchers based at the EPPI-Centre. The perspectives of service-users and practitioners were, however, accessed to different extents across the reviews. Two of the reviews, by inviting organisations to participate, built in the potential for accessing the views of a larger number of people. In the review on PSHE, for example, students and teachers from the collaborating school conducted a survey about relationships in school. Discussion of the survey and its findings within the school informed those who participated in workshops related to the review itself. In the review on HIV prevention for men who have sex with men, organisations that conduct advocacy for potential and actual users of services were invited to participate. The intention was that the representatives of these organisations would have access to a wider network of service users and so have a good understanding of their needs and interests, and the ability to consult further if necessary.

Arguably one of the most important ways in which the three reviews differed was in the opportunities for deliberation and the sharing of perspectives afforded by their different approaches and methods for involvement. In the review of incentives for healthy behaviours, for example, researchers provided a stakeholder group with a set of options for the synthesis stage of the review. Each individual stakeholder had information about the number of different types of study identified by the systematic map; for example, which types of incentives had been studied (financial or otherwise), and how these were made available (to targeted groups or the general population). They were asked to prioritise the different options. This was all done by email exchanges between one researcher and individual stakeholders, with phone calls for clarification if requested. The stakeholders made decisions separately from each other.

The two other reviews, in contrast, used meetings that brought the same people together on several occasions to provide opportunities for the exchange of views between stakeholders. This approach allocated a greater amount of time for eliciting and considering issues as they arose, and partly as a result, both reviews took substantially longer to complete. A case study of one of these reviews (of HIV prevention for men who have sex with men) presented further details of some of the procedures that might be used to elicit ideas and arrive at decisions when working with mixed groups of stakeholders on reviews (see Rees and Oliver 2007). In terms of what was involved, both of these more collaborative reviews required far greater resources for involvement than did the review on incentives. For both reviews, these resources mainly consisted of the time contributed by the various groups of stakeholders in organising and attending events or meetings. This turned out to be a considerable challenge, especially for the students involved in the PSHE review, given the many competing demands on their time within the school day and over the school year. For the HIV review, a large amount of effort was put into preparing information for stakeholders before advisory group meetings, and in minuting and circulating discussions from these meetings. Again, stakeholders spent a great deal of time preparing for and attending meetings.

In terms of influence, all three approaches allowed people other than researchers in the review team to have an impact on the final questions addressed by the review. Their early and repeated involvement in the HIV review appeared to be particularly important. In this review, a range of stakeholders had opportunities over a series of meetings to discuss and help influence decisions on both the conceptual framework and the questions for the review, as well as then providing their reflections on the review's findings as these emerged.

The choice of involvement method will depend upon whether the review team is willing to share decisions about the review with other stakeholders, whether the other stakeholders are networked with easy-to-reach organisations, their familiarity with research and systematic reviews, the time available and the skills of the review team.

Table 2.4 presents the options for review teams that invite stakeholder involvement. If a review team wishes to consult stakeholders, then these stakeholders need to understand the purpose of the research and systematic reviews so that they may also understand why they are being approached for their ideas. This requires the review team to have the research skills for eliciting issues that are important to stakeholders and applying these to the design of the review. In contrast, if a review team wishes to share decisions in order to improve the review in a more collaborative way, it is not enough solely to have stakeholders who understand the purpose of the review. Everyone involved will need to understand and discuss the nature of the review, its potential, its limitations, and options. The review team can either choose stakeholders who already have a sophisticated understanding of reviews, or

**Table 2.3** The approaches to stakeholder involvement used in three EPPI-Centre systematic reviews

| Dimension | Review topic | | |
| --- | --- | --- | --- |
| | Incentives for encouraging healthy behaviour | Personal, social and health education (PSHE) | Preventing HIV among men who have sex with men |
| Brief description of approach | Type D<br>One-off, consultation. Stakeholders voted to select the review's analyses | Type A<br>Collaboration at several points during review between researchers and an organisation (a school), plus consultation with a committee convened for the review, and a student-led consultation of their peers. A teacher co-directed the review | Type A<br>Collaboration throughout review between researchers and a committee convened for the review |
| Perspectives involved | Practitioners<br>Policy-makers<br>Academics/researchers | Service-users<br>Practitioners<br>Policy-makers<br>Academics/researchers | Service-users<br>Policy-makers<br>Academics/researchers |
| Individual and/or organisational participation | Individual stakeholders invited to work with researchers | Individuals invited to represent the school (teachers, pupils, a librarian, a parent governor). Pupils and teachers worked with each other as well as with researchers to study the review topic.<br>Other individuals were invited to work in an advisory committee | Organisations with active service-user networks were invited to participate in review's advisory committee. Other individual stakeholders were also invited to work on this committee |
| Forum for eliciting ideas | Email and telephone conversations | Workshop (pupil, parent and most of teacher participation) to identify review question. Committee meetings once question set (for other stakeholders) | Three committee meetings: (i) before setting review question; (ii) after initial systematic mapping of research so as to identify questions for synthesis; (iii) to comment on interim synthesis findings |
| Techniques for arriving at decisions | Stakeholders presented with review options derived by researchers. Stakeholders voted in isolation for preferred option | School stakeholders discussed PSHE curriculum together with researchers and selected one area for study. Researcher interpretation of these discussions was later used to develop inclusion criteria | Committee chair facilitated informal consensus work and sought clarification of recommendations at each meeting end. A structured voting process was used for one decision |
| Main influences on the review (as identified in review reports) | The stakeholder group identified which out of a range of possible analyses should be conducted (e.g. one analysis was whether schemes using financial incentives were more or less effective than those with other kinds of incentives) | Pupils and teachers at the school chose the topic for review (relationships). This was one that the research team had not previously thought a priority. Additional contact with members of the school helped researchers keep relevance to the school in mind as they worked on the review | The stakeholder group selected a primary outcome that was to receive the most emphasis in the review's report. When the review's protocol was in a draft form they also suggested an alternative conceptual framework for the review (from one centred around risky behaviours to one focused upon individual control over health) |

**Table 2.4**  Options and implications for involvement methods

| | Collaboration | Consultation |
|---|---|---|
| Inviting organised stakeholders | **Stakeholder contributions to the review:** Sharing decisions about the scope of the review, key concepts, search strategies, interpretation of the emerging findings and dissemination of the report | **Stakeholder contributions to the review:** Sensitising review team to issues important to stakeholders |
| | **Involvement methods:** Advisory Group membership; consensus development methods | **Involvement methods:** Interviews, written consultation, outreach meetings |
| | **Stakeholders bring:** An understanding of stakeholders' perspectives An ability to present in discussion a range of stakeholder views An ability to participate in a mixed group discussion Knowledge or an ability to learn about research and systematic reviews An ongoing commitment to the work and mutual learning | **Stakeholders bring:** An understanding of stakeholders' perspectives An ability to present in discussion or writing a range of stakeholder views |
| | **Recruitment:** 'Job description' and person specification sent to stakeholder organisations | **Recruitment:** Invitations circulated to stakeholder organisations |
| | **Review team brings:** Interactional skills, group facilitation skills, and a commitment to mutual learning and sharing decisions | **Review team brings:** Qualitative research skills for collecting and analysing people's views and interpreting their application to the design of a review |
| Inviting individual stakeholders | **Contributions to the review:** Sharing decisions about the scope of the review, key concepts, search strategies, interpretation of the emerging findings and dissemination of the report | **Contributions to the review:** Sensitising review team to issues important to stakeholders |
| | **Involvement methods:** Participatory research | **Involvement methods:** Interviews, focus groups, outreach meetings, e-chatrooms |
| | **Stakeholders bring:** A willingness to reflect on their personal experience A willingness to learn about research and systematic reviews An ongoing commitment to the work and mutual learning | **Stakeholders bring:** A willingness to reflect on their personal experience |
| | **Recruitment:** Invitations sent to workplaces or public services | **Recruitment:** Invitations sent to workplaces or public services |
| | **Review team brings:** Interactional skills, group facilitation skills, and a commitment to mutual learning and sharing decisions | **Review team brings:** Qualitative research skills for collecting and analyzing people's views and interpreting their application to the design of a review |

they can invest time and effort in explaining the issues clearly so as to maximise the value of the discussions. This requires the review team to have interactional skills that will facilitate a constructive discussion.

---

**Box 2.4**

## The practicalities

Review teams need to ask themselves:

1  What judgements about the review is the team willing and able to share with other stakeholders?

   The framing of the question and/or sub-questions?
   The definitions of key concepts? And their relative importance?
   Where to look for literature?
   What the findings mean? And how to report them?

2  Who are the stakeholders who can help make these judgements?

   If members of organisations, they may be able to draw on a wide range of opinions and discuss the review with other types of stakeholder.
   If individuals are not part of organisations, they may be limited to bringing their personal experiences and might be more comfortable talking on their home ground.

3  Who in the review team has the skills to consult or collaborate with stakeholders? (For practical advice, see Cartwright and Crowe 2011.)

4  What advance information would help stakeholders prepare for discussing the review?

5  How much time is there for thought and discussion?

6  What costs will be accrued? For travel, refreshments, a venue, honoraria?

7  How will stakeholders' contributions be acknowledged in the report?

---

## Conclusion

This chapter has described the practical implications of seeing systematic reviews from different perspectives. Towards the end of the second millennium the growing enthusiasm for a more participatory approach to developing services was applied to research and 'evidence-informed decision-making'. These two movements provided the setting that encouraged researchers to draw on the perspectives of policy, professional practice and service use so as to develop a more applied social science. When they recognise that their own perspectives may be limited, systematic reviewers can invite people who will, between them, bring a range of priorities, knowledge and types of expertise to guide the conduct of their review work. By doing so, reviewers can be helped to recognise and check out their own assumptions, and to choose a focus for and a way of communicating the review that is scrutinised and informed by a range of perspectives.

# THREE

## Commonality and diversity in reviews

### David Gough and James Thomas

---

**| Aims of chapter |**

This chapter considers how and why:

- Systematic reviews, despite sharing common principles, vary in terms of their aims, the extent of 'work done' (the amount of the research problem that the review attempts to address), breadth and depth, epistemology, and overarching approach
- Reviews vary in whether they aggregate or configure information, the types of knowledge considered and the heterogeneity and homogeneity of the data included
- Reviews vary in their structure and on many other dimensions of difference in their methods

---

## Introduction

Chapter 1 discussed the ways that reviews examine previous research and how their methods depend upon the questions being asked and the types of study that are to be considered. Primary research asks many different questions from a variety of epistemological, ideological and theoretical standpoints, and this richness of questions and approach is also reflected in systematic reviews. Chapter 2 then considered how individuals and groups in society may have particular perspectives that lead them to ask different questions, each from their own standpoint, raising issues about whose questions are being addressed and how different stakeholders can be involved in asking a review question and undertaking and using a review. Following on from Chapter 2, this chapter considers the many ways in which reviews may differ from each other; differences which often arise because people ask and answer questions in different ways – and also have different needs and requirements of the review. This chapter does not provide a classification of types of review, but instead navigates these differences in terms of:

- differences in extent, detail, epistemology and approach;
- the structure of reviews;
- how the reviewing is conceptualised;
- the further dimensions of difference.

As there are so many ways that a review can vary, it is important to consider the choices available and why one might choose a particular approach. Our aim in this chapter is to provide an overview of these differences that provide a basis for the following chapters on each stage of a review. The chapter may then be useful as a point of reference for potential choices when undertaking or interpreting a specific review.

## Differences in extent, detail, epistemology and approach

Reviews do not exist in isolation; they are commissioned and conducted by people at specific points in time with particular needs, priorities and ways of understanding the issues they address. An important starting point for understanding differences between reviews is therefore understanding the reasons that reviews are conducted, whose perspectives they reflect, and the purpose that they aim to serve in the creation and distillation of knowledge (Gough et al. in press). Differences in perspective and purpose affect the *extent* of the work done by a review (the amount of the research problem that the review attempts to address); its *breadth and depth* (the scope and degree of detail); and the *time period* over which this is carried out (rapidly or over a longer period of time). Cutting across these dimensions is the reviewers' understanding of the nature of knowledge and how knowledge is generated, acquired and used (their *epistemology*). These dimensions can be understood as being similar to the classic project triangle, in which the shape of the project is determined by trade-offs between the review's contribution to knowledge (extent of work done), its breadth and depth, and the time and resources at its disposal (see Figure 3.1). Decisions made in one area will inevitably have a consequences elsewhere, meaning, for example, that reviews with very rapid timetables are unlikely to be broad in scope and have depth of detail.

All of these issues also apply to primary research which, like reviews, varies in the questions asked, extent of work done, breadth and depth and epistemology.

### Extent of a review

We will consider first the extent of the 'work' done by a review in addressing its review question, where 'work' refers to the extent to which a review engages with a research problem. This is difficult to quantify as research questions vary so much in their type and in their level of analysis. The extent of work done in systematic reviews (just as in primary research) is likely to differ depending upon:

- the breadth of the question being asked;
- the depth of detail in which the question is addressed;
- the rigour with which that detail is addressed.

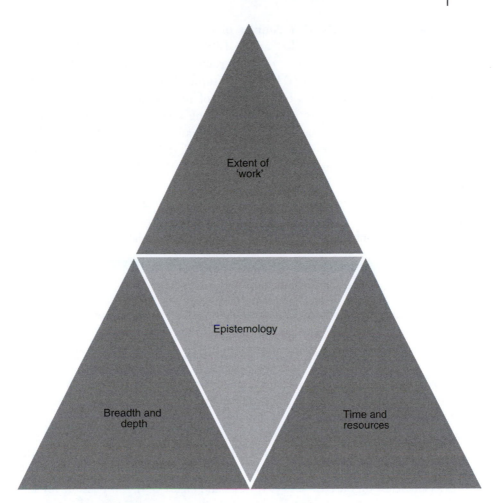

**Figure 3.1**   Differences in extent, detail and epistemology

Some 'what works' reviews, for example, are quite narrow in scope, as they only include studies that evaluate one specific intervention in the lives of a specific population. On the other hand, they may be deep and undertaken very rigorously. The amount of 'work' done by such a review is relatively small, as it aims to be one piece in the jigsaw puzzle of evidence that is available to answer a particular policy or practice question; the review is intended to be placed alongside reviews that evaluate other interventions. In other cases, the review may be very comprehensive and consider many aspects of a complex issue; for example, testing different aspects of a causal model. Whether these broader more comprehensive reviews undertake more or less 'work' than a more narrowly focused review depends on the extent of detail and rigour involved. Both types of review can be useful contributions to knowledge, and each will have strengths and weaknesses in different situations.

Reviews can be part of a series, with each one further exploring aspects of a research question, and each review building on the other sequentially in a contingent way (Sandelowski et al. 2006). Examples of these are programmes of reviews undertaken by the Reviews Facility at the EPPI-Centre funded by the English Department of Health. This project has undertaken groups of reviews that, taken together, provide overviews around key policy topics. For example, it was possible to draw the cross-cutting issues from a series of reviews about young people's mental health, physical activity and healthy eating together in order to identify the main barriers to, and facilitators of, their health and behaviour change in those areas. Alternatively, a series of reviews can be undertaken in parallel and then combined; in such a combined review one synthesises the sub-reviews together in a meta-review (as described later in the chapter).

The extent of work done by a review is not necessarily the same as the contribution of a review to a field, as this contribution can be assessed in so many different ways and a major advance in thinking or practice may be achieved by a relatively modest review.

## Breadth, depth and rigour of reviews

As already discussed reviews can vary in their breadth, depending on their review questions – which in turn depend on the extent of the research 'work' that they are planned to do and the amount of time and resources they have at their disposal. Within the constraints of the breadth of the review question, reviews can be relatively broad or narrow in their inclusion criteria, search strategies, mapping (of the research activity) and synthesis (of findings to answer the review question). If the initial review question is relatively narrow, then all stages of the review, including the synthesis, will also be relatively narrow. If, however, the review question is broad, it is possible for the synthesis to be equally broad or for there to be a narrowing of inclusion criteria after the mapping stage so that only some of the studies in the map are included in the in-depth synthesis (see below on the structure of reviews and Figure 3.4). It is possible for several in-depth syntheses to be undertaken from a single map (see below on the structure of reviews and Figure 3.5). Syntheses can thus be relatively broad or narrow in scope.

Reviews can also vary in their depth, that is, in the amount of detail at each stage of a review. Decisions about limiting the depth of a review are usually related to the breadth of the research question and the time and resources available, though they can also relate to the review's purpose. For example, some reviews will limit the depth of searching by only retrieving electronic documents, or carrying out very specific searches (see Chapter 6). All systematic reviews should be rigorous, but there can also be variation in the rigour with which they undertake their work. Reviews can vary, for example, in the degree that they undertake internal and external quality assurance processes (see Chapter 4). Reviews undertaken with more rigour will need more resources (and will be more reliable) than reviews undertaken with less rigour.

In terms of systematic maps for describing research activity, there is variation in the detail of study descriptions, ranging from listings of a few or many different descriptors of the research studies (mapping keywords) to a more detailed examination of cross tabulations of variables and analysis of the field of research. Maps can thus be described as relatively descriptive or analytic (see Chapter 7).

The purpose of a synthesis is to integrate the findings of different studies to answer the review question. The synthesis should be a proper integration and greater than the sum of the individual studies. In some cases, however, this may not be possible (due, for example, to the heterogeneity of the studies) and the review provides more of a descriptive listing of results rather than a full integrative synthesis (see 'thematic summaries' in Chapter 9).

A synthesis is meant to be an integration of findings from trustworthy and relevant studies that help to answer the review question. In some cases, despite extensive searching, only a few good quality and relevant studies or even no studies at all will meet the inclusion criteria for the review, providing minimal rather than adequate evidence for synthesis. If this is apparent at the mapping stage, there will be an opportunity to redirect the resources for the review rather than investing them in a relatively minimal evidence or even 'empty' review. The resources could, for example, be invested in a more extensive or more analytic map. Taking all of these issues together, reviews may vary in breadth and depth in terms of:

- breadth of question for map: narrow/broad
- breadth of question for synthesis: narrow/broad
- depth of search: scoping search that samples the literature, exhaustive search for unbiased aggregation, or searching for sufficient studies for coherent configuration
- analysis of map: minimal description/detailed description/analytic
- breadth of question for synthesis: narrow/broad
- extent of evidence for synthesis: minimal/adequate
- nature of synthesis: not a synthesis (descriptive)/aggregative/configuring.

As already described in Figure 3.1, the extent of the work done within a review is affected by the nature and breadth of the research question, the breadth and depth of each stage of the review, and the staff, time and resources available (see Chapter 4).

## Limited time and resources

As there are often time and other resource pressures, there has been interest in undertaking rapid reviews. Some use the term 'scoping review' for a quick review that is not undertaken very systematically, though the term is also used by some (for example, Arksey and O'Malley 2005) to denote what we call 'systematic maps' that describe the nature of a research field rather than synthesise findings (see later in this chapter on the structure of reviews and Chapter 7). A scoping review may also be used as preliminary work to inform a fuller systematic review. Another term in common use is 'rapid evidence assessment'.[1] Such a review may be taken rapidly with a greater concentration of staff working over a shorter period of time, resulting in a rigorous, broad and deep review. Alternatively, and probably

[1]Government Social Research Unit Rapid Evidence Assessment Toolkit. Available at: www.civilservice. gov.uk/my-civil-service/networks/professional/gsr/resources/gsr-rapid-evidence-assessment-toolkit. aspx (accessed: 17 November 2010).

more commonly, the review is undertaken with less than ideal resources and so there is some loss of rigour or of breadth and depth (or both) (Abrami et al. 2010).

In general, the authors of this book and other proponents of systematic reviews will prefer detailed, in-depth reviews where more reliance can be given to the review findings. Whether a particular rapid review is fit for purpose depends, of course, on the purpose. If it is to provide a scoping background for a more extensive review, then a rapid review, whether broad or narrow, may be appropriate. If the aim is to examine a very specific issue in depth, then a narrow and deep, rapid review may be more appropriate. If the commissioner of a review has a broad question and yet due to limited resources only funds a rapid, narrow review, then they may receive an unhelpfully narrow answer that they cannot use. It may have been more useful to have commissioned a review of reviews with a broader scope.

In practice, these examples are all extremes. All reviews vary in time and other resources available, and in breadth and depth. The danger is in any lack of rigour, fitness for purpose and explicitness about how the review was undertaken and what it contains.

## Reviewer epistemology

Differences in opinion about how to carry out systematic reviews frequently relate to differences in epistemological viewpoints – how different people understand the nature of knowledge generating activities. These views are often polarised between what are described (in inaccurate shorthand) as quantitative and qualitative positions in the 'paradigm wars' that have occupied (or blighted) social research for many years. They are argued about passionately because they go to the heart of how people make sense of the world they see, and thus raise issues that have occupied philosophers for centuries. They therefore have profound implications in terms of the *overarching approaches* to the activity of reviewing research literature that people adopt, as well as the detail of how *individual methods* are selected and applied.

Some researchers place great emphasis on the importance of considering their position in relation to the philosophy of knowledge, and use this as the starting point for their own investigations and, thus, how they go about conducting a review. Others may take note of learning within the philosophy of knowledge, but will neither see a need for an explicit statement of their position nor adopt any single framework for their research. Most systematic reviews will probably fall within this latter categorisation. Aggregative reviews that 'add up' findings from different studies (see Chapter 1 and later in this chapter for a discussion of aggregative and configurative reviews) are currently the predominant paradigm for reviewing, and most of these reviews do not state their epistemology explicitly. However, this does not mean that they do not have a well-worked out and operationalised epistemological and ontological framework.

Aggregative reviews may assume the independent reality of *naïve realism* (reality exists independent of human constructions and can be known directly (see Box 3.1 and Spencer et al. 2003 for more detail about this taxonomy of epistemologies) or *scientific realism* (knowledge can approximate closely to an external reality). This is necessary for the aggregative logic to apply: that we can expect to observe the same outcomes when the same situations apply.

In contrast, some configurative reviews (that arrange or configure the findings from different studies) do not assume an independent reality. Objective idealism, for example, assumes that there is a world of collectively shared understandings. Critical realism assumes that our knowledge of reality is mediated by our perceptions and beliefs, whilst critical realism reviews which operate using these epistemologies are more concerned with problematising the literature and organising it into a coherent framework which represents how different people understand the phenomenon under investigation. The epistemological stance of subjective idealism is that there is no shared reality that is independent of multiple alternative human constructions. This epistemology calls for the reviewer to adopt a critical stance to the literature being reviewed, and to assert that differences between research findings are explicable through an examination of the assumptions that underpin that research.

While the above definitions of epistemological positions may appear to be fairly orderly, knowledge itself is rarely as precisely organised, and it is possible to detect multiple epistemological perspectives within the same study. Thus, these categorisations should be treated, like the other ways in which reviews differ, as useful *heuristics:* they help us to think critically about the work in which we are involved, but are not necessarily the only – or even the most important – way of thinking about reviewing.

---

| Box 3.1 |

## Key terms – idealism and realism

**Subjective idealism:** there is no shared reality that is independent of multiple alternative human constructions

**Objective idealism:** there is a world of collectively shared understandings

**Critical realism:** our knowledge of reality is mediated by our perceptions and beliefs

**Scientific realism:** it is possible for knowledge to approximate closely an external reality

**Naïve realism:** reality exists independent of human constructions and can be known directly

(Definitions taken from Spencer et al. 2003)

---

## Examples of overarching approaches to reviewing

It is difficult to give examples of implicit frameworks since, by their nature, these frameworks do not contain formal statements of their epistemological position. However, since the way that the EPPI-Centre has carried out reviews falls into this category, our epistemology might be summarised as follows.

**EPPI-Centre reviews** have been developing since their advent in 1993 (Oakley et al. 2005). The approach assumes an external reality but that our experience and understanding of this are socially constructed. Reviews can emphasise social constructionism by investigating the assumptions and theoretical stances held by the authors of primary studies. We would not go so far, however, as to elevate implied systems from the philosophy of knowledge into organising principles for our own research. Rather, we view these critiques as being useful lenses through which we can be critical about our work and as aids to help us expose implicit assumptions. Our reviews recognise that the products of science as textual or numerical statements show degrees of logic and coherence, that at least some of these statements are testable, and that science is largely accumulative. When we carry out reviews that test hypotheses, therefore, we employ accepted methods, such as statistical meta-analysis, understanding that the observations from the studies we include correspond with what is experienced by study participants. However, our social constuctionist position means we also see scientific findings as reflecting the personality, social position and culture of the investigator. We therefore seek to configure our findings in order to locate them within appropriate socio-cultural contexts.

The implications of this epistemological framework for the way that the EPPI-Centre conducts reviews are manifold. To begin with, we take steps to adopt participative approaches to setting research questions, scoping reviews and interpreting findings. This approach emphasises the meaningful nature of people's participation in social and cultural life (interpretivism) and can also be seen in the way this book has been written, emphasising a 'fit for purpose' approach to the selection of methods and the explicit involvement of stakeholders in the review process (see Chapter 2). We have also adapted and adjusted our review methods in order to answer the questions asked by our stakeholders in meaningful and useful ways. This does not mean that we have abandoned the core principles that underpin systematic reviews, but it has led us to examine our methodological assumptions continually, making changes and developing new methods when existing approaches are insufficient. We look on review methods as different tools within our toolbox of review approaches (Oakley 2000b), and use different combinations of these as and when they are needed, often within an explicit mixed methods framework (Brannen 2005; Johnson and Onwuegbuzie 2004).

'What works?' reviews, which test causal hypotheses, are another example of an often implicit epistemological framework. Most commonly associated with reviews conducted by the Cochrane and Campbell Collaborations, reviews within this approach do not concern themselves with issues of reality and instead use empirical data to make empirical measurements and test hypotheses within agreed conceptual frameworks; these may be simple 'black box' hypotheses or more elaborated theories. As has already been mentioned, the approach is largely aggregative with most conceptual work being undertaken before and after the review, though conceptual configuring may be undertaken in examining heterogeneity in the data; particularly in theory driven reviews (Gardner et al. 2010; Petticrew et al. 2012; Rogers 2008). Recently, there has been a growing interest in configuring social, cultural and equity differences in these reviews.

The implications of such assumptions for review methods are that great importance is placed on the review protocol detailing specific methods to reduce hidden bias, the review questions are tightly defined and the review proceeds along a linear process with most methods and concepts defined in the protocol. Searches aim to identify as much relevant literature as possible and any deviation from the protocol needs to be justified since such changes in response to the literature once retrieved might introduce bias.

The above are two examples of often largely implicit epistemologies within reviews, but there are no doubt many others. Approaches that describe their epistemologies explicitly often come from philosophical and research traditions that challenge some of the assumptions made by those traditions that do not. They call for the reviewer to adopt a critical stance to the literature being reviewed, and assert that important differences between research findings are explicable through an examination of the assumptions that underpin that research. Three examples are given below: realist synthesis, critical interpretive synthesis and meta-narrative review.

**Realist synthesis** is a member of the theory-based school of evaluation (Pawson 2006a). This means that it is underpinned by a 'generative' understanding of causation, which holds that, to infer a causal outcome/relationship between an intervention (e.g. a training programme) and an outcome (O) of interest (e.g. unemployment), one needs to understand the underlying mechanisms (M) that connect them and the context (C) in which the relationship occurs (e.g. the characteristics of both the subjects and the programme locality). Realist synthesis asserts that much systematic review activity simply starts from the wrong place; the issue is not which *interventions* work, but which *mechanisms* work in which *context*. Rather than identifying replications of the same intervention, the researcher should adopt an investigative stance and identify different contexts within which the same underlying mechanism is operating.

Realist synthesis is concerned with hypothesising, testing and refining such context–mechanism–outcome (CMO) configurations. Based on the premise that programmes work in limited circumstances, the discovery of these conditions becomes the main task of realist synthesis. The overall intention is to create an abstract model (based on the CMO configurations) of *how* and *why* programmes work. Thus, the unit of analysis in a realist synthesis is the programme mechanism, and this mechanism is the basis of the search. This means that a realist synthesis is not defined by topic boundaries and can range across a wide area, but its search aims to identify different situations in which the same programme mechanism has been attempted.

**Critical interpretive synthesis** (CIS) was proposed by Mary Dixon-Woods and colleagues in 2006 (Dixon-Woods et al. 2006b). The team that created this method had intended to conduct a meta-ethnography of research (an ethnographic review of ethnographic primary studies, see Chapter 9) about access to health care by vulnerable groups but found that, when confronted with the challenges of synthesising a multi disciplinary and multi-method evidence base, changes to this method were required. They see an explicit role for the 'authorial' (reviewer's) voice in the review, and conceptualise the major dimension of difference in reviewing as being aligned between aggregative ('conventional systematic review methodology') and interpretive configuring modes.

The approach is derived on a 'distinctive tradition of qualitative enquiry' drawing on some of the tenets of grounded theory in order to support explicitly the process of *theory generation*. In practice, this is operationalised in its inductive approach to searching and to developing the review question as part of the review process, its rejection of a 'staged' approach to reviewing and embracing the concept of theoretical sampling in order to select studies for inclusion. CIS also prioritises relevance and theoretical contribution in assessing the quality of the studies it includes, over their methodological characteristics (Chapter 8). In particular, and as its name implies, a critical approach to reading the literature is fundamental to CIS, in terms of contextualising findings within an analysis of the research traditions or theoretical assumptions of the studies included.

**Meta-narrative review,** developed by Greenhalgh and colleagues, like critical interpretative synthesis, places centre-stage the importance of understanding the literature critically and understanding differences between research studies as possibly being due to differences between their underlying research traditions (Greenhalgh et al. 2005a, 2005b). Greenhalgh et al. draw on Thomas Khun's (1962) seminal work, *The Structure of Scientific Revolutions*, and understand research as being carried out within specific communities which come to common understandings of what is worthy of study, how phenomena relate to one another, how they should be studied and the tools that define the process of enquiry (Greenhalgh et al. 2005b: 419).

This means that each piece of research is located (and, when appropriate, aggregated) within its own research tradition and the development of knowledge is traced (configured) through time and across paradigms. Rather than the individual study, the 'unit of analysis is the unfolding "storyline" of a research tradition over time' (2005b: 417). Though this may read as a radical departure from many of the systematic review methods described in this volume, the method builds on several of the principles of mainstream systematic reviewing and has similar 'stages', including planning, searching, mapping, appraisal, synthesis and making recommendations. Its key contribution is in answering very broad review questions across heterogeneous literatures in which the 'same' problem has been addressed in different ways by different researchers who came to differing conclusions.

## Linking review methods to overarching approaches

The examples above of overarching approaches to reviewing show that some specific technical methods of review are associated with particular approaches to reviewing. However, as also pertains in the other dimensions of difference discussed in this chapter, it is constructive to consider the *degree* to which this applies (rather than whether it applies), since some methods can be used within a variety of approaches.

This overview of different approaches to research synthesis can seem to be rather abstract, but it is critical to understanding why different methods have been proposed and how one should go about selecting a method for use in a review. It is important to consider which perspective the review team itself takes and to then align this with appropriate methods to answer the review question. There is sometimes no direct correspondence between epistemological framework and selection of method. For example, both CIS and meta-narrative review take a similar epistemological stance, but have important differences that may be due to the preferences of their original developers or the questions they were answering (one takes Thomas Khun as its starting point, whereas the other begins with grounded theory); and a framework or thematic synthesis can be used in reviews taking a range of the above epistemological positions.

Hence, the central concept in Figure 3.1 is epistemology: reviews differ from one another because they have different resources and different requirements in terms of their breadth and in terms of the the extent of work that they do; but reviews that are similar in these dimensions can still be dissimilar in the methods they employ because they are carried out by various people with different understandings about the construction of knowledge.

## The structure of reviews

The previous section has discussed a model which explains the primary reasons for systematic reviews differing from one another. We now move on to examine how these differences are manifested in terms of their basic organisation and structure. In general, reviews can be limited to describing what research has been done (systematic mapping) or they can also include syntheses of findings; they can be single reviews, or mixed methods reviews with several review components, or 'meta' reviews of other reviews.

### Systematic maps and syntheses

One of the most powerful aspects of reviewing the literature systematically is that it is possible to gain an understanding of the breadth, purpose and extent of research activity in a given area. The systematic and extensive searches that are part of most (but not all) systematic reviews gives reviewers confidence that they have not missed any relevant research. They can thus comment with some authority on the relative strengths and weaknesses of how research has been constructed, and they can analyse their findings, identifying specific characteristics of research foci in a given area. This type of reviewing is known as 'mapping' and was first undertaken at the EPPI-Centre in the 1990s (see for example, Peersman 1996; Gough et al. 2001, 2003; and see also Chapter 7).

The aspects of the studies that are described in a map will depend on what is of most interest to those undertaking the review. Just as a geographical map can cover any particular part of the Earth and cover such things as physical geography, transport or political governance, a map of research may describe and analyse such issues as topic focus, conceptual approach, method, aims, authors, location and

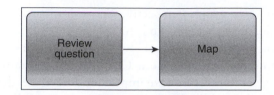

**Figure 3.2** Map as a detailed description of research activity

**Figure 3.3** Review with map and synthesis with consistent inclusion criteria

context (see Chapter 7). Some maps provide very limited descriptions of studies, such as the the names of researchers and country of study. Other maps provide very detailed descriptions and analysis of the research field. The boundaries and purposes of a map are determined by decisions made regarding the *breadth and depth* of the review, which are informed by the review question and inclusion criteria. If the review question is driven by academic interests, then the resultant map may reflect the boundaries of academic disciplines and sub-disciplines. If however, the review is driven by policy, practice or other societal interests, then the map may well cut across such academic boundaries.

The main purposes of creating maps are:

- to describe the nature of a field of research;
- to inform the conduct of a synthesis;
- to interpret the findings of a synthesis.

As Figure 3.2 shows, a map may be the objective of the review. However, it can also be a useful stage in a review where study findings are synthesised as well (Figure 3.3). Most synthesis reviews implicitly or explicitly include some sort of map in that they describe the nature of the relevant studies that they have identified. An explicit map is likely to be more detailed and can be used to inform the synthesis stage of a review. It provides information on the individual and grouped studies in the synthesis and thus also provides insights to help inform the strategy used in the synthesis (see Chapters 7 and 9).

A map may also be used as part of a consultation process with stakeholders. This is particularly valuable for two purposes: first, for when the likely quantity of studies in a given area is unknown; and second, when the specific priority for a synthesis review is unknown at the beginning of the review.

In the first instance, once the map has been produced it may lead the reviewers to consider whether or not to include all of the studies in the map in a subsequent

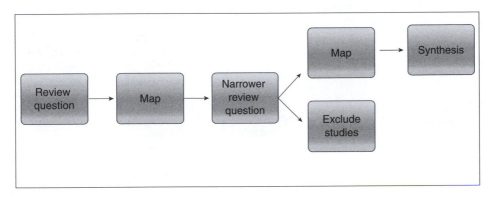

**Figure 3.4**  Review with map and synthesis with narrowing of inclusion criteria

synthesis. The review authors may decide that the studies in the map are not all relevant, are too homogeneous (in the case of configuring) or too heterogeneous (in the case of aggregating) to be synthesised together, or simply too numerous to be synthesised with the current resources for the review. The authors may then decide to synthesise only a sub-group of the studies in the map. In practice, this is a narrowing of the review question and of the inclusion criteria (as in Figure 3.4). In the second instance, the map can be used as part of a conversation with stake-holders to elucidate their key interests and help to focus subsequent reviewing. A map is thus both a key intellectual part of reviewing, and thus determined by the decisions concerning the *breadth* of the review, and can contribute to ensuring the review is carried out within its existing *time and resource* constraints.

Where there is the possibility of narrowing the review question at the review stage, a broad initial question (and inclusion criteria) may be chosen, in the knowledge that a narrower question can be addressed later on. This can be particularly useful when the scope of the question or the types of method for relevant studies are not known in advance or when it will be helpful to have a broader map within which to interpret the synthesis. If these processes of narrowing the review question are explicit, then this guards against hidden factors biasing the way that the review is undertaken.

This approach also allows a broad map to form the basis of a programme of reviews in a topic area (as in Figure 3.5). Using this strategy, one review group sup-ported by the EPPI-Centre undertook a series of five different syntheses from studies in one initial broad map on Information Communication Technology (ICT) and literacy (see Andrews 2004; and Chapter 7).

## Mixed methods and mixed knowledge reviews

Where studies included in a review consist of more than one type of study design, then there may also be different types of data. These different types of studies and data can be analysed together in an integrated design or segregated and analysed separately (Sandelowski et al. 2006; Thomas et al. 2003). Such reviews are usually necessary when they contain multiple layers of review question or when one study design alone would be insufficient to answer the question(s) adequately.

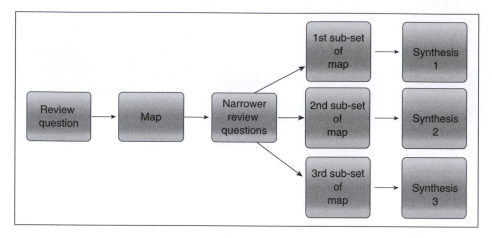

**Figure 3.5**  Review with broad map and several syntheses

They are usually required, therefore, to have both *breadth* and *depth*, and, in covering a broad area, they can undertake a greater *extent of work* than is typically the case. As they are major undertakings, containing what would normally be considered the work of multiple reviews, they are demanding of *time and resources* and cannot be conducted quickly.

In a segregated design, two or more separate sub-reviews are undertaken simultaneously to address different aspects of the same review question and are then compared with each other. For example, a review by the EPPI-Centre (Thomas et al. 2003) undertook a review of the barriers and facilitators of increased vegetable and fruit intake by children and young people (discussed in more detail in Chapter 9). One of the sub-reviews asked about the efficacy of health promotion interventions to increase vegetable and fruit intake by synthesising the results of experimental quantitative studies on this topic. The other sub-review asked about children's and young people's understanding of fruit, vegetables and health by synthesising the results of qualitative studies on children's and young people's views. Both sub-reviews provided useful information independently, but together they allowed a third synthesis that compared the two sub-reviews (as in Figure 3.6) thereby giving insights into why some health promotion interventions to increase fruit and vegetable intake might be more or less effective (Thomas et al. 2004). Such mixed methods reviews can be produced from a single map of the broad research topic (as in a review with a broad map and multiple syntheses; see Figure 3.5) or the maps can be produced independently.

The mixed methods approach can also be used to mix different types of knowledge: for example, knowledge from independent research on the efficacy or implementation of services with survey information on organisations', practitioners', service-users', and policy-makers' understandings (Pawson et al. 2003; see Chapter 2). In a mixed knowledge review, a review of research evidence can be compared with a review of other types of knowledge. In one review, for example, a review of research on the efficacy of a particular approach to mental health

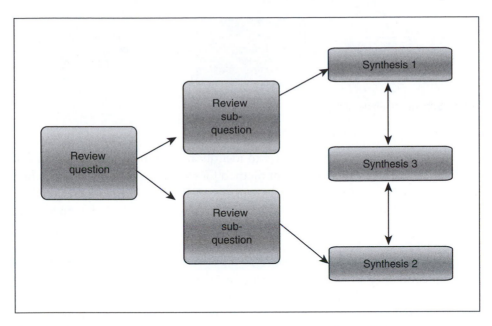

**Figure 3.6**  Mixed methods review with two sub-reviews and three syntheses

services was compared with a practice survey of practitioner views about the most appropriate approach to service provision (Dickson and Gough 2008).

## Reviews of reviews

A review of reviews is a systematic map and/or synthesis of previous reviews (as in Figure 3.7). The 'data' for such reviews of reviews are previous reviews rather than primary research studies (see Ioannidis 2009; Smith et al. 2011; Thomson et al. 2011). In aggregative reviews of reviews, care has to be taken to check whether the same primary studies may occur in more than one review and so risk being double counted.

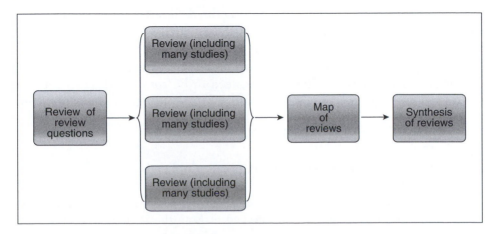

**Figure 3.7**  Map and synthesis of reviews (review of reviews)

**Figure 3.8**  Meta-epidemiology

Some reviews use previous reviews to identify both primary research data and synthesis data. This can be an efficient method for examining previous research but, in reviews purporting to provide an exhaustive overview of the research literature (see Chapter 6), there are possible dangers of bias in selecting which data to include.

## Meta-epidemiology

Meta-epidemiology is where a series of reviews are analysed to ask questions about the nature of the research field (as in Figure 3.8); for example to examine the implications of methodological characteristics of studies (e.g. Oliver et al. 2010; Savović et al. 2010). This approach maps aspects of studies from previous reviews (and so is in essence a special form of systematic 'review of reviews' map).

## Meta-reviews

There is also the concept of 'meta-reviews'. Both 'reviews of reviews' and 'meta-epidemiology' can be considered to be meta-reviews in that they all in some way review other reviews. Mixed methods reviews that synthesise sub-reviews (as in Figure 3.5) are also meta-reviews. Review methods such as realist synthesis and meta-narrative synthesis also have some similarities with meta-reviews as they similarly explore and synthesise different types of evidence and then synthesise these together to address the overall review question.

The different ways that reviews can be structured all relate to the discussion at the start of the chapter on the extent of the research work done by a review. Some of these structures are well suited to quite narrowly framed reviews while others are examining much broader issues and so are aiming to contribute to a broader research question. These issues need to be considered when framing the review question, conceptual framework and appropriate methods of review (see Chapter 4).

## How reviewing is conceptualised

The first section of this chapter has considered the reasons reviews differ from one another and the second section looked at how the structure of reviews is

**Figure 3.9** Configuration (mosaic) and aggregation (cairn)

determined by these reasons. We now move on to describe how the differences in reviewing activities are conceptualised. Rather than seeing these conceptualisations as being either/or, it is more helpful to view them as being useful ways to think about the problem of reviewing, with very few reviews having only one characteristic to the exclusion of the others.

## Configuration and aggregation

Chapter 1 and earlier sections of this chapter have already explained that, although it is important to be aware that reviews can differ from one another across a large number of dimensions, it can be useful to think about two main types of review, depending on the degree that the mode of synthesis is *configuration* or *aggregation* (see the discussion and box definitions in Chapter 1) (Voils et al. 2008; Sandelowski et al. 2011). Aggregating reviews predominately add up (aggregate) the findings from primary studies to answer a review question. Configuring reviews predominately arrange (configure) the findings from primary studies to answer the review question. Figure 3.9 provides an illustration of the different strategies taken by aggregative and configuring reviews.

Syntheses that configure their findings tend to be associated with questions that generate new theory or explore the salience of existing theory in particular (or differing) situations. The studies in such syntheses tend to be different from one another (heterogeneous) and, as the aim of the synthesis is the generation of new theory, the reviews will have few tightly pre-defined concepts. Configurative syntheses can be likened to the patterns in a mosaic, in which the findings from each study are slotted together to form a coherent whole. This idea of piecing research knowledge together from different contexts is not peculiar to research

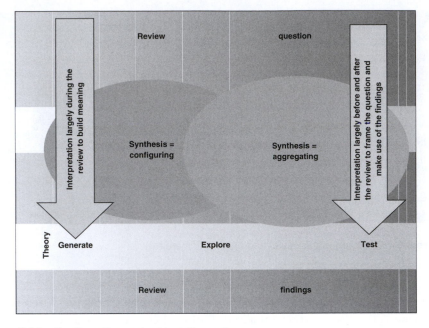

**Figure 3.10**   Configurative and aggregative reviews

synthesis, but has long been considered to be a useful heuristic in primary research too.[2]

Configuring data involves some form of interpretive conceptual analysis and is thus particularly associated with reviews where: (i) the concepts are the data for analysis; (ii) before conceptual analysis is within rather than before or after the review; (iii) the review is aiming to generate and explore theories, taking what is sometimes called an inductive approach; and (iv) the review is an iterative exploration rather than using pre-defined, pre-specified methods. Good examples are meta-ethnography, developed by Noblitt and Hare (1988), and thematic synthesis (Thomas and Harden 2008), where a range of concepts from primary studies is interpreted and configured to create higher order or meta-concepts (see Chapter 9).

Aggregative reviews, on the other hand, are more closely associated with testing theories or hypotheses. The studies in these syntheses are much more homogeneous, usually using the same methods and having commensurate conceptual frameworks (i.e. their conceptualisations of the phenomena of interest are broadly the same). Aggregative syntheses can be visualised as working in a different dimension (or plane) to configurative syntheses since they 'pile up' similar findings in order to gain greater precision (or confidence) in their results. Figure 3.10 encapsulates these two modes of synthesis of configuring patterns and aggregating data in a visual form as overlapping ovals.

Aggregative reviews can ask many different questions and have many forms. Particularly well known are reviews with pre-specified concepts and research

---

[2]See, for example, Chapter 4 of Becker (1970): 'The Life History and the Scientific Mosaic'.

methods that use empirical data to test the evidence for the efficacy of a theory; sometimes described as a deductive approach. The theory often concerns the hypothesis that a service, treatment or other intervention in people's lives produces a different outcome compared with another intervention or no intervention. The purpose is to aggregate the findings of different studies that test this theory by comparing the effect of the intervention with a different intervention or no intervention. There can be many different ideological and conceptual assumptions and the hypothesis can be simple or complex. The important point is that these issues are determined in advance. This approach is thus accepting a pre-determined conceptual view and is often concerned with general rather than individual effects (sometimes known as ideographic rather than nomothetic research, see Thomas 2004).

Aggregative reviews may be quantitative, using statistical methods to provide an overall quantitative finding from individual quantitative findings in the studies included in the review. Aggregative reviews can also summarise qualitative data (though the more interpretive the process of summary, the more the process is likely to become one of configuring the data). Aggregating information without statistics will require grouping and summarising information using words (thematic summaries).

All reviews have some aspects of configuration and aggregation. Some reviews, however, have substantial aggregative and configurative components; theory driven reviews that aim to test the empirical evidence for a program theory (Chen 1994, Weiss 1997) may unpack (configure) the components of such theories and also aggregate the data to test all or part of those theories. This may be undertaken under a mainly a priori paradigm, as in a statistical meta-analysis of complex interventions (maybe also with iterative configuring as in retrospective analysis of review components as in, for example, subgroup analyses); or with iterative aggregation and configuring as in the detective-like approach of collecting evidence about how the theory does or does not apply in different situations. The approach is to test a theory with any form of empirical evidence. Stakeholders may be well placed to provide some of that evidence. The conceptual framework is largely emergent as part of the purpose of the review is to identify the assumptions within the theory and, having made these clear, to seek out evidence to test these assumptions. The aim is to discover general theories that apply to specific groups of individuals.

It is important to bear in mind that configuration and aggregation do not simply reflect the standard qualitative/quantitative paradigm divide in different words, but also represent genuine differences in how to conceptualise the activity of synthesis. For example, a statistical meta-analysis is often used to test the balance of benefit and harm attributable to a given intervention. It will combine the results of the studies it includes statistically in order to gain more precision and confidence in its findings than any one study can give. Such a meta-analysis would fall squarely within the aggregative mode of synthesis. However, if the meta-analysis were extended to include a regression that, for example, examined the impact of interventions on different population groups, the mode of synthesis will have changed to configuration, because the results from different studies (or groups of studies) will be being compared and contrasted with one another. In the same way, one can imagine a synthesis of 'qualitative' research which configured the results of individual studies employing an aggregative logic by treating concepts that had been found in many studies as more important than those that were only found in a few.

## Interpretation and innovation

Another issue of relevance to synthesis is *interpretation*. Again, this is not a binary issue, as all synthesis involves interpretation, but an issue of degree and the role that it plays in the synthesis. In aggregative syntheses, interpretation occurs largely before and after the synthesis to frame the question and make use of the findings. Interpretation in configurative synthesis happens during the synthesis itself as well, as judgement is involved whenever the findings from one study are being compared (translated) with another (see Figure 3.10 and Chapter 9).

In a statistical meta-analysis a reviewer interpretation is often implicit, but also always present. For example, determining how and whether differences in interventions and outcome measurement tools should be accounted for in the analysis and how significant the results might be is a matter for reviewer judgement.

Some definitions of synthesis describe the activity as one that results in a *conceptual innovation* or the generation of *new knowledge*. But does a synthesis or systematic review *have* to be innovative in this way? And does the activity of synthesising the findings of studies always result in new knowledge? Again, this definition is merely a useful heuristic. It helps us to understand some of the relevant issues, but in any given review it should be taken as being a matter of degree rather than one of presence or absence. Nearly all synthesis reviews will have some conceptual innovation, but some will have more than others.

In a statistical meta-analysis, the final summary statistic (see Chapter 9) represents new knowledge; it is a statistic, together with an estimate of its precision, which is entirely new and something unknown before the analysis was carried out. In other types of review, new knowledge or a conceptual innovation might be an original understanding of why people react in a given way in particular circumstances, or the development of a theory that explains how an intervention works in different contexts. In all cases, the innovation represents the contributions of all relevant studies and takes account of how and why these might differ from one another. It will also be provisional; contingent on the participants, circumstances and temporality of the studies in the review.

Critical to the thinking contained in the previous paragraphs is separating the *method* – the detail of how one goes about combining/transferring findings across studies – from our *understanding about the nature* of what is being combined. For example, Chapter 9 discusses the method, 'thematic synthesis', which is a way of systematically synthesising study findings in a textual form. The method itself is agnostic with regard to what is being synthesised; it can be used to combine the results of ethnographic studies, outcome evaluations or other types of data, such as interview transcripts or newspaper articles. It can also be used both to configure and aggregate findings.

Likewise, statistical methods for meta-analysis can be utilised to evaluate the effectiveness of interventions as well as to aggregate correlations from epidemiological studies. Similar methods can also be used to configure statistical findings. While the method might be the same, the reviewer's understanding of *what* is being combined will determine how the synthesis is conducted and how its findings will be interpreted.

## Heterogeneity

In many areas of research there are rarely exact studies that replicate one another precisely, and reviewers thus always need to confront the fact that we are synthesising studies from different places, involving different people, at different times – and often using different measurement tools and evaluating different interventions. The question for the reviewers is less one of 'do we have heterogeneity?' and more one of 'what are the differences between the studies in my synthesis, and how do these affect my findings?'

Aggregative syntheses will tend towards combining homogeneous groups of studies, whereas in configurative syntheses differences between studies are necessary in order for configuration to be possible. For example, a meta-analysis examining the impact of a given intervention will need to have quite homogeneous studies in order for the statistical tests to be meaningful and valid. However, a 'meta-narrative review' which aimed to explore how differences between research paradigms explained differences in research findings requires diversity in the studies it includes in order to make comparisons possible (Greenhalgh et al. 2005a, 2005b). Gene Glass, one of the pioneers of meta-analysis, encapsulates the importance of heterogeneity in the quotation in Figure 3.11 (Glass 2000).

While many texts on meta-analysis treat heterogeneity as a problem, and something to be avoided if at all possible, it is worth remembering Gene Glass's view. Systematic reviews of social scientific literature will almost always contain heterogeneous sets of studies. This should be seen as a strength and an opportunity for analysis rather than as a problem and a barrier to producing clear findings. Some theory-driven reviews therefore plan to examine heterogeneity to test out different aspects of a theory (Gardner et al. 2010, Petticrew et al. 2012, Rogers 2008, Shepherd et al. 2009).

## Types of data

The types of data that are synthesised in a systematic review will be determined by the review's question (see Chapter 4). The most clear-cut difference in type of data is whether we are dealing with *numbers* or *text* in the synthesis. While this does affect whether or not it is possible to do a statistical meta-analysis which may be easier to do and easier to control for hidden interpretation, it makes surprisingly little difference apart from this. Many of the same judgements about study relevance, quality and how results should be interpreted apply across these data types.

> Of course it mixes apples and oranges; in the study of fruit nothing else is sensible; comparing apples and oranges is the only endeavor worthy of true scientists; comparing apples to apples is trivial (Gene Glass 2000)

**Figure 3.11**   Heterogeneity

More important is the reviewer's understanding of *what* the data that are being combined actually represent. One potentially helpful dimension to consider here is the extent to which a study's findings are based on empirical research or theoretical/philosophical concepts (though with the acknowledgement that all are likely to contain elements of both). Sometimes it will be easy to see that a finding is based on direct observation in a research study and at other times it will be more difficult to assess when findings are less concerned with reporting empirical facts and are really theoretical and interpretive extrapolations on the part of researchers.

This thinking can also apply to the type of synthesis conducted. For example, the findings of a statistical meta-analysis can be considered to be *empirical*, because they are derived directly from the data of included studies, whereas a synthesis that develops new theory is more *conceptual*. Again, this is simply a way of thinking about synthesis; the conceptual synthesis is still based on data, in this example on the studies that informed the development of the theory in the first place. Dixon-Woods et al. (2006b: 37) put it like this:

> ...it is important not to caricature an interpretive synthesis as floating free of any empirical anchor: an interpretive synthesis of primary studies must be grounded in the data reported in those studies.

## Further dimensions of difference of reviews

The chapter has described differences in the extent, detail, approach, structure and the conceptualisation of reviews. This final section lists some of the major dimensions of difference in terms of stakeholder roles and the stages of a review (Gough 2007b). The remaining chapters of the book examine many of these issues in more detail. The purpose here is to provide a quick overview of some of the main issues.

The number of possible combinations of these many dimensions of differences is immense, which creates problems for those selecting the methods to use
in their reviews. In order to provide some insight into the relevance of
these choices for different types of review, there is a brief discussion of how
these dimensions commonly relate to aggregative, configurative and mixed
aggregative/configurative reviews (such as theory-driven reviews). In deciding
on the strategy for conducting a particular review, consideration should, of
course, also be given to the other issues discussed in this chapter (such as epistemology, extent, detail, approach, structure) and the rest of the book (such as
coding frameworks and the communication of findings). It must also be stressed
that reviews will vary in degree on most of these dimensions of difference rather
than being either/or alternatives.

## Stakeholder role

As discussed in Chapter 2 on participation, a variety of users of research can participate in many different ways at different stages of a review. These include users'
perspectives and knowledge, users' power in the review, and the stages of the
review in which they are involved.

---

### Box 3.2

## Stakeholder role: summary of dimensions of difference

- *Perspective and knowledge*: different people bring different perspectives,
  ideologies, conceptual assumptions, knowledge, and priorities to the review
  process.
- *Power and role in the review process*: how different stakeholders participate in
  decisions about the focus and conduct of the review ranges from: (i) control/
  manage the review; (ii) engage/participate in the review; (iii) inform directly in
  the review; or (iv) inform indirectly (implicitly or explicitly) via: (a) representation;
  (b) new data collection/research; (c) the existing literature; or (d) reviews of the
  literature on user views.
- *Stage of the review process for the user role*: (i) selecting the focus of the review
  question, such as in user-driven or user-informed review questions; (ii) process of
  review: informing or engaging with the process of the review; (iii) communication
  of review findings, such as user-directed or user-informed review reports and summaries; (iv) interpretation of the findings, such as methods for user interpretation
  of review findings; (v) application of the findings, that is methods of application
  of the interpreted/contextualised review findings.

---

The role of stakeholders does not necessarily vary between aggregative,
configurative or mixed reviews though in aggregative reviews there is often
more pre-specification of the question and detailed method (rather than

being emergent within the review) and so user involvement needs to start early on in that process. Also, as many current configurative reviews come from a critical analytic tradition, they may be particularly concerned with identifying hidden conceptual positions and underrepresented perspectives in society.

## The review question

The review question drives all other aspects of the review (just as research questions drive the focus of primary research). The review question is thus the basis of many of the other ways in which reviews vary.

There are many overlapping aspects to how a review question is determined and applied, and some of these are listed in Box 3.3 below (see also earlier this chapter on conceptualising reviews and Chapter 4 on questions and conceptual framework). As is explained in more detail in Chapter 4, aggregative reviews often use pre-existing conceptual frameworks and aggregate data to test general theories. Configuring reviews, on the other hand, may be more concerned with generating or exploring theories. Between these two extremes are reviews that both explore and test theories.

---

### Box 3.3

### Review question: summary of dimensions of difference

- *Question identification*: how a question is identified as important and requiring an answer may influence both aspects of the question and how it is addressed.
- *Purpose of asking the question*: why a question is being asked will influence the scope and resources brought to bear and the methods used to address the question. The ultimate aim may be to provide enlightenment and understanding of a phenomenon or a more immediate instrumental use of the findings to inform action. This may be achieved by a review designed to: (i) describe a research field; (ii) analyse a research field; (iii) summarise the findings from research; (iv) analyse the nature of the knowledge of a research field; or (v) generalise the findings from research to different contexts and situations.
- *Nature of the question*: there is a lack of a clear taxonomy of research questions for primary social science research and thus also for secondary research, such as reviews, but studies can be described pragmatically as addressing questions that may: (i) aim to generate, explore or test theory; and (ii) use methods that describe, measure, compare, relate or ascribe value (Gough et al. 2009). Testing theory can be: (a) deductive, by checking data against empirical evidence through description, comparison and examining relatedness; and (b) inductive, through ascribing theoretical and ideological values.
- *Conceptual framework*: this is a fuller specification of the meaning of the research question. It may include: (i) ideological assumptions; (ii) theoretical assumptions

---

(including sometimes logic models) underlying the question; and (iii) epistemological stance: the assumptions within the question of the social construction or independent existence of the issues ('reality') to be studied (Barnett-Page and Thomas 2009).

- *Focus on the individual or the group*: the degree to which the interest is in examining general rules or the nature of individuals and their experiences. For example: (i) approaches concerned with large datasets; or (ii) approaches more concerned with the individual case.
- *Extent of the work to be done by the review*: the breadth of the question, the structure used to answer the question, the depth of detail for the data and analysis, and the rigour with which the work will be undertaken.

## Inclusion criteria

All research has to make decisions about which information or ideas it is going to consider when addressing the research question. As reviews examine pre-existing research, they need to decide which information from that primary research is going to be used in the review (see also Chapter 4).

---

**| Box 3.4 |**

## Inclusion criteria: summary of the dimensions of difference

- *Specification of inclusion criteria*: the type of boundaries on the research studies included in the review (such as topic, method, date, source, etc.). This may depend on: (i) the degree of iteration, that is the extent to which the methods for undertaking a review are pre-specified or will develop during the review; and (ii) the breadth of review, with broader reviews having a broader specification of the criteria for inclusion than more narrowly specified reviews.
- *Nature of the inclusion criteria*: the types of features of information that determine whether it is included in the review. For example: (i) the relative homogeneity or heterogeneity in types of information to be included; (ii) the type of knowledge, which is normally research but can also be special types of knowledge gathered through research such as practice or organisational knowledge (Pawson et al. 2003); (iii) whether any practice or organisational knowledge concerns what is 'known' or what is most common 'practice'; (iv) the level of any research information, which can be: (a) raw data from primary research studies; (b) research results from primary studies (which may require some further analysis before entry into synthesis); or (c) other reviews, thus producing reviews of reviews.

---

*Aggregative reviews* tend to decide in advance (*pre-specify*) what will be considered by a review. The criteria for which studies will be included in a review are mostly decided at an early stage of that review and are driven by the question (and the associated assumptions that are made explicit in the conceptual framework). In reviews testing quite simple hypotheses, these may use similar types of data from the included studies which can be analysed together in the same way. More complex hypotheses may require greater variations in the data to test all aspects of the hypothesis. The data can be raw data from primary studies that are reanalysed in the review or they can be the results of the primary studies. The data may be numerical and so potentially allowing for statistical analysis or may only be available in text form. These aggregative reviews are often very concerned about the methods used to produce the data that will be in the synthesis and avoiding any hidden bias from confounding variables. Reviews on the effectiveness of interventions are likely to seek research methods that are most powerful at addressing effectiveness, such as randomised controlled trials.

*Configurative reviews* are seeking to include studies that will provide richness in terms of making distinctions and developing and exploring theory. The reviews may be able to specify in advance the general types of study to be included in terms of both topic and the primary research methods that will provide the sources of data that are to be synthesised. In mixed reviews such as theory-driven reviews, some inclusion criteria may be specified in advance; other reviews may be more iterative with criteria that will emerge through the process of the review. The research and the data are likely to be heterogeneous as different parts of the model will require different types of evidence.

## Search strategy and screening

Reviews vary in their strategies for identifying relevant material that meets the *pre-specified* or emergent criteria for inclusion in the map and or synthesis (see Chapter 6).

---

| **Box 3.5** |

### Search strategy and screening: summary of the dimensions of difference

- *Nature of sufficiency in search*: (i) to identify sufficient material to avoid bias, usually this is an attempt to be exhaustive in a search; or (ii) to identify sufficient material for coherent configuration and this may be based on: (a) a range of examples with definitions of sufficient examples (saturation); or (b) on emergent criteria as to what is relevant for inclusion in the review; or (iii) a more emergent strategy of searching in response to emergent inclusion criteria in a very iterative review.

- *Search sources*: where to look for relevant materials. For example: (i) hard copy publications such as books, journals and reports; (ii) electronic databases; (iii) web search engines; (iv) web pages; (v) personal recommendations; (vi) items referred to in relevant materials already found.
- *Extent of search*: whatever the strategy there can be variation in the extent of searching in terms of: (i) the range of sources; (ii) the comprehensiveness of the search strategy in regards to the search terms used; and (iii) the investment of time and energy in searching.
- *Screening methods*: the search strategy is implemented to identify potentially relevant material and these are then checked (screened) against the inclusion criteria. Screening can vary in, for example: (i) checking the material is relevant in one stage; and (ii) a two-stage process where summary information (such as an abstract) suggests the material is relevant and its full contents are then sought for screening.

*Aggregative reviews* are normally attempting to collate as much relevant research as possible to avoid a bias from having only partial data. The aim is to be as extensive and exhaustive as possible (for a sufficient unbiased aggregation). The sources searched will depend upon the research topic and the methods for the primary research studies being sought. The approach to screening will depend upon the search sources, but in being exhaustive this is likely to include many sources, including electronic databases and thus two-stage screening (see Chapter 6).

*Configurative reviews* are likely to pre-specify the nature of the topic and thus likely search sources; they do not necessarily have to be exhaustive in their searching. Aggregative reviews are aiming not only to represent all of the findings, but also to give weight to the extent of different findings. For configurative reviews, the quantity of studies reporting certain concepts may be of less interest. The focus is more likely to be on the range and nature of concepts found (for a sufficient coherent configuration). The sources searched will depend upon the topic and research method of interest. Where these feature outside the mainstream research literature, electronic databases may be less useful. Screening will be based upon the inclusion criteria and the rules for searching, which may include stopping when enough of one type of study has been found (saturation) (see Chapter 6).

With some mixed reviews searching will be specified in advance; in others the process will be more iterative; with the reviewer following up different types of leads to explore different avenues of enquiry for relevant evidence. Once one piece of evidence is found, this will suggest other avenues to be further explored. Screening is simply the process of checking whether the data found by a lead are actually fit for the purpose of assessing that part of the theory.

## Mapping

Maps can be undertaken for several reasons that relate to the method by which they are produced and used (see earlier in this chapter).

---

**Box 3.6**

## Mapping purpose: summary of dimensions of difference

- *Purpose*: maps can be used: (i) to describe the nature of a field of research; (ii) to inform the conduct of a synthesis; and (iii) to interpret the findings of a synthesis.
- *Coding for mapping*: this can vary in the use of: (i) pre-assigned versus open-ended categories; (ii) the focus of the coding categories (such as descriptors of method or topic or theoretical focus); and (iii) the extent of coding information.
- *Mapping analysis:* maps can be: (i) relatively descriptive; or (ii) more analytical, such as examining the differential conceptual approaches undertaken across studies in the map (so some analytical maps are like some forms of conceptual synthesis (see Chapter 9).

---

Mapping can describe the research field as a description of the research effort or to inform the process or interpretation of synthesis, though many narrowly specified reviews have only simple maps describing the basic publication details and methods for each included study.

As *configurative reviews* are not usually aiming to be exhaustive in their searches, they are also not so likely to produce systematic maps of the literature. In some cases, though, a broad map of studies will be produced which will then be searched for relevant studies for a configurative synthesis. Configurative reviews are similar to analytic maps in that they are arranging and analysing the nature of the research. The difference is that maps tend not to consider the findings from studies whereas synthesis reviews do (though these are often not absolute distinctions).

In iterative mixed theory-driven reviews there is less interest in mapping out the research in an area of enquiry. The final synthesis, however, does provide an overall description of research related to the theory being assessed and so has some similarities to a map.

### Quality and relevance appraisal

Inclusion criteria and screening aim to ensure that relevant material is identified and used in a review. Quality and relevance appraisal processes also aim to assess the appropriateness of material for drawing conclusions but can occur at many different stages of a review and use a variety of methods of appraisal (see Chapter 8).

---

| Box 3.7 |

## Quality and relevance appraisal: summary of dimensions of difference

- *Quality and appraisal stage*: this can occur: (i) as part of the initial inclusion/ exclusion criteria; (ii) at the mapping stage when there is narrowing of inclusion criteria; (iii) as an appraisal of studies included in the map; (iv) as an appraisal of studies being considered for synthesis; and (v) post synthesis.
- *Dimensions of quality and relevance appraisal*: these include: (i) how well conducted the included studies were; (ii) how well the study methods suited the review question; and (iii) how closely the study focused on the review question (Gough 2007c).
- *Methods and criteria applied within and across dimensions of quality and relevance appraisal*: reviews can vary in: (i) the criteria used to make judgements on the three dimensions; (ii) the criteria for combining judgements across the three criteria; and (iii) the methods used to apply these criteria, such as coding frameworks and standardised tools criteria (Gough 2007c).
- *Decisions made on the basis of the appraisal*: (i) remove a study from the review or from the synthesis; (ii) retain a study but qualify the synthesis results; (iii) check the effects of removing or retaining the study (sensitivity analysis); and (iv) just describe the quality of the research and thus the nature of the findings.
- *Levels of the appraisal*: whether the appraisal is of: (i) individual studies; (ii) individual studies as part of a review; (iii) the totality of evidence provided within a review; (iv) whole reviews; or (v) whole reviews as part of a review of reviews.

---

*Aggregative reviews* are often very concerned about the quality and relevance of the studies included in the review because any lack of trustworthiness undermines the empirical tests of any hypothesis. As the reviews are 'adding' up results the aim is to avoid bias by: (i) only including results that are reliable and valid; and (ii) including all such results from all relevant studies. When the aggregation is of statistical data, these reviews often use standardised tools to assess such threats and test the effects of including or not including particular studies through sensitivity analysis (see Chapter 9 on statistical meta-analysis).

*Configurative reviews* can also be concerned about quality. As these reviews are often more concerned about the richness of data than bias, the quality appraisal is often about basic levels of quality with more of a focus on the relevance to the configuration of data. Quality and relevance are also important for iterative mixed theory driven reviews, although: (i) the issue of relevance is not specified in advance and only emerges during the review; (ii) the criteria are not uniform across the review but depend upon the particular aspects being investigated in the assessment of different assumptions of the theory under test (which may be an aggregative sub-review); (iii) the relevant piece of data may not be the whole findings of a research study, it may just be one small piece of information in the research study which would be of use in testing one particular part of the theory.

## Synthesis

The synthesis is the analysis of the data obtained to address the review question (see Chapter 9). The method of synthesis, like all stages of a review, is largely driven by the review question, the conceptual framework, the reviewers' epistemological stance and the types of research that the review has considered.

---

| Box 3.8 |

## Synthesis: summary of dimensions of difference

- *Aggregation and configuration*: (i) to aggregate or add together data in some way (statistically or through thematic summaries) to provide a summary finding (usually where the conceptual assumptions are largely agreed or pre-specified); and/or (ii) to organise and configure data to create new interpretations and understandings.
- *Analytic tools*: even within one approach to synthesis there may be a range of different tools to assist with the specific tasks involved in synthesis. In systematic reviews of impact questions, for example, there is a range of statistical and textual approaches to synthesis. Similarly, techniques such as thematic analysis can be used in reviews answering rather different types of review question.

---

In *aggregative reviews* the approach to synthesis is one of aggregation of data and this often requires ensuring that the data are translated into a common format. The approach used to undertake the aggregation depends on the review question and the data available. Quantitative data may be in a form that allows statistical synthesis or, if not, will require grouping (see the description of *thematic summaries* in Chapter 9).

There are a number of tools available for the coding, configuration and synthesis of concepts. Meta-ethnography assumes a particular sociological stance to data, framework synthesis (Oliver et al. 2010) pre-specifies some aspects of synthesis but as others emerge the framework evolves as a consequence, and thematic synthesis (Thomas and Harden 2008) takes a more iterative approach than framework synthesis to identifying and synthesising concepts found in the studies.

In many theory-driven reviews, the process of synthesis starts from the point at which the theory's assumptions and components have been unpacked. The process of seeking out relevant information to test each a part of the theory builds up a picture of the applicability of the theory in different situations on different topics.

The final synthesis is mainly a bringing-together of what has been found out about the different parts of the theory to provide an overall view of what is known.

## Conclusions

This chapter has considered the many ways in which reviews can vary. This variation depends upon different aims (review questions) and the different assumptions arising from different research and personal and political perspectives, paradigms and purposes. The structure of the review and the extent of work it carries out are limited by the time and resources at the review's disposal. The variation in reviews, not surprisingly, relates to similar differences in aim and method in primary research. In addition, there are review-specific issues relating to organisational structural aspects of reviews and specific methodological issues. Although there is an infinite variety of possible types of review, a distinction in the extent that reviews are aggregative and configuring is useful for understanding the variations in reviews' aims and methods.

---

### Box 3.9

## The practicalities

Planning a review includes a clarification and determination of:

- The overall research issue and who determines this and how
- The aim of the review

  o how the review is part of a wider research issue and the amount of 'work done' by the review to address this research issue;
  o how broad and deep the review needs to be, and its epistemological stance;

- The time and resources allocated to the review
- The structure of the review
- The specific review question, conceptual framework and method to achieve this aim
- Whether the review will mainly aggregate research or configure research, and how much interpretation and innovation is expected before, during or after the reviewing
- Other specific dimensions of this method of review

---

# FOUR

## Getting started with a review

*Sandy Oliver, Kelly Dickson and Mark Newman*

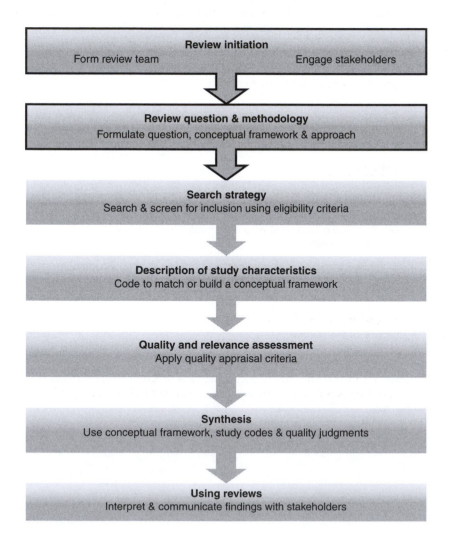

**Review initiation**
Form review team          Engage stakeholders

**Review question & methodology**
Formulate question, conceptual framework & approach

**Search strategy**
Search & screen for inclusion using eligibility criteria

**Description of study characteristics**
Code to match or build a conceptual framework

**Quality and relevance assessment**
Apply quality appraisal criteria

**Synthesis**
Use conceptual framework, study codes & quality judgments

**Using reviews**
Interpret & communicate findings with stakeholders

---

**Aims of chapter**

This chapter addresses the first tasks of the review team. It helps reviewers:

- With the intellectual challenge of deciding what and/or who a review is about
- Choose appropriate review methods and the scale of the work
- Build a review team
- Consider the quality assurance of the review process and product
- Plan and manage the review

---

## Introduction

The first step in any review is deciding what the review is about. Some reviews may have a very specific scope, where all the key concepts are defined in advance. For instance, aggregative reviews usually define the populations, interventions and outcomes of interest as part of the protocol. Others may have only some of the key concepts defined in advance, where the purpose of the review is to identify and configure other concepts from the literature. (This diversity is described in Chapter 3.) Which concepts are important and how they are defined will depend on who is involved in shaping the review (Chapter 2). Early work for the review team is to start combining important concepts into a framework that will allow the evidence to be laid out in a consistent manner to ascertain what is already known within the scope of the review.

Whatever the type of research question or systematic approach, getting started will involve some consideration of the phenomenon, topic, issue or question and the responsibilities of the review team. This chapter deals with these issues by first considering the conceptual framework of a review and then by examining the practical challenges faced by a review team and how they may be met.

## Building the scope of the review: the conceptual framework

Research can be driven by a desire to extend our understanding of the world around us or by a desire to solve the practical problems faced by individuals or organisations, or both. Whatever the starting point, clarifying the precise research question, and how that question should be answered, will involve considering philosophical assumptions about the nature of the world and how it can be understood, often with reference to relevant prior research. Good research rests on clarity about any prior assumptions, and a careful consideration of what is already known, or not, from related research and other sources of knowledge. These assumptions and knowledge, whether implicit or explicit, will include epistemological frameworks about knowledge and how we obtain it, and theoretical frameworks, whether tentative or firm, about the phenomenon that is the focus of study. Taken together, these produce a conceptual framework that informs and helps to structure clear research questions and the choice of appropriate research designs and methods.

The conceptual framework may be viewed as a working hypothesis that can be developed, refined or confirmed during the course of the research. Its purpose is to explain the key issues to be studied, the constructs or variables, and the presumed relationships between them (Miles and Huberman 1994). Developing the conceptual framework requires considerable thought and discussion to explore ideas and challenge assumptions. As for any piece of research, this is the starting point for a systematic review.

> When clearly articulated, a conceptual framework has potential usefulness as a tool to scaffold research and, therefore, to assist a researcher to make meaning of subsequent findings. Such a framework should be intended as a starting point for reflection about the research and its context. The framework is a research tool intended to assist a researcher to develop awareness and understanding of the situation under scrutiny and to communicate this. (Smyth 2004: 167)

---

| **Box 4.1**

## MYTH: Systematic reviews are atheoretical

Systematic reviews have been criticised for being atheoretical. Although this may be so for individual, poorly designed pieces of work, where the evidence from randomised controlled trials is prized above the need for theory (as in a systematic review of intercessory prayer, critiqued by Giacomini 2009), far from being atheoretical, reviews can generate, explore or test theory. Reviews of effects are based on hypotheses constructed from theories and evidence about how interventions might work. Reviews of medicines may be based on theories drawn from pharmacology. Reviews of mental health care may be based on theories of psychology. Although hypotheses provide their theoretical foundation, reviews may be more or less explicit about the basis of their hypotheses.

---

Typical conceptual frameworks for reviews of effects specify a causal link between who the review is about (the population), what the review is about (an intervention and what it is being compared with), and the possible consequences of intervening in the lives of these people (desirable and undesirable outcomes). This is the shape of many reviews of medical treatments, such as a review of the evidence of the effects of paracetamol given to children with a fever. Fevers, which often accompany infection, make people feel unwell, and a rapidly rising temperature in children may occasionally result in a convulsion. Theoretically, the options are to block the chemical pathway that leads to the fever or to treat the symptoms by removing body heat with water or moving air. Thus the choice of the population, intervention, comparison, outcomes and time is based on theories about how these different interventions work, and how they are likely to be implemented in practice. Box 4.2 shows the conceptual framework for this review. Once the review has been completed, the conceptual framework could be refined in terms found in the included studies, such as dosage (single or multiple).

---

**| Box 4.2 |**

## Conceptual framework for treating fever

**Population**: Children aged 1 month to 15 years with fever of presumed infectious origin. Fever is defined as temperature of 37.5°C or more (axillary); or 38.0°C or more (core body temperature).

**Intervention**: Paracetamol (acetaminophen).

**Comparison**: Placebo or physical methods (sponging, bathing, or fanning).

**Outcomes**: Return of temperature to normal (<37.5 C).
Febrile convulsion after treatment started.
Associated symptoms (discomfort, shivering, chills, anorexia, vomiting, irritability, headache, myalgia).
Adverse events.
Caregiver dissatisfaction.

**Time**: 30 minutes to 6 hours after beginning treatment.

(Adapted from Meremikwu and Oyo-Ita 2002)

---

A conceptual framework such as this, captured by PICOT (population, intervention, comparison, outcomes and time), allows the findings of similar studies to be synthesised to provide an answer from the relevant literature as a whole, rather than multiple answers from multiple studies. In this particular case, the authors concluded that there was no convincing direct evidence that paracetamol was effective in reducing fever or preventing febrile convulsions in children.

As systematic reviews address increasingly complex issues, conceptual frameworks are often expanded to take into account important differences in participant populations, similar interventions or multiple steps in a causal chain. We consider each of these in turn, starting with conceptualising distinguishing populations.

Much national and international health policy focuses on inequity,[1] or unjust and avoidable differences in health, that arise from complex interactions linking environmental, economic, social, 'lifestyle' and biological factors (Dahlgren and Whitehead 1991). A mnemonic PROGRESS (Evans and Brown 2003) has been used as a framework to prompt thinking about several social dimensions that may have implications for health inequalities (see Box 4.3). Additionally, there are personal characteristics such as age, disability and sexual orientation that often present barriers to a full integration in society, including the use of health

---

[1]Within the UK, the term 'inequality' is often used for the same meaning.

and other public services, and are subject to anti-discrimination law (Krieger 1999). Moreover, there may be other people who are vulnerable, or socially excluded, who are best described with additional details about their circumstances, depending on the focus of the study. For studies of unborn babies and infants, details may include parental lifestyle, such as smoking and drug abuse. For school-based or other studies of young people, relevant characteristics may include those excluded from school, being 'looked after' or runaways. For older people, it may include those returning home from hospital or respite care. Thus PROGRESS-Plus (see Box 4.3) provides a conceptual framework that is now being used in systematic reviews (Kavanagh et al. 2008, 2009a; Oliver et al. 2008a).

---

**Box 4.3**

## Conceptual framework for distinguishing populations

Progress:

Broad social determinants of health: Place of residence, Race/ethnicity[2], Occupation, Gender, Religion, Education, Socio-economic position and Social capital

Plus: Other

Personal characteristics attracting discrimination, such as age, disability and sexual orientation.

Features of relationships, such as smoking parents, being 'looked after' or excluded from school.

Time-dependent circumstances, such as leaving hospital or respite care.

---

Conceptualising interventions can be similarly complex. A Cochrane review of social franchising could not begin until the team had defined the intervention. Being familiar with social franchising, each member of the team had a mental picture of the intervention but it took discussions spread over two days, with reference to policy and research literature, before those mental pictures could be amalgamated and refined into text sufficiently clear for a naïve reader to understand. This discussion required asking: What is social franchising? Does all social franchising look the same? What is the minimum required for social franchising? How do I recognise social franchising in a research report or policy paper? Why is social franchising designed as it is? How is it meant to work? This led to definitions of both the scope of social franchising and variations in social franchising.

---

[2]The term 'race' relates to human population types based on external phenotypes. It is now understood that such categorisation is not meaningful and can be considered pejorative.

Box 4.4

## Conceptual framework for a review of a complex intervention: social franchising

Social franchising is an adaptation of commercial franchising (such as McDonalds for 'fast food'), in which the developer of a successfully tested social concept (franchiser) enables others (franchisees) to replicate the model using the tested system and brand name to achieve a social benefit. The franchisee, in return, is obligated to comply with quality standards, report sales and service statistics, and in some cases, pay franchise fees. All service delivery points are typically identified by a recognisable brand name or logo (WHO and USAID 2007).

The elements that typify a social franchising package are:

- training (e.g. in clinical procedures, business management);
- protocolised management (e.g. for antenatal care, childhood diarrhoea);
- standardisation of supplies and services (e.g. birthing kits, HIV tests);
- branding (e.g. use of a logo on signs, products or garments);
- monitoring (e.g. quarterly reports to franchiser, reviews);
- network membership (e.g. more than one franchisee in the organisation).

Social franchising can be further categorised according to the following models:

- stand-alone model practices established to provide exclusively franchise-supported services or commodities;
- fractional model: franchise services are added to an existing practice.

(Koehlmoos et al. 2009)

The framework was essential for defining the intervention being studied, and its variations, in order to decide which studies to include in the review and which interventions to compare. Only once there was consensus within the team about the conceptual framework could the tasks of seeking, assessing and synthesising all relevant studies begin.

Conceptual frameworks are important not only for describing accurately the interventions of interest, but also for clearly delineating the steps between the intervention and the desirable and undesirable outcomes. This is the putative causal pathway, the programme theory or theory of change. For instance, a flow diagram illustrating the paths that lead to the faecal contamination of food and drinking water reveals opportunities for interrupting pathways with different types of interventions: water treatment, sanitation and good hygiene (see Figure 4.1).

Conceptual frameworks that can be elucidated as detailed putative causal pathways (such as paracetamol for reducing childhood fever, social franchising for increasing access to quality care, or interventions for preventing diarrhoea) form the basis of systematic reviews that test hypotheses.

Alternatively, the purpose of a review may be to build or further develop a conceptual framework from the literature. This was the purpose of a systematic review

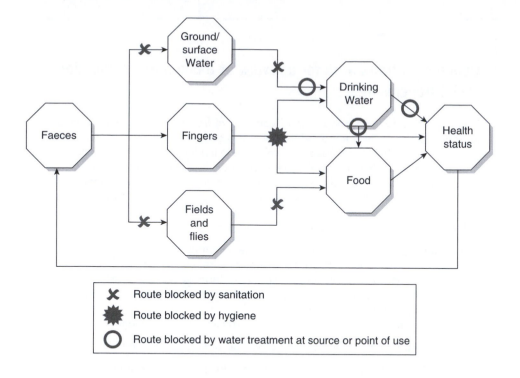

**Figure 4.1**   Faecal oral contamination: arrows representing transmission routes for pathogens (adapted from Waddington et al. 2009).

investigating adherence to treatments for tuberculosis. The conceptual framework in this case was the product of a meta-ethnography that included several steps. The starting point for these was a working hypothesis based on the epistemological and theoretical position that adherence is a complex, socio-culturally specific phenomenon which can only be understood by examining the different perspectives of patients, caregivers, and health care providers. A detailed thematic analysis of the research reporting on these perspectives (from any discipline or theoretical tradition that used qualitative methods) and team discussion to merge themes was followed by comparing themes from different reports, considering their meaning in the context of successive studies, and identifying key categories as they emerged from this interaction with the studies. A table was constructed to show each theme, sub-theme and their explanations. Each reviewer worked independently to construct an overarching framework and then together to produce a model and generated hypotheses about patients' adherence to treatments (Figure 4.2).

> The researchers identified eight major factors associated with adherence to treatment. These included: health service factors such as the organization of treatment and care; social context (family, community and household influences); and the financial burden of treatment ... a simple model [combined] four interacting sets of factors – structural factors (including poverty and gender discrimination), social context factors, health service factors, and personal factors (including attitudes towards treatment and illness). (Munro et al. 2007)

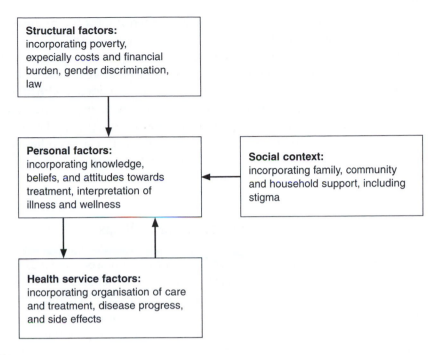

**Structural factors:**
incorporating poverty,
expecially costs and financial
burden, gender discrimination,
law

**Personal factors:**
incorporating knowledge,
beliefs, and attitudes towards
treatment, interpretation of
illness and wellness

**Social context:**
incorporating family, community
and household support, including
stigma

**Health service factors:**
incorporating organisation of care
and treatment, disease progress,
and side effects

**Note:**
↓ ↑ suggest a bi-directional relationship between factors. For example, health service interventions directed at patients are likely to influence patient adherence behaviour through the filter of 'personal factors.' Similarly, patients' interactions with health services are likely to be influenced by their knowledge, attitudes, and beliefs about treatment as well as their interpretations of illness and wellness.

**Figure 4.2** Conceptual framework for a qualitative review of adherence to TB treatment

Where concepts are complex and causal pathways unclear, conceptual frameworks can be partially developed before a review begins (the working hypothesis) and refined during the course of reviewing the literature (the resulting conceptual framework). These are mixed methods reviews that involve some configuring of findings and some aggregation of findings. An example of such complexity is the provision of financial services (such as banking, credit or insurance) to low-income clients with the intention of helping them lift themselves out of poverty. A systematic review of the impact of such services (collectively called microfinance) began by searching for all possible studies of evaluations of micro-credit or micro-savings in sub-Saharan Africa (Stewart et al. 2010a). The reviewers then summarised the evidence of impact and synthesised the findings of qualitative studies. Once familiar with these results, they pushed their analysis further by using the studies to test the assumptions driving microfinance in different circumstances to develop a causal chain of events to explain an array of possible consequences of microfinance and arranged the available evidence along this causal chain. The synthesised findings showed what works, for whom and when: microfinance improves the lives of many clients, but some people are made poorer, and not richer, particularly micro-credit clients. Micro-saving may be a better model than micro-credit because it does not require an increase in income to pay high interest rates and so the implications of failure are not so high; a further rigorous evaluation is needed.

A clear conceptual framework is characteristic of all good systematic reviews, although the clarity of the conceptual framework may be more a product than a starting point for some reviews. Some reviews may be conducted with the primary purpose of generating or exploring theory. In contrast, an explicit framework combining well-defined concepts is a prerequisite for testing causal relationships. Nevertheless, the process of reviewing the literature to test a hypothesis may reveal unexpected findings that could encourage a refinement of the conceptual framework (see, for example, Chapter 9).

## Choosing appropriate review methods

Having chosen the topic, review question and conceptual framework (as far as is possible), the next step is to choose between the diverse synthesis methods used in reviews (see Chapter 3). There is a vast array of methodological issues involved in undertaking a review and, as mentioned in earlier chapters, a key issue for any review is the degree to which it aims to *configure* and the degree to which it aims to *aggregate* the findings from individual studies (see the dimensions of difference in the reviews in Chapter 3).

Figure 4.3 illustrates a spectrum of synthesis methods that spans:

- syntheses that mainly aggregate the findings of studies to test hypotheses constructed with concepts well defined in advance (right-hand side); and
- syntheses that mainly configure the findings from studies to generate theory from early tentative assumptions and concepts that emerge from the data (left-hand side).

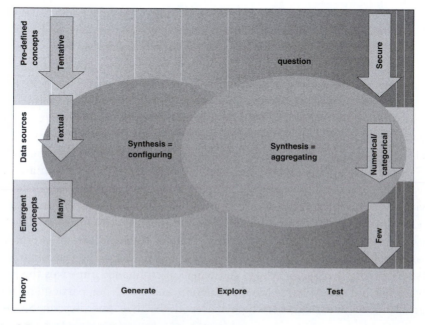

**Figure 4.3**   A spectrum of approaches to synthesis

The former typically aggregate quantitative data and, where it is justifiable, pool the data in a statistical meta-analysis. The latter typically configure qualitative data, for instance using meta-ethnography or grounded theory. However, reviews may configure quantitative data by analysing sub-groups, or they may aggregate qualitative data by identifying common themes across studies. Between the extremes are mixed synthesis methods such as framework analysis or realist synthesis, which both configure and aggregate study findings. The challenge for would-be systematic reviewers is not only to recognise this spectrum of methods, but also to choose appropriately between them.

---

| **Box 4.5** |

### Key terms and how we use them

- **Causal pathways** link a series of events that result in effects some time or distance later; they may be hypothetical (particularly before a piece of review) or supported by evidence. Other similar terms (which have slightly different meanings) include programme theories, logic frameworks and theories of change.
- **Transformative reviews** are designed with the perspectives of marginalised or disadvantaged people in mind and the intention of synthesising the evidence to improve their situation.
- A **theoretical lens** focuses a review on a particular way of analysing the evidence, such as an 'equity lens' focusing a review on unjust differences between groups of people, or an 'advocacy lens' with a goal of social change.

---

Where all the key concepts are well defined in advance, research questions will ask whether they are related and how they are related. Whether they are related is addressed in 'black box' reviews that test the links between well-defined problems, well-specified interventions (or exposures) and judiciously chosen outcomes (as in the review of interventions for reducing fever above). Testing how they are related requires more details to be specified in advance about how interventions vary (as in the review of social franchising above) or about the causal pathway (as in the review of interventions to combat childhood diarrhoea). In each case, the purpose of the review is to test the hypothesis by synthesising the findings of the included studies, where possible with a statistical meta-analysis (illustrated by the right-hand arrows in Figure 4.3). The review process may confirm, refute or refine the hypothesis.

Where key concepts are less well defined in advance, research questions ask about how concepts are perceived and related, and how salient, important or valuable they are. The purpose of such a review is to understand a situation better and build a theory about that situation by identifying concepts and how they are related by synthesising qualitatively findings from the included studies, perhaps using meta-ethnography or grounded theory (see Chapter 9) (illustrated by the left-hand arrows in Figure 4.3). This is illustrated by the review of TB adherence interventions above. Another such review increased understanding of how mothers experience their first year of caring for twins, triplets or more: 'bearing the burden, riding an emotional roller coaster, lifesaving support, striving for maternal justice, and acknowledging individuality' (Beck 2002: 214).

Where some, but not all, key concepts are well defined in advance, and there is already a partial understanding of how they relate to each other in terms of theory or policy intentions, the purpose of the review is to build on this prior understanding, explore the theory and policy implications, and identify new concepts and relationships by bringing together the findings within a conceptual framework that is amended during the course of the review. When this approach is applied to an observed causal relationship, the appropriate choice of method is quantitative for assessing the strength of a causal relationship, combined with qualitative methods for explaining the relationship. Such a combined approach was taken to review systematically the literature about children and healthy eating (Thomas et al. 2004). A thematic analysis of studies of children's views revealed children's understandings and experience of healthy eating, and their attitudes towards healthy eating. A parallel statistical meta-analysis measured the effect sizes of different interventions designed to increase children's healthy eating. The two together identified likely active components of complex interventions.

Where the purpose of the research is to drive change, a review requires a theoretical lens or perspective that underpins the drivers of change and informs all aspects of the research design and methods. For primary research methods this approach has been described as transformative-emancipatory research (Mertens 2003). Cresswell (2003) has summarised the criteria of transformative-emancipatory primary research which are also applicable to the early stages of systematic reviews, whether these reviews intend to generate, explore or test theory:

- Did you deliberately search the literature for concerns of diverse groups and issues of discrimination and oppression?
- Did the problem definition arise from the community of concern?
- Did your research approach arise from spending quality time with these communities, building trust, showing respect, active listening, anticipating mutual learning?

Transformative reviews may use the views of less powerful groups to:

- drive the analysis of quantitative data (Thomas et al. 2004 on children's healthy eating, and Lorenc et al. 2008 on walking and cycling);
- explore the role of social inequalities in shaping people's views (Oakley et al. forthcoming on women's views of antenatal care) or the impact of intervention (Kavanagh et al 2009);
- use a framework that explicitly acknowledges power relations (Oliver et al. 2004 reviewing public involvement in research agenda setting);
- focus the review by spending time with people (in schools, Garcia et al. 2006; or in local authority services, Members of the Children's Active Involvement Service, Islington and Liabo, K. 2010; or with recently pregnant mothers, Oliver et al. 2001b) to allow service users to shape a review from their own perspective.

In sum, an array of methods exists for conducting systematic reviews that either generate, explore or test theory. The appropriate choice of review methods depends on: (i) the review question(s); (ii) whether the data available are qualitative, quantitative or mixed; and (iii) how well defined concepts are before the review begins. In primary research, mixed methods have been chosen for different reasons (Cresswell 2003), and the same arguments apply to systematic reviews:

1 To combine the strengths of different research methods, as with the review of children and healthy eating where the findings of a configurative review were used to interrogate the findings of an aggregate review (Thomas et al. 2004). For longer discussions about mixed methods in reviews, see Harden and Thomas (2010) and Pope et al. (2007).

2 For one method to inform or develop another by applying them sequentially (for example, a configurative synthesis of parents' and children's views to refine the conceptual framework for shared decision-making followed by an aggregative synthesis of intervention studies to evaluate the effects of shared decision-making: Sutcliffe 2010); or a subsequent configurative review of adherence to TB treatment conducted to explain the disappointing findings of an aggregative review (as described above: Munro et al. 2007; Cochrane 1972/1989).

3 To provide insights at different levels of analysis by nesting one method within another, for example, reviewing process evaluations associated with trials, as in a review of incentives for changing young people's behaviour (Kavanagh et al. 2011); or a systematic map aggregating research about incentives for behaviour change to inform the choice of an in-depth systematic review of processes and impact, and provide a context for the review findings (Kavanagh et al. 2009a, 2010).

4 To apply a theoretical lens to frame the collection and analysis of diverse studies to answer 'transformative-emancipatory' questions, as with the review of public involvement in research agenda setting (Oliver et al. 2004); or aggregative reviews followed by configuring a PROGRESS-Plus framework to explore inequalities through sub-group analysis (Kavanagh et al. 2009b).

The result is reviews with different structures (see Chapter 3). Chapter 9 describes in more detail methods for aggregative and configurative syntheses.

---

### Box 4.6

## The practicalities

1 If the aim of the review is to test a hypothesis, work begins with the development of the conceptual framework to match the question and include clearly defined concepts to frame a review. Aggregative methods are appropriate.

2 If the aim of the review is to generate or explore a theory, and there are few concepts clearly defined in advance, work begins with delving into the literature for key concepts. Configurative methods are appropriate and employed to build a conceptual framework or theory.

3 If the aim of a review is to explore implicit or partially developed theories, or policy or practice options, initial assumptions are tentative and gradually develop into a stronger theory, and work begins as findings emerge from the research literature. Mixed methods, such as framework synthesis or realist review, are appropriate.

4 If the aim of the review is ultimately to lead to change, work begins: by involving stakeholders to collaborate in developing the hypothesis (for 1 above); with reviewers listening to stakeholders to sensitise themselves to some of the key issues (for 2 above); or by bringing together key stakeholders to contribute to the initial assumptions and framework, and interpret the emerging findings (for 3 above).

## Choosing the scale of a review

Reviews can vary in the breadth and depth of the question that they seek to address (see the discussion of this issue in Chapter 3). The scale of a review will depend upon such things as the need for evidence, what is already known about the evidence likely to be found, the methods appropriate for answering the review question and the time and resources available for the review. A review for generating theory requires reviewers to be immersed in detailed analysis to such an extent that approaches such as meta-ethnography or thematic synthesis are most appropriately applied to a small number of studies. In contrast, framework analysis for scoping an area of the literature can be applied to hundreds of reports to produce a 'map' of the available research.

Many systematic reviews of the effects of interventions will address a focused population that has been offered a single intervention and comparison, evaluated with a range of outcomes (similar to the review of paracetamol mentioned above). Investment in Cochrane Review Groups has provided the infrastructure for volunteers to conduct such reviews, and they have been very successful in generating evidence for the Cochrane Database of Systematic Reviews within the Cochrane Library. Broader reviews that include a range of interventions seeking similar or overlapping outcomes (for instance, interventions for encouraging children's physical activity) will better inform decisions about which interventions to implement. This evidence may be particularly useful when facing a range of options. However, these are likely to be more time-consuming and will need a larger team.

## Building a review team

Systematic reviews are better conducted by teams, partly because a single person is unlikely to hold all the necessary knowledge and skills, and partly because coding studies benefits from being done by two people independently to assure the quality of the work. Systematic reviews require a combination of substantive knowledge (sometimes spanning different topics or disciplines) and methodological skills (including skills for literature searching, analysis and writing) that are rarely found in a single author. A team for designing and implementing a review consists of people who have different roles and responsibilities at each stage of the review process. Working together, the team aims to complete the review, on time, to a high standard.

Either the review question and its appropriate methods will determine the choice of review team, or the review team will choose questions which they will have the appropriate knowledge and methodological skills to address. The knowledge and methodological skills of the review team can be supplemented by an advisory group whose members may bring research expertise in the topic and/or the methodology, or expertise from the perspectives of policy, practice or service-use. How these people are brought together, to take into account different perspectives when specifying the review question, was addressed in Chapter 2.

## Key skills for review teams

All reviews, as with all research, need to be led by someone who is experienced in *managing research* projects: managing the tasks, the people and the resources. When conducting a systematic review, this includes taking responsibility for establishing the review team, engaging with potential users of the review, setting and managing review-specific milestones (see planning a review below), co-ordinating the completion of the protocol and overseeing the quality of the final review product. The person leading the review needs to work closely with the other review team members to ensure they are clear about their roles and responsibilities, to facilitate others contributing to the review, to be available to discuss and make decisions at each stage of the review, and to manage any risks to the project. It is advisable to designate the team leader before the review begins and to allocate this to a member of the team who is both interested in or familiar with the review topic and who has the systematic review skills to lead and conduct the review.

The quality of the review will be enhanced when it is informed by team members who can engage with the review topic from different standpoints. If some (but not all) of the review team are familiar with the topic, they bring valuable background knowledge and understanding of relevant issues, and their assumptions can be challenged by other members of the team who are new to the topic but bring methodological expertise. A team that includes *experts in the topic* being reviewed and *newcomers* to that topic benefits from their interaction. The experts offer their relevant knowledge and interrogation by the newcomers clarifies explanations and reveals hidden assumptions. These discussions are essential for defining ideas in advance to frame hypotheses about the cause and effect that are tested by a review. They also contribute to generating or refining conceptual frameworks in mixed methods reviews, and to interpreting and communicating the findings of all types of reviews.

Topic knowledge engagement is not the only criteria for ensuring the success of a review. Each stage of the review requires *methodological expertise* from the team to guide the review. This includes developing the protocol, designing and running search strategies, retrieving studies, designing and using coding tools, synthesising studies, and drawing conclusions and implications from the findings. A core team of systematic reviewers needs to be supplemented by specialist staff. Information scientists for developing search strategies may be found in institutional libraries. Some synthesis methods require particular expertise, such as a statistician or economist. Additional staff can help with the resource-intensive work of retrieving, screening and coding studies. Additional input, perhaps from an advisory group, can guide the team in moving from the synthesis to the conclusions and implications (see Chapter 2).

*Achieving the balance* between topic expertise and methodological skills is important. A team that is very knowledgeable on the topic, but without methodological skills in review may: (i) struggle to complete the review at all; or (ii) harbour a vested interest in a particular outcome of the review, for instance if they are authors of included studies. The opposite imbalance of all review skills and little familiarity with the topic can lead to: (i) missing important contextual details, particularly when developing the conceptual framework; or (ii) neither understanding the broader theoretical or political position nor understanding where the review fits in a particular body of knowledge. The result may be a superficial review which is methodologically robust (systematic, transparent, replicable) but does not have depth and fails to engage with important issues.

All research is open to interpretation, particularly at the stages of setting the research question, deciding which literature to include, being sensitive to patterns in the data, making judgements about the quality and relevance of the evidence, and drawing conclusions and implications for policy and practice. Accommodating and managing this process requires a careful choice of review team and advisors to provide a balance of key perspectives for the work. Making good use of that balance requires excellent interpersonal skills. Managing a team of highly skilled and independent-minded researchers is not merely a technical project management issue. Researchers largely manage themselves, and group management is concerned with the creation of shared values and norms to facilitate self-management and create mutual trust so that the team gels, and works within their agreed framework to achieve their shared goals (Ernø-Kjølhede 2000).

## Quality assurance for reviews

The quality of a review can be enhanced and monitored using both internal and external quality assurance procedures (see Box 4.7 on the practicalities). In terms of internal procedures, good quality reviews result not only from good research design and methods, but also from good research management. Essential for success is good project management, formal quality assurance procedures for the review team, and formal procedures to support external quality assurance.

Key project management includes staff planning and the allocation of tasks. How these relate specifically to reviews was considered above. Information management systems are vital for keeping track of the literature, monitoring the progress of reviews and running many analyses. These are described in Chapter 5.

Ensuring the quality of the review rests on specific procedures, such as double coding, for each stage of the review. These relate particularly to searching (Chapter 6), screening and coding studies (Chapter 7), and appraising their quality (Chapter 8). Authors can refer to the PRISMA (Preferred Reporting Items for Systematic Reviews and Meta-Analyses) statement for guidance.[3] PRISMA is an evidence-based minimum set of items for reporting in systematic reviews and meta-analyses and can provide the basis for reporting templates.

Exposing the review to external quality assurance takes a number of forms. The first is convening an appropriate advisory group (see Chapter 2) or making good use of external consultants (see 'Building a review team', above). The second is the time-honoured tradition of peer review, where 'peers' with an appropriate specialist interest comment on draft review protocols and draft review reports.

---

[3] www.prisma-statement.org/

These people may work in academia, policy development, service management or delivery, or have a personal, family or community interest in the topic of the review. Academics with a methodological interest provide an additional check. Inviting comments from the author of an included study can be challenging, but does ensure a particularly relevant academic input. A third approach is to maximise the transparency of the work by making it public every step of the way. Protocols can be made publicly available on institutional websites representing the topic area or a reviews programme or both. In health research, for example, *The Cochrane Library* publishes and invites feedback on the protocols for Cochrane reviews. More inclusive is PROSPERO, which invites the registration of protocols for systematic reviews of the effects of interventions and strategies to prevent, diagnose, treat and monitor health conditions, for which there is a health-related outcome.[4] These outlets also make it possible to publish and obtain feedback on review reports with all their details, including the data extracted from included studies and how these have been coded and analysed.

---

> ### Box 4.7
>
> ## The practicalities
>
> The quality of reviews is assured by:
>
> 1  **Internal project management**: such as the planning of staffing, finances and other resources, work to be done by whom, when, procedures, information management systems (related to IT and EPPI-Reviewer; Thomas et al. 2010), project monitoring, checking progress against milestones, risk assessment).
> 2  **Internal formal quality procedures**: piloting and checking some or all of the review stage actions (such as searching, screening, coding, quality and relevance appraisal, synthesis), face-to-face or virtual team meetings.
> 3  **External formal quality procedures**: advisory groups, consultants, the web publishing of process data (such as study codes), draft or final products (protocol, final report), the peer refereeing of draft products (by, for instance, an academic expert, policy expert practitioner, service user and an expert systematic reviewer).
> 4  **Product management procedures**: filing systems for paper and electronic documents, excellent record-keeping for all decisions, reporting templates that match PRISMA standards for reporting reviews, good writing skills, plagiarism rules and citation systems.
> 5  **Financial management**: including the costs of: staffing (management, researchers and information specialists); inter-library loan costs (perhaps hundreds of papers can be needed at short notice); external advice (convening advisory group meetings or other approaches to stakeholder involvement); other communication costs (conference presentations); publication costs (copy editing, formatting, typesetting, printing); software (reference management software, specialist reviewing software, statistical meta-analyses software); office and IT costs (for maintaining and running the offices in which the team works).[4]

---

[4]www.crd.york.ac.uk/prospero/

## Conclusion

By their very nature, as pieces of research, systematic reviews need a clear plan to get started. This plan includes all the issues considered in this chapter: deciding who and what the review is about; the choice of review methods; the team skills and ways of working together; and systems for managing information and preparing the report to ensure the quality. If the review is to be funded, a proposal will need to convince the funders that the review question is important and the conceptual framework is clear and justified, that the chosen methods are appropriate, and that the review team has the skills and resources to do the work. A timetable with clear milestones will allow the monitoring of progress.

# FIVE

## Information management in reviews

*Jeff Brunton and James Thomas*

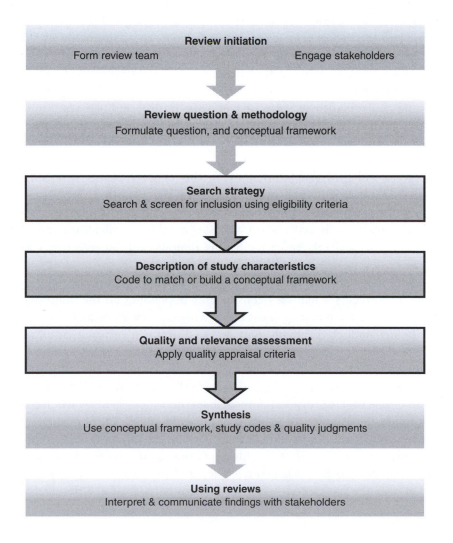

---

**Aims of chapter**

This chapter aims to:

- demonstrate that good information management is vital for systematic reviews
- examine the types of information that need management in systematic reviews
- discuss tools, processes and methods that will assist good information management

---

## Introduction

Systematic reviews involve the generation and management of a great deal of information. This chapter discusses the importance of good information management and the use of appropriate tools through an examination of the volume and types of information that a reviewer will make use of during the course of a review. Looking at the challenges encountered while handling this volume and range of data, the chapter considers how bibliographic, word-processing and spreadsheet software can assist in different aspects of information management. The chapter then examines the use of specialised systematic review software, and outlines the functions available in one tool in particular: EPPI-Reviewer 4.

Reviewers will find the information in this chapter useful when planning their review, as it will alert them to various common pitfalls. Commissioners of reviews will also find it useful to know about the challenges involved in systematic reviewing, both to assist when assessing funding applications and also to understand what is likely to be happening operationally at different stages of the review.

As Chapter 3 discussed, there is no one model for carrying out reviews, and methods and processes will vary considerably depending on the question being addressed. Information management needs will also vary according to the type of review being conducted though some areas will remain constant, as all reviews involve searching for literature and therefore have similar bibliographic information management needs. Reviews differ significantly in their analytical approaches, and it is here that the supporting tools vary the most. We will begin with an example of one type of review, acknowledging that most reviews will have similar information management needs in their early stages. Our consideration of data management tools is in two sections. First, we consider the different types of data management needs that different phases of reviews have and how generic software (such as Microsoft Office and bibliographic tools) might be used. Later in the chapter we discuss specialist software for different types of review.

## Systematic reviews generate significant amounts of data

In June 2003, a systematic review entitled 'A systematic map and synthesis review of the effectiveness of personal development planning [PDP] for improving student learning' was carried out at the EPPI-Centre (Gough et al. 2003). The method chosen followed fairly standard stages that are typical in many reviews which pre-specify their search strategy and involve little iteration throughout (see Chapter 3). Its mode of analysis was aggregative, though the mapping also involved some configuration. It included the creation of a systematic map to answer the question 'What empirical research has been undertaken on the use of PDP in higher and related education?' and a synthesis review with the question 'What evidence is there that processes that connect reflection, recording, planning and action improve student learning?' A brief summary of the flow of references through this review showed that:

- 14,439 references were found by searching;
- 982 references were found to be potentially relevant from the titles and abstracts;
- 813 full reports were obtained;
- 157 of these reports met the review's inclusion criteria and were described in the map;
- 25 studies were relevant to the focused review question and so were included in the in-depth review.

Systematic reviewers typically represent the flow of studies through a review using a PRISMA diagram (Moher et al. 2009). These diagrams are an important part of the process of reporting reviews as they enable readers to see how the review authors accounted for all the references retrieved in their review. The PRISMA diagram for the review about PDP being discussed here is shown in Figure 5.1. The diagram summarises the many reasons for why, out of the 14,439 references found initially by an extensive search strategy, 25 were eventually identified as being relevant for the in-depth review. It enables readers to see at a glance that, for example, 1,394 were duplicates, 10,302 were not about PDP, 1,164 were not empirical, etc.

What these figures do not show, however, is that even as the number of studies decreased, the amount of information created to complete the work increased steadily throughout the review. Each reference was read at least once by one person, and some were read multiple times. To ensure consistency across the team, references were screened multiple times and all decisions were recorded. The retrieval of the full text of documents was tracked along with final decisions about whether a study should be included or excluded.

All of the additional pieces of information about decisions taken in the review generated 30,246 new pieces of data that supplemented the original 14,439 references. In addition to these predicable information categories, there will be many other instances in which reviews need to keep track of information, such as:

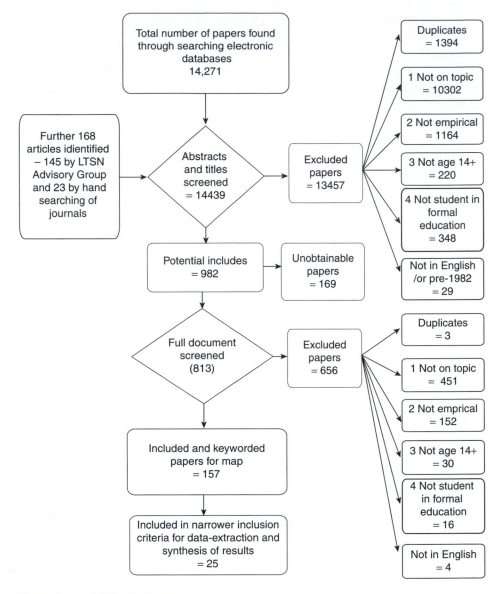

**Figure 5.1** PRISMA diagram

recording contact with authors and any information gleaned; noting the methods used and any assumptions that were made in calculating effect sizes for included studies; and mapping out relationships between concepts in the final synthesis. The types of data include: search 'strings' for searching electronic databases; the records retrieved from database searches; bibliographic information, full-text reports; categorical, free-text and numeric information about studies including inclusion/exclusion decisions; and information about the methods and findings of the synthesis.

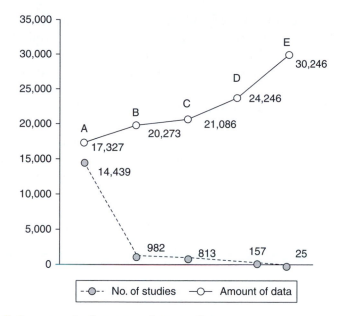

**Figure 5.2** Reference reduction versus data creation

**Table 5.1** Data increase through a review

| Stage | Number of references/studies | Amount of data |
| --- | --- | --- |
| A | Search results: 14,439 items available for title and abstract screening | 17,327 pieces of data after screening criteria applied (10% double screening) |
| B | After title and abstract screening: 982 potential includes require retrieval | 20,273 pieces of data after full-text retrieval |
| C | After full-text retrieval: 813 items remain for full text screening | 21,086 pieces of data after full-text screening |
| D | After full-text screening: 157 items remain for keywording | 24,246 pieces of data after application of keywording tool |
| E | After keywording: 25 items remain for data extraction | 30,246 pieces of data after application of data extraction tool |

As Figure 5.2 shows and Table 5.1 summarises, the number of references that the reviewers were actively considering reduced during the review process, from 14,439 to 25, but the amount of information that had to be stored more than doubled from 14,439 to in excess of 30,000 pieces of information.

Of course, not all reviews will take precisely the same approach to finding research (see Chapters 3 and 6). Some will have more specific search strategies and will therefore start with fewer studies. Others, usually reviews which aim to *configure* the research they identify, will take a more iterative approach to searching, and conduct multiple 'rounds' of searching, screening and document retrieval. The numbers of documents retrieved with each iteration may well be smaller than the above example, but the challenges of information management will be similar. Indeed, in reviews which have multiple iterations of searching, some items of information will need to be stored multiple times, such as the search strategy used with each iteration, how the strategy was implemented and during which iteration(s) each piece of research was identified. Aggregative reviews, too, will sometimes have more than one 'round' of searching, as some reviews will perform a quick update search at the end of the review to identify studies that have been published during the time that the review was being undertaken (Chapter 6).

In addition to the bibliographic information that was the focus of the above example, reviewers typically need to deal with process and management information as well as, for example, any text-mining operations (see later in this chapter) that might be applied to the original references, or keeping track of team members and their allocated tasks. (There is increasing interest in using text mining in systematic reviews to reduce the amount of time that identifying relevant documents can take. See Chapter 6 and Thomas et al. 2011 for further information.) For many reviewers, especially those new to the process, trying to manage this volume of information becomes a challenging task. Lost, misplaced or uncategorised data can lead to delays and wasted effort in the review and have the potential for biasing its findings. Good information management is therefore a critical part of a successful review.

## What is information management and why is it important?

Information management is the collection, storage, categorisation, analysis, manipulation and presentation of the data that are created while carrying out a systematic review. Throughout the process the types of information will vary and the volume of data will continue to increase. There are many important reasons for having clearly defined processes and tools to manage this information.

The first reason is to be sure that the process is explicit and replicable. By explicit we mean that there is a clear description of what has occurred and what will happen throughout the review. By replicable we mean that the reviewer or someone else looking at the review can recreate the process. (NB replicability is a contested subject, but in the context of information management it can mean that, in and of themselves, information management systems should not be responsible for differences in findings.)

A second reason is to guard against the loss or distortion of information and the wasting of time in duplicating effort (i.e. redoing some of the review because data have been lost). While being a simple idea on the face of it ('let's collect all the research about…'), systematic reviews are complex operationally (O'Blenis 2004) and conceptually – as Chapters 3 and 4 demonstrate. Keeping track of the quantity of data collected and created in a systematic review can be difficult, especially if members of the review team are in different locations and not always present when all the key decisions are taken. The allocation and co-ordination of reviewer tasks, tracking revisions of instruments such as coding tools, quality control with respect to, for example, the interpretation of coding tools, are all activities that can lead to lost or distorted information if not carefully managed.

A third reason is so that the review team can justify or defend their decisions. At the end of the process, reviewers may be required to defend an action such as why a particular study was or was not included in the review. With a record of all the steps and decisions made during the review, information should be available about what happened to each study identified, and with a good record of all searches and the results they returned, it is possible to see if a study appeared in the initial references. If the reasons for including or excluding all studies are recorded, it is possible to determine at what point and on what criterion a study was excluded. With clearly defined quality assessment tools and the ability to query the application of that tool, it will be apparent whether a study was left out because it did not meet a given quality threshold and on what basis that decision was made.

A final reason for clear processes and tools for information management is so that the systematic review can be updated. Many systematic reviews are never considered finished: there is an expectation that the review will be updated periodically to include any new relevant research that exists. If a clear process has been followed, a reviewer, who may or may not have been in the original research team, should be able to conduct new searches, insert any new results into the existing review, follow the same processes as before, and determine if the new studies change the original results in any way.

## What types of information will be managed?

In the process of carrying out a systematic review there are many types of information that must be generated and stored. These can be categorised into four groups:

- Bibliographic;
- Substantive;
- Process;
- Management.

Bibliographic information consists of the individual references obtained by searching different sources to find documents related to the subject of the review. These sources might include online databases, journals, secondary references and other authors.

Substantive information is information that the reviewer creates. These are the summary descriptions, categorical classifications and judgements made about the primary studies that are created throughout the review process. In the early stages these will be the criteria that are used to determine whether a study is within the scope of the review and that are applied to each reference (known as 'exclusion' or 'eligibility' criteria). In the latter stages they will be the observations and judgements about the studies collected during data extraction and quality assessment. In the final synthesis they will be the reviewer's interpretation and presentation of the data.

Process information explains what has occurred throughout the review. It provides an audit trail informing the reader of the decisions made and the reasons why they were made. This contains details such as which studies were excluded for which specific reason or the reason that apparently relevant studies (based on their titles and abstracts) were not retrieved. It provides the reviewer with data which can be used to justify the decisions made during the review.

Management information gives a snapshot of progress being made during the course of the review. It helps with the management of resources by indicating whether the review is on schedule or whether more effort is required for a particular activity. Good records of which studies within the review have been inspected and at what stage mean that a clear picture of likely timelines can be established.

## What devices can be used to help manage review information and when should they be used?

To help manage the wide range and volume of information collected while carrying out a systematic review the reviewer can call upon a number of devices or tools. These devices can exist in many different forms and can range from paper records to generic software applications. At this point we are not considering software created specifically for systematic reviewing, but rather devices in the researcher's general toolbox that can help store data and order the process.

A list of devices to help manage the information could include:

- databases;
- manuals, strategies, coding guidelines;
- paper records of individual reports;
- records of the review stages;
- report structure.

A database is one of the most important electronic tools a reviewer will use, and can be considered to be analogous to an index card system. References are one of the types of information indexed, and it is common practice to store all of the references that were collected after searching in a database. Some reviews utilise a series of databases to hold items as they proceed through the review, so others might include databases that hold the items that need full-text screening or references that require retrieval. A well-constructed database is 'normalised', meaning that each item in the database is unique. This can be accomplished by giving every item a unique identifying number. A good database allows the reviewer to 'query' its contents in many different ways. Being able to retrieve information entered into a database easily makes them very powerful tools. Reference management software is ideal for this purpose and we discuss how they can be used in reviews later in the chapter. Two typical examples are RefWorks[1] and EndNote.[2]

---

[1] www.refworks.com/

[2] www.endnote.com/

Manuals, strategies and coding guidelines help direct the reviewer through the review process. An example of such a tool is the inclusion/exclusion criteria sheets that describe each individual criterion and how they should be applied to each reference. These ensure that each reviewer has the same criteria and guidance on how to apply those criteria to the references. A similar tool is the data extraction form (see Chapter 7). It will direct the reviewer through a series of questions to be sure the information required for the review is extracted from each study. As these tools are often revised during the review process, it is important to have a revision control system to avoid the situation where different versions of the same coding tools exist and are being used by different reviewers. Word-processing software or spreadsheet software is ideal for these activities.

Despite the importance of electronic information storage, paper records associated with individual studies in the review are still part of the data management challenge. In the absence of electronic tools, paper records must be kept of all coding decisions. A completed coding sheet stating the outcome of screening should have an identifier written on it to match the reference's unique identifier. Many full reports are not available in an electronic format and will need to be stored in a filing system. As with coding sheets, these paper reports should be assigned the same unique identifier that was used in the inclusion/exclusion stage to identify the item. An important point to bear in mind when designing any filing system for a systematic review is that the later unit of analysis is the *study*, rather than the paper, so it should support the grouping of papers according to study for analysis. (It is often not possible to group papers according to study at the beginning of the review; it is only when reviewers begin the process of reading them in detail that the links between papers will become apparent.)

Records of the review stages can be in a paper or electronic format. Complete records for each stage of the review allow anyone to follow the process and re-create any steps if necessary. Full records include a search log that records all of the databases and locations that were searched and the search strategy that was used. A record of screening at both the abstract level and the full-report level for each document allows the progress of each item to be traced. Time and resources often prevent the reviewer from obtaining all studies that might be relevant, so a record needs to be kept of all attempts to retrieve full reports and why certain studies were not retrieved. Records of decisions involving double coding must include the independent work as well as any meetings to reconcile differences.

The structure of the report that will be used for the completed systematic review is an important device that is often overlooked. If the reviewer knows ahead of time the information that they wish to present, they will also know what information they need to be collecting (or do not need to collect) during the course of the review. For example, to present a breakdown of the number of items excluded and with which criteria from the screening stage, relevant information needs to be collected at the time of screening. If a particular type of summary table is required in the final report, then the reviewer can ensure that the necessary questions are asked during the data extraction stage to complete this table (very common in the appendices of full technical reports of reviews). It will be easier to present this type

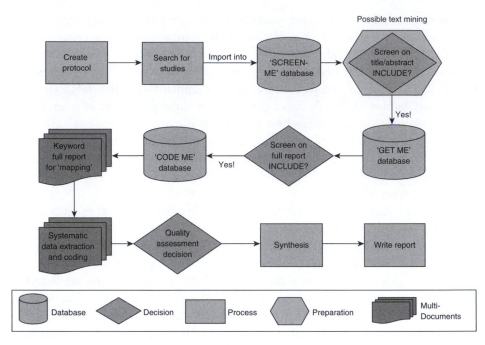

**Figure 5.3** Flow of references through a review

of information at the end of the review if the reviewer has been identifying and collecting these data throughout. (Additionally, rather than waiting until the very end, the report can be written up as the review progresses. One approach to doing this is to use the protocol as the basis for the report, and to amend it as each stage of the review is completed.) To demonstrate examples of where and when to use these devices or tools in the systematic review process, we can follow the flow of references through a review depicted in Figure 5.3. Although a systematic review can take many forms, this example should be sufficient. (As mentioned above, some reviews have an iterative approach to searching; in these cases some of the stages and procedures involved will simply occur more than once.)

Based on Figure 5.3, the first step in the review is to **determine the methods that are to be used**. This is sometimes described as 'creating a protocol', though protocols contain varying amounts of detail, depending on the type of review being undertaken. As described in Chapter 4, this will contain the review question, the conceptual framework, and help to determine the search strategies and inclusion/exclusion criteria that will be applied to the search results. The production of a protocol can be assisted by the support of good information systems. While the use of word-processing software with 'tracked changes' facilities is becoming commonplace, and is very useful in this situation where a document is often being edited by many people, mistakes – such as the creation of different versions – still occur. Setting up an online area (e.g. Google Docs or a shared network drive) where files can be shared throughout the team (and version control established) can avoid some of these problems.

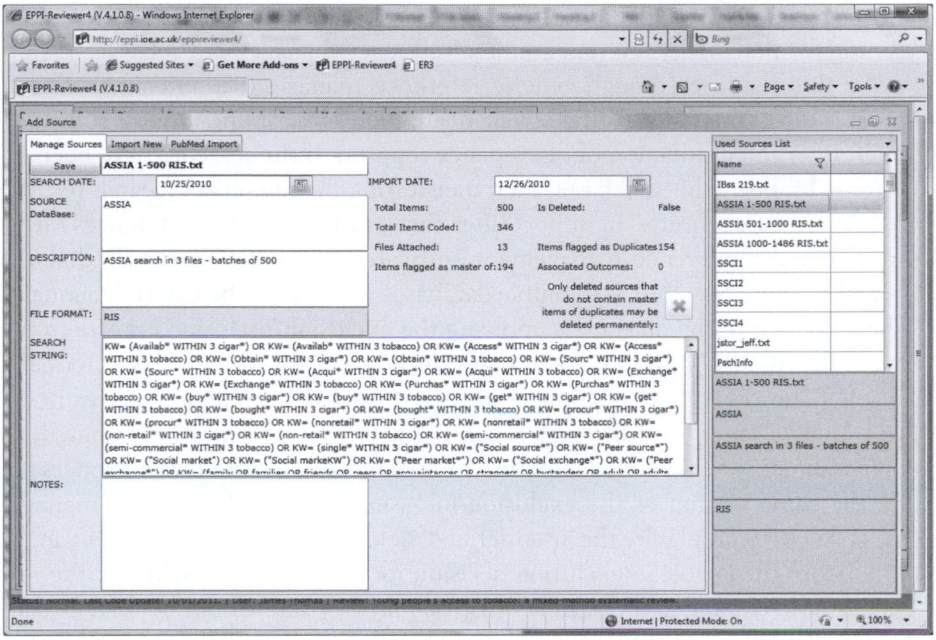

**Figure 5.4**  Keeping track of where and how references were obtained

The next step in the review is **searching for studies**. While many search strategies will include website searching and personal contact, electronic searches are usually the least specific (i.e. retrieve most irrelevant 'hits') and require the most data management. Each electronic source to be searched may have its own interface and be more or less sophisticated in terms of its functionality. This means that each source will require its own specific search strategy that may in turn require a unique search string to be used (see Chapter 6). As well as managing the results of the search, a log of search strategies must be kept to provide the reader of the review with a detailed record of the searching. The log for search strategies must include what search parameters were used for each database, when the search was carried out, who carried out the search and the number of results returned. The search results can be in many different formats so the method of transferring the references into the reviewer's database of references may vary.

If many sources are being searched, there is a good chance that some references will be found multiple times. **Removing duplicates** will reduce the number of citations that need to be examined manually, but records of the removed items will need to be kept if the reviewer is able to account for all references identified throughout the review. Figure 5.4 shows an example of software that allows the sources of references to be recorded. Along with the date of the database search, and the filter used for importing, this software also stores the full search string and shows the reviewer how many items were imported, how many were duplicates and how many have the full text of papers attached.

The next operation illustrated in Figure 5.3 is to take the results of the searches and **create a database of references**. The name of the database in the diagram is identified as 'SCREEN ME', indicating that everything in the database will require screening for potentially relevant studies. Reference management software is suitable for this purpose (though generic reference management software will not support some of the tasks that reviewers need, such as the 'blind' double screening of references and production of discrepancy reports). If the searches have been on electronic bibliographic databases, then transferring the references (search results) into this database requires an import filter that can translate the references into a format that the reference management software can read. References that are obtained from places other than online databases will need to be entered manually.

The next step in the diagram is **applying the exclusion/inclusion criteria** to the items in the SCREEN ME database to decide whether the reference is potentially relevant. (The criteria being applied will have been determined at the protocol stage.) Ideally, some form of version control will be used (either automated, or using a manual system such as structured file names) to ensure that all coders are using the same version of the exclusion/inclusion criteria. If reference management software is available, the user-defined fields or the keyword fields can be used to store the inclusion/exclusion decision for each item (i.e. whether the reference is not relevant to the review or is (or may be) and should be further considered). The term added to this field describes the criterion being applied and at what stage. For example, 'Excl Abstract' can mean 'Exclude on criterion 1 based on the citation's title and abstract'. It is possible to search individual fields in most reference management software, so it should be possible to retrieve all items coded a particular way. The same functionality can also be achieved in a spreadsheet by having all of the references listed by rows. Inclusion/exclusion will be in columns and the user can indicate a criterion selection with a marker. Spreadsheet software has many functions that allow the user to query individual cells to find items coded in a particular fashion as well as requiring the reviewer to select a category from a pre-defined list.

Once the references that are potentially relevant (based on their titles and abstracts) have been identified, their **full text will need to be retrieved**. As well as ensuring that these references are easily distinguished from those that have been deemed to be irrelevant, systems and procedures will need to be established in order to keep track of which items are 'In file', 'On order', 'Out of file' and 'Not available'. Some reference management software will have a field reserved specifically for this purpose while others will require the use of user-defined fields. Once the full papers are 'In file', a filing system will be needed to store them. Some documents will be available in an electronic format; others will be hard copies. The item's unique identifier, generated when the item was placed in the database, is applied to each retrieved document; applying the same identifier to the front page of hard copies allows filing for easy access and retrieval. Electronic copies will need to be stored in a dedicated file directory on a computer. Reference management software will normally have 'link fields' allowing the user to link a reference to a location on their computer's file system. If this is not available, the user can preface the name of the file with the unique identifier to make it easier to locate the saved file. A record of retrieval attempts should be kept. If an item identified as being potentially relevant is not retrieved, a reason should be recorded. This reason can be added to the notes field of the reference.

The full copies of the references will now need to be assessed using the same **exclusion/inclusion criteria** as were earlier applied to titles and abstracts. If reference management software is being used, then the user-defined or keyword fields are again suitable for this purpose. The term added to the field should have a name that will identify the stage at which the criterion is being applied (e.g. 'Excl Full' can mean 'Exclude on criterion 1 based on full report').

After applying the Inclusion/Exclusion codes to the full reports of studies, some items will move forward in the process. The next step is to **place these items in a new database**. In our example, the items that have moved forward are now coded (keyworded) to create a map of studies (maps are described in Chapter 3) so the database can be called, for example, 'Code Me' (see Chapter 7 on coding). Not all reviews contain a 'map' of research activity, and will move straight to data extraction at this point. The keywording coding tool normally consists of a number of questions with potential answers. Some of the answers may also require a textual response. If the user can restrict the keywording tool to pre-set responses only with no textual responses needed, it should be possible to use the keyword or user-defined fields found in reference management software to record the response. In the case where textual responses are required, the user may need to set up a spreadsheet to record the keywords applied and the textual responses given. Ideally, the same data storage tool will hold both the keywords applied and any textual responses given, making searching the data less cumbersome. If the reviewer is looking at the data at a study level, they may find different papers referring to the same study. Since the 'unit of analysis' in a systematic review is the primary research study, and not individual research reports, a single account is required, which draws on all published papers of the study in question. In these cases, the papers should be considered 'linked' and the 'user-defined fields' in standard reference management software can be used to hold the unique IDs of the linked papers. Occasionally, more than one study will be reported in the same publication. In these situations a new record should be created for each study.

In our example review about personal development planning, the map of studies is now examined and a review question is formed based on the initial coding (keywording) exercise. Items relevant to answering the review question are selected for more detailed coding. As Chapter 7 describes, detailed coding or '**data extraction**' means collecting the results of the studies based on a number of questions the reviewer has created. A set of such questions is called a 'data extraction tool'.

As many of the questions require textual and statistical responses, in addition to categorical answers, reference management software will not be able to provide the functionality required, although most word-processing software allows the user to create a 'form'. Such a form can contain all of the questions in the data extraction tool, accommodating the entry of textual data. These forms are essential to enable the standardised abstraction of information from studies as well as facilitating independent data extraction in teams of reviewers. Although forms based on standard word-processing software cannot easily be queried, and thus it is difficult for the reviewer to summarise information across studies, with fewer studies to inspect at this point than was the case when potentially thousands of references were being screened, a visual comparison of the data extracted from each included study may be sufficient. As well as textual information, studies may include numeric outcome data that could be used in a statistical meta-analysis. Although all of the formulae required for running a meta-analysis can be placed in a spreadsheet, there are statistical software packages available to deal with statistical data collection and analysis too. The **quality assessment** of included studies can be a separate activity or part of the data extraction stage of review. It normally involves answering a number of questions about the studies. Again, this can take place in the same word-processing software that was used for data extraction.

The next stage of a review is **synthesis**, usually involving analytical tools that are discussed in the next section. After synthesis, the final stage of our example, **report writing**, is communicating the findings and how they contribute to knowledge (see Chapter 10). This involves bringing together all of the information collected and created in the review process. Many different tools were used at the various stages of the review, so the relevant content from each will need to be extracted and then combined in the presentation of the results. This will include reference lists, report tables, statistical results, graphical representations and a narrative summary. Word-processing software should provide most of the functions required to format and present the results, and reference management software will help create a formatted reference list. Functions such as 'cite as you write' enable reviewers to insert citations in a consistent way and when this is being used, the people working on a report need to co-ordinate their activities carefully in order to avoid corrupting the reference list. The summary in Table 5.2 shows the stages from Figure 5.3 depicting the flow of references through a review, and which device applies, and gives examples of available tools. The aim is to suggest options when systematic reviewing software is not available, but the use of generic software for specialist tasks is not always straightforward. (NB this table focuses on the data stored at each stage of the review, rather than the flow of data through the review, and so has a slightly different structure from that given in Figure 5.3.)

Much of the above discussion has focused on the use of information technologies to support good information management throughout a review. This is because, while it is possible to conduct a review using paper records only, we feel electronic data storage offers many advantages over paper, especially considering that reviews are often conducted by teams working in different locations. Reviewers often do use paper for specific parts of the review. For example, they may print out the data extraction form and complete this offline before later transferring their data to a computer. Likewise, some review teams print out the many hundreds (or thousands) of titles and abstracts retrieved in electronic searching and 'screen' these from the printout. Again though, their decisions are usually stored electronically. Sometimes, teams will find that some types of synthesis (usually those *configuring* findings to generate new theory) are best completed using pencil and paper, coloured

**Table 5.2**   Review stages and devices that may be used

| Stage | Device | Examples |
| --- | --- | --- |
| Create protocol | Manuals, strategies, coding guidelines | Word-processing and spreadsheet software |
| Search for studies | Manuals, strategies, coding guidelines | Word-processing and spreadsheet software |
| Store search results | Database | Reference manager, Endnote |
| Screen studies on title and abstract | Manuals, strategies, coding guidelines | Word-processing and/or spreadsheet software |
| Store included studies | Database | Reference manager, Endnote |
| Retrieve full studies | Paper records of individual reports | Word-processing and/or spreadsheet software |
| Screen studies on full report | Paper records of individual reports<br>Manuals, strategies, coding guidelines | Word-processing and spreadsheet software |
| Store included studies based on full report | Database | Reference manager, Endnote, RefWorks |
| Keyword studies for map | Paper records of individual reports<br>Manuals, strategies, coding guidelines | Word-processing and/or spreadsheet software |
| Data extract studies for synthesis | Paper records of individual reports<br>Manuals, strategies, coding guidelines | Word-processing and/or spreadsheet software |
| Quality and relevance appraisal | Paper records of individual reports<br>Manuals, strategies, coding guidelines | Word-processing and/or spreadsheet software |
| Synthesis | Manuals, strategies, coding guidelines | Word-processing and/or spreadsheet software |
| Write report | Report structure<br>Paper records of individual reports<br>Manuals, strategies, coding guidelines | Word-processing and/or spreadsheet software |

pens, stickers and scissors. Other types, such as meta-analysis, can also be carried out manually, but it would be difficult to argue that this is more reliable than using a computer. Ultimately, the selection of data management medium is a matter of personal choice, with the core principle being that decisions should be recorded and available for later scrutiny. Good practices when keeping records in paper form are storing data extraction records in wallets along with the study article, filing according to study rather than paper (thus keeping papers about the same study in the same place), and cross-referencing the data on forms with the specific paper – and the point in the paper – from which the data were abstracted.

## Analytical tools

The previous section has outlined the many ways that different software applications can contribute to information management in a review. In addition to these, the type of software application needed will also vary according to the type of review being conducted and, in particular, to the type of synthesis (see Chapter 9).

Figure 5.5 contains the conceptual model of reviews that we are using throughout this book, showing how different review purposes (moving from generating to testing theory) involve the analysis of different types of data and therefore different types of analytical software. The arrow on the left indicates the progression of reviews that are well supported by qualitative analytic software and the arrow on the right indicates the progression of reviews requiring statistical software. The large arrow in the centre, 'database software', indicates that there is a substantial overlap in this area and we anticipate all reviews will need to make some use of database software to keep track of the different types of information described earlier in this chapter. In addition to this, there are data management tasks that are quite different from review to review.

Reviews that are located towards the left of the diagram are those in which pre-defined concepts tend to be few, with the aim of the review being to *configure* the included studies and to generate new concepts and theories inductively. These types of review often involve the 'open coding' of documents and the identification of themes. Thus the software often used to analyse qualitative data in primary research is suitable for use in these sorts of synthesis. Examples include some of the specialised review applications listed below and generic tools such as NVivo, NUD*IST and Atlas.ti.

Reviews that lie on the extreme right-hand side of the diagram *aggregate* their findings and sometimes use statistics as the main data for synthesis. Most concepts are pre-defined and the aim of the review is not to develop new concepts but to test pre-existing hypotheses. In these cases, software that supports open coding is not required. Rather, software that supports meta-analysis and the storing of structured data is needed. Examples here include the specialised review applications mentioned below (Table 5.4) and generic statistical packages such as stata, SPSS and Excel. Some reviews *configure* statistics from their included studies (e.g. meta-regressions – see Chapter 9); while being located in the centre or towards the left of the diagram, they will still need suitable tools such as stata and SPSS (Excel would not be suitable for a meta-regression).

## Text-mining tools

As well as the above analytical tools, which are an established part of the research landscape, new developments in 'text-mining' technology are now beginning to be evaluated in systematic reviews (Ananiadou et al. 2009; Thomas et al. 2011) (see Chapter 6). Sometimes called *text data mining*, text mining involves the identification of patterns in text, either within individual documents or across multiple documents.

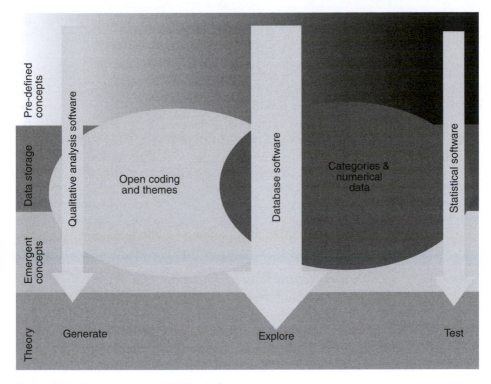

**Figure 5.5** Conceptual model of reviews

Currently, the use of text-mining tools in systematic reviews is in its infancy, but the tools being used include 'term extraction' (or 'recognition'), 'clustering', 'classification' and document 'summarisation'.

Term extraction involves the automatic identification of key terms from within documents. This can help with, for example, the identification of relevant search terms to put in a search strategy. As outlined in Chapter 6, this technology can also be employed to identify 'priority' citations for screening.

It is possible to use document clustering to group similar documents together automatically. One use of this technology in a systematic review is to gain a quick overview of the topics discussed in a set of titles and abstracts, providing a very quick 'map' (see Chapter 7). While this is useful in some situations, the categories identified are completely dependent on the text in the documents, and so cannot be guaranteed to align with the categories in a review's conceptual framework.

Document classification technologies are able to assign pre-existing keywords to documents. In systematic reviews these technologies are used to determine whether a given study should be included or excluded, and also to assign keyword descriptors (such as topic, methodology, participant characteristics). Classification depends upon a pre-existing set of data on which to learn, such as existing include/exclude decisions, or a set of keyworded studies. See Chapter 6 for a more detailed examination of the potential of this technology to help when screening thousands of titles and abstracts.

Finally, summarisation enables reviewers to view a quick summary either of a single document or across multiple documents. Useful in mapping, this technology operates best on homogeneous sets of documents.

The use of text-mining tools in systematic reviews currently (summer 2011) requires specialist text-mining expertise. None of the tools is yet integrated within standard 'office' software, although some are now in specialist systematic reviewing tools (see below). A good example of automatic term recognition is the TerMine tool, available on the National Centre for Text Mining (UK) website.[3] Automatic clustering can be seen operating in some search engines, such as Yippy[4] and Carrot2[5], although online summarisation tools are less common.

## How specialist tools assist in managing information in a systematic review

One of the issues with using generic software is that the reviewer will need to use many different programs throughout the systematic review process. This adds to the complexity of conducting the review and increases the chance that mistakes will be made. There is a growing number of specialist reviewing tools now on the market that offer many of the necessary functions described above. Some focus on specific parts of the review process, whereas others support all aspects of review information management and thus provide the benefit of having all data in one location. Another advantage of using specialist reviewing software is that their functionality is tailored to systematic reviews in a way that generic software is not. Table 5.3 provides a summary of the capabilities that review tools can contain for different parts of the review process, although not all will support (or aim to support) every capability listed.

As shown in Table 5.3, specialised systematic review tools offer the reviewer capabilities that generic tools do not provide. We will examine them briefly according to the various different stages of the review process to highlight some of their advantages.

Some specialised reviewing software applications support the significant data and work management associated with screening many thousands of studies: allocation of batches to different reviewers; screening through multiple 'rounds'; independent 'double' screening; the uploading and storage of electronic documents.

To support the descriptive mapping and quality appraisal of research studies, some specialist systematic review software supports the creation and editing of keywording tools, and provides a mechanism to store the keywords assigned to individual studies as well as to present the data in figures and tables. As for screening, some applications allow single- or multiple-user data entry and a mechanism to compare entries. As there are often many papers published from a single research

---

[3] www.nactem.ac.uk/software/termine/

[4] http://search.yippy.com/

[5] http://search.carrot2.org/stable/search

**Table 5.3** Capabilities of specialist systematic review tools

| Activity/Function | Capabilities |
|---|---|
| Searching and screening | Manage the search process |
| | Reference the import functions |
| | De-duplication functions |
| | Creation and management of the inclusion/exclusion tool |
| | Support the multiple level application of the inclusion/exclusion tool |
| | Support multiple data entry |
| | Manage full document retrieval |
| | Support the uploading of full documents |
| Characterising studies | Creation and management of keywording tools |
| | Store the coding responses |
| | Support multiple data entry |
| | Provide linking mechanism for studies with multiple references |
| Data extraction and quality assessment | Creation and management of keywording tools |
| | Store the coding responses |
| | Support multiple data entry |
| | Provide the linking mechanism for studies with multiple references |
| | Allow input of textual response |
| | Provide the indexing of textual responses for querying and searching |
| Statistical analysis | Import/export data |
| | Allow the input of numerical outcome data |
| | Support multiple outcomes per study |
| | Allow the combining of outcomes from multiple studies |
| | Perform a statistical meta-analysis and mechanisms for exploring heterogeneity (sub-group analysis; meta-regression) |
| | Present the results in a clear format including forest plot and funnel plot |
| Thematic summaries/framework synthesis | Facilitate analysis and synthesis using searching and reporting engines |
| | Allow querying, both codes and textual responses |
| | Provide reports of categorical, numeric and textual data |
| | Present frequency, crosstabs and full-text reports |
| | Present configurable tabular summary reports |
| Thematic synthesis/meta ethnography and other conceptual methods | Allow the line-by-line coding of textual data from uploaded electronic documents |
| | Permit the matching of highlighted text to codes |
| | Present codes graphically in conceptual relationship diagrams |

**Table 5.3** (Continued)

| Activity/Function | Capabilities |
| --- | --- |
| Online application | Support individuals located in different geographical locations |
| | Allow the sharing of information between the reviewers |
| | Allow for variations in internet connection speeds |
| | Allow multiple users to be logged in concurrently |
| Data security | Provide confirmation dialogs for any data removal operations |
| | Have functions that auto-save data |
| | Provide back up of user data |
| | Allow password protected user access |
| Review management | Support reviewer management through access restriction |
| | Permit configurable levels of user access |
| | Should provide real-time summary of coding tasks and review progress for management purposes |
| | Allow commenting features for multi-user collaboration |

study, a way of linking multiple documents to the same study is often supported and as reviews often share generic data extraction and quality assessment tools, it makes sense to be able to use the same tool in multiple reviews.

Specialist tools support the three main types of data generated in reviews (see Chapter 7 for further discussion of data types): categories can be pre-specified as well as emerge as part of the review process; free-text entry to explain or elaborate on categorical assignment and interpretation; fully searchable text data; quick reports such as listing all studies with a given category, frequencies and crosstabs are all supported by some applications. Some tools also allow the reviewer to construct customised reports and can produce summary tables for insertion in the appendices of reviews.

Statistical information is required if a meta-analysis is to be conducted. Necessary functionality includes the storage of summary statistics that represent multiple measures (e.g. outcomes) for each study (see Chapter 9). As well as this, reviewers need to be able to calculate such statistics from the wide range of statistics presented in published reports (e.g. to be able to calculate a standardised mean difference from an exact $p$ value or an odds ratio from percentages), so many specialised tools offer some support for this often tricky process. Methods for synthesising (and partitioning variance) in reviews are developing all the time, so some of the 'generic' tools, such as stata and $r$, may have the latest techniques and be able to respond more quickly to changes in methods. More standard analyses, such as those combining studies using fixed and random effects models and providing forest and funnel plots, are common to many reviewing tools.

Some specialist reviewing tools support thematic, or more conceptual, methods of synthesis. The functions associated with these analytical methods are the line-by-line coding of text, and a mechanism to generate and store new codes while coding, to organise them, and to view the text associated with particular codes. Associated functions also include the ability to draw diagrams to show the relationship between concepts in a similar way to software for the analysis of primary qualitative research.

Many systematic review teams are spread across many locations, and so some reviewing tools support this working practice by being available online, with review data stored in a central server. While this sort of system has many advantages, supporting centralised backups, version control and the logging in of many reviewers simultaneously, it does require a reliable internet connection (something which cannot always be guaranteed).

Robust specialised tools provide advanced functionality in the often overlooked field of data security. While generic software may appear to offer sufficient functionality, there are likely to be multiple points of potential data loss because reviewers will need to manage moving data between multiple software applications. Most specialist tools will have been designed by systematic reviewers, who will be aware of the danger of data loss. In addition, they will usually prevent accidental deletions by having a user interface that provides confirmation dialogs for any data removal operations, and functions that save data automatically. Systematic reviews sometimes synthesise confidential information and the ability to protect data by requiring user authentication with a password is required.

Finally, and as alluded to above, reviewing tools often help with the management of a review (see Chapter 4). They allow different parts of the review to be accessible or editable only by specified members of the review team, and they provide a real-time summary of how the review is progressing.

## Examples of specialised systematic review software

There are a number of specialised systematic review applications available that provide some or all of the listed desired functions (see Table 5.4).

### Example of a specialised systematic review tool: EPPI-Reviewer 4

The EPPI-Reviewer software was developed to help conduct the systematic reviews being carried out at the EPPI-Centre. It was created out of a need to deal with the challenges of systematic reviewing in complex areas, as described throughout in this volume. Over time, as other systematic reviewers learned of its capabilities and requested access to it, it was made available online. EPPI-Reviewer 4, the latest version of the program, has been developed based on the experiences and feedback from over a thousand users in hundreds of reviews carried out using earlier versions. The current functions of EPPI-Reviewer are listed below to provide an example of what specialist software can offer to systematic reviews.

EPPI-Reviewer 4's many functions include:

**Reference management**

- Managing the thousands of references that often result from comprehensive searches of electronic databases.
- Importing references in a wide variety of 'tagged' formats.

- Duplicate checking using 'fuzzy logic' (potential duplicates can be checked manually and/ or automatically classified as duplicates, depending on how similar they are).
- Storage of the original document file (such as pdf, doc, etc.) along with the study record.
- 'Linked documents': the 'unit of analysis' in a systematic review is usually the study, but there are often multiple publications originating from the same study. EPPI-Reviewer 4 helps reviewers to use the correct 'unit'.
- Direct access to PubMed through web services. EPPI-Reviewer makes use of this capability to allow direct searching and search result data transfer from PubMed.

**Table 5.4**   Specialised systematic review applications

| Name | Organisation | Web | Notes |
|---|---|---|---|
| ASSERT | NaCTeM | www.nactem.ac.uk/assert | Text-mining demonstrator project |
| Comprehensive meta-analysis | Comprehensive meta-analysis | www.meta-analysis.com/ | Standalone |
| | | | Provides statistical meta-analysis functionality |
| Distiller SR | Evidence Partners | http://systematic-review. net/ | Online |
| EPPI-Reviewer | EPPI-Centre | http://eppi.ioe.ac.uk/ | Online |
| Mix 2.0 | Leon Bax | http://www.meta-analysis-made-easy.com/ | Provides statistical meta-analysis functionality within excel |
| RevMan | Cochrane Collaboration | http://ims.cochrane.org/ revman | Standalone (with online interface to create/update Cochrane reviews) |
| Sumari | Joanna Briggs Institute | www.joannabriggs.edu.au/ services/sumari.php | Online with installed modules |

*For full details of each application please consult the relevant website

## Study classification and data extraction

- Flexible coding schemas for classifying studies:
  - Inclusion/exclusion/eligibility criteria;
  - Codes for descriptive 'mapping' of research activity;
  - Codes to capture detailed information about a study.

- Concurrent multi-user classification: multiple users can classify studies independently and then compare their results. EPPI-Reviewer supports this process, producing summary discrepancy reports and an interface to facilitate the process of agreeing final decisions.
- Bulk application/removal of codes to selected studies.
- Text-mining facilities, including term identification, document clustering and document classification.
- Calculation of common measures of effect (odds ratios, risk ratios, risk differences, standardised mean differences, mean differences, correlation coefficients) from a variety of statistics ($2 \times 2$ tables, means, standard deviations, confidence intervals, $p$, $t$ and $r$ values).

## Synthesis

- Running meta-analyses (fixed and random effects models), calculating I-squared and supporting sub-group analyses.
- A powerful search engine enabling users to search by categories and text and combine searches using Boolean terms.
- Producing reports of categorical, numeric and textual data in a wide variety of formats from frequency reports, crosstabs and full-text reports, to tabular summary reports and summary statistics of numeric data (for export into other statistical software).
- Inductive coding functionality. This allows line-by-line coding of textual data and organising and structuring these codes graphically into conceptual relationship diagrams to display analytic and descriptive themes found through inductive coding.
- Full-text reference searching using the uploaded pdfs.
- Diagrams to summarise, e.g. qualitative syntheses and theories of change for interventions.

## Review management

- The ability to create an unlimited number of reviews.
- Allocation of classification tasks (e.g. screening/data extraction) to individual users.
- Work progress reporting.
- Individual reviewer permissions.
- Review flow charts which update automatically (e.g. with counts of how many studies have been included/excluded according to which criterion).

---

### | Box 5.1 |

## The practicalities

When planning a review, or reviewing a proposal for a review, it is important to consider all data management, analysis and reporting needs. The following questions may assist this process:

- Does the team have good document versioning processes agreed to avoid competing versions of documents being created?
- Does it need to obtain a shared server or an area online where documents can be shared?
- Which tools will be needed for screening studies? (Does the review have access to specialist bibliographic software and/or specialist reviewing software?)
- How will the review *processes* will be managed? (For example, independent data extraction.)
- How will studies be described in reviews and what will the summary tables (often presented in review appendices) contain? Which tools are needed for (a) developing the tool; (b) capturing the codes, text and statistics entered by reviewers; (c) producing the summary tables; (d) providing the data for quality assessment and synthesis.
- What type of synthesis will be conducted? Which software is needed for which task?

*Where different tools are to be used, check that the data can be stored, exported and imported in the correct format.*

## Conclusion

There is a great deal of information to handle in a systematic review, and it is essential to have clearly defined processes and tools to assist in the management of that information. The idea of collecting research together about a particular issue appears to be simple enough, but this simplicity belies the information management challenges that will confront anyone embarking on a review. Where resources are tight, it is possible to conduct a review using no more than commonly available desktop software to manage its information. This chapter has outlined some of the issues that need to be considered should this approach be taken, but it also concludes that there is no substitute for a bespoke reviewing solution. Good information management does not guarantee that a review will be successful, but it does lay the groundwork on which a successful review can build.

# SIX

## Finding relevant studies

*Ginny Brunton, Claire Stansfield and James Thomas*

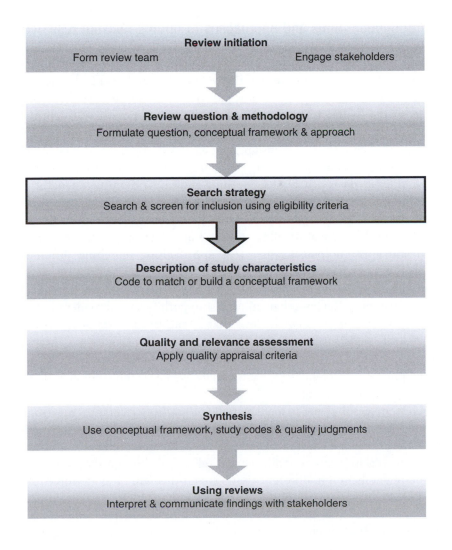

---

**Aims of chapter**

This chapter addresses:

- Why reviews with different purposes require different approaches to finding studies
- How different approaches will influence how research is located and what happens to it once it is found
- The value of planning a search strategy
- Various techniques to locate and consider potentially relevant research, including new developments using text mining

---

## Introduction: Aims and approaches to finding relevant research

Thinking about how to find relevant research for reviews begins with the research question and the purpose of the review. Researchers need a rationale for where and how they search for studies, part of which was discussed in Chapter 3 in terms of the 'work' to be done in the review, its breadth and depth, and – critically in the case of searching – the amount of time and resources available. Cutting across these three dimensions, and again an important driver for searching, are people's priorities and understandings about how knowledge is constructed: their *epistemology*. Drafting, testing and implementing a structured plan for searching is known as developing a *search strategy*. In this chapter we detail methods for how to find relevant research for inclusion in a systematic review, considering both practical details (e.g. searching electronic databases) and conceptual and epistemological issues (e.g. approaching searching differently in different types of review).

As discussed in Chapter 3, different types of review can have different starting points for searching. Reviews that aim to test hypotheses need to identify *sufficient studies for unbiased aggregation*; reviews that intend to generate or explore theory aim to identify *sufficient concepts for coherent configuration* (Figure 6.1 encapsulates this model). As well as this key distinction as to the purpose of the search, there are some practical differences, in terms of *how often* a search strategy is developed and implemented in a review.

Search strategies that aim to identify *sufficient studies for unbiased aggregation* are sometimes presented as being 'exhaustive' and aiming to identify every relevant study (though may fall short of this in practice). The reason for this is that aggregation aims to gain greater confidence and reliability through the examination of the same phenomenon in different contexts and this will be undermined if there is a systematic bias in the set of studies being synthesised. (For example, if the set of studies identified was affected by *publication bias* – see later in this chapter – it might conclude that an intervention was more effective than it actually was.)

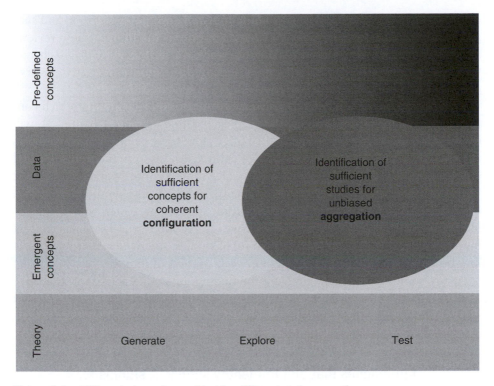

**Figure 6.1** Different aims of searching for different review questions

Other reviews aim to identify *sufficient concepts for coherent configuration*. For these reviews, the issue is not one of finding every relevant study, as the review may not necessarily place more emphasis on concepts that are replicated across many studies compared with those that are only reported in one or two. Rather, the utility of these reviews rests on their ability to piece together insightful and relevant research. They therefore aim for conceptual saturation, and a poor search strategy in this instance would yield an incomplete range of concepts to be configured. Searching for studies in these reviews may be either very specific and linear (taking place only once in the review), or may have multiple iterations as part of an 'investigative' approach to reviewing. Such reviews (e.g. realist and critical interpretive synthesis – see Chapter 3) respond to new concepts as they are revealed in the studies already identified by opening new lines of investigation until no new concepts emerge, borrowing the principle of 'saturation' from qualitative primary research. At the time of writing, these reviews are the exception rather than the rule, and most reviews define their inclusion criteria in advance and only search for relevant studies once.

While most reviews follow these general principles, there are exceptions. Some reviews that aggregate their findings will also use configuration. The first examples of these are reviews that use statistical methods such as meta-regression and sub-group analysis (see Chapter 9) to configure the results of studies. These reviews *aggregate* findings with the same characteristics (covariates) and *configure* characteristics across and between them. They therefore follow the aggregative logic of needing an unbiased set of studies on which to operate.

Similarly, reviews which do not synthesise findings statistically, but which contain a similar structure of configuring aggregated findings (see Chapter 3), will need to employ an exhaustive search strategy. A notable example of this logic is realist synthesis, discussed in Chapter 3. Realist synthesis examines the empirical evidence supporting theories about how a given intervention works (or does not work) for different people, in different circumstances. Realist syntheses follow an investigative mode of enquiry with multiple phases of search and synthesis. However, claims as to the effect of a given intervention in a particular context may be undermined if based on a biased set of studies, and reviewers would therefore be advised to search exhaustively in each context of interest.

Finally, some reviews that configure the findings of studies adopt an exhaustive search framework, as there are situations in which trying to find every relevant study is the easiest way of identifying sufficient relevant concepts.

## Approaches that aim to identify sufficient studies for unbiased aggregation

The aim of an 'exhaustive' search strategy is to find *sufficient studies for unbiased aggregation*, identifying as many (ideally all) studies which fit the inclusion criteria as is possible to locate, thus being as comprehensive as possible. In practice, reviewers cannot know how many studies have addressed their research question so cannot be sure that *all* potentially relevant studies have been located. Further, available resources often do not allow such exhaustive searching. A review may have misleading results if, potentially, studies that are easier to find have results that are systematically different from studies that are more difficult to find (see *publication bias* below). Decisions relating to the methods of searching in a review are therefore of critical importance.

For an 'exhaustive' search, reviewers need to be clear about the types of study they are seeking: what and who the studies are about, in what setting, and with what study design. In a review of effectiveness examining 'what works', these can be structured as criteria for including or excluding studies for the review, depending on the study design and the population, intervention/issue, comparison, outcome and context/time (PICOC/T) of a research question (as described in Chapter 4).

For an 'exhaustive' approach to be manageable, the scope of the review needs to be limited. Where the authors decide to include only controlled trials, or randomised controlled trials, 'exhaustive' approaches are feasible. For instance, a systematic review comparing paracetamol with physical methods for reducing fever in children (see Chapter 4) sought only randomised or quasi-randomised trials, and appropriately applied their strategy to search only Cochrane databases that specialised in registering controlled trials and four other major commercial databases that were searchable by study design.

Sometimes the scope of the review can be limited by insights from prior research. A recent EPPI-Centre review on social exclusion and teenage pregnancy and parenthood identified multiple prior research syntheses on behavioural-level interventions for pregnancy prevention, such as 'just say no' programmes and sexual health education strategies (Harden et al. 2006). However, other research highlighted that young people sometimes made informed decisions to become young parents (Berthoud et al. 2004; Lawlor and Shaw 2002). Findings from these studies of young people who wished to become pregnant were not going to be relevant for a review examining teenage pregnancy prevention. This illustrated the need to look for and include references that specifically researched *unintended* teenage pregnancy.

The scope of a review may also be limited by using a particular date as an inclusion or exclusion criterion. If an intervention was only implemented from a certain date, searching prior to this may not be necessary. In other cases, a cultural or policy 'watershed' occurs which influences how an issue is perceived or managed. Research occurring before this date may be less relevant to a particular review question and can then be excluded. An example of this occurred in an EPPI-Centre review of HIV/AIDS prevention strategies for men who have sex with men (Rees et al. 2004), in which only interventions in place in or after 1996 were a priority. This was because breakthroughs in Highly Active Anti Retroviral Treatment (HAART) were announced at the XI International Conference on AIDS in Vancouver that year (Walters 1996). This date was considered to be a key turning point not only for the treatment of HIV/AIDS, but also for how men viewed HIV/AIDS as a treatable condition and consequently colouring their attitudes towards sexual health promotion. Making searching more manageable by only including reports published in English is a common but more risky strategy, as it allows 'publication bias' to creep in and reduces external generalisability.

## Publication bias

Empirical research has shown that statistically significant 'positive' research results are:

- more likely to be published (publication bias);
- more likely to be published rapidly (time lag bias);
- more likely to be published in English (language bias);
- more likely to be published more than once (multiple publication bias);
- more likely to be cited by others (citation bias) (Alderson and Green 2002).

Collectively, these biases are known as *publication bias*. The key problem with publication bias is that the bias is *systematic*; if the chance of publication was random, with no consistent impact on results, then it would be less critical. However, since the studies included in reviews that aim for *unbiased aggregation* need to be representative of all possibly relevant studies, a systematic bias in favour of positive results may lead to misleading conclusions. The extensive searches carried out for such reviews aim to minimise this bias, recognising that it may not be possible to overcome publication bias entirely.

Publication bias has been identified empirically relatively recently through systematic review activity (see Dickersin, 2005, for a recent summary), but it is not a new issue. In 1975, Anthony Greenwald carried out an empirical investigation into some of the causes of publication bias, written up in a paper entitled 'Consequences of prejudice against the null hypothesis'. In this paper, Greenwald considers all the different points in the research process that a systematic bias in favour of positive results might originate. He demonstrated that researchers are more likely to investigate problems that confirm their personal viewpoints (and, we might add, in which they are personally invested), that they are more likely to publish positive findings, and that editors are more likely to accept papers that report positive findings. Thus, bias in reviews needs to be considered from many angles, and the way a particular field has been conceptualised and investigated may, to some extent, lead to bias in the way that results are reported (see Chapter 2).

Publication bias means that even 'exhaustive' searches are less likely to find negative and non-statistically significant findings, and that systematic reviews affected by publication bias are likely to overestimate positive results. Given the long list of potential biases identified above, it seems possible that most searches are affected by publication bias to some extent, and the key question for the reviewer, after attempting to minimise the bias by conducting a thorough search, is assessing the extent to which it affects an individual review's findings. While publication bias may affect any type of synthesis, and it should be considered whatever the synthesis method being used, there are a number of techniques that attempt to identify publication bias in the context of meta-analysis. Please see Chapter 9 for further information on this.

## Strategies for searches that aim to identify sufficient studies for unbiased aggregation

Although many systematic research syntheses, especially in the health sciences and in government policy, have advocated searching exhaustively for all potentially relevant research (DeLuca et al. 2008; Jackson et al. 2005), 'exhaustive' searching assumes that the entire 'universe' of potentially relevant literature can be located. Being comprehensive requires the use of sources that will uncover published and unpublished, easily accessible and harder to find records of research studies. While some researchers have developed methods to estimate the theoretical 'horizon' of this universe (Kastner et al. 2007), searching exhaustively has obvious challenges for most systematic reviewers; their searches are practically constrained, due to database and reviewer limitations, the restricted time and resources available to reviewers, and the nature of the academic publication itself. For these reasons, exhaustive searching is usually an aspiration rather than something that can be fully achieved in practice. We have therefore used apostrophes around 'exhaustive' to denote our provisional use of the term.

---

| **Box 6.1** |

## MYTH: Every relevant study for a review can be located

Exhaustive searching is improbable, because the total 'universe' of potentially relevant literature is unknown. Just as primary research deals with theoretical populations and actual samples of participants, so reviews have theoretical populations and actual samples of studies. Rather than trying to search everywhere for every possible study, the obligation on reviewers is to plan a thoughtful and clearly described plan to locate the sample of studies most likely to answer their research question(s) reliably.

---

Many reviewers opt instead to consider the ideal as having access to *all* studies (a 'universe' of studies) that could answer the review question, but make clear decisions about how best to get at *the maximum* studies possible from within that universe of potentially relevant literature.

A good 'exhaustive' search leaves researchers surprised by what research they find. An example of this occurred in a review examining the effect of travel mode on children's health (Gough et al. 2001). Searching for research assessing the impact of how children travelled to school on their subsequent mental, cognitive and social outcomes identified several American studies on racial bussing policies. While these were not ultimately relevant for this UK-focused review, their identification during searching confirmed to the team that they were not being led by their expectations and that a systematic search for what might meet the inclusion criteria also helped them to tighten up their inclusion and exclusion criteria.

The issues discussed above help authors to decide upon a careful selection of key sources most suited to the review's question. The search strategy is thus developed in a way to avoid the biases outlined. In doing so, it could be considered a 'reasonable' search strategy. Such a strategy may be more thorough than those used, for example, in rapid reviews, as more time and resources are devoted to developing and implementing a good search strategy. When it is not possible to access this 'universe' of studies, the strategy should attempt to identify an unbiased sample of sources.

## Approaches which aim to identify sufficient concepts for coherent configuration

Some reviews aim to generate theory, seek important themes, or sufficient key concepts for a coherent theory; these may be found without identifying all the relevant studies, making exhaustive searching unnecessary. The aim of searching when carrying out these reviews is to seek selected exemplars to provide a sufficiency of breadth and representation (within the constraints of their interests) rather than attempting to be exhaustive. This approach to searching is sometimes described as 'purposive', although this term can be confusing as all searching is purposive (in that all searches have a purpose).

The term **purposive** is commonly used in primary qualitative research to encompass a range of approaches and strategies to sampling. In a chapter entitled 'Purposeful sampling', Patton (1990: 230) states that 'the logic and power of purposeful sampling lie in selecting *information-rich cases* for study in depth' [emphasis in original]. Thus, in a review the aim is to treat individual studies as cases, **selecting** those that provide the most valuable information for the review. Patton describes how selection can have many principles, including 'maximum variation', 'intensity' (information-rich), 'extreme/deviant case', 'confirming' or 'disconfirming', and 'politically important', also pointing out that a useful strategy is 'snowball' or 'chain' sampling, in which leads are followed from one case to another. Thus, part of the aim of a 'purposive' search (sample) can only be understood in terms of the studies (cases) already identified: configuration is not concerned with piling up examples of the same finding, but in identifying studies that contain new conceptualisations of the phenomena of interest.

Following on from this, then, is the concept of **saturation**. In attempting to identify a range of concepts, the review may therefore reject studies that, although on topic and method, do not contribute any new concepts to the synthesis. Saturation has been reached for those concepts in the review. For example, a recent meta-ethnography (see Chapter 9) of women's experiences of birth trauma was prompted by the argument that current maternity services do not recognise or understand women's responses to a traumatic birth (Elmir et al. 2010). Their search strategy could be described as selective, purposive and very specific. They searched only four databases using a few keywords: birth trauma, traumatic birth, qualitative research, birth narrative and birth stories. They limited the search further to reports published in English between 1994 and 2009. This very specific search allowed them to draw on ten qualitative studies from which they developed 'six major themes: "feeling invisible and out of control", "to be treated humanely", "feeling trapped: the reoccurring nightmare of my childbirth experience", "a rollercoaster of emotions", "disrupted relationships" and "strength of purpose: a way to succeed as a mother"'. Assuming the ten qualitative studies in the review captured all the relevant perspectives, even if the review had included ten times as many studies, its findings may not have been any different.

## Strategies for searches that aim to identify sufficient concepts for coherent configuration

When it is unclear at the beginning of a review what specific types of study are needed, or where the review is proceeding along an 'investigative' line, pursuing conceptual and evidential 'leads' as and when they arise, an **iterative search strategy** is appropriate. A review of access to health care by vulnerable groups provides a good example (Dixon-Woods et al. 2006b). Searching on the broad topic of 'access' among databases, websites, reference checking and contact with experts elicited over 100,000 records – too many to consider for the review. Reviewers decided that this broad search, coupled with the broad and emergent review question, was well suited to an iterative search strategy. This required the reviewers to be 'led' from the findings in one research article to inform where and how next to look for the next potentially relevant reference in order to create a 'sampling frame'. While iterative searching is a very broad issue requiring searching, learning about the search, and then searching some more based on what is learned, it is also a very empirical method. Finding out what is needed when searching becomes a part of the findings of the review: reviewers are a bit like detectives seeking out some information on an issue, which then leads them to ask new questions.

In iterative reviews, the search strategy evolves as reviewers encounter important new concepts from studies identified as the review progresses. Another example of an iterative approach to reviewing is realist synthesis, which evaluates the theories that underlie social interventions: for example, a health care intervention begins as an idea along the lines of 'because the world works this way, if we provide this service, then that will happen' (Pawson et al. 2004). Realist reviewers structure a synthesis to locate evidence testing the theory that underlies the existing phenomenon or intervention in order to assess what works, in what circumstances, and with whom (Pawson et al. 2004). The evidence that might help test the theory may come from many different types of research and it may not be known what these are at the start of the review. It is only through doing the review, and following different leads, that the relevant types of research evidence come (iteratively) to light.

Iterative reviews can be systematic in having clear overarching rules for inclusion, but the specific detailed criteria for meeting those rules may only become apparent in the process of doing the review. Instead of applying particular inclusion or exclusion criteria to each located study, reviewers taking an iterative approach would be systematic about their methods of thinking about (and keeping track of) which studies they are looking for and why. In the critical interpretive synthesis (see Chapter 3) by Dixon-Woods et al. (2006b) mentioned above, the team examined the literature on access to health care by vulnerable groups in the UK. Because this was a broad policy topic, a necessarily broad research question was addressed and refined as the literature was identified, and studies were chosen to develop theory and concepts rather than attempting to be an exhaustive summarisation of the all the literature about their initial broad topic.

## Developing search strategies

A search strategy, which is derived from the review question and its conceptual framework, contains a description of the search concepts and terms to be used in the search, sources to be searched (e.g. electronic database searching or hand searching journal contents), and the search limits. As in other stages of the review, the search strategy (or 'strategies' for reviews with multiple iterations of searching) needs to be as systematic as possible, in line with the general principles of systematic reviews to be transparent, accountable and replicable (Hammerstrøm et al. 2010; Lefebvre et al. 2010). It is also a useful record for reviewers at the reporting stage, when an account is written of how and where included research was found. Developing a search strategy allows reviewers to search systematically in order to reduce bias, which is of key importance in approaches that aim to identify all relevant studies. It is important that a well-planned search strategy is developed and implemented, and authors need to be aware of, and report on, any limitations in their search and the impact that these may have had on their review.

An explicit search strategy needs to be developed and systematically applied to a range of research sources. A thoughtful search strategy considers:

- the aim of searching, ensuring that the appropriate methods are used;
- what the most relevant sources of studies are likely to be;
- the benefits and drawbacks of searching each source;
- the resources available; and
- the benefits and costs of different combinations of sources within the available resources.

Searching begins with clarifying the scope of the review, and setting the criteria for including or excluding studies. A recent EPPI-Centre review for the Department of Health examined research on the relationship between fathers' familial involvement and their families' mental health (Brunton et al. 2010). Having clear definitions of the meaning of 'fathers' (e.g. resident, non-resident, biological, but not adoptive or recently bereaved) and 'involvement' (e.g. accessible, responsible and engaged) allowed decisions to be made about which sources to search and how to structure searches within those sources.

Where searching is not limited to an easily identifiable group of studies, searching more sources inevitably means even more cost and more time to locate, retrieve and assess potentially relevant records (Harden et al. 1999). Reviewers also need to consider how many abstracts they can reasonably screen and how many full-text reports of research they can afford to purchase, collect or retrieve (see below under 'screening located studies').

The dangers of limiting reviews to the English language have already been discussed. Many non-English studies are indexed in English language databases, and sometimes include a translated English abstract. However, the cost of translating all the *potentially* relevant articles that may be found into English may be prohibitive (Egger et al. 2003; Moher et al. 2003; Song et al. 2010). One option is to search for potentially relevant research in all languages (using databases that can be searched in English), but exclude those not in the language of choice. This ensures that all potentially relevant research has been searched for and is more readily available for researchers who may have the ability to translate. It might be possible either to gain help from other researchers with knowledge of the language or contact the authors of the research. It is equally important to search in databases whose first language is other than the reviewers' as, for example, potentially relevant non-English language studies may be more likely to be indexed on non-English language databases. Some recent reviews have experimented with using Google Translate and other online translation tools to gain a rough translation of the title and abstract of a study to screen for relevance. However, this technique has not yet been formally evaluated.

Searching for potentially relevant research can continue throughout the review process while researchers also code, assess and extract studies right up until the point of synthesis. Indeed, in some reviews, synthesis is the way in which additional lines of investigation are identified and thus further searches specified. However, setting a discrete end date for the retrieval of studies (or a time limit after which further iterations of searching will cease) is a more common practice. This is done for practical reasons. Individual researchers must decide where the balance point is for them in terms of locating as many articles as possible, while still having time to code, assess, extract and synthesise them. (Some reviews will carry out an extensive search at the beginning of the review and then a smaller 'catch-up' search at the end to identify research that has been carried out during the intervening period. The catch-up search should have the same scope as the original search or the review may risk introducing publication bias, so this approach may only be practicable for reviews with tightly focused searches.)

Search strategies need testing for their ability to locate sufficient relevant research and/or concepts both across and within sources, and that they are doing so as efficiently as possible – without retrieving a large number of ultimately irrelevant records in the process. When testing the search strategy, researchers will scan or 'screen' (see below) through a sample of the retrieved records using the inclusion and exclusion criteria developed earlier in order to identify any potentially relevant records.

Search strategies should be carefully thought through for several reasons, but perhaps most importantly because findings can evade us: there is a profusion of published and unpublished material available to search, and much of the unpublished material is hidden. Box 6.2 outlines some of these considerations.

---

| **Box 6.2** |

### Some considerations in seeking specific types of study

Beware of variation in the ways study types are understood and labelled, e.g. 'survey', 'controlled trial'.

- Studies using particular methods do not always identify themselves as such in publications.
- Methods are often poorly indexed by commercial databases.
- A *search filter* is a group of search terms that have been developed to locate types of literature. Published search filters developed for specific study designs in the literature can be a useful aid.

*(Continued)*

*(Continued)*

Avoid searching by outcome.

- Outcomes are less well indexed and may be subject to outcome reporting bias.

Systematic reviews (and other literature reviews) are worth seeking.

- They are sources of primary studies as well as being studies in their own right.
- They may also be labelled as meta-analysis, research synthesis, systematic narrative, meta-ethnography, and others.
- They tend to be clustered on websites of review-producing organisations.

Searching for English language studies.

- There is potential bias within the literature if the search is limited to English language records only, and potentially if only English terms are used. Strategies described in the text can help generate an awareness of potentially relevant research citations from other languages even if there is no resource for translation.

Different databases catalogue different journals, often with a geographic bias (Gomersall and Cooper 2010; Stansfield et al. 2010), using different terms to catalogue or classify studies and offering different interfaces for access. Other issues to be considered, regardless of the approach taken while searching, are the implications for search strategies of academic discipline, geographic area, key dates and languages. Key studies can be missed if sources or search terms are poorly chosen. For example, Taylor et al. (2003) examined the unique articles from a systematic review in the area of social care. A total of 213 studies met the inclusion criteria: over half of the located studies were found only through searching the Social Science Citation Index, almost a third only on MEDLINE (a medical database), and some were only obtained from other sources in the fields of nursing and social care. This illustrates that there are often disciplinary boundaries around research knowledge, and it is important to consider searching databases of different disciplines. Further, teams are each individually constrained by their own disciplinary and policy area knowledge: which journals, books or databases are unfamiliar to the research team? It is worth considering, when developing a search strategy, to be as broadly-based as possible in order not to be biased by your own preconceptions.

Finally, consideration should be given as to how to handle studies in different geographical locations. During the review of social exclusion and teenage pregnancy (given earlier), searchers identified over 34,000 references. Of these, 2,550 were non-UK and would have been missed completely if the search strategy was limited to seeking out UK studies only. Those non-UK records are available for others to utilise in future. Conversely, for some reviews, limiting by country can help in making the review more focused and more manageable as it lowers the number of results retrieved from bibliographic databases. This approach was used in an EPPI-Centre review of UK young people's views of obesity, body size, shape and weight (Rees et al. 2010) and involved consideration of both search sources and search terms for locating UK-specific literature. Other types of publication bias have been considered earlier in this chapter.

## Implementing a search strategy

This section discusses the detail of methods for searching for studies. It applies equally to all types of search strategy, though some searches will implement different aspects of the content of this section to greater or lesser degrees, depending on their different needs.

There is a variety of types of source where research information is located: bibliographic databases (e.g. Education Resources Information Centre database (ERIC), MEDLINE), specialised databases of primary and review research (e.g. Educational Evidence Portal, BiblioMap, Index to British Theses), specialist registers, internet search engines, websites of organisations, hand-searching books and journals, scanning reference lists, and professional and personal contacts. Web-based information sites such as Evidence Network at www.evidencenetwork.org, low and middle income country (LMIC) resources available on http://epocoslo. cochrane.org/lmic-databases, and gateways including Intute and ELDIS may provide previously unknown sources to search. For exhaustive searching it is recommended that reviewers include all these elements, although the choice and extent of these sources can depend on the nature of the review, subject area and the type of information sought. Each of these types of source is further discussed below. Searching disciplinary topic-specific bibliographic databases, for example, ERIC in education, MEDLINE in medicine, or PsycInfo in psychology, is a convenient way to search for studies published in journals. However, searching in only one database may miss key studies of interest published by professionals in other disciplines. Bibliographic databases rarely cover all the relevant journals within the scope of the systematic review, even across databases that cover the same subject area. There is also a significant body of research that is published as non-journal reports, books, book chapters, unpublished theses and conference proceedings which may not be available in large bibliographic databases. Specialised databases are often focused on a precise research area or a type of study design (e.g. controlled trials, theses) and they tend to be compiled from a range of search sources. However, it is also important to seek out literature from non-electronic sources as well. These can include contacting authors and other key experts, and reference checking. All are important methods to supplement electronic searches and add currency to the review, particularly as there can be time lags in between journal publication and the indexing of that publication in a bibliographic database.

A recent analysis that identified 230 'views' studies (studies about people's perceptions, beliefs and experiences) across four systematic reviews found that although a majority of the studies were located in bibliographic database sources, some studies were only found using other sources, such as reference checking, author contact, websites, specialised registers and library catalogues (Stansfield et al. 2010). For some review questions, bibliographic databases may not even be the most important source of studies. For example, web-based searching of government websites may be important for some reviews, such as the recent review on non-retail access to tobacco by youth (Sutcliffe et al. 2011). For some discipline-focused reviews, such as a recent review on women's experiences of first-time motherhood (Brunton et al. 2010), book chapters were an important outlet for academic research. These are not always well indexed on bibliographic databases and tend to be identified through other areas of the search strategy.

## The basics of bibliographic databases

There are many bibliographic databases, and just a few are named in this chapter. Factors in choosing which database to use are considered under the section 'Developing search strategies' (above). It is useful to think broadly when considering which sources will best locate relevant studies. For example, an EPPI-Centre review (Stewart et al. 2010a) focusing on the impact of microfinance on poor people in sub-Saharan Africa includes details of where the included studies were found. Seven out of 15 studies were found in bibliographic and specialised databases across the fields of social science (International Bibliography of Social Sciences, Sociological Abstracts), economics (Econlit, IDEAS) and health (Cochrane Library, PsycInfo). The remaining eight studies were found from reference lists, citation searching, contacting authors and specific websites.

Most bibliographic databases focus on broad subject areas; they vary in the nature of the literature covered, search functions and indexing. A database consists of a collection of research records, where each record is comprised of different fields (e.g. title, abstract, keywords or controlled vocabulary, author, journal, date). These fields are searched either by selection or by default. Some databases may have further fields, such as language of the report, publication type, and date added to the database.

Database records are indexed manually according to a classification system or thesaurus that is standardised for a specific database. For example, in MEDLINE and PubMed, the system used is called 'Medical Subject Headings (MeSH)'. In EMBASE, the 'EMTREE' thesaurus is used, and in the Education Resources Information Centre database ERIC, the system is called 'ERIC Descriptors'. Thus, 'socio-economic factors' is a MeSH term in MEDLINE, while 'socio-economic influences' is a descriptor term in ERIC. Without these terms, the user is reliant on identifying research by using their own choice of terms in the title and abstract fields (i.e. 'free-text') in the hope that they match those that have been used by the authors. Using the controlled vocabulary enables a greater objectivity and consistency to locate similar records. The user is able to browse the thesaurus to identify appropriate terms, and sometimes it will contain definitions on the meaning of each keyword term. For example, in MEDLINE, 'Health Literacy' is a MeSH term introduced in 2010 to describe the 'Degree to which individuals have the capacity to obtain, process, and understand basic health information and services needed to make appropriate health decisions'. Without this keyword term, it could be difficult to easily locate all relevant records based on choosing terms that might be in the title or the abstract. Controlled vocabulary terms are also very useful when terms have more than one meaning or can be used in different ways. For example, the controlled term 'art' can be used to locate studies which discuss the use of artwork in hospital settings without identifying studies that for example, refer to the 'art of midwifery'.

In addition to using controlled vocabularies, it is also important for the user to search the free-text fields (commonly the title and abstract). Not all databases have controlled vocabularies (for example, Social Science Citation Index) or where they do the terms may not adequately describe the research concept desired by a user, or may be inadequately applied to research records through indexer interpretation or error. PubMed publishes a list of recently published records that are awaiting indexing, and free-text searches are the only way to find these studies. In order to identify relevant research and minimise bias in search results, it is essential to use a variety of search terms, which search both the controlled vocabulary and free-text fields.

The thesaurus tools available in mainstream bibliographic databases can be used to identify controlled terms for each of the concepts in the review, which are then supplemented with free-text words and phrases for each concept. The terms *within* each concept are combined using the Boolean operator 'OR'. Once these are linked together, the concepts are *combined* using the Boolean operator 'AND'. This Boolean structure is critical to a well-performing search: it enables reviewers to cast their net very widely and identify as much research as possible within each concept (using 'OR'), while insisting at the same time that all records retrieved contain *all* the concepts they are interested in (using 'AND'). An example is shown in Box 6.3.

It is important to test a search strategy before conducting electronic searching, as additional free-text and controlled terms of relevance may be identified. Consideration of language and terminology is important for free-text terms, such as synonyms (similar terms) and antonyms (opposites), international spelling variations and word forms of the same word. Some databases enable the truncation of word forms, synonym searches and 'proximity' searching (which can be used to identify words within close vicinity to other words).

A search using some common terms may locate tens of thousands of records – not all of which may be relevant. For example, the term 'weight' could have a range of meanings. It may be appropriate to use an alternative term, or use it in combination with qualifying terms or phrases such as 'body weight' or 'weight of evidence'. Alternatively, a large number of results may be eliminated when combined with another concept using the Boolean AND operator, as outlined above. Searches can be limited by date limits and, in particular cases, by study design (though limiting searches according to research method is not always reliable). Some organisations and groups, such as InterTASC Information Specialists' Sub-Group (ISSG), publish search filters (or hedges) that may provide useful terms for locating, for example, specific study designs (ISSG 2010). Some databases include a 'related items' function, which might also locate relevant records that were not identified. Examining 'related items' is a useful technique when testing a search strategy, as if this method identifies relevant studies that were not picked up by the original search, an examination of their index terms and language used might suggest ways in which the search strategy should be amended.

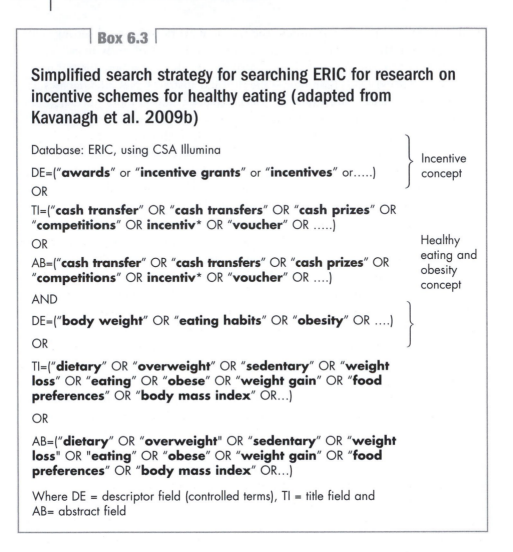

**Box 6.3**

## Simplified search strategy for searching ERIC for research on incentive schemes for healthy eating (adapted from Kavanagh et al. 2009b)

Database: ERIC, using CSA Illumina

DE=("**awards**" or "**incentive grants**" or "**incentives**" or.....)

OR

TI=("**cash transfer**" OR "**cash transfers**" OR "**cash prizes**" OR "**competitions**" OR **incentiv***  OR "**voucher**" OR .....)

OR

AB=("**cash transfer**" OR "**cash transfers**" OR "**cash prizes**" OR "**competitions**" OR **incentiv***  OR "**voucher**" OR ....)

AND

DE=("**body weight**" OR "**eating habits**" OR "**obesity**" OR ....)

OR

TI=("**dietary**" OR "**overweight**" OR "**sedentary**" OR "**weight loss**" OR "**eating**" OR "**obese**" OR "**weight gain**" OR "**food preferences**" OR "**body mass index**" OR...)

OR

AB=("**dietary**" OR "**overweight**" OR "**sedentary**" OR "**weight loss**" OR "**eating**" OR "**obese**" OR "**weight gain**" OR "**food preferences**" OR "**body mass index**" OR...)

Where DE = descriptor field (controlled terms), TI = title field and AB= abstract field

*Incentive concept*

*Healthy eating and obesity concept*

Testing and refining the search involves scanning some of the results and considering if some records include terms that have been missed, and if the records retrieved contain studies that are both expected and unexpected. It is worth circulating a search strategy among other researchers, research commissioners and other users of the research to check that the search terms used are appropriate.

As different databases have different search interfaces, functions and controlled vocabularies, after the search has been tested in one database, it will need to be translated to operate in a consistent way on other databases. EPPI-Centre reviews typically develop a search string in a large database first, which is then adapted for use in other databases. Translating a search usually involves identifying controlled terms that are specific to a given database and allowing for the variation in focus and technical functionality of each database. For example, if a given search includes a broad education concept, it may be appropriate to omit this concept when translating the search from the health database MEDLINE into ERIC, an education database (since, by searching ERIC, one is already limiting the search to literature in the field of education). Additionally, some databases use different symbols for truncating word forms or proximity searching (or simply do not support some of these functions). Many database providers facilitate access to a database though an interface, and the functions of the fields for searching may differ. ERIC is searchable from its own website, and also from commercial database providers such as CSA Illumina and ProQuest, EBSCOhost, OCLC FirstSearch, Ovid, H.W. Wilson, and Dialog.

When putting together an exhaustive search, it is important to find a balance between being able to find everything within an electronic source and finding exactly what is desired. To be exhaustive one needs to have a broad search strategy with many search terms and look in many different sources. This will increase the number of relevant studies identified, but will also increase the number of studies that, when screened, turn out not to be relevant.

Harden et al. (1999) examined the range of results obtained from using different numbers of controlled vocabulary terms for identifying trials of sexual health promotion in MEDLINE. The original search used ten sexual health terms and 22 health promotion terms. Altering the search to use four sexual health terms and two health promotion terms reduced the retrieval of relevant studies to 65%. Thus, using fewer search terms would have meant that they missed 35% of their relevant studies. However, although the results were lower, the total number of records retrieved and number of records that needed to be screened was also lower, and thus the work involved in identifying those 65% of relevant studies was considerably reduced. This example illustrates some important concepts in searching: *sensitivity* and *precision*. The first search by Harden and colleagues is known as a *sensitive* search, as its aim is to identify as much relevant material as possible. As a by-product of being as inclusive as possible, sensitive searches usually retrieve large numbers of irrelevant studies too. The latter searches had more *precision*; they retrieved fewer irrelevant documents compared to the number of relevant ones, but they also found fewer relevant studies.

While sensitivity and precision are not polar opposites, this illustrates the need to find a balance between: (i) searching sensitively, which would retrieve a high proportion of the total number of relevant articles in existence plus (usually) a high yield of irrelevant items to screen, and (ii) searching precisely, in order to identify a high proportion of studies that meet the inclusion criteria, but risking the loss of relevant studies. (In information science, these concepts are understood slightly differently from those in medical testing, which would normally test for sensitivity and specificity.) These concepts are illustrated in Box 6.4. Using the Boolean operator AND to combine concepts can also help achieve a balance between sensitivity and precision.

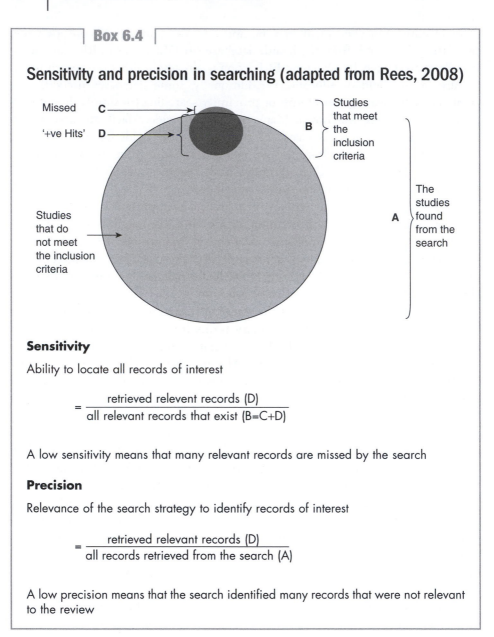

Box 6.4

## Sensitivity and precision in searching (adapted from Rees, 2008)

**Sensitivity**

Ability to locate all records of interest

$$= \frac{\text{retrieved relevent records (D)}}{\text{all relevant records that exist (B=C+D)}}$$

A low sensitivity means that many relevant records are missed by the search

**Precision**

Relevance of the search strategy to identify records of interest

$$= \frac{\text{retrieved relevant records (D)}}{\text{all records retrieved from the search (A)}}$$

A low precision means that the search identified many records that were not relevant to the review

### Specialised registers and library catalogues

The line between specialised bibliographic registers and bibliographic databases is often blurred. They are mentioned separately here as specialised registers and catalogues are important sources of research on focused topic areas but typically have less functionality than commercially available bibliographic databases. They could contain specific index terms, depending on the focus of the register or catalogue, and they vary in size. For example, PopLine is a freely accessible register containing a large number of records on reproductive health, and has many index terms. Zetoc contains the British Library's electronic table of contents of journals and conference proceedings, but has limited search functionality. When searching specialised registers it is often only possible to combine two of the search concepts together, and to use a limited number of terms within a search concept.

Methods for searching specialised registers for reviews are not well documented and systematically searching these sources can be challenging. Seeking out any advanced searching options and help files is crucial as specialised registers often have very different options for searching. Generally, the search strategy used for bibliographic databases will require modification and simplification when translated for use on specialised registers, while adhering to the review's conceptual framework; in effect, it may need to be tailored to the subject nature of each register. These limitations are sometimes offset by the increased precision of specialised registers. For example, when searching a register of controlled trials, the study design concept can be omitted. If the search functions are limited, it may be more appropriate to carry out a number of different searches using different terms, or use a mixture of broad and specific terms to capture the relevant literature. Sometimes browsing or searching with the database's controlled vocabulary is more appropriate than carrying out Boolean searches. In some databases, it is only possible to search titles of records whereas others may also search, for example, data in the contents pages and summaries of books. A book containing research could have a much broader title than a specific journal paper or report. Using subject keywords and broad free-text searches may be of particular use here.

## Hand searching

'Hand searching' is the process of manually scanning the contents pages of journal issues and book chapters to identify relevant research. Just as with approaches to searching sources such as bibliographic databases, the journal titles and the years to be searched are decided in advance. The aim of hand searching is to counter any limitation that arises from using pre-determined search terms and a controlled vocabulary. It can be used for searching journals and books that are not well indexed by a database or have not been covered by the databases. Hand searching can also be used as an aid to support the bibliographic database search for journals that should have been covered within the databases, adding an extra layer of protection in case relevant research was missed by the electronic search.

## Reference list checking

Scanning the titles of citations in the reference lists of potentially relevant literature is known as 'reference list checking'. Reference list checking has two components. One component is to scan references cited within a research report ('backward' or 'retrospective' reference list checking). The other component is to use citation databases (outlined below) to identify research where others have cited included studies ('forward' or 'prospective' reference list checking). Forward reference list checking can be undertaken on a number of different databases, for example Google Scholar, Web of Science Cited Reference Search, Scopus and others. Utilising at least two of these sources is recommended since individually these sources may not cite all referencing papers or reports. For example, forward reference checking using Google Scholar will identify research reports and dissertations as well as some journal papers; however, forward reference checking with Web of Science might cite additional journal papers.

Reviewers should consider the resource implications of utilising these strategies as each can significantly increase the number of references that then need to be screened. Screening reference lists from all retrieved references may result in reviewers scanning thousands of mostly irrelevant references. Reviewers may choose instead to screen only the reference lists from all studies that meet the eligibility criteria for the review, or from other studies and reviews that are related to the topic.

Reviewers also need to decide how potentially relevant references are to be selected when checking reference lists. References can be screened simply as they appear by title in the reference lists. Reviewers may choose to include references that seem relevant based on their citation in the text instead. A third option is for reviewers to search for the abstracts of all relevant references identified from the reference lists for judgements about inclusion. Reference list checking is a time-consuming but often a fruitful aspect of a well-rounded search strategy.

## Internet searching

Generic search engines, such as Google and Bing, can be useful sources for research, can check searching already undertaken, and can also identify organisations that may contain relevant research. For some reviews, internet searching may be the primary method of obtaining research not indexed in bibliographic databases. However, it is difficult to undertake large Boolean searches on most internet search engines, and to manage their results. The scope of internet search engines tends to be far less clear than is the case for bibliographic databases and the methodology for ranking results and the regularity of updating is also unclear. It is also not possible to search specific fields in the same way as is possible in a bibliographic database (e.g. 'title' or 'abstract'), although the ability to search the full text of journal articles is often valuable. Search engines are not manually indexed, although they may identify descriptive keyword data created by the authors of a record. As with searching registers, it may be necessary to undertake several searches or to use a mixture of broad and narrow terms. It is worth reading help screens and looking at advanced search functions to check if these offer, for example, phrase searching, synonym searching or assigning words that must or must not appear within a record. Some academic libraries offer online tutorials on utilising search engines.

As with other sources, a balance between sensitivity and precision must be found when using search engines. For more precise searches, the order of results in search engines could be ranked by date (when this option is available), popularity, relevance to the search terms used, or a mixture of these. It is often impossible to know, however, how a search engine has operationalised 'relevance'. Adopting a sensitive search in a search engine will elicit millions of potentially relevant hits to screen. Rather than selecting all the results, a more common approach errs on the side of precision. For example, researchers may opt to select a specified number of records to scan through or to scan pages until reaching a page where no further potentially relevant items are found. Some search engines offer additional features such as related documents (Bing, Google Scholar and Scirus) and an automated clustering of results (Scirus). The search strategy should be carefully documented, detailing all of the decisions made about how to use search engines during the search process.

An adjunct to internet searching is 'hand' (or 'eye'!) searching online. Web pages are designed to link to one another, containing hyperlinks that will entice reviewers to investigate leads and click from page to page and site to site. There is little empirical evidence or guidance on how to use such technologies in systematic searches, but they clearly have value in some reviews. The best advice we can offer is that the same principles apply to this type of searching as to any other and it is important to document what is done so that valuable information is not lost and the way that studies were located can be described accurately.

## Professional and personal contacts

Obtaining information from authors of research studies and professional and personal contacts can be a significant source for identifying further studies. This can take the form of direct emails, or be indirect, through newsletters, web pages, discussion groups and other social network tools. The method and rationale for selecting contacts – including how non-replies are to be followed up – should usually be decided beforehand. When contacting authors, it is vital to be clear about the types of research that are being sought and what recipients are being asked to do as authors of primary research studies may not necessarily be aware of the significance in attempting to identify and obtain all research of interest for a systematic review. Explaining the importance of their research's contribution to the overall review's findings may help (Higgins and Green 2011).

## Searching requires skill and time

It can take time and skill to develop and implement a successful search strategy, and it is worth bearing in mind that the skills required are fairly specialised, including knowledge and experience of using search interfaces, database functions and exporting results. It is worth consulting an information scientist or librarian on these technical issues, timetabling their input at key stages: for example, search development and testing, contacting authors and reference list checking.

## Keep track of searching contemporaneously

To enable transparency and reproducibility in the review process it is good practice to keep records of the search process. This will also facilitate any updating
of the review. A record-keeping log includes the full search strategy, the search
date, which database (if relevant) and interface was used and searcher name. An
example is shown in Table 6.1. Further record-keeping is needed for author contact, citation checking and decisions made when searching and scanning websites.
The EPPI-Centre is collaborating with other information professionals to promote good practices on techniques for search documentation and their rationale.

## Exporting the results of searching into reference management software

Once the research records have been identified they need to be stored to retrieve and
use them throughout the rest of the review. Large numbers of records are typically
identified from bibliographic databases, and these records can usually be retrieved
in a format that is operable with reference management software (see Chapter 5).
Some databases will specifically indicate the output format of the report and
provide tools for transferring outputs into specific reference management software. Most databases facilitate a generic output of records in a tagged text format.
This enables the fields within a research record to be transferrable between different
database systems.

The way a record is tagged is often unique to the database provider or individual database. A second step is therefore sometimes required which converts the
tagged text format into a format that can be used for importing into the reference
management software. Import filters have been created for this and are sometimes
available through academic libraries and commercial reference management software providers. The EPPI-Centre has a tool that enables conversion from many
bibliographic databases into RIS formatted text. This is freely available from the
EPPI-Centre website at http://eppi.ioe.ac.uk.

**Table 6.1**  Example of record-keeping log

| Database searched | ERIC |
|---|---|
| Database interface | CSA Illumina |
| Date of search | 29 June 2009 |
| Person searching | Claire Stansfield |
| Timeframe of search | 1999–2009 |
| No. of records obtained | 466 |
| Search string | (((DE=("awards" or "incentive grants" or "incentives" or "motivation" or "rewards" or "token economy")) or(TI=("cash transfer" OR "cash transfers" OR "cash prizes" OR "competitions" OR incentiv* OR "reward" OR "rewards" OR "lottery" OR "lotteries" OR "raffle" OR "raffles" OR "voucher" OR ... |

## Screening located studies

Searching will often elicit a large number of records providing data on study titles, abstracts, author names, source, date of publication and keyword terms. These data will usually be uploaded to suitable reference management software. A proportion of these records will be relevant to the review, but the only way to know for sure is to read them (though see below for new approaches to screening). The process of reading each title and abstract to ascertain its relevance is known as *screening*. Explicit criteria, based on the review's scope and question(s), are applied to each record in order to determine if it should be included in or excluded from the review. Criteria often cover the range of dates that the review covers, characteristics of the study population (and intervention, if applicable) and methods used in the research. Clear criteria and records which detail which studies meet which criterion help users of the review to see why some studies are included and others not.

To be included in the review, a study needs to meet all its inclusion criteria and not meet any exclusion criteria. 'Excluded' records may have a useful contribution to make elsewhere, even though they are not considered relevant to the current review. For example, in the review by Harden et al. (2006) examining social exclusion and teenage pregnancy, having detailed exclusion criteria allowed the authors to describe the reasons why specific numbers of records were not included. This created a sub-set of records containing, for example, similar research in other countries, which might be reviewed in the future.

Finally, it is useful to consider the order in which criteria are applied to determine the inclusion of studies in the review. In the social exclusion and teenage pregnancy review described earlier, reviewers ordered the exclusion criteria in such a way that the largest body of literature would be excluded first (e.g. the study is not about pregnancy), and more specific criteria (e.g. the report does not contain data for synthesis) occurring further down (Harden et al. 2006). This hierarchical approach to excluding studies gives reviewers extra information for potential future use. For example, if a study is excluded on the third criterion, it will have met the first two criteria. This may be useful if, in future, reviewers want to use the same body of literature in a different way. For example, they may wish to relocate the studies which met certain criteria – perhaps those which were 'on topic' even if they did not use the right methods for the review in question or were published within the specified date ranges. Hierarchical screening criteria will allow this kind of 'sorting' of records for future use.

Screening should be as consistent as possible in order to reduce any risk of systematic selection bias. If more than one person is screening, they must ensure that they are consistent with one other. Testing for inter-rater reliability is achieved by having two reviewers screen the same records independently using the inclusion criteria, then meeting to compare how often they agreed and disagreed. Disagreements are resolved by an independent third reviewer or through team discussions. In order to assume that both reviewers are screening articles similarly, there must be a high level of inter-rater reliability. (This is sometimes quantified using Kappa scores, though these are rarely more informative than examining simple percentages.)

## New approaches to screening: sampling and text mining

Screening every potentially relevant reference is sometimes not possible, and the exponential growth of publications on electronic databases means that it is becoming more and more time-consuming to screen every reference. For example, in 1998/1999 a broad systematic review of peer-delivered health promotion interventions for young people identified 5,124 citations in its exhaustive search (Harden et al. 1999). Ten years later, reviewers in a narrower systematic review of mostly 'qualitative' research found themselves ploughing through 11,128 citations (Rees et al. 2009). These examples are fairly typical of the scale of task when reviewing social research, but some reviews involve screening many tens of thousands of citations – a very expensive exercise! Some reviews lessen the problem of having unmanageable numbers of citations to screen by limiting their search strategy in some way, for example, by reducing the number of sources examined or the number of terms used. As discussed above, however, such an approach is likely to mean that relevant studies are missed.

Where it is not practicable to screen every reference manually, alternative methods are employed. These methods can shorten considerably the amount of time spent on screening. Some will 'borrow' from sampling theory in primary research whereas others will use emerging methods in information science around new technologies called 'text mining'. One critical principle to bear in mind when these new techniques are used is that the set of studies that are identified for in-depth reviewing should not be biased in a *systematic* way. Namely, while every relevant reference may not be identified (and this cannot be guaranteed in any review), the studies that are found should be representative of the entirety of the studies that might be relevant. If this principle is not adhered to, the findings of the review may simply reflect, for example, the studies that are easy to find, rather than the full extent of knowledge about a particular issue. One recent EPPI-Centre review used methods to get at the most representative sample of all located references using random sampling, whereas another tried a different approach and attempted to use text mining to reduce its screening workload.

### *Random sampling*

During a recent research synthesis about women's experiences of becoming a mother (Brunton et al. 2010), searching elicited over 13,000 records. This large number of records exceeded the research team's capacity to screen and retrieve. However, since this was a two-stage review of a map of research and an in-depth review, we decided to screen only a random sample of the 13,000 records for inclusion in the mapping stage, the aim of which was to aggregate studies. A random sample was chosen because each record had an equal probability of being selected for screening, meaning that the records located would represent the 'true' distribution of records across the entire sample of all those 13,000 located records.

A 10% random sample was chosen for screening because this proportion matched the team's capacity to screen in the available time.

### Text mining

Text mining is another approach to consider when there is neither the time nor resource available to screen tens of thousands of citations. Sometimes called 'text data mining', this relatively new technology is currently being evaluated for use in systematic reviews (Ananiadou et al. 2009; Thomas et al. 2011). One potential application lies in its ability to 'learn' to apply particular classifications to text, such as knowing which titles and abstracts should be 'included' or 'excluded'. A text-mining *classifier* does this by examining the titles and abstracts that have been screened manually and then building up sets of rules to apply to future titles and abstracts. Wallace and colleagues have been testing approaches to classification in systematic reviews and have found that a process called 'active learning' (in which the classifier identifies the most informative items to screen manually) is highly promising for use in systematic reviews (Wallace et al. 2010a, 2010b).

Two other text-mining technologies are also useful in reviewing: *term recognition* and *automatic clustering*. Term recognition involves the identification of key terms from text. For example, the term recognition tool TerMine (www.nactem.ac.uk/termine) identified the terms in Table 6.2 as being the most significant in a draft of this chapter (only the top ten are shown; the tool identified many more than this). It shows that 'systematic review' is the most important (as determined by its 'C-Value' score: see Frantzi et al. 2000), followed by 'search strategy' and 'bibliographic database'. It also picked out 'inclusion criterion' and 'exclusion criterion' and 'relevant research', which indicates that the tool is good at identifying the most important concepts in a body of text. Term recognition can aid the screening process because it is able to identify the language used in sets of titles and abstracts and enables us to prioritise items for screening that 'look' most similar to other already included studies.

We tested one potential way forward using this method in a recent review about young people's access to tobacco (Sutcliffe et al. 2011). We deliberately

**Table 6.2** Automatic term recognition

| Rank | Term | Score |
|------|------|-------|
| 1 | systematic review | 30 |
| 2 | search strategy | 24 |
| 3 | bibliographic database | 18 |
| 3 | social science research unit | 18 |
| 5 | research question | 11 |
| 5 | inclusion criterion | 11 |
| 7 | research synthesis | 10 |
| 8 | relevant research | 10 |
| 8 | exclusion criterion | 10 |
| 10 | social science | 9 |

**Figure 6.2** Automatically generated clusters

searched broadly and sensitively and, as a result, our searches yielded about 36,000 titles and abstracts, of which we had time to screen manually only about a quarter. In order to evaluate the effectiveness of this approach, we compared the number of studies we identified with a 'baseline inclusion rate' (BIR). The BIR was estimated by screening a random sample of 661 citations manually, the appropriate size of the sample being identified using standard power calculation methods. The BIR was 1.81%, i.e. about 1.81% of all the 36,000 citations we had identified were likely to be relevant (652). After using the prioritisation method to screen a little over 9,100 titles and abstracts manually, we had marked 656 as being potentially relevant: a rate of 7.16%. If our initial results are confirmed, this method has enabled us to identify the expected number of relevant studies with only 25% of the usual manual work. We have obtained similar results in two other reviews in which we have tried this out. However, while these tests demonstrate the applicability of the approach, and a proper evaluation is needed before this technique can be considered as anything but experimental.

The final technology to mention here, *automatic clustering*, can be used to gain a quick overview of a set of titles and abstracts. It does this by looking across the text (e.g. titles and abstracts) and identifying groups that use similar combinations of terms. Figure 6.2 is an example of automatic clustering in a recent review about the sources of tobacco for young people.

Each term listed in Figure 6.2 represents a 'cluster' of titles and abstracts that use similar combinations of words. Some of the main topics in the review have been correctly identified, such as 'buy cigarettes', 'underage youth' and 'tobacco control', showing that automatic clustering can be a useful aid to identifying the broad areas into which a set of studies falls. However, the limitations of these tools are also clear, as clusters such as 'corresponding figures', 'conducted in 2002' and 'higher risk' are possibly not useful sub-divisions for the reviewer. (The clusters generated are completely dependent on the text submitted to the clustering engine; the reviewer cannot pre-select areas of particular importance.)

Text mining offers many possibilities to the systematic reviewer. For a more comprehensive overview of how this technology can assist in systematic reviews, see Thomas et al. (2011).

## Conclusion

Planning and executing a search and ensuring consistent screening takes considerable time. By reflecting on the review's research question, its conceptual framework and the types of study that should be included or excluded, researchers can plan an efficient and effective search strategy aiming to identify either sufficient studies for unbiased aggregation or sufficient concepts for coherent configuration. A good search strategy will identify which sources will be searched and why they were chosen, and will be as transparent, accountable and replicable as possible. Searching and screening can be seen as a circular process: while searching and screening, reviewers refer back to earlier stages of the review process and think about the next stages.

Understanding the logic that underpins the search activity can be instructive. If an aggregative approach to synthesis is planned, then an exhaustive approach to finding an unbiased set of *studies* is probably required; if the synthesis will configure study findings, then the strategy needs to ensure that sufficient relevant *concepts* are found.

New methods to shorten the searching and screening process are under development and over the coming years, they may change the methods described here substantially.

---

| Box 6.5 |

## The practicalities

- Decide whether your review question means that you should identify sufficient studies for unbiased aggregation or sufficient concepts for coherent configuration and think about what this means in terms of your search strategy.
- Develop a search strategy that balances your need to find sufficient studies and/ or concepts with the time and resources at your disposal.
- Ensure that you keep good records of your searches and what was retrieved.
- A search strategy involves more than a search of electronic databases: identify the key sources of relevant studies for your review, both electronic and other (e.g. books, organisations and personal contacts).
- Consider the structure of your search and how different parts of your conceptual framework break down into different components of a Boolean search.
- Ensure that screening is conducted consistently across your team.
- If you have large numbers of studies and access to technical support, consider the use of emerging technologies in order to reduce the amount of manual screening you need to do.

# SEVEN

## Describing and analysing studies

### *Sandy Oliver and Katy Sutcliffe*

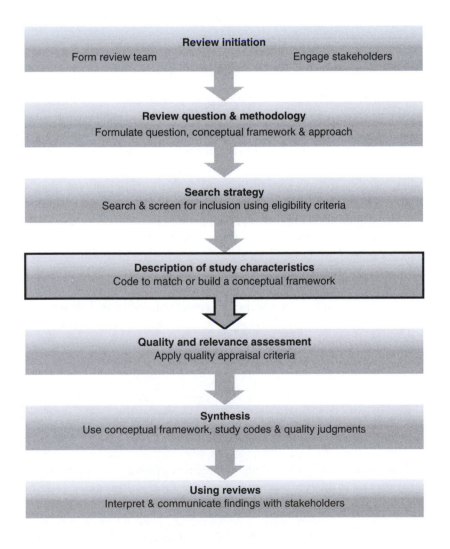

## Introduction

Characterising individual studies is an early step in analysing a body of research whether the purpose is to describe the focus of research effort (a systematic map) or to appraise the studies and collate their findings (a systematic synthesis). Capturing information about the content of each study, what is being researched and how, in a structured format facilitates analysis of themes and trends across all the studies being addressed. Description and analysis of the content of studies to answer a review question is perhaps the primary function of coding studies. However, the utility of coding goes far beyond this.

The chapter opens with a brief consideration of the different reasons for describing individual studies and for describing a body of literature. Next it considers each of these reasons in greater detail, describing the utility of such coding and how to go about capturing, organising and presenting the details of studies for each purpose. Finally, it links the technical aspects of describing studies (applying keywords, or extracting text and coding or categorising studies) to the intellectual effort of systematically reviewing research literature within an explicit conceptual framework, illustrating how the approach to coding is shaped by the nature of the review question.

## Why describe studies?

This section describes why describing studies by applying codes can be useful in different ways and at different stages in a review. Table 7.1 provides a summary of the reasons for coding discussed in this chapter. The various benefits of coding studies have been revealed over the course of conducting many systematic reviews, so this list should be considered illustrative rather than exhaustive.

**Table 7.1** Reasons for describing studies in a review

| | |
|---|---|
| (i) | To manage a review |
| (ii) | To include or exclude studies |
| (iii) | To create a map |
| | to describe the nature of a field of research |
| | to inform the conduct of a synthesis |
| | to interpret the findings of a synthesis |
| (iv) | To gather data for quality and relevance appraisal |
| (v) | To gather data for synthesis |
| (vi) | To accumulate a body of literature |

Table 7.1 illustrates how coding is an integral part of the review process. Coding also has a particular value at specific points within a review, such as the mapping and synthesis stages. However, the final purpose listed in the table, developing resources for researchers, illustrates the value of coding beyond an individual review. The following section takes each of these reasons in turn, providing detail about the utility of each type of coding and how to describe studies to meet that purpose.

## (i) Review management

### How does coding help manage a review?

From the very beginning of a systematic review, coding can be used to support the flow of the review process. Individual studies are coded to keep track of their progress through the review, to allocate tasks to review team members and to monitor the progress of the review as a whole (see Chapter 5 on information management). This coding can also provide an audit trail for reporting how the work was conducted. Although it is only the reviewers who need to know the operational codes for managing the review process, readers and users can legitimately have more confidence in a review if they know the reviewers were supported by a sound information management system, and if they can read an audit trail of how the studies were found and how they either contributed to the map or review or were justifiably excluded from the review.

### What needs to be described for effective review management?

The reliability of a review rests in part on the ability of the systematic reviewers to keep track of the studies they have found and the plans they have for them. It can be beneficial, therefore, for reviewers to capture and describe information about the studies from the point at which they are first identified. The initial information they find in a search may be a publication's title and abstract. To find out how fruitful were their different sources of searching for studies, reviewers can add to the title and abstract information about where or how the study was found – the name of an electronic database that was searched, an internet or web search, a journal whose list of contents were inspected systematically, a study's list of references, or a personal approach to an expert in the field (see Chapter 6 on searching). Chapter 5 provides a detailed description of managing studies through a review. It highlights the critical points at which assessments are made about each study, such as the application of inclusion criteria and the problems that can occur when dealing with a large number of studies. Coding the results of assessments for each study ensures it follows the correct path through the review.

---

**Box 7.1**

## Key terms and how we use them

**Scoping:** preliminary examination of a field of research

**Mapping:** describing the nature of a field of research

**Keywording:** describing studies in terms of their bibliographic details, focus of interest and study design

**Data collection or data extraction:** taking from the studies information about their focus of interest, methods, findings or authors' discussion

**Coding:** any keywording, data extraction or other annotation of studies in order to conduct a systematic review

---

## (ii) Including or excluding studies

Search strategies often identify more reports than are ultimately required in the review. Coding at this stage records which studies are eligible for the review and which are not.

### Why code eligible and ineligible studies?

Applying codes to explain why studies are excluded from an aggregative review records decisions that can later be used to justify or check detailed methods. Applying codes to explain why studies are included in a configurative review tracks the evolving scope of the work.

### How to code when screening for eligibility?

For aggregative reviews, where the key concepts are clearly defined in advance, the eligibility criteria can be translated into exclusion codes which are applied to each study in turn. For configurative reviews, where the scope of the review may initially be fluid, codes can be applied to signify why a study is of interest and may be included in the review. More detail about coding studies to screen for eligibility can be found in Chapter 6.

## (iii) Creating a systematic descriptive map of a body of literature

Systematic maps for describing a field of literature, or to inform or interpret syntheses, were introduced in Chapter 3. This section provides more detail on the coding issues relevant to creating and using maps.

### Why describe the contextual feature of studies?

#### *To describe the nature of a field of research*

One of the key functions of coding in systematic reviews is to capture the characteristics of individual studies in order that they may be described as a set or a body of literature, for instance, to consolidate the literatures of health promotion (Peersman 1996) and neurotrauma (Bragge et al. 2011). As a body of coded research accumulates electronically, it becomes a convenient starting place for scoping the size of a literature addressing key concepts and for revealing gaps in that literature, either gaps in primary research, or gaps in systematic reviews where primary research is already available (see Box 7.2).

---

| Box 7.2 |

## Map as a product – describing studies and revealing gaps

A review on the effectiveness of interventions to support pupils with emotional and behavioural difficulties (EBD) in mainstream primary school classrooms classified the interventions into four groups:

- Behavioural – using techniques to modify behaviour in the short term, e.g. rewards and sanctions.
- Cognitive behavioural – in which children reflect on their behaviour to support long-term behaviour change, e.g. peer modelling of self-instruction techniques to keep 'on task'.
- Systemic or ecological – which emphasises the importance of understanding the situational context in which any particular behaviour occurs, e.g. disruptive behaviour in the classroom, might be 'caused' by the classroom layout.
- Psychotherapeutic – which emphasises the deep and complex roots of behaviour problems and the possibility of long-term change through personal development, with an emphasis on building relationships, e.g. 'nurture groups' in schools.

These categories enabled the reviewers not only to describe the interventions that had been evaluated as a set, but also to identify gaps in knowledge about the different theoretical approaches for supporting children with EBD in mainstream classrooms. In particular, they found no studies evaluating psychotherapeutic techniques.

> Psychotherapeutic approaches have yet to be fully evaluated, but may lead to some understandings of the behaviour of more seriously disturbed children, who may otherwise not be able to be supported in mainstream. (Evans et al. 2003: 52)

A body of literature may also be described in terms that refer to policy or practice options to provide a framework for assessing the degree to which policy questions have been addressed by research. Policy options were a key dimension for coding the literature about public involvement in setting research agendas (Oliver et al. 2004), where reports were coded according to how involvement methods matched the three degrees of involvement recognised by national policy (Hanley et al. 2000).

Where policy or practice options reach beyond the scope of an individual piece of work, applying the same codes to successive reviews builds a growing set of coded studies addressing similar or overlapping bodies of literature. Consistent coding allows individual studies to be retrieved for use in successive reviews with overlapping scopes. For instance, a review of children's healthy eating and a review of children's physical activity included many of the same studies because some interventions target both these issues at the same time. Similarly, a review of workplace health promotion included studies also reviewed for their contributions to the evidence about peer-delivered health promotion.

### Mapping to inform a synthesis

'Mapping' the research in this way can also inform decisions about the final scope of a review that focuses in detail on one or several portion(s) of the literature in a synthesis rather than the whole. A descriptive map may be an important first stage in a review where the literature is unfamiliar so that the size and content of the area can be understood. If an extensive literature is found, the map enables reviewers to frame a narrower, answerable research question and specific criteria for including studies in a synthesis. A detailed map of a large body of research may be the precursor to a series of systematic syntheses addressing related issues (see Box 7.3).

---

| **Box 7.3** |

## A broad map and a series of in-depth reviews

In 2001 a group of reviewers working with the EPPI-Centre embarked on a series of reviews on the impact of Information and Communication Technologies (ICT) on literacy learning in English. The reviews set out to gather evidence as to whether the investment in ICT was resulting in benefits to learning and specifically literacy learning. The work began with a map describing the range and type of research studies addressing the impact of ICT on literacy learning in ages 5 to 16 (Andrews et al. 2002) and was followed by a series of five in-depth reviews with the following foci:

- networked ICT (Andrews et al. 2002);
- a meta-analysis on ICT in literacy learning (Torgerson and Zhu 2003);
- English as a second or additional language (Low and Beverton 2004);
- literature (Locke and Andrews 2004);
- moving-image texts (Burn and Leach 2004).

---

As well as informing the choice of studies to include in a review, a map can inform the choice of sub-group analyses. Describing the population and context of each study within a review provides a picture of how much studies differ and whether some sub-groups might usefully be analysed separately. Knowing whether differences in populations and contexts give rise to differences in the findings is important for drawing conclusions about whether findings can be applied universally (they are generalisable) or under what circumstances it is justifiable to apply the findings of a set of studies elsewhere (they are transferable).

*Mapping to interpret the findings of a synthesis*

In reviews where a map is succeeded by a narrower in-depth review and synthesis, reviewers may return to the findings of the map to further understand and contextualise the findings of the synthesis. By comparing the mapped and synthesised literatures, reviewers may reveal patterns, gaps or associations with the attributes of studies which determined their inclusion in the in-depth review but which without comparison to the wider mapped literature were not readily apparent. This approach provides reviewers with an important understanding of how representative the synthesised research is of the wider literature, and allows them to determine whether further synthesis is appropriate or whether further primary research should be recommended (see Box 7.4).

---

| **Box 7.4** |

## Using map findings to contextualise synthesis findings

A map of the literature on Personal Development Planning (PDP) explored the available research on how individuals reflect upon and plan their own learning (Gough et al. 2003) and led to a number of outputs, including:

- a descriptive map;
- a searchable database of coded studies; and
- the identification of a sub-set of studies for in-depth review, i.e. studies where PDP interventions had been formally implemented and assessed.

A key benefit of the map was, however, that it enabled the findings of the synthesis to be contextualised. For example, reviewers could see that in many ways the studies in the synthesis did not differ from the rest of those in the map. However, there were some key differences, such as in outcome measures. The synthesised studies were more likely than the mapped studies to have measured educational attainment and less likely to have measured attitudes to learning. This contextualisation supported the development of recommendations for future research, including a recommendation for further research that evaluates the impact of PDP on broader self-development in addition to attainment.

## How to describe studies for a map?

A descriptive map describes research activity (what sort of research has addressed what sort of issues), but does not usually describe the findings of the studies. Whether or not this is a precursor to a synthesis, research activity can be described in terms of variables such as the following:

1 Geographical distribution of studies: the country setting, urban or rural, and organisational setting (regional, local, institutional).
2 Research methods used: qualitative research, observational studies or experimental designs.
3 Research participants: their age, gender, ethnicity, education or other characteristics, and their social and economic circumstances or health status.
4 Particular contexts, policies and practices studied: e.g. interventions, delivery mechanisms, duration and intensity of an intervention.
5 Conceptual issues, such as theoretical approaches.
6 Anything else providing a rational focus for study.

A standard and well-defined set of codes is vital to enable studies to be described as a set. Deciding which of a set of codes to assign helps reviewers seek out key aspects of each study in a systematic way. The focus of the study can be described in terms of the participants and their context. Codes can be developed to capture important differences in these dimensions. These dimensions may be applicable to research generically (such as types of publication), to particular disciplines or policy areas (such as theories or study designs within disciplines or types of educator or clinician within policy sectors), or dimensions specific to an individual review. Capturing the details of the research focus and research design is sufficient to produce a simple map describing what research has been undertaken in an area.

An analytical map is more than descriptive. Where there is a strong external conceptual framework, analysis within that framework can offer more learning, even without looking at the findings of the included studies. For instance, a map of methods for involving clinicians and patients in setting research agendas showed how over time methods have involved patients more directly, allowed them greater thinking time, and involved them in decision-making processes (Stewart et al. 2010b). Similarly, an analytical map revealed differences in fundamental approaches to Personal Development Planning (see Box 7.5).

---

| **Box 7.5** |

## Learning from the characteristics of a set of studies

In a map of research on Personal Development Planning (PDP) (Gough et al. 2003) (see Box 7.4 also), reviewers were able to explore the relationship between different features of PDP approaches. The majority of PDP approaches evaluated were part of a course requirement and within this group of studies PDP was predominantly aimed at achieving course-specific outcomes. Conversely, the PDP approaches that were 'optional' were more likely to be aimed at broader self-development. Capturing this information enabled the reviewers to explore the reasons for such associations, illustrating the learning that can be gained from contextual information about the studies.

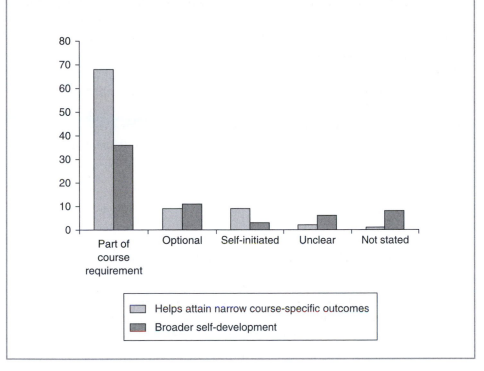

## (iv) Gathering data for quality and relevance appraisal

### How does coding support quality appraisal?

In a systematic synthesis, the work of reviewers goes beyond simply describing research. A systematic synthesis attempts to advance understanding to bring together evidence to support the decision-making of individuals, policy-makers and practitioners. It is therefore important that the evidence is well suited to answering the review question by being both trustworthy and relevant. As such, much more detailed coding, or 'data extraction', is required to describe the methods used in the study, the phenomenon under study, and its context. This detailed coding provides information on which to base judgements about the trustworthiness of a study and its relevance to the review question before taking note of the study findings. Quality and relevance codes may be applied as eligibility criteria, and in order to characterise included studies.

## What to capture for appraising studies?

Detailed coding is required to enable the findings of studies to be synthesised, taking into account how well the studies were conducted in order to address a specific research question. The question asked, the mode of synthesis and the methodology of included studies will determine how studies are appraised and what needs to be captured. For example, a set of codes for determining whether the findings of an experimental study are trustworthy will be very different from the set of codes for appraising a study capturing views using focus groups. Comprehensive recording of the methods employed by studies involves far more than just coding the basic design. Describing the methods for sampling, recruiting, collecting and analysing data is usually a prerequisite for judgements about whether these methods were conducted well (see Chapter 8 on the quality and relevance appraisal of studies). A quality appraisal of the methods is an essential step for reviews that aggregate the findings from studies addressing similar issues, but for reviews that configure, the quality of studies may depend more on the trustworthiness or credibility of the findings (see Box 7.6).

---

### Box 7.6

### Excerpt from a quality appraisal coding framework

In a review about the barriers to and facilitators of healthy eating for children (Thomas et al. 2003), the methods employed by the studies were appraised to judge whether the study findings were rooted in *children's own perspectives*. In relation to this, reviewers were asked to capture relevant data from studies to assess whether they:

1 used appropriate *data collection* methods for helping children to express their views;
2 used appropriate methods for ensuring the *data analysis* was grounded in the views of children;
3 actively involved children in the *design and conduct* of the study.

---

## (v) Gathering data for synthesis

### How does coding support synthesis?

The main product of many systematic reviews is a synthesis of research findings to answer a review question, for example 'What are effective strategies to support primary-aged pupils with emotional and behavioural difficulties in mainstream classrooms?' or 'What are children's views about the meanings of obesity or body size, shape or weight?' A synthesis involves pooling the details and results of a group of studies (see Chapter 9 for how this is done). In order to compare findings across studies, each study must be scrutinised and its data coded using an approach appropriate to the nature of the review question and the nature of the data used to answer that question. A consideration of the different approaches to coding for synthesis is provided later in this chapter.

## What to capture for synthesising studies?

The results or findings of each study, whether these are qualitative or quantitative, also need to be described and coded for analysis before they can be synthesised into the findings of a review. This 'data extraction' stage of taking from each study descriptions of how the study was conducted and what it found is analogous to data collection in primary research. Coding the content of individual studies may be very detailed. Coding the content of a set of studies multiplies the complexity of the task. The approach used for capturing and interrogating the findings of studies in a review depends largely on the nature of the review question. The range of approaches and details of how to capture detailed data for different types of review question are described in the final section of this chapter.

In summary, coding has benefits for the wider research community, in particular the research synthesis community, in addition to the obvious benefits to the review team and the review's potential audiences. As such, the approaches to coding, the stages in a review at which coding will take place and the ways in which these descriptions will be stored all merit careful consideration. The following section considers how the review aims and questions can inform considerations about how to capture information from studies.

## (vi) Accumulating a body of literature

### How can coding develop resources beyond the review?

The storage of detailed information on individual studies and sets of studies, in particular in an electronic format, allows the development of resources for other researchers or reviewers. Storing detailed descriptions about the content or trustworthiness of a study electronically not only facilitates analysis for the current review, it also provides a sustainable record to allow the reviewed study to be included in other subsequent reviews addressing cross-cutting issues. For instance, some studies included in a review about young people and healthy eating evaluated complex interventions that were also relevant to a subsequent review about young people and physical activity. In addition, describing studies with a set of codes that reaches beyond the individual piece of work also allows a body of evidence to accumulate with each successive piece of work. This approach provides an opportunity for analyses encompassing many reviews, as in meta-epidemiology. An example of this was a systematic review and meta-regression to investigate how randomisation can influence the findings of controlled trials (Oliver et al. 2010). Individual studies can be stored electronically and retrieved efficiently in the course of personal academic work. Programmes of work can be supported by pooling the resources of teams of researchers: a shared set of codes consistently applied to studies soon generates a specialist database. The Trials Register of Promoting Health Interventions (TRoPHI) at the EPPI-Centre is a web-based database of randomised controlled trials and controlled trials (non-randomised) of Public Health and Health Promotion interventions. It grew out of successive reviews of effectiveness in the area of health promotion. Its counterpart, the Database of Promoting Health Effectiveness Reviews (DoPHER), is a specialised register of health promotion reviews. Although both of these databases were initiated to support the work of a single team, they are now publicly available on the internet and used as a source by other systematic reviewers.

### What to capture to develop research resources?

Using standardised coding tools to capture characteristics of research across a number of reviews enables individual research reports captured in different reviews to be compared across reviews and retrieved for further work. As successive reviews are conducted in the same area, studies are reviewed with a generic coding tool. The example in Box 7.7 highlights some of the dimensions that have been useful for capturing information to support future work in the area of health promotion.

---

**Box 7.7**

## Standardised coding tools for developing resources

The EPPI-Centre Health Promotion Keywording Strategy (1997) has been used to capture the details of thousands of health promotion studies on a variety of dimensions, including:

- how the report was located;
- the publication language;
- the country in which it was carried out;
- the area of health promotion focused on;
- the characteristics of the population;
- details of the intervention site – (as illustrated here).

**Q.12 What is/are the intervention site(s)?**

A.12.1 community site
A.12.2 correctional institution

---

A.12.3 day care centre
A.12.4 educational institution
A.12.5 family centre
A.12.6 health care unit
A.12.7 home
A.12.8 hospice
A.12.9 hospital
A.12.10 mass media
A.12.11 outreach
A.12.12 preschool
A.12.13 primary care
A.12.14 primary education
A.12.15 residential care
A.12.16 secondary education
A.12.17 specialist clinic
A.12.18 tertiary education
A.12.19 workplace site
A.12.20 intervention site unspecified

## Tailoring descriptions to meet the needs of different types of reviews

This section of the chapter considers how coding approaches need to be appropriate for the type of review question and the type of research being analysed. For example, some reviews aim to aggregate or pool the findings of empirical studies to test a theory, while others aim to create new interpretations or ways of understanding by organising and integrating or configuring data. Figure 7.1 presents a range of review types and illustrates how coding procedures will vary depending on the aims of a review.

For reviews that are designed to aggregate data to test a specific hypothesis, all key concepts within the hypothesis are clear in advance. Each of these concepts provides a code that can be attached to the relevant studies. These codes, and others for the methods and findings of the studies, are combined in a coding framework that is largely designed in advance of data extraction and describes the studies in terms that are suitable for subsequent analysis across all the studies.

For reviews that are designed to configure, generate or explore a theory, although some important concepts may be recognised in advance, many may emerge from the process of reading and re-reading studies. As such, pre-specified coding categories or questions to ask of the data are undesirable. An approach to coding in which both questions and answers are open allows new knowledge and understandings to emerge from the data. This is analogous to qualitative analysis of primary research data and is an iterative process, moving between studies and the review question repeatedly (see Figure 7.1).

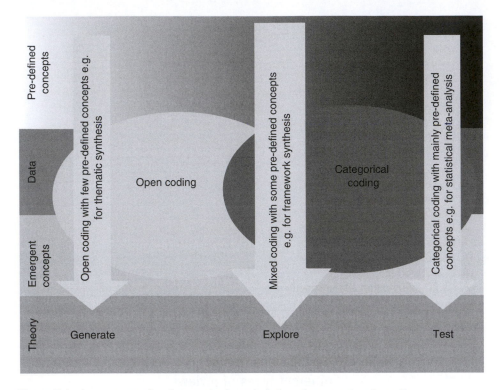

**Figure 7.1** A spectrum of review methods and choice of approaches to coding

## Categorical coding

When aggregating textual or numerical data to test hypotheses, pre-specified codes are systematically applied to individual research reports prior to analysis to produce a systematic map or a synthesis. As mentioned above, coding the focus and overall design of studies for a map or for building a database is often called keywording, whereas the more detailed task of describing the methods and findings of studies is 'data extraction'. The validity of a review depends in part on how well the codes have been applied.

For data to be categorised, categories (or codes) need unambiguous definitions that are consistently applied. Consistency is greater if definitions are accompanied by hints, including examples, about how to apply them. The definitions for codes and hints for applying them are together termed 'review guidelines'. Each study is reviewed and coded in turn using the same guidelines. Typically, these will ask a series of questions which will be used to interrogate the studies. The same set of questions is asked of each study in turn, with sets of multiple choice answers, and allows free text to explain the choice of category and the degree of certainty. Reviews can have their own specific guidelines, although if they share some questions and answers with other related reviews, this opens the possibility of cross-cutting analyses. Some questions and answers may be applicable across reviews very broadly, such as the coding of bibliographic data, including the type of publication, for instance, a book or academic journal article. Other questions and answers may be chosen for particular disciplines or policy sectors. Each review is likely to have its own specific combination of common and unique questions and answers.

Developing or adapting guidelines for extracting data is an important step in each review. Guidelines can be piloted on a few research reports by two or more reviewers working independently and then comparing how these are applied by different reviewers. Discrepancies may reveal oversights or they may reveal differences in their understandings of the definitions, so that definitions and hints will need refining and the guidelines piloting again. Once definitions and their interpretation are agreed, there is the option of measuring the degree of agreement between reviewers applying the same guidelines. This is a measure of 'inter-reliability' and can be presented as a 'kappa' statistic (Orwin 1994). Decisions will need to be made about how to handle disagreements between reviewers, as even with a well-considered coding guideline there will inevitably be studies that are difficult to code or borderline cases.

## Open coding

If the purpose of a review is not to test a well-constructed hypothesis, but to advance understanding by generating or exploring theory, many key concepts may not be known in advance, and codes that have not been pre-specified (open codes) will be applied to the data. Identifying these concepts, and coding them, through a growing familiarity with the studies and a qualitative analysis of the data, is one of the products of the review. In this case, discrepancies in coding will raise issues to be discussed in order to explore the meaning of key concepts and to build theories rather than to report the reliability of coding pre-specified concepts.

Exploratory analysis of qualitative data in a configurative systematic review may be very similar to the analysis of the primary research data, such as grounded theory (Glaser and Strauss 1967). Open coding can also contribute to exploring some details of aggregative reviews, for instance when describing the context of studies or the underpinning theories of interventions. In contrast to the categorical approach detailed above, open coding is organic and iterative as opposed to pre-determined.

However, notable differences exist between the use of open coding applied to primary research and open coding applied in systematic reviews. One key difference is that in addition to coding raw data, such as participants' own accounts of phenomena, or first-order constructs, reviewers are able to code and describe the study authors' analysis of and conclusions about that data, or second-order constructs. Reviewers' interpretations of both the participant data and author analysis can therefore be considered as 'third-order' constructs (Britten et al. 2002; Schutz 1971).

A second difference is that, in conducting secondary analysis, systematic reviewers will have to work harder to ensure that the context and original meaning of the raw data are preserved (Sandelowski et al. 1997). Systematic approaches to coding and organising qualitative data have been integrated with the open coding approach to address this issue (see Box 7.8).

---

## Box 7.8

## Maintaining context in a qualitative synthesis using framework analysis

A review of qualitative studies on decision-making between children with chronic conditions and health care practitioners (Sutcliffe, 2010) used a systematic approach to ensure that the meaning and context of the primary data were not being lost in the synthesis. Framework analysis was used to organise systematically the results of an open coding synthesis to make clear whether the themes in the synthesis reflected both participant accounts and the analysis of the primary author. The work involved placing the first-order constructs, or participant data, in grids alongside corresponding second-order constructs and both of these alongside the reviewers' interpretation of this data, or third-order constructs. Coding and organising the data in this systematic way made transparent the thread from the contextualised participant views, through to the second- and third-order interpretations.

| Third-order constructs | Second-order constructs | | First-order constructs | |
|---|---|---|---|---|
| Reviewer analysis | Author analysis | Author theme headings | Participant views/ perspectives | Participant description |
| Lack of continuity or consistency can undermine trust in technical competence as families receive contradictory messages | (Inconsistent messages) *can confuse mothers; encourage mothers to question provider competence; and permit mothers to accept only the information they can cope with easily* | Validity of the diagnosis<br><br>Level of service provision | ***It didn't inspire my confidence that much*** (Mother 2 on receiving contradictory information from different providers)<br><br>*Lack of consistency raised concerns for this mother about GPs' technical competency and was, she said, a disincentive to getting GP care for her son's asthma* | ***Different doctors have told me different doses to give her*** (Mother 1)<br><br>*Mixed messages from GPs on diagnosis and treatment were reported in our study* |

Data from Buetow et al. (2003)

As has been described throughout this book, but particularly in Chapter 3, individual reviews need not be confined to one type, or indeed one end of the spectrum represented in Figure 7.1. Approaches to coding should reflect the needs of each individual review question and reviewers should consider the benefits of integrating a number of approaches to coding data within one review.

---

| **Box 7.9**

## The practicalities

### For all reviews

1 Choose management codes to identify reviewers and stages in the review process (see Chapter 5).

### For aggregative reviews

1 Bring together stakeholders to refine the question and clarify the conceptual framework.
2 Choose codes for eligibility criteria that match the question and apply these consistently to potentially relevant studies (see Chapter 6).
3 Choose codes for key concepts in the conceptual framework.
4 Design a coding tool: 'double' code (two reviewers working independently) a subset of studies and discuss discrepancies to eliminate errors, identify different understandings, and refine key concepts and their definitions. Repeat on successive sub-sets until satisfied that all key concepts are clearly defined and the tool is reliable to use.
5 Analyse the completed coding to describe the studies.

### For configurative reviews

1 Consult stakeholders to ensure reviewers are sensitised (but not limited) to the key issues.
2 Read studies, get immersed in the data, code the participant data and authors' themes (first- and second-order themes).
3 Systematically organise the findings to enable a comparison of these across studies and to check that the context and meaning of the original data are preserved.
4 Translate studies into one another – assess how they correspond/contrast, taking into account differences in context (third-order themes and 'lines of argument', see Chapter 9).

### For mixed methods reviews

1 Bring together stakeholders to refine the question and explore their conceptual frameworks.
2 Set initial eligibility criteria, taking into account the question and conceptual frameworks.
3 Choose codes for key concepts in the conceptual frameworks.
4 Read the studies, code for key concepts in the conceptual frameworks and code themes emerging from the data.
5 Discuss with the stakeholders the evolving conceptual framework in light of the emerging findings. If necessary, amend the framework and eligibility criteria, extend the search and inspect the studies again (see Chapter 9).

## Conclusion

This chapter has considered the rationale for describing studies, the technical procedures for describing studies and the range of resulting products. It describes how coding can support the management of the review, lead to a descriptive map of the relevant literature, gather data about the research methods to appraise the quality of studies, gather textual and numerical data in categories for aggregating the research findings from similar studies, and employ open coding for a synthesis that configures research findings from related studies. Most challenging is setting up an initial coding framework that is coherent and useful. This is only possible if the review authors are thinking clearly about the key concepts and how they may be interrelated.

Chapter 4 described how a conceptual framework may be defined in advance, or generated or refined during the course of the review. Once the initial key concepts have been defined, reviewers can decide which of these to use to define the boundaries of the review (the inclusion and exclusion criteria) and which to use to describe key dimensions within the review (the coding framework). Each key concept is likely to have some synonyms and these will translate into terms for the search strategy. Thus, the coding framework provides a tool to compare the literature with the conceptual framework.

The range of approaches to coding and the resulting benefits described in this chapter have been identified as reviewers' experience at the EPPI-Centre has accumulated. The great variety in types of review, illustrated in this chapter and others, means that being sensitive to novel ways in which coding can potentially support reviews of different types is an important part of methods development for systematic reviewers.

# EIGHT

## Quality and relevance appraisal

### *Angela Harden and David Gough*

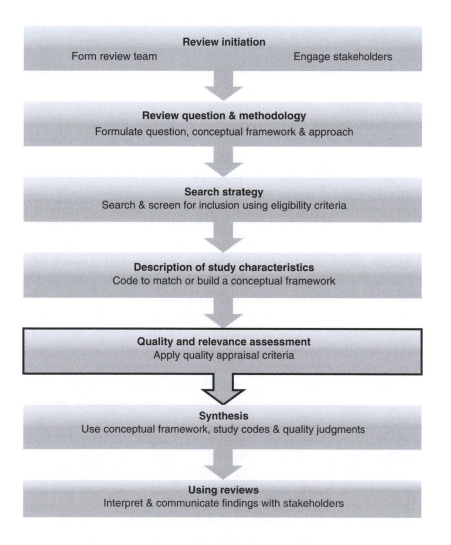

---

┌─────────────── **Aims of chapter** ───────────────┐

This chapter discusses:

- Different approaches to assessing quality in research and review
- The appraisal of relevance to the review questions under study
- A 'weight of evidence' approach to quality and relevance appraisals
- Appropriate critical appraisal tools
- The stages at, and ways in which, quality and relevance appraisals are made in reviews
- Broader debates about research quality

└────────────────────────────────────────────────────┘

## Introduction

Previous chapters have discussed searching for relevant studies to include in reviews and describing the key features of the research found. Chapter 7 described the use of coding frameworks for gathering information about the studies identified. An important reason for gathering this information is to examine the nature of the results of the studies and assess how relevant and useful the studies are for answering the review questions. By appraising the quality and relevance of studies, reviewers can ensure that only the most appropriate, trustworthy and relevant studies are used to develop the conclusions of the review. Assessing the quality and relevance of individual studies within a review is a crucial part of the review process and contributes to the quality and credibility of a review itself. Research varies in its quality and relevance and study quality can have an impact on the findings of reviews (see Box 8.1). Engaging in any type of review of research offers the opportunity to examine issues of quality in research in detail. Systematic reviews, by their very definition, *demand* such a detailed examination. As noted in Chapter 3, the past decade has seen the development of different types of systematic review, ranging from the most traditional aggregative empirical models, in which review methods are largely pre-specified, through to more configurative reviews using iterative and/or conceptual approaches, such as realist synthesis or meta-ethnography. These different approaches vary in how they make and use quality and relevance appraisals, but all types of review provide guidelines on quality and relevance assessment regardless of whether the review is a statistical meta-analysis of the findings of controlled trials, a meta-ethnography of qualitative research or a theory driven synthesis of diverse study types. In EPPI-Centre reviews, two key principles are that: (a) judgements about quality and relevance are always made in relation to a particular review question and purpose; and (b) the criteria and methods used should be made as explicit as possible so that readers of the review can understand and assess how judgements about quality and relevance have been made.

This chapter begins by locating quality and relevance appraisal within broader debates about the multidimensional nature of quality in research. The layers of complexity in discussions of research quality and relevance are: the diverse range of research questions that is asked; the array of study types, designs and epistemologies that are available to answer those questions; and the wide variety of contexts in which research is undertaken. There is also the issue of the diversity of systematic review methodology and the various ways that quality and relevance appraisal are approached within different types of review. As a way to navigate this complexity, we outline a framework for considering quality and relevance – 'weight of evidence' – which was developed at the EPPI-Centre in the course of conducting systematic reviews to answer different types of question across a range of domains, such as education, health promotion and social care. We also discuss the range of ways in which the results of quality and relevance appraisals can be used in the synthesis stage of a review and illustrate different approaches to quality and relevance appraisal using several examples. Because the weight of evidence framework is flexible enough to be applied to a variety of review questions and to accommodate a variety of research designs, it is not prescriptive in terms of the exact criteria to be used to assess quality and relevance. In this chapter we therefore also signpost a number of critical appraisal tools that can be used in conjunction with a weight of evidence approach.

---

| **Box 8.1** |

## Does the quality of studies change the conclusions of a review?

As noted at the beginning of this chapter, by appraising the quality and relevance of studies, reviewers can ensure that only the most trustworthy and relevant studies are used to develop the conclusions of the review. This argument makes intuitive sense, but is also illustrated by empirical work on the impact of quality on review findings. Glass (1976: 4) stated that 'It is an empirical question whether relatively poorly designed studies give results significantly at variance with those of the best designed studies'. In the health care field, there is now a large body of work that has examined empirically the question of whether the design, quality of execution and analysis of studies evaluating the effects of interventions make a difference to the findings of reviews (e.g. Abraham et al. 2004; Moher et al. 1998; Schulz et al. 1995). Similar findings have been produced within other public policy areas too (Goldring 1990; Guyatt et al. 2000; Oliver et al. 2010; Peersman et al. 1999). Although it is not yet possible to predict the way in which the results of poorly designed studies will vary from better designed studies (Britton et al. 1998; Kunz and Oxman 1998; MacLehose et al. 2000), a number of reviews have found that lower quality studies – where quality is measured by how well the study design and methods have minimised the introduction of bias and error through, for example, the employment of an equivalent control or comparison group – tend to overestimate the effects of interventions. Evidence from higher quality studies can therefore serve as a 'reality check' for the overly optimistic claims that are often made about new approaches to solving health, educational or other social problems. (Also see 'Hearing the grass grow' chapter in *Experiments in Knowing* for some examples of where choosing different research designs mean you get different answers; Oakley 2000b.)

## Conceptualising quality and relevance in research

Research knowledge is one of several types of knowledge useful for engaging with the world. Compared to other types of knowledge, such as practice knowledge or organisational knowledge, research knowledge is usually explicit rather than tacit and is produced in a purposeful way in relation to a research goal or question (Gough 2007c; Furlong and Oancea 2005; Pawson et al. 2003). This latter point is important because although the quality of research can be judged by very abstract and generic criteria, specific criteria are required in order to judge whether it is fit for purpose.

The term 'quality' can refer to a particular standard or a specific characteristic of somebody or something. The term 'relevance' – whether something is closely connected or important to the matter at hand – can be viewed as a particular aspect or dimension of quality. Assessing quality and relevance in the context of evidence-informed policy and practice is often referred to as 'critical appraisal', which has been defined as 'the process of carefully and systematically examining research to judge its trustworthiness, and its value and relevance in a particular context' (Burls 2009: 2). What is clear from these definitions is the necessity of judgement. Who defines the standard required for a piece of research to be judged as high quality? How might reviewers judge whether it is highly relevant to our context? Ways of making these judgements are of crucial importance, not only to those who conduct systematic reviews but also to the whole research community and wider society. Individual researcher reputations and the status of research as a legitimate and useful activity depend on research being of good quality and high relevance (Hargreaves 1996; Oakley 1998). Explicit systems have been devised to ensure quality and relevance (e.g. peer review, ethical codes, guidelines for research reporting) and notions of quality are at the heart of the norms and principles of working within a scientific or social scientific research community (for example, a culture of reflection, criticism and debate). These principles and norms are a key starting point for thinking about judging quality and relevance in a systematic review.

Within the research community there has been a focus on assessing the quality of research on the basis of the way the research has been designed and the methods used to conduct the research. Collectively, these kinds of criteria can be referred to as *epistemic*. Once you begin to think about how the findings from research may be used or applied, other dimensions of quality become pertinent, in particular, relevance. Apart from producing findings that are useful in an applied context, doing research can also lead to other benefits, such as new skills and learning for the team involved in carrying out or shaping the research. This way of thinking about research reveals other quality dimensions on which research might be judged. For example, in relation to practice-based and applied educational research Furlong and Oancea (2006) argue for a much wider conceptualisation of quality in research, which not only includes, but also goes beyond, the traditional epistemic dimension of methodological and theoretical robustness. They propose three other dimensions: the *technological* dimension, which refers to the value of the research in an applied context; the *capacity-building and value for people* dimension, which refers to the extent to which the research has stimulated personal growth and has involved partnership, collaboration and engagement with users; and the *economic* dimension, which refers to whether the research is, for example, cost-effective and competitive.

A particular piece of research can be judged on all or any one of the above dimensions depending on the perspective of those judging the research and the questions they bring to it. A funding body, for example, may want to know the quality of the research on all four of Furlong and Oancea's dimensions before making the final funding payment to a research group. A policy-maker, on the other hand, who has a specific policy problem to address, may be less interested in the capacity-building dimension of the research in favour of its robustness and its relevance in supporting proctical decision making. In other words, in an applied context, question-specific quality and relevance criteria are used to determine how much 'weight of evidence' should be given to the findings from a research study in answering a particular question.

The TAPUPAS framework developed by Pawson et al. (2003) to define types and quality of knowledge in social care is a useful way of thinking in more detail about how to judge the epistemic quality and relevance of a piece of research. TAPUPAS involves assessing a piece of research (or any other type of knowledge) along seven dimensions: *transparency* – whether the process of knowledge creation is open to outside scrutiny; *accuracy* – whether knowledge claims are supported by the data or information on which they are based; *purposivity* – whether the methods used in the research were suitable for the 'task in hand'; *utility* – whether the knowledge generated is a useful answer for the question posed; *propriety* – whether knowledge has been created with a due respect for legal and ethical matters; *accessibility* – whether the knowledge has been presented in a way that meets the needs of the knowledge user, such as whether it is easy to read and understand; and *specificity* – whether the knowledge meets the specific standards that are associated with that type of knowledge.

The transparency dimension with TAPUPAS highlights an important distinction between the quality of research reporting and the quality of the research itself. Reporting quality in research is hugely variable, with much effort in recent years dedicated to improving reporting standards. Although how well a piece of research is reported may be a proxy for the quality of the research itself, there is a danger of missing a good piece of research due to poor quality reporting; or wrongly judging a polished report as being indicative of a well-conducted piece of research. Sandelowski and Barroso (2002), on the other hand, argue that the research cannot be separated from its communication in a research report and that the epistemic value of a study includes its rhetorical and aesthetic qualities of how the report represents the research and the reader's response to this. The reader is attempting to make the research reports meaningful just as a qualitative researcher may seek meaning.

Quality and a relevance appraisal of the individual studies combined in the synthesis stage of a review can impact on the conclusions of a systematic review and their interpretation and implementation by policy, practice and individual decision-makers (see Chapter 10). Even if some further analysis has been undertaken to convert the findings of a review in a way that is more easily understandable in terms of everyday policy and practice, this does not in and of itself indicate what, if any, action should be taken. This is largely because much of the knowledge and information needed to make such a decision lies outside a review. The researchers' role in making recommendations for action on the basis of their research findings is a matter for debate. But it is important that reviews describe intervention content and the context of the individual studies.

In research on the effectiveness of health interventions, the GRADE system has been developed to provide a framework for judging and reporting: the quality of individual findings, the overall body of evidence, the underlying quality of evidence, key statistical results, and the quality of evidence for each health outcome (Guyatt et al. 2008). Randomised controlled trials are considered to provide good evidence but may be downgraded if there is an inconsistency to the results, an indirectness to the evidence, imprecision or a reporting bias. Similarly, observational studies provide low-quality evidence but may be rated higher if the magnitude of the treatment effect is very large, if there is evidence of a dose–response relation, or if all likely causes of bias would decrease rather than amplify the apparent treatment effect. GRADE also distinguishes the quality of evidence from recommendations about the use of the intervention. The recommendation is based not only upon the quality of evidence, but also on uncertainty about the balance between desirable and undesirable effect, uncertainty or variability about values and preferences of those affected, and uncertainty about whether the intervention is a good use of resources (Guyatt et al. 2008). In this way, Guyatt and colleagues argue that 'GRADE provides a systematic and transparent framework for clarifying questions, determining the outcomes of interest, summarizing the evidence that addresses a question, and moving from the evidence to a recommendation or decision' (Guyatt et al. 2011: 380). As the concern of GRADE is primarily with the effectiveness of health interventions, the definition of quality of evidence is based on confidence in estimates of the effect of these interventions (Guyatt et al. 2011). The strength of evidence can of course be crucial, but it is not always the only concern. There may also be issues about the applicability of that evidence to the situation in which it is going to be used or the fit-for-purpose – 'purposivity' – dimension of quality in the TAPUPAS framework.

The above frameworks are useful for highlighting the variety of dimensions upon which the quality of research can be judged. TAPUPAS and the dimensions of quality offered by Furlong and Onacea do not, however, offer a ready-made framework for assessing the quality of research in the context of systematic reviews. Within reviews, judgements about quality and relevance are always made in a specific context and need to consider the particular review question and purpose.

In the next section we discuss the specific issues associated with appraising quality and relevance in reviews and outline the 'weight of evidence' framework as a useful heuristic in which to make sense of these issues and structure quality and relevance appraisals.

## Appraising research in reviews

There are several issues to consider when appraising the research in reviews, including the points at which appraisal will take place in the review process, the criteria to be used to judge quality and relevance, whether judgements will be made by more than one reviewer, and how the results of the appraisal process will be used. Different types of review will vary in how quality and relevance appraisals are undertaken, depending on, for example, the type of question asked, the research included, or the mode of synthesis. For example, a review focused on a question relating to people's perspectives and experiences on a particular health or social issue that aims to include only qualitative research is likely to use quality criteria specifically developed to judge qualitative research. On the other hand, a review focused on the effectiveness of interventions is likely to opt for a set of criteria developed to assess studies according to the extent to which their methodology is able to rule out alternative explanations for any observed effect of the intervention(s). In terms of our typology of review methods introduced in previous chapters, another key distinction relates to where a particular review lies on the 'generate–explore–test' theory continuum (Figure 8.1).

In reviews towards the theory-testing end of the continuum, in which the major concepts of interest are largely pre-defined and the mode of synthesis is primarily

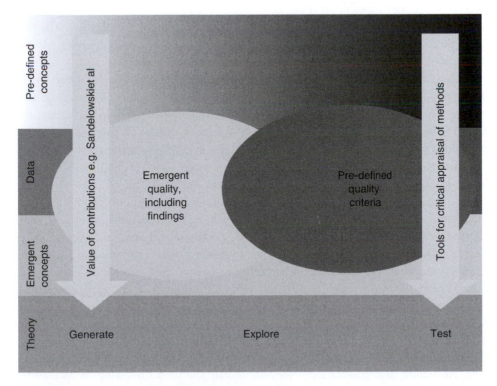

**Figure 8.1** Types of review and quality assessment

aggregative, a quality and relevance appraisal is usually done before the synthesis takes place using pre-defined criteria and quality assessment tools (see later in chapter), with an emphasis on the appraisal of the methods used to conduct the research. In a sense, the criteria for quality are inclusion criteria for the review. In a statistical meta-analysis to test questions about the efficacy of interventions, for example, a common concern will be to assess whether any part of the method could have introduced a hidden bias and so would lessen confidence in the experimental results (as with the GRADE system previously mentioned).

At the other end of the continuum, in reviews which aim to generate theory, a quality and relevance appraisal is more likely to be emergent rather than pre-defined, with both quality and relevance assessed on the basis of the findings of studies as well as, or instead of, methods. Noblit and Hare (1988), who developed meta-ethnography, for synthesising the findings of qualitative research, argue that the quality of 'qualitative' research will only emerge in the synthesis stage of a review. According to them and, more recently, Pawson (2006b), judging the quality of a study in relation to a particular research synthesis is not just about determining whether the research has been carried out according to sound procedures. Assessing quality is also about examining how study findings fit (or do not fit) with the findings of other studies. How study findings fit with the findings of other studies cannot be assessed until the synthesis is completed. Quality is perceived in term of its value; as Pawson (2006b: 141) puts it, the 'worth of a study is determined in the synthesis'. However, in practice, many reviews towards the configuring end of the continuum do use pre-specified methods such as critical appraisal tools to assist with making judgements about quality.

As noted earlier, in a systematic review, the quality and relevance of a particular study are ultimately judged in relation to the research question(s) asked in the review. Reviewers at the EPPI-Centre have often found it useful to structure thinking about a quality and relevance appraisal in terms of three dimensions which involve both generic standards and review specific assessments (the Weight of Evidence Framework (Weight of Evidence); Gough 2007c). The first dimension is the quality of execution of the study in its own terms or the 'soundness' of the study or the quality of a study according to the generic and accepted standards associated with that particular type of study: for example, judging whether a randomised controlled trial had been designed, executed and analysed according to the accepted standards of this study type to minimise the effects of, for instance, hidden bias. This first dimension is therefore a generic assessment. The second and third dimensions are review-specific. The second dimension is the appropriateness of the study design and analysis for answering the review question under study. It is important to note that the emphasis here is on the *review question*, not the original research question of the study. The third dimension is how well matched the study is to the focus of the review in terms of its topic and its operationalisation, its sample and population, context, and/or any measures used or its usefulness in other ways. In practice, reviewers may not always overtly address each of these dimensions. They may be implicit or may be dealt with by some other part of the review process, such as screening out particular research designs or outcome measures at the inclusion/exclusion criteria stage of a review.

The Weight of Evidence Framework can be used as a practical strategy for critical appraisal to ensure that all three dimensions are systematically considered in a review. Each study in a review can be judged on each individual dimension and given an assessment (for example, a numeric or categorical rating such as high, medium or low). A final step involves reviewers making an overall judgement about the three dimensions combined to provide an overall appraisal of the weight of evidence of a study's findings in relation to a review. The EPPI-Centre does not have specific scales for measuring the three dimensions in a study, but it has developed a series of questions for coding studies in a review (see Chapter 7 on gathering data for quality and relevance appraisal).

In a systematic review of factors promoting participation in further and higher education by minority ethnic groups, Torgeson et al. (2008) used Weight of Evidence to structure the quality and relevance assessments of their included studies (see Box 8.2). Using Weight of Evidence, they were able to break down step by step, and make explicit, the judgements they needed to make to identify the most trustworthy and relevant studies for their synthesis.

---

| **Box 8.2** |

## Use of weight of evidence in an education review (adapted from Torgeson et al. 2008)

**Review question**:  What are the factors that promote high post-16 participation of many minority ethnic groups?

**Review overview**: The desire to widen participation in formal post-compulsory education and training is a policy agenda common to most developed countries. Given that some minority ethnic groups have higher rates of post-16 participation in the UK than both the majority white cohort and some other minorities, identifying potential determinants could lead to a method of increasing participation for all. The aim of this review, therefore, was to determine the factors that drive the high post-16 participation of many minority ethnic groups. Studies had to be conducted in the UK, have a key focus on post-16 aspirations, provide a distinct analysis of different minority ethnic groups and either (a) elicit student aspirations about education (cross-sectional survey or qualitative study) or (b) investigate the statistical relationship between aspirations and educational variables (secondary data analysis). A conceptual framework for the synthesis was constructed to capture post-16 'promoters' and 'non-promoters' within the following categories: government policy; institutional practices; external agencies; work; religion; family; individual aspirations; and other factors.

**Weight of Evidence (WoE)**: Separate ways of assessing studies were put in place for the two different types of study included in the review. For all dimensions of WoE,

*(Continued)*

*(Continued)*

studies were given a rating of low, medium or high. Examples of how the studies were judged 'high' or 'medium' are shown below. A standard formula was used to calculate the overall weight of evidence for a study (e.g. for a study to be rated overall 'high', it had to be rated 'high' for WoE A and B and at least 'medium' for WoE C). Only the findings from studies rated 'high' or 'medium' were used in the synthesis stage of the review.

| | **Cross-sectional surveys and qualitative research** | **Secondary data analysis** |
|---|---|---|
| **WoE A: Soundness of studies** | High: Explicit and detailed methods and results sections for data collection and analysis; interpretation clearly warranted from findings. Medium: Satisfactory methods and results sections for data collection and analysis; interpretation partially warranted from findings. | High: Explicit and detailed methods and results sections for data analysis; interpretation clearly warranted from findings. Medium: Satisfactory methods and results sections for data analysis; interpretation partially warranted from findings. |
| **WoE B: Appropriateness of study design for answering the review question** | High: Large-scale survey methods using questionnaires and/or interviews. Medium: Survey methods using questionnaires and/or interviews. | High: Large-scale secondary data analysis; origin of dataset clearly stated. Medium: Secondary data analysis; origin of dataset partially indicated. |
| **WoE C: Relevance of the study focus to the review** | High: Large sample, with diverse ethnic groups, with good generalisability and clear post-16 focus. Medium: Adequate sample, with diverse ethnic groups, with generalisability and partial post-16 focus. | High: Large sample, with diverse ethnic groups, with good generalisability and clear post-16 focus, and low attrition from original dataset. Medium: Adequate sample, with diverse ethnic groups, with generalisability and partial post-16 focus, and any attrition indicated. |

NB: Additional guidance was provided for reviewers for making judgements on, for example, what constituted a 'large sample'.

Although the appraisal stage of a review usually refers to the point at which a detailed assessment of quality and relevance occurs, some judgement about quality and relevance can occur much earlier in the review process, especially in the case of reviews which pre-specify at least some of their methods. For example, the application of inclusion and exclusion criteria is an attempt to sift out studies that are outside the scope of the review. The inclusion and exclusion criteria may also specify that only studies of a particular design will be included. In the review of factors promoting the participation of minority ethnic groups in further and higher education (Box 8.2), two broad types of study were included in the review (cross-sectional surveys and qualitative studies and secondary analyses of existing datasets). The review authors argued that these types of study were the most appropriate for addressing their review question.

When the inclusion criteria of a review limit the study types to be included, judgements about the quality of execution of method are therefore limited to the study types specified by the inclusion criteria for a review. Judging the appropriateness of the included studies' design for answering the review question in these cases is also likely to be fairly straightforward and limited. For example, in a Cochrane or Campbell Collaboration review in which the review authors plan to conduct a statistical meta-analysis and limit the inclusion of studies in the review to randomised controlled trials, one would expect all included trials to be rated highly on appropriateness of design. The trials may, of course, be judged differently on execution and relevance. In more broad based reviews, however, there may be a range of types of research study included and so considerations of quality of execution of the method and the fitness for purpose of that method will be more complex. In the case of our participation review example, although appropriate study types for addressing the review question had been specified by the inclusion criteria, there was still a need for further assessment. In judging the appropriateness of the research design, review authors assigned a higher weight of evidence to those studies that were 'large scale' in design.

Whatever the type of review or the stage that a quality and relevance appraisal is considered, there needs to be some basis for making decisions on the various dimensions of Weight of Evidence, whether these are specified in advance or emerge iteratively as the review progresses. The basis for making these judgements may be precisely or loosely specified and can involve the use of coding frameworks and standardised tools to inform judgements (see the 'critical appraisal tools' section of this chapter for a discussion of such tools). As there are several dimensions to making weight of evidence judgements, there also needs to be some consideration of how judgements on individual dimensions are combined to make an overall judgement.

An issue not yet covered by the discussion in this chapter so far is how to use the results of the quality and relevance appraisal in the review. There are at least four options here. First, studies which do not meet a particular quality threshold or those judged as 'low' within a weight of evidence framework can be removed from the synthesis stage of the review (the 'threshold' approach). This is similar to applying exclusion criteria. Second, all studies, regardless of the result of the quality and relevance appraisal, may be included in the synthesis but less weight may be given to those which were assessed as 'low' on quality and relevance (a 'weighting' approach). A third option is simply to describe the quality and relevance of each study for the reader of the review to make their own conclusions. Fourth, a sensitivity analysis may be carried out in which the effects of excluding or including studies of lower quality are examined. In the statistical meta-analysis of trials, a sensitivity analysis examines whether variations in the findings of individual studies can be accounted for by variations in methodological quality (see Chapter 9). On the basis of the results of this analysis, a decision can be made on whether to focus the interpretation on those trials which show strengths on the items that have been identified as protecting against the production of biased effect estimates (Moher et al., 1998). In a sensitivity analysis, the quality and relevance appraisal thus become a component of the synthesis. (The debate introduced in Box 8.1 is informed by the results of sensitivity analyses.) As noted earlier, in reviews towards the theory- generating end of our continuum of reviews, judging the quality and relevance of studies may not be considered complete until the reviewer has been able to get a handle on how well each of the individual studies fits together within the synthesis. In other words, in more iterative reviews there may be a process of interpreting what contribution the results of a particular study (or part of a study) makes towards answering the review question and thus the synthesis.

## Levels of critical appraisal

The previous section was concerned with the evaluation of studies within a review but mention was also made earlier of the GRADE system, where not only are individual studies appraised but so is the totality of evidence with the review (which is really part of the conclusions of synthesis). In addition, whole reviews can be critically appraised using tools specially designed for the purpose (Moher et al. 2000, 2009; Shea et al. 2007) or by applying study-level tools at the review level. In the Weight of E system, for example, a review can be appraised as to its execution of review methods, appropriateness of that review method and focus of the review for answering the review question or your question, if different. Reviews may be produced for a particular audience but still be of use (or may be apportioned a lower weight) to other users (just as primary studies may be undertaken for one purpose but still may have use in a review with a different purpose). A review may also be assessed using other criteria, as discussed at the start of this chapter (such as Furlong and Oancea 2006). A rhetorical review of the literature aiming to make a case for a particular point of view (and probably not using explicit systematic review methods) may be more useful in producing, for example, personal growth than a more methodologically sound systematic review.

In addition to the synthesis of individual reviews, there are also reviews of reviews (see Chapter 3), where the studies included within a review are previous reviews rather than primary research studies. The approaches to critical appraisal for such reviews can be the same as for reviews of primary research.

In sum, there are at least six levels of critical appraisal:

1  Primary research studies assessed on their own (i.e. can the findings of a primary study be trusted as an answer to the study question?)
2  Primary research studies in terms of their contribution to a review (i.e. can the findings of a primary study be trusted in answering the review question? – which may not be the same as the study's question)

3 Summation of evidence provided by a review (i.e. how evidence is appraised in the process of combining it together to produce the review findings)

4 Value of whole reviews (i.e. can the conclusions and/or recommendations of a review be trusted?)

5 Summation of evidence in a review of reviews (i.e. can the findings of a review of reviews be trusted?)

6 Value of review of reviews (i.e. can the conclusions/recommendations of a review of reviews be trusted?)

## Appraisal tools

Critical appraisal tools provide a structured approach for assessing quality and relevance. They usually consist of a list of questions with fixed response options which prompt the reviewer to make an evaluative judgement. For example, Tables 8.1 and 8.2 shows the critical appraisal tools used in a recent EPPI-Centre review on the

**Table 8.1** Critical appraisal tool used to assess the quality of outcome evaluations in a review of behavioural interventions to prevent sexually transmitted infections among young people (Shepherd et al. 2010)

| Assessment item | Response options |
| --- | --- |
| J.1 Was a selection bias avoided?<br>i) Study can 'pass' if participants were allocated using an acceptable method of randomisation (i.e. answer at G1.1) OR: ii) studies can 'pass' if (1) the baseline values of major prognostic factors are reported for each group for virtually all participants as allocated (i.e. answer at G3.1) AND if the baseline values of major prognostic factors are balanced between groups in the trial (i.e. answer at G4.3) OR the inbalances were adjusted for in analysis (i.e. answer at G5.3). | J.1.1 Yes<br><br>J.1.2 No |
| J.2 Was a bias due to loss to follow-up avoided?<br>Study can pass this component if: (1) the attrition rate is reported separately according to allocation group (i.e. answer at H1.1), AND if (2) the attrition rate differs across groups by less than 10% and is less than 30% overall (i.e. answer at H2) OR the baseline values of major prognostic factors were balanced between groups for all those remaining in the study for analysis (i.e. answer at G5). NB: For studies which are not trials, this question should simply read 'Is the attrition rate less than 30% of the original participants?' | J.2.1 Yes<br><br>J.2.2 No |
| J.3 Was a selective reporting bias avoided?<br>Studies can pass this component if authors report on all the outcomes they intended to measure as described in the aims of the study. | J.3.1 Yes<br><br>J.3.2 No |
| J.4 Is the study sound?<br>To be sound a study has to avoid all three of the specified types of bias. | J.4.1 Not sound<br><br>J.4.2 Sound<br><br>J.4.3 Reviewers judge the study sound despite the discrepancy with quality criteria (clarify) |

**Table 8.2** Critical appraisal tool used to assess the quality of process evaluations in a review of behavioural interventions to prevent sexually transmitted infections among young people (Shepherd et al. 2010)

| Critical appraisal item | Response options |
|---|---|
| E.17 Were steps taken to increase rigour/minimise bias and error in the sampling for the process evaluation? Consider whether: <br>* the sampling strategy was appropriate to the questions posed in the process evaluation (e.g. was the strategy well reasoned and justified?) <br>* attempts were made to include all relevant stakeholders and/or obtain a diverse sample (think about who might have been excluded, who may have had a different perspective to offer) * characteristics of the sample critical to the understanding of the study context and findings were presented (i.e. do we know who the participants are in terms of, for example, role in the intervention/evaluation, basic socio-demographics, etc.) | E.17.1 Yes, a fairly thorough attempt was made (please specify) <br><br> E.17.2 Yes, several steps were taken (please specify) <br><br> E.17.3 Yes, a few steps were taken (please specify) <br><br> E.17.4 Unclear (please specify) <br><br> E.17.5 No, not at all/Not stated/Can't tell (please specify) |
| E.18 Were steps taken to increase rigour/minimise bias and error in the data collected for the process evaluation? Consider whether: <br>* the data collection tools were piloted (if quantitative) or validated <br>* the data collection was comprehensive, flexible and/or sensitive enough to provide a complete and/or vivid and rich description/evaluation of the processes involved in the intervention (e.g. did the researchers spend sufficient time at the site/with participants? Did they keep 'following up'? Were steps taken to ensure that all the participants were able and willing to contribute? (e.g. confidentiality, language barriers, power relations between adults and young people); Was more than one method of data collection used? Was there a balance between closed- and open-ended data collection methods?) | E.18.1 Yes, a fairly thorough attempt was made (please specify) <br><br> E.18.2 Yes, several steps were taken (please specify) <br><br> E.18.3 Yes, a few steps were taken (please specify) <br><br> E.18.4 Unclear (please specify) <br><br> E.18.5 No, not at all/Not stated/Can't tell (please specify) |
| E.19 Were steps taken to increase rigour/minimise bias and error in the analysis of the process data? Consider whether: <br>* the data analysis methods were systematic (e.g. was a method described/can a method be discerned?) <br>* the diversity in perspective was explored <br>* the analysis was balanced in the extent to which it was guided by preconceptions or by the data (i.e. participants' views, researcher observations, etc.) <br>* the analysis sought to rule out alternative explanations for findings (in qualitative research this could be done by, for example, searching for negative cases/exceptions, feeding back preliminary results to participants, asking a colleague to review the data, or using reflexivity; in quantitative research this could be done by, for example, significance testing) | E.19.1 Yes, a fairly thorough attempt was made (please specify) <br><br> E.19.2 Yes, several steps were taken (please specify) <br><br> E.19.3 Yes, some steps were taken (please specify) <br><br> E.19.4 Unclear (please specify) <br><br> E.19.5 No, not at all/ Not stated / Can't tell (please specify) |
| E.20 Were the findings of the process evaluation grounded in/supported by the data? Consider whether: | E.20.1 Very well grounded/supported (please specify) |

**Table 8.2** (Continued)

| Critical appraisal item | Response options |
|---|---|
| * enough data have been presented to show how the authors arrived at their findings<br>* the data presented fit the interpretation/support claims about patterns in the data<br>* the data presented illuminate/illustrate the findings<br>* (for qualitative studies) quotes are numbered or otherwise identified so that the reader can see that they don't just come from one or two people | E.20.2 Fairly well grounded/supported (please specify)<br><br>E.20.3 Limited grounding/support (please specify) |
| E.21 Please rate the findings of the process evaluation in terms of their breadth and depth<br>Consider whether:<br>(NB: it may be helpful to consider 'breadth' as the extent of description and 'depth' as the extent to which data have been transformed/analysed)<br>* a range of processes/issues is covered in the evaluation<br>* the perspectives of participants are fully explored in terms of breadth (contrast of two or more perspectives) and depth (insight into a single perspective)<br>* both the strengths and weaknesses of the intervention are described/explored<br>* the context of the intervention has been fully described/explored<br>* richness and complexity have been portrayed (e.g. variation explained, meanings illuminated)<br>* there has been a theoretical/conceptual development | E.21.1 Limited breadth or depth<br><br>E.21.2 Good/fair breadth but very little depth<br><br>E.21.3 Good/fair depth but very little breadth<br><br>E.21.4 Good/fair breadth and depth |
| E.22 To what extent does the process evaluation privilege the perspectives and experiences of young people?<br>Consider whether:<br>* young people were included in the process evaluation<br>* there was a balance between open-ended and fixed-response options<br>* young people were involved in designing the research<br>* there was a balance between the use of an a priori coding framework and induction in the analysis<br>* the position of the researchers mattered (did they consider it important to listen to the perspectives of young people?)<br>* steps were taken to assure confidentiality and put young people at their ease | E.22.1 Not at all<br><br>E.22.2 A little (please specify)<br><br>E.22.3 Somewhat (please specify)<br><br>E.22.4 A lot (please specify) |
| E.23 Overall, what weight would you assign to this process evaluation in terms of the reliability of its findings?<br>Guidance: Think (mainly) about the answers you have given to questions E17 to E20 above. | E.23.1 Low<br>E.23.2 Medium<br>E.23.3 High |
| E.24 What weight would you assign to this process evaluation in terms of the usefulness of its findings?<br>Guidance: Think (mainly) about the answers you have given to questions E20 to E22 above and consider:<br>a) how well the intervention processes are described (e.g. do they provide useful information on barriers and facilitators to implementation – factors that others implementing the intervention would need to consider?)<br>b) whether the findings can help us to explain the relationship between intervention process and outcome (e.g. why the intervention worked or did not work; factors influencing effectiveness; how the intervention achieved its effects) | E.24.1 Low<br><br>E.24.2 Medium<br><br>E.24.3 High |

effectiveness of behavioural interventions to prevent sexually transmitted infections (STIs) among young people (Shepherd et al. 2010). This review included outcome evaluations (randomised and non-randomised trials) to estimate the effects of interventions to prevent STIs and process evaluations (using mainly qualitative methods) to assess the appropriateness of interventions and implementation issues.

These tools were embedded within the larger coding tool used for the whole review. Much of the information needed to make the evaluative judgements had been collected earlier on in the review process during the coding and data extraction stage. For example, in Table 8.1, the reviewer is directed to questions that appear in earlier parts of the coding framework to help reviewers make their evaluative judgements.

While the use of a tool does not eliminate the need for reviewers' judgement, it does help reviewers to treat each study in the same way and can provide a means for reviewers to record, and make explicit, their judgements. In the context of conducting a meta-ethnography, Campbell et al. (2003) found that in addition to helping to weed out inappropriate and poor quality papers, appraising study quality with the help of a critical appraisal tool acted as a first stage for synthesis by helping reviewers to engage with studies and identify key concepts from study findings. Attree and Milton (2006), who also conducted a synthesis of qualitative studies, noted that the use of an appraisal tool in their reviews provided a thorough and systematic basis for comparing the strengths and weaknesses of different studies and stimulated debate among reviewers. Like other stages of the review, it is important for the quality and relevance appraisal to be undertaken independently by more than one reviewer. Outside of doing reviews, tools and checklists are a useful way for researchers to debate and communicate common standards of research quality in their field. Reviewers may well be drawing on common standards enshrined in tools when making their judgements, even if a particular tool is not used.

Although there are some exceptions (see the tool illustrated in Table 8.2), appraisal tools have usually been developed for specific types of research rather than specific types of research or review questions. For example, there are tools for assessing the quality of randomised controlled trails (RCTs) or non-randomised trials, cohort studies, diagnostic tests (Whiting et al. 2003), surveys, qualitative studies (Spencer et al. 2003), and systematic reviews (Moher et al. 2000; Shea et al. 2007). There are many tools available but there is much duplication of effort, especially for RCTs and qualitative studies (Dixon-Woods et al. 2005; Juni et al. 1999; Moher et al. 1995). As the vast majority of these tools focus on the quality of studies in terms of the methods used and their implementation, existing critical appraisal tools will, from a weight of evidence perspective, tend to be most useful for helping reviewers to assess the methodological quality of studies in their own terms rather than fitness for purpose or relevance of the focus of the study to the review question.

In the health field, a good starting place to identify tools is the Critical Appraisal Skills Programme (CASP)[1] run by the UK-based Public Health Resources Unit. This

---

[1]www.phru.nhs.uk/casp/casp.htm

programme has developed user-friendly tools for a variety of study designs from RCTs to qualitative research. Another useful reference is the Cochrane Collaboration handbook (Higgins and Green 2011). This argues that a study may be undertaken well yet still create a risk of bias whilst a study with methodological flaws may still provide accurate results. As it is so difficult to provide reliable and valid scores of actual bias, the Cochrane 'risk of bias' assessment tool does not lead to a summary score but instead provides a structure for examining the domains under which a risk of bias may occur and so enable an overall judgement as to the level of risk of bias (Higgins and Green 2011).[2] Although the tools developed within the health field can be used in other domains, resources outside the health field, in areas such as education and social care, are much less well developed. An exception here is the US-based 'What works clearing house' for evidence-informed education, which has published criteria for assessing the quality of a range of study designs for assessing the effects of educational interventions.[3] The resources of the international Campbell Collaboration,[4] focused on the effects of interventions in education, crime and social welfare, are also worth checking, although at the time of writing there were no specific tools on offer.

Given the number of tools available, reviewers are likely to be faced with the question of 'Which tool should I use?' A first step in choosing a tool is to be clear about the review purpose and question and the types of study likely to be included. If the review purpose is to test a theory and its aim is to address a question about the effects of interventions, then the types of study to be included are likely to be RCTs or other kinds of controlled studies. In this situation the reviewer will want to choose a tool developed specifically for these types of study in order to assess Weight of Evidence A, such as the tool illustrated in Table 8.1 or the tool 'Study DIAD' (Valentine and Cooper 2008). Alternatively, if the review purpose is to generate theory, driven by a question about understanding the perspectives and experiences of a particular group of people, reviewers are likely to want to consider using one of the myriad of tools available to assess the quality of qualitative research. If the review purpose and question require the inclusion of a wide variety of study types, a number of tools (one for each study type) will be needed. Faced with the latter situation, some review teams have chosen to apply a number of generic criteria across studies as an initial step in quality assessment. For example, Dixon-Woods et al. (2006b) used the following five prompts to help reviewers make judgements about the quality of papers within their review, which included a diverse range of study types on the topic of access to health care:

1   Are the aims and objectives of the research clearly stated?
2   Is the research design clearly specified and appropriate for the aims and objectives of the research?

---

[2] www.cochrane-handbook.org/

[3] http://ies.ed.gov/ncee/wwc/

[4] www.campbellcollaboration.org/

3   Do the researchers provide a clear account of the process by which their findings were produced?
4   Do the researchers display enough data to support their interpretations and conclusions?
5   Is the method of analysis appropriate and adequately explicated?

Not all of the tools available to assess the quality of, say, RCTs or qualitative research are equally valid or useful. For example, nearly two decades ago Moher et al. (1995) surveyed 25 tools for assessing the quality of RCTs. The number of items within the tools ranged from three to 34 and covered different dimensions of quality, including items related to trial organisation and reporting quality as well as internal validity. Not surprisingly perhaps, it has been found that applying different tools to the same trials will result in different assessments of quality which in turn will have an impact on the conclusions and implications of a review (see Box 8.3). Katrak et al. (2004) systematically reviewed 121 tools in applied health and also came to the conclusion that there is considerable variety in the properties of tools.

---

**Box 8.3**

## Choice of critical appraisal tool can impact on the conclusions and implications of reviews

In a study examining whether the type of quality assessment tool affected the conclusions of a statistical meta-analysis, 17 trials comparing two different types of a drug for use in preventing deep vein thrombosis in surgery (low molecular heparin and standard heparin) were assessed using 25 different critical appraisal tools (Juni et al., 1999). The high-quality trials identified by six of the tools showed that there was no difference between the two drugs in preventing deep vein thrombosis, while the low-quality trials showed low molecular heparin to be superior. However, with seven different tools the opposite was the case. Trials of high quality revealed low molecular heparin to be superior, while low-quality trials showed that there was no difference between the two drugs. Juni et al. (2001a, 2001b) argue that there are weaknesses in many of the tools they tested because they include items which are not relevant to assessing internal validity – the extent to which a trial has minimised the introduction of bias and error into estimates of the effects of interventions.

---

Juni and colleagues (1991) argue that a good appraisal tool should only assess study qualities that have been related, either empirically or theoretically, to biased effect estimates. For example, with one of the first tools to be developed (Chalmers et al. 1981), a composite quality score is calculated from scores on individual items covering the dimensions of external validity (e.g. were the interventions described?), trial organisation (e.g. were the starting and stopping dates of the trial provided?), and presentation of data (e.g. were the test statistics and $p$ values provided?), as well as items assessing internal validity. With the summary score reflecting scores on all these dimensions, trials which have low internal validity may score just as highly as those with high internal validity as the former may have scored higher on other dimensions. Three other tools that meet this criterion are the risk of bias tool (Higgins and Green 2011), the Study Design and Implementation Assessment Device (Study DIAD) (Valentine and Cooper 2008) and the tool developed by researchers at the EPPI-Centre illustrated in Table 8.1.

In relation to qualitative research, Harden (2007) found that in a survey of 31 tools for assessing the quality of qualitative research, many were 'manifestos' for qualitative research which suggests an agenda to demonstrate the superiority of qualitative research over quantitative research rather than to identify the highest quality qualitative studies. When the items in tools were allocated and analysed within five study domains – background, theory and research questions; sampling, sample and setting; methods of data collection and analysis; findings; and ethics and write-up – three types of tool emerged. *Methods-orientated tools* had a predominant focus on fieldwork, data collection and analysis, and were often very specific with regard to strategies to increase rigour and reporting. *Findings-orientated tools* included less detail on methods but had more extensive coverage of findings. Methods-orientated tools focused on whether findings were supported by data, generalisable and useful, whereas findings-orientated tools covered a greater range, including whether findings were clear and distinguishable, whether concepts or theory were well developed, whether diversity in meaning, perspective and experience were captured, and whether the findings resonated with readers and participants. *Methods-and findings-orientated tools* struck a balance between items about methods and findings, with some managing to retain a fairly detailed coverage of both domains.

Although we do not yet have a full understanding of how variations in study quality may influence the findings of a synthesis of qualitative studies, or of the types of problem that are likely to undermine the credibility of qualitative research as opposed to more minor problems or weaknesses, empirical and theoretical work to date suggests that a good critical appraisal tool for qualitative research should enable reviewers to assess quality through engaging with *both* the methods and findings of the research study. The methods employed need to be rigorous, but rigorous methods may not always lead to greater insights or coherent and explanatory concepts, which are the building blocks of configurative syntheses. Campbell and colleagues in the UK, who undertook a synthesis of 'qualitative' research on lay experiences of diabetes and diabetes care using meta-ethnography, found that the most useful quality appraisal items in their tool were those that required reviewers to engage with the findings of studies: (a) that the concepts and interpretations should be grounded in the data gathered; and (b) that the concepts and interpretations posed were cogent and original (Campbell et al. 2003). Similarly, Sandelowski and Barroso, who undertook a synthesis of qualitative research on women's experiences of living with HIV found the most useful appraisal items to be those in the 'findings' category which included items such as "concepts or ideas are well-developed and linked to each other" and "the results offer new information about, insight into, or formulation of the target phenomenon" (Sandelowski and Barroso 2002: 40). Popay et al. (2003: 50) argue that 'qualitative' process evaluations should be assessed according to the 'explanatory quality of evidence on implementation' that they provide, which requires a reviewer to engage with the findings of studies as well as methodological rigour (e.g. reporting quality, quality of design). The study appraisal of qualitative research should therefore not be restricted to reporting quality, methodological rigour and the appropriateness of methods for the research question, but should instead extend to a consideration of the conclusions of the research and whether these conclusions were warranted given the methods used.

There are a number of tools which include a balance between items on methods and findings (Campbell et al. 2003; Cesario et al. 2002; Corbin and Strauss 1990; Critical Appraisal Skills Programme 2002; Giacomini and Cook 2000; Greenhalgh and Taylor 1997; Kuzel and Engel 2001; Mays and Pope 1995; Sandelowski and Barroso 2002). As part of a project examining tools to assess the quality of qualitative research, the EPPI-Centre convened a small group of experienced systematic reviewers to develop a set of criteria to evaluate the utility of critical appraisal tools. Although this exercise was focused on qualitative research, the results revealed a set of general factors to consider in choosing/adapting an existing tool or developing a new tool (see Box 8.4). The 31 tools included in the survey by Harden (2007) were subjected to these evaluation criteria. The tools scoring highly on these criteria were those developed by Campbell et al. (2003) and Sandelowski and Barroso (2002). The tool illustrated in Table 8.2 was designed to contain a balance of items related to methods and findings and was also developed in line with these same criteria.

Given the range of review questions and study types and the fact that quality and relevance assessments will need to draw on review-specific criteria as well as generic criteria, reviewers need to be aware that there may not be a ready-made tool available for them to 'pick off the shelf' to use. In these circumstances, existing tools will need to be adapted or a new tool will have to be developed.

---

| **Box 8.4** |

## Factors to consider in choosing/adapting an existing tool or developing a new tool to assess the quality and relevance of studies within a systematic review

1 Is the information provided to help the reviewer judge the fit between the tool, the studies and the appraisal context?
2 Is a distinction made between the quality of the study and the quality of the report that describes it?
3 Is guidance provided to help reviewers arrive at the quality judgements required by the tool?

4  Is a distinction made between the collection of descriptive information and judging quality?
5  Is a means to record judgements about quality provided?
6  Are reviewers helped to assess whether the study conclusions are warranted, given the study design, methods and sample?
7  Is evidence provided for why particular characteristics of research are assumed to constitute 'good' or 'bad' quality?
8  Are reviewers helped to identify the 'fatal flaws' in a study?
9  Are reviewers helped to make an overall judgement about study quality?
10  When an overall scoring system is provided, does it: (i) give appropriate weight to different items in the overall score; (ii) allow flexibility in the weight that can be given to individual items; (iii) differentiate the WoE dimensions of quality of execution, the fitness for purpose of methods and relevance of focus?

## Examples of quality and relevance appraisal

To illustrate some of the issues discussed in the preceding section, in this part of the chapter we present some detailed examples of quality and relevance appraisal in action in systematic reviews. The reviews we have chosen are deliberately diverse in terms of methodology. Some of the review methods are very new and there are only one or two worked examples of the methods. We have still included these reviews as they illustrate the potential of research synthesis methods beyond its more widely known examples of statistical meta-analysis.

The reviews in Table 8.3 are organised broadly according to where they lie on the theory generating–theory-testing continuum shown earlier in Figure 8.1. The first review by Coren et al. (2010) represents the classic 'what works?' theory testing review while reviews towards the bottom of the table, such as those by Campbell et al. (2003), Greenhalgh et al. (2005a) and Dixon-Woods et al. (2006b), represent the theory-generating reviews. Those in the middle of the table have some elements of theory testing and some elements of theory generation. For example, the review by Harden et al. (2009) not only aimed to test the effectiveness of interventions for reducing unintended teenage pregnancy but also aimed to generate new ideas for appropriate and promising interventions to test, based on a synthesis of the findings of studies analysing the perspectives and experiences of young people.

Another feature of the reviews in the first few rows of Table 8.3 is that they are also more likely to be addressing pre-specified concepts (at least in part), while those reviews in the bottom half of the table are more emergent in nature. Although there are exceptions, theory-testing reviews tend to undertake quality and relevance appraisal before the synthesis stage of the review (using pre-specified critical appraisal tools largely, but not exclusively, focused on methodology) whereas in theory-generating reviews at least some aspects of quality and relevance

**Table 8.3** Examples of quality and relevance appraisal (QRA) in different types of review

| | Review question or purpose | Type of review | Included studies | When QRA took place | How QRA was undertaken | How appraisals were used |
|---|---|---|---|---|---|---|
| **Coren et al. (2011)** | To assess the effectiveness of parent training interventions to support the parenting of parents with intellectual disabilities | A Cochrane and Campbell effectiveness review with statistical meta-analysis | RCTs | Before synthesis | Two review authors independently assessed the trials for risk of bias using a pre-specified tool (Higgins et al., 2008) | All trials contributed to the synthesis regardless of quality. The risk of bias for each trial was explicitly reported for readers |
| **Brunton et al. (2006)** | How do children's, young people's and parents' views of the barriers to, and facilitators of, walking and cycling match interventions evaluated for their effects on walking and cycling? | Framework synthesis | Qualitative and other studies of people's perspectives | Before synthesis | Tool developed for review based on items in existing tools and new items. Tool aimed to assess "the extent to which the reviewers can be confident that a particular study's findings make a valuable contribution to the review" (p17) | Low quality studies were excluded from the synthesis |
| **Harden et al. (2009)** | To determine the impact on teenage pregnancy of interventions that address social disadvantage, to assess the appropriateness of such interventions for young people | Mixed methods combining thematic synthesis with statistical meta-analysis | Trials / Qualitative and other studies of people's perspectives | Before synthesis | Trials: The EPPI-Centre quality assessment tool for outcome evaluations (Peersman et al., 1997) / Qualitative: A tool specifically developed to assess the quality of research assessing people's perspectives and experiences | Trials and qualitative and low quality studies excluded from the synthesis |
| **Campbell et al. (2003)** | To synthesise qualitative research on lay experiences of diabetes and diabetes care | Meta-ethnography | Qualitative studies | Before synthesis | Adapted the CASP tool for qualitative research | Low quality studies excluded from the synthesis |
| **Dixon-Woods et al. (2006b)** | How can access to health care services, particularly for potentially vulnerable groups, be best understood? | Critical interpretive synthesis | A diverse range of study types | Before and during synthesis | All studies assessed for fatal flaws using criteria proposed by the National Electronic Library for Health | Only fatally flawed studies with little relevance/ contribution to the review were excluded |

**Table 8.3** (Continued)

| | Review question or purpose | Type of review | Included studies | When QRA took place | How QRA was undertaken | How appraisals were used |
|---|---|---|---|---|---|---|
| **Greenhalgh et al. (2005a)** | How can we spread and sustain innovations in health service delivery and organisation? | Meta-narrative review | A diverse range of study types | Before synthesis | a) Seminal papers identified using three criteria<br><br>b) Empirical studies were assessed according to quality criteria appropriate for the research tradition which the study was undertaken within. | Unclear |
| **Pawson (2006b)** | To develop a theory of mentoring relationships and address questions such as: What makes for an effective partnership between mentor and mentee? How does the relationship develop? | Realist review | Evaluations (all types of designs) of mentoring schemes | During synthesis | Not specified in the review report, but of note in Pawson (2006b):<br><br>'the whole study is not the unit of analysis but the relevant 'evidential fragment' | |

appraisal takes place during the synthesis itself. Theory-generating reviews are also less likely to use pre-specified critical appraisal tools, or if these are used, they are utilised as prompts to alert the reviewer to potential problems rather than as a basis for excluding or including studies in a synthesis.

In the Cochrane review, the quality and relevance appraisal began at the very early stages of the review with screening titles and abstracts. The reviewers were only looking to include randomised controlled trials (RCTs) that were highly appropriate designs for questions about the effects of interventions – that evaluated their interventions and outcomes of interest. Three trials met the inclusion criteria. Before the synthesis, the included trials underwent a further quality assessment process using a standardised 'risk of bias' tool used across the Cochrane Collaboration.[5] At this stage, all trials were considered to be relevant (having met the inclusion criteria for relevance) and so no further relevance assessment took place. Due to the small number of included trials, the review authors were unable to undertake a sensitivity analysis to assess whether studies with different quality characteristics would have different results. A similar process was followed in reviews by Brunton et al. (2006), Harden et al. (2009) and Campbell et al. (2003), albeit with a wider range of study designs than was included in Coren et al. (2010), and consequently using a 'fit for purpose' range of existing, adapted or newly developed pre-specified quality assessment tools.

Despite the employment of meta-ethnography, Campbell et al. (2003) excluded lower quality studies before the synthesis. As noted earlier, the original specification of meta-ethnography suggests that the worth of the studies is determined in the synthesis. In their reflections on this, Campbell et al. (2003) argued that a pre-specified critical appraisal process also helped them to weed out poor quality and 'inappropriate' papers and that the process also helped them to prepare for the synthesis. (The team used the critical appraisal tool to also collect the raw data for the synthesis.) It is interesting to note that the tool the team used to appraise papers included several items focused on the quality of the study findings as well as the methods. In fact, the items in the critical appraisal tool that Campbell et al. (2003) felt were most useful were both focused on findings ('Are concepts and interpretations grounded in the qualitative data gathered?' and 'Are the concepts and interpretations posed cogent and original?').

As noted above, in theory-generating reviews, reviewers will be less driven to exclude studies prior to synthesis on the basis of methodological quality. A study finding or concept may still be useful to a synthesis even if the method of producing it was not ideal methodologically. In other words, its usefulness may not be compromised as much by methodological flaws as by poor-quality compromises of the 'what works?' reviews. (Although of course this may depend upon the methodological problem – if the concepts or findings were not at all grounded in the data then one might be concerned about including it in the review.) In the review undertaken by Dixon-Woods and colleagues (2005), it was important that

---

[5]http://www.cochrane-handbook.org/

their methodological and relevance focus was kept very open in the early stages of the review so as not to lose potentially useful studies. While they did assess studies for 'fatal flaws' – those that would undermine the credibility of the research findings rather than more superficial areas or omissions in reporting – using pre-specified criteria related to study methods, they were unwilling to exclude studies solely on that basis until the value of the studies could be fully assessed during the synthesis. They suggest that 'some limited formal appraisal of methodological quality of individual papers is likely to be appropriate' but that the overall aim of quality and relevance appraisal when conducting a critical interpretive synthesis is to 'maximise relevance and theoretical contribution of the included papers' (Dixon-Woods et al. 2006b: 10)

Greenhalgh and colleagues (2005a) were also concerned with ensuring that their review did not exclude relevant studies early on in the process. They abandoned their initial set of inclusion criteria, which turned out to be far too narrow, in favour of their meta-narrative approach. This started with an initial search to map the diversity of perspectives and approaches on 'innovation' across the research literature of many disciplines. This search was guided by intuition, informal networking, 'browsing' and tracking the references for references, and aimed to identify seminal papers relevant to the diffusion of innovations. Thus the first stage of the quality appraisal process in this review was to evaluate whether or not papers were seminal (e.g. has the paper been cited as a seminal contribution by competent researchers?).

Seminal papers were used to identify the different research traditions or 'meta-narratives' of research on the diffusion of innovations. A search for empirical papers by electronically searching key databases, hand searching key journals and 'snowballing' (references for references or electronic citation tracking) followed. Each empirical paper was then evaluated for its validity and relevance to the review question, as in more traditional systematic review methods.

The process by which the worth of studies emerges (at least partly) within the synthesis stage in theory-generating reviews can be difficult to describe explicitly. Very iterative reviews, such as realist synthesis, are more like detective work – unpacking the nature of a theoretical claim (including the logic model) and seeing what evidence supports the components of the claim and also its applicability in practice. The investigation may lead reviewers to explore many avenues so it is difficult to specify in advance the quality and relevance criteria. But it may be possible to specify (a) the general nature of those criteria and perhaps also (b) the type of criteria that would be applied down different types of avenue. These avenues are akin to empirical sub-questions and so studies could still be assessed within a weight of evidence framework. A distinctive feature of realist synthesis with respect to quality and relevance appraisal is that the unit of assessment for critical appraisal is not the whole study but the relevant 'evidential fragments' from the study (Pawson, 2006b). Thus the purpose of a quality appraisal in a realist review is to assess the quality of the 'evidential fragments' from a study that are to be put to use in the synthesis. In practice, this can also be true of other types of review in that it is the particular findings from a study being included in a review that are being appraised. In contrast to all the other reviews discussed in this section, realist synthesis is the only approach that has not so far made use of an appraisal tool.

## Conclusion

In this chapter we have unpacked the nature of the quality and relevance appraisal within reviews and described the diverse approaches to this aspect of reviews within the range of established and emerging research synthesis methodologies. The quality and relevance appraisal is dependent upon the purpose of the review, so, as with all stages of a review, the review question, the conceptual framework and review method are crucial. As with other aspects of reviews considered in this book, there are general differences between aggregative and configuring reviews. Aggregative reviews tend to have pre-specified methods, including method for quality and relevance appraisal. Configuring reviews can be more iterative, whereby quality appraisal issues will emerge during the process of the review. However, in practice, many reviews towards the configuring end of the continuum do use pre-specified methods such as critical appraisal tools to assist with making judgements about quality.

---

**Box 8.5**

## The practicalities

Consider the following questions:

1 Why quality and relevance might be issues in a review?
2 What level of quality appraisal would be involved?
3 At what stage or stages of the review would these be applied?
4 What aspects of study execution, appropriateness of study design, and relevance and focus would be applied and how would they be combined?
5 What specific tools, if any, would be applied?
6 What are the consequences of any appraisal judgement?

---

# NINE

## Synthesis: Combining results systematically and appropriately

*James Thomas, Angela Harden and Mark Newman*

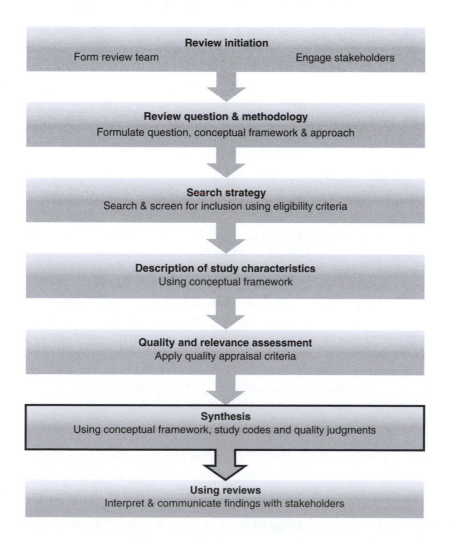

**Review initiation**
Form review team                              Engage stakeholders

**Review question & methodology**
Formulate question, conceptual framework & approach

**Search strategy**
Search & screen for inclusion using eligibility criteria

**Description of study characteristics**
Using conceptual framework

**Quality and relevance assessment**
Apply quality appraisal criteria

**Synthesis**
Using conceptual framework, study codes and quality judgments

**Using reviews**
Interpret & communicate findings with stakeholders

> ⌐ **Aims of chapter** ⌐
>
> This chapter:
>
> - Describes critically the range of purposes, data types and analytical approaches underlying different forms of research synthesis
> - Gives guidance about the relevance and use of different approaches to, and methods for, synthesis
> - Describes the principles and stages of synthesis
> - Gives an overview of different methods of synthesis and how these methods may be conceptualised

## Introduction: conceptualising synthesis

This book has thus far discussed how to conceptualise, locate, describe and assess the quality and relevance of studies in systematic reviews. This chapter now focuses on the detail of synthesis: how you actually go about combining the results of research studies. In this sense, while analytical, synthesis is a quite different activity from analysing the characteristics of research activity outlined in Chapter 7, as we now need to understand the *results* of individual studies and ascertain what they mean as a *collective* body of knowledge.

The *Oxford English Dictionary* defines synthesis as:

> The process or result of building up separate elements, especially ideas, into a connected whole, especially a theory or system.

Under this definition, a synthesis is not just a list of the findings of individual studies, it also involves a transformation of the data from the primary studies in order to build a 'connected whole'. Strike and Posner (1983: 346) put it like this:

> ...[synthesis is] the product of activity where some set of parts is combined or integrated into a whole. ... [Synthesis] involves some degree of conceptual innovation, or employment of concepts not found in the characterisation of the parts and a means of creating the whole.

According to these definitions, then, synthesis is an activity that generates new knowledge – knowledge that is grounded in the information gleaned from multiple research studies. While grounded in the studies that it contains, there is the notion that it 'goes beyond them', that the product of a synthesis is more than simply the sum of its parts. But does a synthesis or systematic review *have* to be innovative? And does the activity of describing the findings of studies always result in conceptual innovation? As with many of the ways in which it is possible to think about synthesis, this definition is merely a useful *heuristic*; it helps us to understand some of the relevant issues, but in any given review it should be taken as being a matter of degree, rather than one of presence or absence. Nearly all syntheses will have some conceptual innovation, but some will have more than others. In the same way, the *dimensions of difference* described in detail in Chapter 3 should be taken as useful ways of thinking about synthesis, rather than being hard-and-fast categories of synthesis which each systematic review either does, or does not, fall into.

As Chapter 3 described, it is possible to think about systematic reviews as differing from one another across a number of dimensions, and the same applies to synthesis. We have conceptualised the main dimensions in Figure 9.1, showing how different types of question are broadly associated with different methods of synthesis. In addition to those depicted in Figure 9.1, other important concepts to consider are interpretation, conceptual innovation and the ontological and episte-mological nature of the knowledge being synthesised and generated.

The bottom row of Figure 9.1 encapsulates the type of question being addressed, and the type of answer given. Some syntheses aim to *test* a theory or hypothesis (e.g. 'Does intervention x work better or worse than intervention y?'); some aim to *explore* a range of possible answers and approaches within a given theoretical framework (e.g. 'Which interventions are most effective at reducing problem x within population y?'); and some aim to *generate* new theories, conceptualisations and under-standings (e.g. 'What are the meanings of phenomenon x within population y?').

As already discussed in Chapter 3, it is helpful to think about two broad modes of synthesis: *configuration* and *aggregation* (the two overlapping ovals in Figure 9.1), which correspond to varying degrees with the generate–explore–test taxonomy

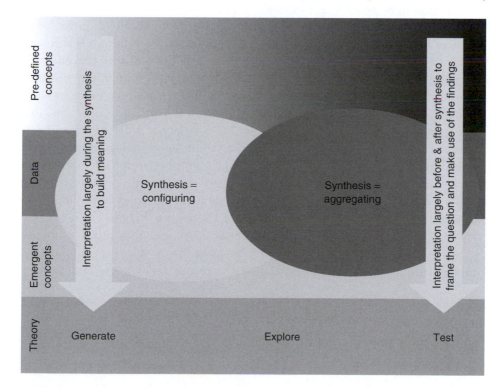

**Figure 9.1**  Conceptualising synthesis

of questions, though it is of course important to bear in mind that most syntheses will both configure and aggregate their findings (Sandelowski et al. 2011).

Syntheses that *configure* their findings tend to be associated with questions that generate new theory, or explore the salience of existing theory in particular (or differing) situations. The studies in such syntheses tend to be different from one another (heterogeneous) and, as the aim of the synthesis is the generation of new theory, there are few pre-defined concepts prior to synthesis. Configurative syntheses can be likened to a mosaic, in which the findings from each study are slotted together to form a coherent whole. This idea of piecing research knowledge together from different contexts is not peculiar to research synthesis, but has long been considered to be a useful heuristic in primary research too.[1]

*Aggregative* syntheses, on the other hand, are more closely associated with testing theories or hypotheses. The studies in these syntheses are much more homogeneous, usually using the same methods and having commensurate conceptual frameworks (i.e. their conceptualisations of the phenomena of interest are broadly the same). Aggregative syntheses can be visualised as working in a different dimension (or plane) to configurative syntheses, since they 'pile up' similar findings in order to gain greater precision (or confidence) in their results.

Possibly the most important concept in any synthesis is *heterogeneity*. Aggregative syntheses will tend towards combining homogeneous groups of studies, whereas in configurative syntheses the differences between studies are necessary in order for configuration to be possible. For example, a meta-analysis examining the impact of a given intervention will need to have quite homogeneous studies in order for its statistical tests to be meaningful and valid. As outlined so far, synthesis is a process that is not just a matter of listing what each study says, but is also about constructing a piece of knowledge that aggregates and configures the findings from multiple research studies, taking into account differences in their conduct, contexts – and findings. As we go through the methods of synthesis, it is worth bearing in mind that these are methods of analysis that can be used on a variety of different types of data and any of them could have a place within the various epistemological frameworks outlined in Chapter 3. While one obvious distinction is between those that do and do not use statistical methods, they are all concerned with the detail of how the findings of studies can be combined in a systematic way and how differences between studies can be explored and explained. Please note that this chapter is concerned with the details of methods for synthesis – how one goes about combining the results of individual studies. Chapter 3 discusses the overarching approaches to synthesis, such as realist synthesis, meta-narrative review and 'what works?' reviews.

## Variation in methods of synthesis

There are many ways of combining the results of studies in a synthesis and different methods are appropriate in different circumstances.

---

[1]See, for example, Chapter 4 of Becker 1970, 'The Life History and the Scientific Mosaic'.

The role that *configuration* is to play in the synthesis is an important factor in determining the appropriate method (which relates in turn to the question being asked), and an important issue when configuring studies is how and when the concepts by which studies will be configured are determined. Chapter 7 described how studies might differ (or be similar) in their methods, participants, contexts and, where appropriate, types of intervention. These dimensions are all used in a synthesis in order to organise groups of studies along lines of similarity, with an additional dimension for some methods of synthesis being the *findings* of the studies as well. There are many ways of grouping studies in a synthesis, and they differ from one another principally in terms of when in the process the distinguishing categories originate; whether they are determined at the outset of the review as part of its conceptual framework ('deductive'), derived from the studies themselves ('inductive'), or a combination of the two. This chapter does not aim to cover all methods comprehensively, rather it selects approaches that fall into each of these categories: topic-based summaries (fully deductive); framework synthesis (mainly deductive); thematic synthesis (mainly inductive); meta-ethnography (mainly inductive); and mixed methods synthesis (both deductive and inductive). It is possible to think about these methods as operating over a continuum with all the themes being pre-specified at one extreme and all the themes generated inductively at the other (Figure 9.2).

The first method, thematic summaries, is probably the most widely used in systematic reviews. Many reviews asking 'what works?' questions employ this method, sometimes in conjunction with a meta-analysis, meta-regression or economic analysis, but often without. For example, a synthesis might begin with a topic-based summary in order to configure studies appropriately (in terms of conceptually coherent sub-divisions of studies), and then use a statistical meta-analysis to aggregate their findings and draw conclusions about how the findings vary according to, for example, context and population.

The term 'theme' is employed very broadly in this chapter, and is shorthand for any means by which studies might be thought of as being similar to or dissimilar

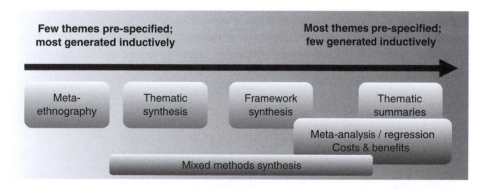

**Figure 9.2** Variation in methods for synthesis

from one another (i.e. a 'theme that runs through' a set of studies). In Chapter 7 the idea of 'coding' studies was discussed and the fact that some codes are pre-specified, whereas others are generated inductively, was observed. In an aggregative review, a theme would be described as an independent variable: a characteristic that studies have in common and one that might explain the differences in findings. The same might be the case in a configurative review, though in these reviews themes may be generated inductively in a synthesis. The key point to bear in mind is:

> Whether they are pre-specified or generated inductively, themes (or 'codes' or 'independent variables') have much the same purpose in a synthesis: they are the mechanism by which studies are compared, contrasted, and sub-divided; and their findings are configured.

For example, the results of studies from similar socio-economic groups ('low', 'medium' or 'high') may be grouped together in a *thematic summary* and either summarised using text or statistics. Some authors write about synthesising 'concepts', 'theories' or 'metaphors'; these also might all be understood as being themes which run through particular studies, or groups of studies, in a synthesis. When we are considering complex (or complicated) interventions (Rogers 2008), themes can be the different components that make up complicated interventions or the reinforcing loops and 'tipping points' that characterise highly complex causal relationships. In a realist synthesis, one of the key dimensions of difference between interventions will be their mechanisms – sometimes operating in different ways in different contexts (Pawson 2006).

The final point to bear in mind about inductively generated themes is that they can simply be a theme (or concept, etc.) that is described explicitly in one or more studies. They can also be a product of synthesis, whereby themes arising from multiple studies are joined together to create a new conceptualisation that may be implicit in the primary studies, but which has taken insights gained from examining multiple studies together to surface.

## Stages of synthesis

Characteristics that are common to many reviews and the various stages that they go through are illustrated in Figure 9.3. While not a linear process (and, as mentioned in Chapter 3, reviews involve differing amounts of iteration), there are seven main stages in the conduct of most reviews:

- What is the question (including the conceptual framework)?
- What data are available?
- What are the patterns in the data?
- How does integrating the data answer the question?
- How robust is the synthesis?
- What is the result?
- What does the result mean?

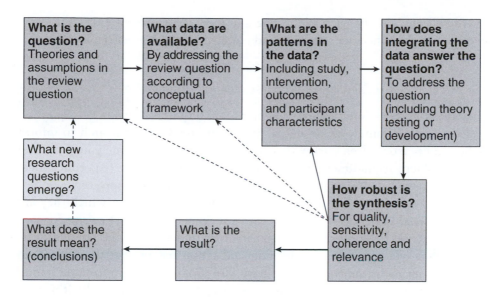

**Figure 9.3**  Stages of synthesis (Cooper 1982; see also Popay et al. 2006)

These stages of synthesis will be operationalised in different ways, depending on the type of synthesis being conducted, but most will appear in all systematic reviews in some way or another. For example, the stage of synthesis entitled 'How does integrating the data answer the question?' might involve a meta-analysis or meta-ethnography to combine the results of studies, but reviews involving both of these methods will also contain stages that examine the data they have available and a check of their robustness.

The outcome of the synthesis is a narrative that tells a trustworthy story (see Popay et al. 2006), answering the review question and also telling the reader what the findings *mean*. The stages of research synthesis can also be conceptualised as a cycle, or as several cycles. A cycle arises when the review question itself has been generated by a previous systematic review or research, and the review itself might then suggest further avenues of enquiry. Within a review, some models of synthesis involve examining the literature ('What data are available?' through to 'How robust is the synthesis?'), seeing how it addresses the review question(s) and then reformulating the question and/or search strategies to bring in more research. This process can proceed through multiple iterations before the review is complete. Some reviews are based on detailed formal protocols, which specify each step of the review in detail. The review itself proceeds along a 'straight line', with searching being completed before the data extraction takes place, and synthesis only beginning once the final set of quality appraised studies has been arrived at. Others are more iterative, and though they may still pre-specify the methods they will use, will have a more flexible structure, with searching, data extraction and synthesis happening multiple times in order for the search strategy, eligibility criteria and, sometimes, review question itself to be developed and informed by previous iterations.

We will now discuss each of the stages in turn, acknowledging that they may occur more than once per synthesis, and not always in the order depicted.

## Review question and conceptual framework

Chapter 4 has considered the starting point for all synthesis, the review question and conceptual framework, in detail. Systematic reviews of research to inform policy and practice often start with a population (e.g. low income young people) and a 'problem', sometimes with a set of outcomes to improve (e.g. educational attainment, etc.). From this starting point will come one or more review questions and a conceptual framework which defines the context in which they are to be answered and understood. Aggregative reviews need to have secure conceptual frameworks before synthesis begins in order to determine the population of studies they will search for and include, and those that present their results in terms of a *thematic summary* tend to have fairly well-defined conceptual frameworks from the outset, as the studies are grouped and summarised within this framework.

## What data are available?

The starting point for reviewers examining the data available for the synthesis is describing the scope of the research contained in the review. Chapter 7 contains a detailed account of this. Using similar methods (and data) to 'mapping' research activity, we can arrange the data from the studies in our synthesis in order to answer the questions: 'what are the results of individual studies?' and 'what are the characteristics of each study?'. We can organise results in terms of: their directions and sizes of effects; different factors and processes present in their interventions (where present); which themes in our conceptual framework they speak to (and which new themes they contribute); or the characteristics of the studies' samples and interventions (where appropriate).

Examining the studies in this descriptive way helps us to understand similarities and differences in the data we have available for synthesis, and also helps us to see how we might be able to answer our review questions and whether there are additional issues arising that we should include in the synthesis. Examining the studies in terms of the data that are available enables reviewers to identify gaps in the research activity, as well as identifying groups of studies that may be able to answer particular aspects of the review's question.

## What are the patterns in the data?

Once the data have been organised in a descriptive way, it is possible to begin the process of identifying patterns. Again, this can overlap with 'mapping' the research activity (Chapter 7), but contains the additional component of including

**Table 8**  Study design and reported effects in category 'Approaches to learning'

| Author | Design | Random | Comparison | Sample size Int. Start/Effect | Sample size Control Start/effect | Similarity of control | Assessment Blinding | Contamination | Baseline | Reliability | Outcome measure | 1- Int. group (s.dev) | 2- Cont. group (s.dev) | 1-2 | 3-Int. change | 4-Cont. change | 3-4 | Standard deviated effect size $d$ | Gain effect size |
|---|---|---|---|---|---|---|---|---|---|---|---|---|---|---|---|---|---|---|---|
| Moore 2 | RC T | 9 | 2 | 61/61 | 61/58 | 1 | 9 | 1 | 1 | 1 | Discovery | 31.4 (3.75) | 27.2 (4.06) | +4.15 | −0.27 | −2.23 | +1.96 | 1.0 | −0.5 |
| Moore 4 | | | | | | | | | | | Receptive | 16.64 (2.51) | 17.98 (2.64) | −1.34 | −0.61 | −0.58 | −0.03 | −0.5 | 0.02 |
| Coles 1 | CB A | na | 2 | ? | ? | 2 | 1 | 2 | 1 | 1 | Reproducing | 10.8 (3.1) | 14.6 (3.6) | −3.8* | −1* | +1.3* | −2.4 | −1.1 | 0.7 |
| Coles 3 | | | | | | | | | | | Meaning | 15.7 (4,1) | 13.7 (3.9) | 2* | −0.9 | −2.4* | +1.5 | 0.5 | −0.5 |
| Coles 5 | | | | | | | | | | | Versatility | 32.9 (6.3) | 30.2 (6.3) | 2.7* | −1.5 | −3.3* | +1.8 | 0.4 | −0.3 |

*statistically significant

**Table 4.3**  Relevance of studies to aspect of provision of schooling

| Aspect of Provision | Studies |
|---|---|
| Learning and Teaching | Clare et al., 1996; Day, 2002; Deakin Crick, 2002; Holden, 2000; Maslovaty, 2000; Mooji, 2000; Russell, 2000 |
| School Ethos and Context | Behre et al., 2001; Carter and Osler, 2000; Flecknoe, 2002; Gillborn, 1992; Naylor and Cowie, 1999; Taylor, 2002 |
| Leadership and Management | Carter & Osler, 2000; Deakin Crick, 2002; Flecknoe, 2002; Holden, 2000; Maslovaty, 2000; Mooji, 2000; Taylor, 2002 |
| Curriculum Construction and Development | Clare et al., 1996; Day, 2002; Deakin Crick, 2002; Holden, 2000; Russell, 2002; Williams et al., 2003 |
| External Relations and community | Day, 2002; Gillborn, 1992; Holden, 2000 |

**Figure 9.4**  Examples of describing patterns in the data*

*From: Newman, M (2003) A Pilot Systematic Review and Meta-analysis on the Effectiveness of Problem based Learning. Newcastle: Learning & Teaching Subject Network Centre for Medicine, Dentistry and Veterinary Medicine; and Deakin Crick R, Coates M, Taylor M, Ritchie S (2004) A systematic review of the impact of citizenship education on the provision of schooling. In: Research Evidence in Education Library. London: EPPI-Centre, Social Science Research Unit, Institute of Education, University of London.

the findings from studies. Figure 9.4 contains two examples of this process. In the first example ('Table 8'), the characteristics of studies in the category 'approaches to learning' have been listed. It is possible to look across this table and examine the types of research design used, the results of the quality assessment process and the calculated effect sizes. The second example (Table 4.3) has organised its studies according to different aspects of provision of schooling. This tabulation enables reviewers to see the extent of evidence available for each type of provision.

## How does integrating the data answer the question?

There are different ways of integrating data from primary research studies depending on the type of review question being asked, the types of data available, and the methods of synthesis selected, and some of the detailed methods are described later in this chapter. The previous stages – setting out what data are available and examining their patterns – are critical groundwork for a successful synthesis.

In a configurative synthesis, results are placed alongside one another in order to build up a picture of the phenomenon of interest. Such syntheses aim either to generate new (interpretative) constructs or explore the salience of existing theory in detail. Data are heterogeneous and one of the key challenges and purposes of these syntheses is enabling the findings from one study to 'speak' to another. For example, in a thematic synthesis (see below), the key concept here is *translation*: by examining the themes arising in individual studies, the reviewer identifies common themes between them, even though they may be expressed in different words in different studies. Translation is not always interpretive in configurative syntheses, however, and the 'closer' one gets to an aggregative synthesis, the more similar the included studies will be.

In an aggregative synthesis that aims to test a theory or hypothesis, the data need to be checked to ensure that they are sufficiently commensurate and that combining them 'vertically' is appropriate. In this context, *translation* involves examining the context, participants, measurement tools, etc., and coming to a judgement as to the manner of synthesis. Sometimes it will not be appropriate to pool all the studies, but to have a number of mini-syntheses or sub-group analyses as the outcome of the review.

## How robust is the synthesis?

Before the final result can be decided upon, all types of synthesis will usually have a check for robustness – examining the impact of different decisions made throughout the review. This stage of the synthesis is often called a 'sensitivity analysis' in the context of a meta-analysis, though while this term is less frequently employed in other forms of synthesis, the issues it addresses are important whatever the method. Critical questions to ask in a sensitivity analysis include:

- Has the translation of findings between studies been consistent and coherent?
- Do the results vary according to the quality of the studies contributing? (Is the way they are being combined defensible?)
- How reliable are the studies included in the synthesis? Should any issues about their quality affect the strength and credibility of the synthesis?
- Do the results depend heavily on one or two studies, in the absence of which they would change significantly?
- Which contexts can the results be applied to? Do the results vary according to context?
- How well do the results answer the review question?

## What is the result and what does it mean?

Finally, after checking its robustness, the result of the synthesis can be expressed. As described above, sometimes this will be a re-examination or clarification of the review's conceptual framework and can be depicted graphically as thematic relationships or programme theories, as shown in Chapter 4. Presentation techniques for different types of statistical analysis are shown later in this chapter.

Deciding what the result of a synthesis might mean can be examined in two ways. First, the review needs to be reported in a way that is appropriate for those who are going to use its results. The 'metric' that the final synthesis was conducted in may not be accessible or easily applied to different contexts and might require some translation before use. Specific ways of doing this for statistical results are described later in the chapter. Second, the people conducting the synthesis may not be best placed to discern its meaning and implications: other stakeholders need to be engaged in this process, as discussed in Chapters 2 and 10.

We will now begin to consider the specific methods of synthesis outlined in Figure 9.2, starting with thematic summaries, which depend upon themes being pre-specified, and moving through framework synthesis to thematic synthesis and meta-ethnography, which emphasise the inductive generation of themes and concepts as part of the synthesis process. The final section of the chapter then focuses on statistical methods for synthesis, including a brief discussion covering the synthesis of economics evidence and interpreting results.

## Thematic summaries

Many systematic reviews state that a 'narrative' synthesis was conducted, but often do not present any more detail than this on their precise methods for synthesis. In general, they will follow the 'stages of synthesis' as outlined earlier, relying heavily on the conceptual framework that was developed early on in the review process to organise (configure) the studies into groups according to a dimension (e.g. research method or socio-economic group) that would be salient to their intended readership. This involves a detailed assessment of the characteristics of included studies (participants, intervention and programme theory – where applicable – outcomes, etc.) in order to establish which group(s) a study belongs to, followed by a presentation of their results according to these (usually pre-specified) sub-divisions. Procedures described in the 'stages of synthesis' section (above) are used to consider any differences between studies in each group, whether they have similar or divergent findings, and finally the conclusions that should be drawn to answer the review's questions.

Thematic summaries are often carried out when a meta-analysis has proved to be impossible – either because of too much unexplained heterogeneity or because measures of effect could not be calculated. In these situations, reviewers some-times default to 'vote counting': essentially counting up how many studies report statistically significant positive, negative and unclear results and using the balance of positive versus negative to determine the answer to the review question. While an examination of the overall distribution of results can be a first stage of a syn-thesis (e.g. in the stage entitled 'what are the patterns in the data?'), there are four potential pitfalls in using this approach. Most importantly, vote counting takes no note of the relative *sizes* of the studies concerned; all studies are treated equally, whether they have two or 200 participants, whereas a full statistical meta-analysis takes the size of studies into account. Second, a reliance on statisti-cal *significance* can be misleading (Cooper and Rosenthal 1980). For example, a review might have ten studies of which only one observed any difference between the intervention and control group; the review might conclude that there was no evidence of effect. This could be misleading as it takes no account of the *direction of effect*. In reality, all of the studies might be suggestive of a positive result, but lacked the statistical power to demonstrate statistical significance. Third, a simple vote-counting approach takes no account of study *quality*, giving poorer quality studies as much importance as the better ones. Fourth, counting votes does not take account of any differences in the *sizes* of effect across studies.

It is possible to see how some of these problems might be mitigated in certain ways. Tabulating results according to study size and quality might assist with two of the above issues, and noting the direction of effect, rather than statistical sig-nificance, would also be a positive step. Some reviewers have integrated an assess-ment of quality into their vote-counting system by, for example, giving higher quality studies more votes than those of lower quality. Vote counting may also be valid when all the included quality assured studies in a group show a positive effect in the same direction, though its application is still limited, as this only tells us the direction of an effect, and not its magnitude. Thus, while there are ways of limiting some of the weaknesses described above, vote counting is generally thought to be a 'last resort' to be employed when meta-analysis is impossible (Higgins and Green 2011). Thematic summaries are thus summaries of the findings of their included studies that have been arranged into themes, and do not utilise any of the specific methods of synthesis that the remainder of this chapter considers. Since they do not have any method of generating themes inductively from the studies they contain, they usually rely exclusively on their review's conceptual framework to provide an organising structure. Care needs to be taken in summarising study findings in order to avoid some of the weaknesses of 'vote counting'.

## Framework synthesis

Framework synthesis introduces an inductive element to thematic summaries by allowing an initial conceptual framework to evolve during the synthesis as the reviewers become more familiar with the literature being reviewed. (To avoid confusion, in this section 'conceptual framework' refers to the framework that was developed at the beginning of the review, 'framework' to the modified framework that is the outcome of the review, and 'framework synthesis' to the method.) Framework synthesis is an adaptation of framework analysis which was originally developed for the analysis of primary research data (Ritchie and Spencer 1994). It has been used to synthesise research and reflective reports about public involvement in research (Oliver et al. 2008b), studies of attitudes to walking and cycling (Lorenc et al. 2008) and research about the taking of medicines or nutritional supplements to prevent cancer (Carroll et al. 2011). Each review applied framework synthesis slightly differently, thereby taking advantage of different characteristics of the method. The earliest of these examples adapted framework analysis in order to analyse a mixture of research and policy documents while making the analysis open to discussion and influence by co-investigators (Oliver et al. 2008b). The subsequent example applied framework synthesis because it can be applied by a team of novice analysts (Lorenc et al. 2008). In the third example, framework synthesis was chosen for its applicability for reviewing diverse study designs (experimental designs, economic studies and qualitative research) within a tight timeframe (Carroll et al. 2011). Each synthesis applied the same steps, with slight modifications.

### The stages of framework synthesis

Framework analysis (for primary research) has been described as five neat stages (Pope et al. 2000). The reality, however, at least when applied to literature reviewing, is a messier, more iterative experience of finding a way to construct a coherent picture from what initially seems to be an overwhelming pile of studies.

As with framework analysis for primary research, framework synthesis starts with delving into the data, initially reading the abstracts from search outputs, then the full texts as they become available, to get an impression of the key issues and recurrent themes. Some themes will emerge from the data while others will be sought in the data guided by the review question, prior knowledge of the review team, or new knowledge acquired by consulting stakeholders. Once all the key themes have been identified, each study, or piece of text, is coded with themes that will act as an index to navigate the data and allow the literature to be sub-divided into sections, albeit overlapping, that are more manageable for in-depth analysis.

The initial conceptual framework evolves as the importance of different concepts becomes apparent. The initial conceptual framework is tentative either because it is 'borrowed' from elsewhere to provide a pragmatic starting point, or because at the beginning the reviewers will rely more on their prior knowledge, and later this will be complemented by their growing understanding of the literature they have found.

As the conceptual framework crystallises, the task of coding pieces of text or whole studies begins again, more systematically, and themes are expanded with short annotations as their significance becomes clearer. The process may involve a series of frameworks that will become increasingly coherent and simultaneously accommodating of more data, but each evolution of the framework will require another iteration of the coding process.

Once the framework is satisfactorily coherent, and coding is complete, each element of the framework can be tackled in turn, tabulating the data under key themes in order to present distilled summaries.

The last stage is drawing together what can be learnt from the tables and summaries. This is done by creating typologies, mapping the multidimensional nature and diversity of phenomena, finding associations between themes and providing explanations for the findings across the included studies.

## Review question and conceptual framework

The success of the framework synthesis depends on constructing a coherent framework, and this can be done in different ways. Where a review question was rooted in the growing interest in public involvement in research with very little underlying research, the initial conceptual framework was informed by current policy, the direct experience of the research team and themes that became apparent from abstracts identified by the electronic search strategy (Oliver et al. 2008b). Where a review question could be addressed by a well-developed research literature, the initial conceptual framework drew on hypotheses from the directly relevant background literature and on broader prior knowledge about social determinants of health, tackling inequalities and theoretical models in health promotion (Lorenc et al. 2008). Where a review about taking medicines or nutritional supplements to prevent cancer was required to be completed quickly, the review team searched the literature specifically for a suitable initial conceptual framework. A published model about women's attitudes to taking vitamins and minerals was considered a 'best fit' for starting the synthesis (Carroll et al. 2011).

## Configuration and aggregation

In all three of these syntheses, reviewers inspected the included literature for data addressing each theme within the conceptual framework as it was initially configured. Where data could not be accommodated by the themes of the initial conceptual framework, new themes evolved and data were aggregated within initial and emerging themes. Definitions for each theme were developed and refined through reviewers working independently and then comparing and discussing their application of the themes. The first two reviews reported the sources of initial themes and the themes that emerged from the data, thereby reconfiguring the framework. The third example described how the reviewers conducted these steps in detail. In framework synthesis, revealing the data available is an iterative process of aggregating and reconfiguring the data.

Once the data were aggregated according to themes or dimensions within the final configuration of the framework, the reviewers described the patterns in the data, drawing conclusions from across the framework. The strength of the synthesis was considered in two different ways: the number of studies or policy reflections contributing to each theme (Oliver et al. 2008b; Lorenc et al. 2008), and whether the reports about working together were authored by one or both of the parties (Oliver et al. 2008b).

## Thematic synthesis

As with thematic summaries, and framework synthesis, thematic synthesis is a method that can be employed within a review in order to bring together findings of research from many different types (Thomas and Harden 2008). It is not a method (or methodology), such as grounded theory, which brings with it accepted understandings about the nature and meaning of knowledge, but rather is a technique that can be used in a variety of types of review to help the reviewer conduct a synthesis that is systematically grounded in the studies it contains. It is thus a way of systematising an analysis regardless of whether (or if) the analysis itself takes an overtly interpretative or realist perspective (Barnett-Page and Thomas 2009). In either case, the way that the thematic synthesis itself is conducted would be broadly constant. As discussed in *conceptualising synthesis*, one of the key activities in synthesis is the *translation* between the results of studies. Thematic synthesis can be understood as a technique to achieve this systematically, though it has important roles to play in analysis as well. When discussing the equivalent method in primary research, thematic analysis, Richard Boyatzis asserts that thematic analysis is particularly suitable for analysing multidisciplinary datasets, and offers a way of enabling people across the paradigm divide to share a common understanding about their endeavour. The 'interpretative' social scientist's understanding of the social construction of meaning is satisfied, as 'social "facts" or observations seem to emerge' inductively. Likewise, the systematic 'identification of these observations satisfies the positivist social scientist's conceptual definition of discovery' (Boyatzis 1998: xiii). These characteristics may be one reason that it works so well when synthesising multiple research studies, which are often multidisciplinary and require the researcher to consider their analysis from different sides of the paradigm divide.

At the heart of a thematic synthesis are thematic codes that are applied to, and across, studies. These codes (and the difference between a theme and a code is discussed later) may be both pre-specified and generated inductively and, according to Boyatzis, a good thematic code has five principal elements:

1  A label (i.e. a name).
2  A definition of what the theme concerns (i.e. the characteristic or issue constituting the theme).
3  A description of how to know when the theme occurs (i.e. indicators on how to 'flag' the theme).
4  A description of any qualifications or exclusions to the identification of the theme.
5  Examples, both positive and negative, to eliminate possible confusion when looking for the theme. (Boyatzis 1998: 31)

A theme therefore has a great deal of information associated with it, some of which is built up during the conduct of the synthesis and, for pre-specified codes, some will be available at its outset. While it may seem to be tedious and overly detailed to spend time carefully defining a theme while identifying it within a study, the time spent is paid back later since the information associated with the theme will form a large part of its description when writing up the review.

A thematic synthesis can take many forms, ranging from a largely 'deductive' model, in which themes are set up in advance of the synthesis itself, to one that emphasises the 'inductive' generation of themes. As is frequently the case when thinking about how methods differ from one another, most thematic syntheses will have elements of both, and the extent to which a given synthesis can actually be characterised as one or the other is purely a matter of degree. Situations in which a developed framework of themes is established prior to the thematic analysis are similar to framework synthesis (Carroll et al. 2011; Oliver et al. 2008b). Outlined below is the process that has been employed in carrying out thematic syntheses in a number of reviews of health promotion and public health research. It neatly distinguishes the inductive generation or 'discovery' of themes (which might be characterised as being more descriptive than analytical) from an examination of what the previously discovered themes might *mean* in the context of a given review (an activity that emphasises interpretation and analysis over description).

## Stage one: coding text

The first stage of a thematic synthesis involves the identification of themes across the included studies. As discussed above, this activity is primarily concerned with *translating* the findings of studies into a common 'metric' so that it is possible to compare and contrast them. The aim at this stage is to be fairly descriptive, remaining 'close' to the text contained in the primary studies. A phase that often overlaps (Stage 2) with this is organising the initial themes into a framework that relates them to one another. The final, third stage of the synthesis aims to answer the review questions in the light of the descriptive themes.

*Identifying the 'findings'*

One challenge when undertaking a thematic synthesis is deciding what constitutes the 'findings' of primary studies. Some reviews which have employed thematic synthesis are quite selective about this, and only take, for example, what the study authors report participants to have said – either individually or as a group – as the findings of a study. Other thematic syntheses take a broader perspective and treat the authors' conclusions as also being part of the 'findings' of the study as well. As the reports of all studies are mediated by the studies' authors, it is important to acknowledge that even when the more selective approach is adopted, any findings that are presented will reflect the authors' original perspectives and priorities.

Whichever method of selecting findings has been adopted (and one approach we are currently trying is simply treating the whole paper or report as 'data'), the principles of systematic reviewing mean that we should take steps to ensure that our analysis is systematic and that we do not 'cherry pick' convenient or attractive findings from the studies, but are as even-handed as possible in our treatment of the material we have to synthesise. We use computer software to help us in this as it is able to keep a permanent record of our interpretative and analytical decisions, and ensures we consider each piece of evidence, or at least reveals where we may not have done so. Standard software for undertaking qualitative analyses is suitable, such as NVivo or Atlas TI, as is some more specialist reviewing software (see Chapter 5).

*Line-by-line coding*

Having identified the 'findings' of the studies in the synthesis, analysis proceeds using the line-by-line coding of text stored on a computer. This method will be familiar to those who have conducted thematic analyses of, for example, interview transcripts in their primary research. Each sentence and paragraph is read carefully with a view to identifying its underpinning themes and concepts. Text is highlighted and associated with a particular code (or theme). As mentioned above, some analyses will begin with quite a detailed list of themes (e.g. framework synthesis), whereas others will be entirely inductive and the first study will be analysed with very few pre-existing themes to choose from. Whichever method is adopted, the aim is to associate all relevant text with one or more themes or codes and, where no pre-existing theme exists to encapsulate the meaning of the text, a new code is created. At the beginning of a synthesis new codes are created very frequently, but as the synthesis progresses, the set of themes and codes becomes more stable.

The terms 'theme' and 'code' have been used almost interchangeably in the previous paragraph and this is because there may be very little difference between the two, especially when a pre-existing conceptual framework is being used as the starting point for the synthesis. However, it may be useful to think of a 'code' as being a short phrase that summarises the content of the text to which it is applied; it contains no analysis or abstraction, and is simply concerned with data reduction (reducing the amount of text to read so that concepts can be more clearly visualised and organised). A 'theme' is a concept that has been identified in more than one study and, as a result, may either be more refined or contain a higher level of abstraction.

For example, text in one study in a review about healthy eating might refer to the 'temptation of having confectionary at home' and be coded as such; another study might refer to the availability of cakes and biscuits. Unless the reviewer needs to distinguish between different types of food at home, the first code might be renamed to encompass the second, by abstracting 'confectionary' and 'cakes and biscuits' and referring instead to 'the availability of sweet food'.

When themes have been applied to the first study, the next study in the synthesis is considered. As soon as this happens, and as the above example shows, the key task of *translation* is underway. The reviewers' judgement and interpretation are critical parts of this process, as they need to determine when the theme underpinning the text is sufficiently similar to be *translated* into an existing theme or sufficiently dissimilar to warrant the creation of a new theme. As will be discussed below in the section about meta-ethnography, Noblit and Hare (1988) outline two different types of translation, *reciprocal* and *refutational*, whereby commensurate themes are analysed in terms of whether they agree with one another or not (as well as whether they refer to the same underlying concept). The use of computer software ensures that the themes are always associated with the text on which they are based. This aids consistency, as this text can be referred to whenever there is doubt about the applicability of the theme to another study. Software also facilitates *axial coding*, where all the text about a particular broad theme or concept is identified and then coded in more detail.

## Stage two: developing descriptive themes

The descriptive codes and themes generated above (and those originating from the conceptual framework) are then organised into descriptive themes. Sometimes this happens concurrently with the coding of studies and sometimes it is a separate stage in its own right. The aim is to develop and articulate relationships between the themes and associate conceptually similar themes with one another. Essentially, this is much the same as building a theory which explains how the population in question understand or experience a particular phenomenon. Again, the interpretation and judgement of reviewers plays an important part, even though the aim is for this to be an essentially descriptive process.

For example, in a review about healthy eating, one code might be: 'eating with friends makes me break my diet'; another, 'friends help support my healthy eating'; and another, 'I want to eat what I see advertised'. All these themes might be organised under an overarching theme of 'influences affecting food choice', with a sub-category covering the range of influences (themes) that friends might have.

In some reviews, the descriptive themes will answer the review questions sufficiently well for the analysis to stop at this point. Other reviews will progress to a more analytical final stage.

## Stage three: generating analytical themes

The final stage of a thematic synthesis is generating analytical themes. These themes usually take the synthesis 'beyond' the content of the primary studies, offering new conceptualisations and explanations. Sometimes the generation of descriptive themes (above, stage two) moves naturally in a more analytical direction. In other situations, the descriptive synthesis is 'pushed' into analysis by considering how the descriptive themes answer the review's question(s). In the later situation, it is helpful to consider each theme (or group of themes) and ask 'how does this theme address/answer this question?'. This process generates a set of statements which can themselves be analysed thematically, generating the analytical themes.

For example, in a recent synthesis of children's views about body size, shape and weight, we synthesised a number of 'qualitative' studies that led us to conclude that participants considered discrimination against overweight children to be normal and expected (Rees et al. 2009). We named the theme in our synthesis 'discrimination is normal', as that encapsulated what we understood the text in many studies to be saying. The word 'discrimination', however, does not appear in any of the texts we used to generate the theme: it was our interpretation, based on our reading of the studies (and on our understanding of the synthesis activity being interpretative, and our findings being our interpretations of the primary studies, which were in turn researchers' interpretations of what children had been saying to them). This theme itself has been organised within a set of themes on the subject of 'body size matters' and, as Figure 9.5 shows, most of the themes in the synthesis are of an analytical kind (e.g. 'using body size to judge people'; 'adult control of children's eating behaviour') in that they describe concepts that the children themselves will not have expressed explicitly, but will have emerged as part of the analyses presented in the individual studies and our synthesis.

## Checking the robustness of the synthesis

As outlined above in the discussion about *stages of synthesis*, there are a number of questions that can be asked of a synthesis in order to test its robustness. The relative contribution of each study to the synthesis can be assessed by compiling a grid like the one depicted in Figure 9.6.

Such a grid helps the reviewer determine whether important parts of the synthesis depend upon relatively few studies – and whether or not this matters – and whether there are associations between particular populations and quality judgements about the studies and groups of themes. It is important to bear in mind that in a synthesis that configures studies, the fact that some areas of the synthesis are based on more studies than others does not necessarily mean that these areas are more trustworthy or that they should be given greater weight. A *sensitivity analysis* of this kind simply raises questions which assist the reviewer to be critical about their work.

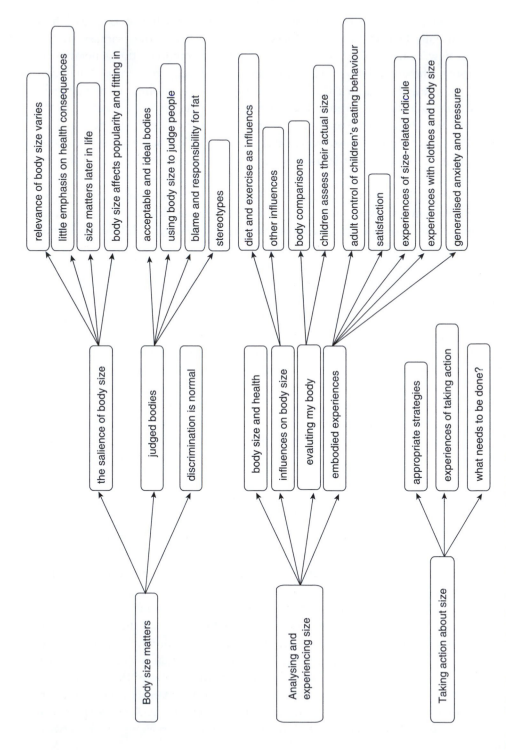

**Figure 9.5** Themes identified across studies of children's views

Themes from the interpretive synthesis: the contribution of each study

| No. | Study name* | Relevance of body size varies | Health consequences | Size matters later | Popularity/fitting in | Body size and judging people | Acceptable/ideal bodies | Blame/responsibility for fat | Stereotypes | Discrimination is normal | Body size and health | Diet & exercise as influences | Other influences | Body comparisons | Assessing actual size | Adult control | Satisfaction | Size-related ridicule | Clothes & body size | Generalised anxiety/pressure | Appropriate strategies | Experiences of taking action | What needs to be done? |
|---|---|---|---|---|---|---|---|---|---|---|---|---|---|---|---|---|---|---|---|---|---|---|---|
| 1 | Burrows et al. (1999) | ✓ | | | | | | | | | ✓ | | | | | | | | | | | | |
| 2 | Cole et al. (2005) | | | | | | ✓ | | ✓ | | | | ✓ | ✓ | ✓ | | | | | | ✓ | ✓ | ✓ |
| 3 | Dixey et al. (2001) | | ✓ | ✓ | ✓ | ✓ | ✓ | ✓ | | ✓ | ✓ | ✓ | ✓ | ✓ | ✓ | | | ✓ | ✓ | ✓ | ✓ | ✓ | |
| 4 | Edmunds (2000) | ✓ | | ✓ | ✓ | ✓ | ✓ | | ✓ | ✓ | ✓ | ✓ | ✓ | ✓ | ✓ | ✓ | ✓ | ✓ | ✓ | ✓ | | ✓ | |
| 5 | Girlguiding UK (2007) | ✓ | | | ✓ | ✓ | ✓ | ✓ | ✓ | ✓ | | | | ✓ | | | | ✓ | ✓ | | ✓ | ✓ | ✓ |
| 6 | Grogan and Richards (2002) | | | | | | ✓ | ✓ | | ✓ | | ✓ | | | | | | | | | | ✓ | |
| 7 | Kurtz and Thornes (2000) | ✓ | ✓ | | | | | | | | | | | | | | | | | | | | |
| 8 | Ludvigsen and Sharma (2004) | | | ✓ | | ✓ | | ✓ | | ✓ | | ✓ | | | ✓ | | | | ✓ | | | | |
| 9 | McKinley et al. (2005) | | | | | ✓ | | | ✓ | | ✓ | | | | | | | | ✓ | | | ✓ | ✓ |
| 10 | Mulvihill et al. (2000b) | | | | | | | | | | ✓ | | | | | | | | | | | | |
| 11 | Murtagh et al. (2006) | | ✓ | | ✓ | | ✓ | | | ✓ | | | ✓ | | | | ✓ | | ✓ | ✓ | | | |
| 12 | NCB (2005) | | ✓ | | ✓ | | | | | ✓ | ✓ | | ✓ | | | | | ✓ | ✓ | | | | ✓ |
| 13 | Robinson (2000) | | | | | ✓ | | ✓ | | ✓ | | | | | | ✓ | | | | | | | |
| 14 | Stewart et al. (2006) | | | ✓ | | | | | | ✓ | | | | | | | | | ✓ | | | | |
| 15 | Walsh-Pierce and Wardle (1997) | | | ✓ | | ✓ | | | ✓ | | ✓ | | | | | | | ✓ | ✓ | | | ✓ | |

*Shading indicates a study was rated as having a low quality, both in terms of reliability and usefulness for this review.

**Figure 9.6** The contribution of each study in a thematic synthesis

## Meta-ethnography

Like thematic synthesis above, meta-ethnography is another flexible method for synthesis that can be used in a range of settings. Originally conceived by Noblit and Hare in 1988 as a way of thinking about drawing conclusions across multiple meta-ethnographic studies, it has since been used by reviewers to synthesise many different types of research, going far beyond the ethnographies (studies of human societies and cultures usually collecting data through participant observation) that give it its name (e.g. Britten et al. 2002; Campbell et al. 2003). Noblit and Hare (1988) outline three distinctive types of synthesis that correspond to how the studies concerned relate to one another. *Reciprocal translation* refers to situations in which the concepts in multiple studies correspond and agree with one another and their results can thus be aggregated in some way. Likewise, *refutational synthesis* depends on the ability of concepts to translate into one another, but this type of synthesis concerns the situations in which accounts in different studies conflict with one another. The final type is a *line of argument synthesis*, in which results are not seen so much as being supportive or in conflict, but rather can be configured to produce a wider narrative.

Britten and colleagues have produced a useful example of the application of meta-ethnography to other types of qualitative research concerning the lay meanings of medicine (i.e. not ethnographies at all) (Britten et al. 2002). Their synthesis moves through three distinct phases: the identification of concepts in the primary studies; the description of the original author's findings; and the construction of the reviewers' interpretation. Identifying concepts in the primary studies primarily involves *reciprocal translation*, the activity of translating concepts from one study to another,

Table 1 Completed grid: lay meanings of medicines

| Methods and concepts | Donovan and Blake[14] | Morgan[16] | Britten[15] | Rogers et al[17] |
|---|---|---|---|---|
| Sample | 54 patients with suspected inflammatory arthropathy | 60 white and Afro-Caribbean patients treated for hypertension for at least one year | 30 patients, attenders and non- attenders | 34 patients with a diagnosis of schizophrenia or schizo-affective disorder |
| Data collection | Home interviews pre and post consultation: observation of consultations | Home interviews | Home interviews | Interviews |
| Setting | Three rheumatology units | 15 general practices | Two general practices | Different points in the mental health |
| Type(s) of medicine | NSAIDs and second-line drugs | Antihypertensive drugs | Unselected | Neuroleptic medication |
| Adherence/ compliance | (Patients do not perceive compliance to be an issue) | Stable adherence and problematic adherence | Correct behaviour and routine medicine-taking | (Patients mention benefits of taking medicines] |
| Self-regulation | Levels of non-compliance | Leaving off drugs | Preference for rot taking drugs | Adjustment of medication, self-regulation |
| Aversion | Dislike of taking drugs, fear of side-effects, weakness. dependence | Fear of side-effects, addiction. harmful effects of drugs | Aversion to medicines, medicines as harmful | Wide range of side-effects |
| Alternative coping strategies | Range of alternative remedies | Traditional (herbal) remedies | Use of alternative medicine | Alterative coping strategies |
| Sanctions | – | Patients warned by doctors and told severely about the need to take the tablets regularly | – | Coercion from significant others, fear of coercion from mental health professionals |
| Selective disclosure | Patients did not tell doctors of altered doses | – | Patients may not articulate views that they do not perceive to be medically legitimated | Management of information to psychiatrists |
| Explanation/ theory (second-order interpretation) | 'Patients carry cut a "cost-benefit" analysis of each treatment, weighing up the costs/risks of each treatment against the benefits as they perceive them' | Medicine-taking is influenced by cultural meanings and cultural resources | | 'the self-regulations of medication appear to have been circumscribed or inhibited by the impact of the threat of social and professional sanctions' |

Figure 9.7  Meta-ethnography grid 1

NSAIDs, non-steroigdal anti-inflammatory drugs.

Note: Entries in parantheses are explanationa for what would otherwise be empty cells; enties in quotation marks are the original authors own words (see previous page)

**Table 2** Synthesis, including concepts and second- and third-order interpretations

| Concepts | Second-order interpretations | Third-order interpretations |
|---|---|---|
| ADHERENCE/COMPLIANCE: stable adherence; correct behaviour and routine medicine-taking | (a) Patients carry out 'cost-benefit' analysis of each treatment, weighing up the costs/risks of each treatment against the benefits as they perceive them | (c) Self-regulation includes the use of alternative coping strategies |
| SELF-REGULATION: problematic adherence; levels of non-compliance, leaving off drugs; preference for not taking self-regulations | | |
| AVERSION: dislike of taking drugs; fear of side-effects; aversion to medicines; harmful effect of drugs | (b) Medicine-taking is influenced by cultural meanings and cultural resources | |
| ALTERNATIVE COPING STRATEGIES: range of alternative remedies; traditional remedies | | |
| SANCTIONS: patients are warned by their doctors and told severely about the need to take the tablets regularly; coercion from significant others, fear of coercion from mental health professionals | (d) Self-regulation is…inhibited by….the threat of social and professional sanctions | (e) Self-regulation flourishes if sanctions are not serve |
| SELECTIVE DISCLOSURE: patients do not tell doctors of altered doses; manangement of information to psychiatrists | (f) Patients may not articulate views that they do not perceive to be medically legitimated | (g) Alternatve coping strategies are not seen by patients as medically legitimate (h) Fear of sanctions and guilt produce selective disclousure |

**Figure 9.8** Meta-ethnography grid 2

recognising that they will often be expressed in different ways. The data created in this phase are summarised in the first column of the table depicted in Figure 9.7. The second phase, the identification of explanations from the original authors' accounts, is also summarised in the table, and makes up the bottom row. Britten et al. conceptualise these stages in terms of Schutz's notion of first- and second-order constructs: the 'everyday understandings of ordinary people' (first order), and the 'constructs of the social scientists' (second order) (Britten et al. 2002: 211).

The table in Figure 9.7 summarises the first two phases of synthesis. The four studies in the sample make up the four columns and the translated concepts are listed on the left. We can see that the four studies had different ways of expressing the concept 'self-regulation', with only one study using that exact term (Rogers et al.) and the other three talking about 'levels of non-compliance' (Donovan and Blake), 'leaving off drugs' (Morgan) and 'preference for not taking drugs' (Britten). The bottom row in the table is qualitatively different from the other rows. Rather than containing translated concepts, this row contains the key finding from each study that addresses the review question. (While each study has only one entry in this example, there may be multiple entries for each study in more complex syntheses.)

The final phase of the synthesis is summarised in the table shown in Figure 9.8. The first column contains the concepts that were summarised in Figure 9.7 and the second column the second-order interpretations which made up the bottom row of Figure 9.7. The reviewers have arranged (or *configured*) these concepts and second-order interpretations in order to build up a *line of argument* that is depicted by the letters a–h. Taking one of the lines of argument, we can see that the bottom row is concerned with selective disclosure – that patients do not inform their doctors when they deviate from their prescribed regimen of medicine. The original study authors concluded that 'patients may not articulate views that they do not perceive to be medically legitimated'. Based on their readings of the texts across the studies, the reviewers concluded that 'alternative coping strategies are not seen by patients as being medically legitimate' and also that the 'fear of sanctions produces selective disclosure'. Neither of the two conclusions reached by the reviewers might be found in any of the studies in the synthesis: this is an example of a synthesis 'going beyond' the studies it contains and generating new theoretical explanations. A strength of this method of reporting is that the reviewers' interpretations are made explicit, so the reader should be able to judge for themselves whether or not they feel the interpretation is warranted.

## Mixed methods synthesis

Interest in the potential of studies that combine qualitative and quantitative research has been growing over the past 20 years (e.g. Tashakkori and Teddlie 2010). There has also been a parallel interest in mixing methods in systematic reviews (e.g. Dixon-Woods et al. 2005), and while the vast majority of systematic reviews do not use a mixed methods paradigm, there is increasing acceptance of the potential of qualitative research to strengthen reviews of effectiveness (Noyes 2010) and the first Cochrane review to incorporate qualitative research has recently been published (Ryan et al. 2011).

The EPPI-Centre's experience of conducting systematic reviews to inform policy has taught us that policy-makers ask questions of effectiveness that are answerable by an aggregative review (with or without a meta-analysis), but they also ask questions that precede (e.g. 'what might work?'; 'what is feasible?'; 'what are people's needs?') as well as questions that go beyond effectiveness (e.g. 'why did/didn't this work?'; 'how does it work?'; 'under what circumstances does this apply?'; 'is it acceptable/appropriate?'). Answering these adequately requires that the reviews incorporate a broad range of research since we need the studies that assess the balance of benefit and harm attributable to an intervention to be accompanied by studies that have the explanatory power to answer the 'how' and 'why' questions. To this end, we developed an approach to mixed methods synthesis that uses the results of a synthesis of qualitative research to interrogate and interpret the results of a meta-analysis.

One of the first reviews we used this method in concerned the barriers to, and facilitators of, healthy eating among children aged 4 to 10 years (Thomas et al. 2003). After consulting with the review's steering group (see Chapter 2), our initial review question about healthy eating was focused more narrowly on fruit and vegetable intake and decisions were made about the kinds of research to include. In order to identify the barriers and facilitators we chose two paths:

1 We decided to examine trials which would provide evidence of the effectiveness, or otherwise, of interventions.
2 We included what we term 'views' studies. These are studies which examine children's own perspectives on food and healthy eating using what are often termed 'qualitative' research methods – for example, in-depth interviews and focus groups.[2]

The review used conventional systematic review methods: sensitive searching, systematic screening and an independent quality assessment, giving us 33 trials and eight 'views' studies which met our inclusion criteria. Figure 9.9 illustrates how the two discrete sets of studies were initially dealt with separately in the systematic review process. For example, both sets of studies had their own inclusion criteria; they were assessed for their quality and reliability according to standards for their specific study types; they were synthesised individually using appropriate methods for their data type; and in the last stage of the review they were brought together in the final synthesis.

---

[2]We use the term 'qualitative' research cautiously because it encompasses a multitude of research methods at the same time as an assumed range of epistemological positions. In practice it is often difficult to classify research as being either 'qualitative' or 'quantitative' as much research contains aspects of both (Thomas and Harden 2008; Bryman 1998). Because the term is in common use, however, we will employ it in this chapter.

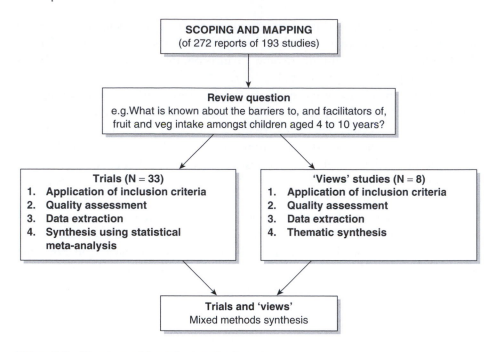

**Figure 9.9** Structure of the mixed methods review

The trials were synthesised in a meta-analysis and a standard sensitivity analysis was used to test the robustness of the synthesis. However, as the interventions in the trials differed from one another, it was difficult to ascribe a specific meaning to the pooled effect size, beyond answering a broad review question concerning the overall effectiveness of this body of research. The 'views' studies were synthesised using thematic synthesis and the analytical stage of this synthesis involved inferring 'recommendations for interventions' that were implied by the descriptive themes. For example, one of the themes was about children not seeing their health as being their personal responsibility. We therefore inferred that interventions should promote fruit and vegetables on the basis that they are tasty (the focus of another theme), rather than them being good for our health.

We then combined the two syntheses by examining the interventions in the trials to identify those that matched, and did not match, the recommendations arising from the views synthesis. This analysis was summarised in a matrix, part of which is shown in Figure 9.10.

The final stage of the mixed methods synthesis was a statistical sub-group analysis which ascertained whether differences in the results of studies could be explained by the sub-divisions arising from the views synthesis. This approach enables us to configure the aggregated findings of sub-sets of trials in accordance with a conceptual framework that is empirically derived from studies with the potential to tell us 'why' and 'how' interventions might be working. It utilises the strengths of both types of research and takes a *dialectical* stance towards mixing methods by using the thematic synthesis to develop hypotheses that are tested in

| Children's views | Number of trials which match recommendation | |
|---|---|---|
| Recommendations for interventions | Good quality trials | Trials which did not reach our quality threshold |
| Do not promote fruit and vegetables in the same way | None | None |
| Brand fruit and vegetables as an 'exciting' or children-relevant product, as well as a 'tasty' one | 5 | 5 |
| Reduce health emphasis in messages to promote fruit and vegetables, particularly messages which concern future health | 5 | 6 |

**Figure 9.10**   Mixed methods synthesis matrix (part thereof)

the mixed methods synthesis. (For further information about this approach, see Harden and Thomas 2005, 2010; Thomas et al. 2004.)

## Statistical meta-analysis

Meta-analysis is a statistical method for combining the numerical results of studies. It is most commonly used to combine the results of controlled trials (e.g. to see which treatment works best), but can also be used to answer questions about the patterns of phenomena across society in observational studies, the accuracy of diagnostic tests, the comparative benefits of different choices in terms of costs and outcomes, and even questions about which research methods are more reliable than others. A straightforward meta-analysis that assesses the extent of benefit or harm that can be ascribed to a particular intervention on a particular outcome can be understood as working primarily within an aggregative mode of synthesis. Other analyses, which examine the effects of an intervention in different contexts/populations, can be considered to be using a combination of aggregative and configurative (when results are compared and contrasted) modes of synthesis.

There are two distinct phases of a meta-analysis: (1) obtaining measures of effect that summarise individual studies; and (2) combining the studies statistically. We will consider both in turn before moving on to discuss more advanced topics and the interpretation of the results of a meta-analysis.

### 1. Calculating effect sizes

The result (or results) from each individual study are summarised as an 'effect size', usually together with some estimate of the precision of that statistic – often its standard error. (Effect sizes are also known sometimes as 'effect estimates'. This is a more descriptive term as it encompasses the idea that we are only able to view an estimate of the true effect of an intervention. While we use the term 'effect size' throughout the chapter, it is helpful to remember that they are all estimates and contain a degree of uncertainty and error.) While a statistical test will tell us the probability (or likelihood) that a given outcome was the result of chance, an effect size tells us the magnitude of the result and its direction. For example, in a standard experiment in which the impact of an intervention with one group of participants is compared with another group which did not receive the intervention, the effect size will be a measure that tells us how big the difference was between the two groups (if there was any difference at all), and in which direction (i.e. which group did better or worse than the other). The estimate of precision is usually expressed as a *standard error*, a statistic that provides information about the replicability of the effect across samples; that is, it estimates how similar the size of the observed effect would be for different samples drawn from the same population. The smaller the standard error, the more precise the effect size. Smaller studies tend to have larger standard errors, which reflects the fact that, as we are only basing our findings on a small number of participants, we are that much less sure that our results approximate to those of the population of interest than we would be with a larger study.

The standard error can be used to create 'confidence intervals' around an effect size, giving an upper and lower boundary to the range of possible results that the study was estimating with the effect size itself in the middle of the two values. The confidence interval gives us an indication of how *precise* the results are. A narrow confidence interval suggests that the estimate of the effect is more precise than would a wide confidence interval. Small studies, often containing only a small proportion of the population of interest, have wide confidence intervals, while the confidence intervals of larger studies tend to be narrower, including a smaller range of possible values. Meta-analyses of many studies can have very narrow confidence intervals, reflecting a greater degree of certainty about the likely size of the effect of the intervention. Typically, we will speak about '95% confidence intervals' which can be interpreted to mean: *if this study was carried out 100 times with a new confidence interval calculated each time, the confidence interval would contain the true effect 95 times out of 100.* In practice, when interpreting a confidence interval, it is useful to ask the question: 'Would I be happy with my intervention if the difference it actually made was at the top (or the bottom) of the range described by the confidence interval?' This enables us to consider whether the practical, real-world implications of an imprecise estimate are of concern: if there is a large practical difference between our estimate and the upper/lower boundaries, then we should be cautious in treating our estimate as an appropriate estimate of the true value.

Effect sizes can be in the same metric as the results of any study, and are usually classified as being 'continuous' or 'dichotomous'. Continuous effect sizes are statistics that are on some kind of scale – e.g. age, weight, and percentages. Long ordinal scales, such as depression and quality of life, are also treated as being continuous when calculating effect sizes. Dichotomous effect sizes are 'either/or' results – e.g. pass/fail or dead/alive. Effect sizes associated with diagnostic tests are also of this variety. The statistical methods used to combine effect sizes are the same regardless of the type of effect size that is being combined. (See the CRD's guidance for undertaking reviews in health care for information about effect sizes, including diagnostic tests and economic evaluations: CRD 2009.)

One type of continuous effect size that deserves special mention is the *standardised mean difference*. In a controlled trial, the difference in outcomes between two groups of participants in a study is often simply the difference between the mean of one group (the intervention group) and the other (the control or comparison group). In a systematic review it is not uncommon to find that different studies measuring the same outcome have used different tools to measure their results (e.g. there are many scales that measure depression) and it is therefore necessary to convert the results on to a common scale in order to compare like with like. The way that this is done is to find the difference in means between the groups and then to divide this by a measure of variance of the population in question. Usually, the variance is either the pooled standard deviation of the two groups or the standard deviation of the control group.

Please see Coe (2002) for further information about the standardised mean difference and the *Cochrane Handbook* (Higgins and Green 2011) for information about dichotomous effect sizes. Formulae for calculating effect sizes can be found in many sources, with Lipsey and Wilson's *Practical Meta-analysis* (2001) being particularly useful as it has valuable material in its appendices. Also see Borenstein et al. (2009), Deeks and Higgins (2007) and the various software utilities listed in Chapter 5 for further guidance.

### Special issues concerning cluster trials

Experimental studies that evaluate the impact of a given intervention prospectively assign some people to receive the intervention and (usually) some to act as a comparison. When the focus of the evaluation is an intervention that operates on groups rather than individuals, allocations are also often done at a group (e.g. school, class, hospital or locality), rather than an individual, level. There are additional complexities to consider when such designs are employed, as people coming from the same group (or location) tend to be more similar to one another than would be the case from a random sample of individuals across the whole population. This matters, as the amount of additional information gained from each additional individual in a group is less than would be the case with a random sample. The 'effective' size of the study, along with its statistical power, is therefore reduced.

The fact that the statistical power of a cluster trial is lower than the total number of participants is significant to a meta-analyst for two reasons. First, care must be taken when calculating effect sizes to ensure that the correct standard error is obtained. Second, many cluster trials incorrectly analyse their results as though their participants had been individually allocated, rather than assigned as a group. The standard errors 'claimed' by these trials will be too small and will need adjusting upwards. Fortunately, there are some fairly simple calculations that can usually be carried out in both situations to ensure that the correct standard error is used. (NB The effect size itself is not affected by this issue, only its standard error.) See Chapter 16 of the *Cochrane Handbook* (Higgins and Green 2011) and White and Thomas (2005) for further details.

### What to do about multiple outcomes

A common issue for meta-analysts is deciding what to do when a study provides more than one result for the outcome of interest. For example, a study might report students' results on two different achievement tests, or at different time points, or report both body mass index and percentage body fat as indicators of weight status. This is problematic because most methods of meta-analysis are based on the assumption that each study only contributes one effect size to the analysis. Including multiple effect sizes from each study violates the statistical assumptions underlying meta-analysis and can lead to incorrect estimates of the effect and its precision (see Gleser and Olkin 2010, for a more detailed discussion of the problem with dependent effect sizes).

Historically, meta-analysts were forced to choose one measure (e.g. only use body mass index and ignore percentage body fat) or to average across related measures of the same outcome (e.g. the average score on two achievement tests). However, these are often poor compromises. Where only one measure is selected, we lose potentially valuable information from the measures that we are excluding. Where measures are averaged, we can end up with downward biased (i.e. lower than expected) effect sizes if the correlation between the different outcomes is not high (Rosenthal and Rubin 1986).

Moreover, some research questions are best explored by including different measures of an outcome so that the impact on different outcomes can be directly compared. For example, we might ask the question: 'Does a study skills intervention improve maths tests scores and English test scores to the same extent?' In this case, it is desirable to include more than one effect size from each study (i.e. an effect size for maths and an effect size for English) so that we can test whether maths or English achievement improves more as a result of the study skills intervention. Questions like this cannot be appropriately answered by traditional meta-analysis techniques using sub-group analyses because including both maths and English test scores from each study in the same analysis would violate the assumption of independence of outcomes. However, if we use multivariate techniques (i.e. models that include multiple outcomes), we can account for the dependence between the outcomes by incorporating the correlation between maths and English test scores into the analyses. By doing so, we can more accurately estimate the impact of the study skills intervention on both subject test scores.

Multivariate approaches should be considered if you have multiple relevant effect sizes in each included study. However, such approaches to analysing multiple outcomes are early in their development and can be difficult to implement because of an inconsistent reporting of data in studies and limitations in the currently available software (see Borenstein et al. 2007; Kalaian and Kasim, 2008a, 2008b; Kalaian and Raudenbush, 1996).

### Aids to calculating effect sizes

While the formulae for calculating effect sizes are fairly simple, their calculation can still take a long time, especially since there is considerable variability across published reports in the way that results are presented. Computer software can help here, by converting a wide range of published statistics into effect sizes. Most of the specialist computer software for systematic reviews outlined in Chapter 5 can calculate effect sizes and there are a large number of online tools too (enter 'effect size calculator' into a search engine to find many hundreds of them). One of the most comprehensive tools was developed by David Wilson, who has been conducting meta-analyses of social research for many years. The software will run in Microsoft Excel[3] and a new online version is available on the Campbell Collaboration website.[4]

## 2. Combining effect sizes in a meta-analysis

The calculation of effect sizes for each study is often the most difficult and time-consuming aspect of a meta-analysis, but once the effect sizes are available, the actual analysis can be completed comparatively quickly. This stage contains several mini-steps, including: selecting the appropriate statistical model; sensitivity analysis; checking for publication bias; sub-group analysis; and interpreting the results.

A meta-analysis is more than a simple average of the results of the studies it contains. Depending on the assumptions that underpin the analysis, it considers that some studies should be awarded more or less significance than others and quantifies this principle by giving different 'weight' to different studies. Most importantly, a study's weight is affected by its variance – heavily determined by its size – which is related to its standard error (see above). Large standard errors are associated with smaller studies and smaller standard errors with larger studies. Thus, if a meta-analysis contains a couple of small studies and one very large study, its result will be more dependent on the effect size of the large study than on the smaller ones. The precise way that weights are calculated depends on the statistical model selected (discussed below).

The result of a meta-analysis is usually expressed in the form of a 'forest plot'. An example plot is given in Figure 9.11.

### Interpreting the results of a meta-analysis

Figure 9.11 actually contains two forest plots, showing the results from two different meta-analyses, each containing a great deal of information. Each row on the plot represents one study. We have the study's name, followed by its effect size (in this case, its standardised mean difference) and confidence intervals around its effect size. These numbers are then represented graphically by squares on the graph (the effect size) and horizontal lines (the confidence intervals around each effect size). The size of the square reflects the relative weight that the study has received in the analysis. This is usually in proportion to the number of

---

[3]Download the Excel version at http://mason.gmu.edu/~dwilsonb/ma.html

[4]The online version is available at: www.campbellcollaboration.org/resources/effect_size_input.php

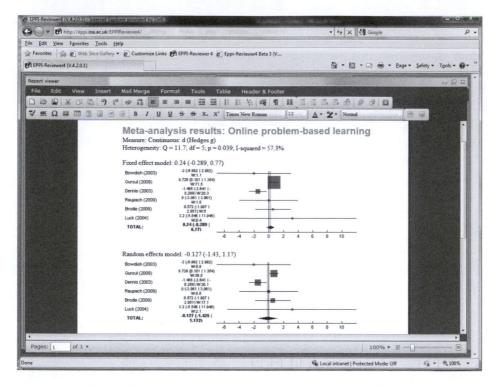

**Figure 9.11** The results of a meta-analysis presented in a forest plot (illustrative data only)

participants in each study with large studies receiving greater weight than smaller ones. The 'line of no effect' (0 on this plot, but 1 on plots with some types of effect size) shows the point at which the two groups (e.g. intervention and control) are equivalent in terms of the outcome of interest. In Figure 9.11, if the block representing the effect size is to the right of the line it means that the intervention group did better than the control; to the left means that the control group did better and that the intervention was possibly harmful. (It cannot be assumed that all effects to the right of the line are beneficial and all to the left are harmful, though: this will depend on the context of the review. For example, beneficial effects would be on the left of the line in a forest plot of interventions that aim to reduce depression.) If the confidence intervals cross this line of no effect, it means the results were not statistically significant; that is, there was no statistically significant difference between the intervention and control groups. If the confidence intervals do not cross the line of no effect, then there was a statistically significant difference between the two groups. The diamond at the bottom represents the result of the meta-analysis; it is the weighted (or pooled) mean of all the effect sizes (see below) and its left and right points indicate its lower and upper confidence intervals.

A number of statistics accompany the forest plot (above the plots in Figure 9.11). The heterogeneity statistic, Q, is a statistical assessment of how heterogeneous the effect sizes in the analysis are. Its accompanying p-value assesses whether Q – and therefore the heterogeneity in the effect sizes – is statistically significant.

$I^2$ (pronounced 'eye-squared') is a percentage which quantifies the amount of heterogeneity that is due to differences between studies, rather than random error. A quick visual check for heterogeneity is to look at the studies' confidence intervals and effect sizes. When the confidence intervals overlap and the effect sizes are in close alignment, there is likely to be little statistical heterogeneity. Divergent results and confidence intervals that do not overlap are indicative of heterogeneity. Another quick check for heterogeneity is to look at the Q statistic and its degrees of freedom *(df)*. When Q is larger than its *df*, the test for significant heterogeneity is likely to be positive; and when Q is equal to, or less than, its degrees of freedom, heterogeneity will not be significant.

The issue of heterogeneity warrants particular attention. First, it should be remembered that the statistical test for heterogeneity is no substitute for reviewers considering carefully whether it is appropriate to combine the studies in their analysis statistically. Only the reviewer can assess how similar participants, interventions, measurement tools etc. are, and whether it makes sense to combine; the heterogeneity statistic can only discern whether heterogeneity between studies is detectable in their results (and it is of course entirely possible for very different interventions to have much the same statistical results). The heterogeneity statistic Q should also be treated with caution: it is underpowered with small numbers of studies (usual in many reviews) and overpowered with large numbers of studies; i.e. it will fail to detect heterogeneity in many situations where results actually are heterogeneous, and will report significant heterogeneity in rarer situations where there are many studies but no statistically noteworthy differences between them. Please see Higgins et al. (2003) for a thorough discussion about this subject, along with information about the $I^2$ statistic. There are a number of other graphical plots that are used in meta-analysis; please see Anzures-Cabrera and Higgins (2010) for a comprehensive overview.

### Statistical models

Figure 9.11 shows the result of a meta-analysis using two different statistical models: fixed and random effects. Opinion is divided about when each model should be used, but it is usually inappropriate to use the fixed effect model when there is statistically significant heterogeneity, as detected by the Q statistic. The assumptions underpinning this model are violated in heterogeneous datasets, as it assumes that the same 'true' effect underlies all studies, and that any differences between them are purely due to sampling errors. A statistically significant heterogeneity statistic is indicating that results differ *more* than this. The random effects model accounts for between-study differences by relaxing the assumption that they are all estimating the same 'true' effect, and instead assumes that each study is representative of its own population of studies. The effect that is being estimated in this model is assumed to be the mean of all these different populations of studies. We should note that the random effects model does not 'fix' heterogeneity, but instead merely supplies a method of incorporating the heterogeneity that cannot be 'explained' by sub-group analysis (see below). When faced with a heterogeneous dataset, the reviewer needs to justify why it is appropriate to combine what are, according to the statistics, studies that will differ from one another in possibly unexplained ways. Sometimes when doing this, it is helpful to think of the question that the heterogeneous meta-analysis answers. It may be so broad (e.g. 'Do interventions to reduce obesity "work"?') as to be unlikely to help people's decision-making. In such cases, a statistical synthesis is usually avoided, or is broken down into more conceptually useful components.

In practice, the calculation of fixed effect and random effects models is quite similar. However, while fixed effect models only weight the effect sizes by the inverse of the sampling error variance, random effects models weight the effect sizes by the inverse of the sampling error variance *plus* the between-studies variance component (which incorporates Q).

As Figure 9.11 shows, the two models can give quite different results, with the random effects model giving comparatively more weight to the smaller studies than the fixed effect model (and less to the larger ones), and having wider confidence intervals around its pooled effect size. The fact that the random effects model downwardly weights the larger studies relative to the fixed effect model can sometimes be problematic, as larger studies are often of a higher methodological quality than the smaller ones. (Having said that, it could be argued that the fixed effect model gives comparatively too much weight to the larger studies, and that the random effects model simply corrects this imbalance!)

The random effects model assumes that the 'study-specific' underlying effects follow a normal distribution, and so the reason that relatively more weight is given to smaller studies in a random effects analysis compared to fixed effects is that in this situation they contribute relatively more information about the (distribution of) underlying effects. In a fixed effects analysis, relatively more weight is given to the larger studies as they are more likely to be closer estimates of the one true underlying effect being estimated.

The choice of model is thus not straightforward, and when there is no obvious way of determining the right way forward, reviewers will often conduct the analysis with both models to report on both sets of results, thus giving greater emphasis to the one that is more appropriate in their judgement. (For further discussion see Hedges and Vevea 1998; Overton 1998.)

### Checking the robustness of the synthesis

The selection of statistical model, while important, is only one of the judgements that are required in a systematic review and meta-analysis. As depicted in Figure 9.3, one of the stages of synthesis is a check of its robustness. The questions outlined above in the section entitled 'How robust is the synthesis?' apply equally to a meta-analysis and there are two statistical techniques to employ at this point: sensitivity analysis and checks for publication bias.

Sensitivity analysis   Sensitivity analysis asks the question: 'how robust is my synthesis?' Many of the ways in which this is done are covered earlier in the chapter in the 'Stages of synthesis' section. Here we will cover the statistical methods for performing sensitivity analysis, which are concerned with the impact of individual studies, the selection of statistical model, the impact of the various assumptions made and whether studies of different types (e.g. methodological quality) have different results.

The investigation of the impact of individual studies is conducted by removing studies from the analysis one at a time and examining how this changes the results. Some software, such as Comprehensive Meta-analysis, has a function that supports this procedure and can produce a forest plot that shows what the pooled effect size would be if any one given study were removed.

As with any assessment of the real significance of an effect size (or in this case, in the difference of an effect size), whether or not these differences are important is a matter for reviewer judgement. In our example, the importance of a difference of 0.1 will vary from review to review (discussed below in 'Interpreting results'). This step is particularly important in meta-analyses with few studies as it may be that the results are overly dependent on a single atypical study. In this sense, a sensitivity analysis is part of an investigation of heterogeneity as well.

The impact of the selection of statistical model was illustrated in Figure 9.11. As well as accounting for why a particular model was selected, a sensitivity analysis of the difference can include an assessment of the relative weights accorded to individual studies. It is also important to evaluate the possible impact that assumptions in calculating effect sizes might have had on the meta-analysis. As discussed above, not all papers will present sufficient information to calculate an effect size accurately, and some statistics can be 'borrowed' from similar studies. As the imputed statistics may not be correct, it is usual to test the impact on the findings under a range of different assumptions. Findings that vary a lot when different assumptions are made need to be treated more cautiously than findings that are relatively stable.

Finally, sensitivity analysis sometimes assesses the consistency of findings between groups of studies, using the methods presented below in the section or 'Sub-group analysis'. When studies of differing methodological quality (or simply different characteristics) are included in the same analysis, reviewers will often check to see whether the findings vary between groups or are consistent. For example, sensitivity analyses will often check whether studies rated 'high' or 'medium' quality have the same results, or whether the results vary according to age and region.

While all these checks have the same limitations as outlined below, they are useful indicators to a reviewer that there may be unexplained issues in the dataset which will either undermine the rationale for combining studies statistically, or require further exploration and explanation.

Publication bias    The possibility that a review's results may be biased systematically due to the way that studies have been selected for publication cannot be ruled out, so checks are usually also made for *publication bias* (see Chapter 6). While none of the following will actually *determine* whether such a publication bias is present, positive results may be suggestive of a bias that requires additional investigation and special care should be taken when drawing conclusions.

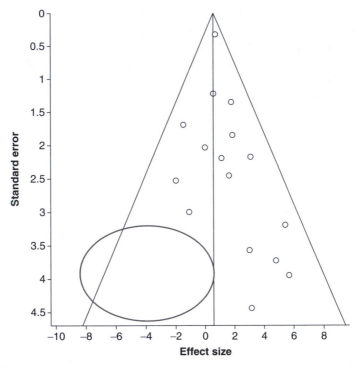

**Figure 9.12** Example of a funnel plot

First, there is the 'funnel plot' (Figure 9.12). These graphics plot the effect size (usually on the X-axis) against a measure of variance (usually the standard error on the Y-axis). The larger studies (with smaller standard errors) will be at the top of the plot and the smaller ones at the bottom. As the estimates of the 'true' effect size are more precise in larger studies, the results of these studies will be less dispersed than will be the case with the smaller studies. This should result in a scattering of dots which will form the shape of an inverted funnel that gets wider towards the bottom of the plot. If a publication bias is present, the dots will create an asymmetric funnel with part of the funnel missing: the area where the less positive studies *should* be, but are missing due to this bias. The missing studies are less likely to be published and thus tend to be smaller and have inconclusive or 'negative' findings.

While funnel plots are useful in theory, they are more suggestive than definitive in practice since many reviews will not have sufficient studies to judge visually whether or not a funnel is asymmetric. There are two statistical tests based on correlations (Begg and Mazumdar 1994) and linear regression (Egger et al. 1997), but both are considered to be underpowered. Additionally, even if the funnel plot or statistical tests do indicate assymetry, it is not possible to tell whether the results are due to this bias or something else. For example, it may be that the smaller studies in a given review are simply different in some ways compared to the larger ones. Duval and Tweedie (2000a, 2000b) suggested a way of 'filling in' the missing studies in a funnel plot by adding hypothetical studies to the analysis. While this method is not all that widespread in use, it can be a valuable aid in sensitivity analysis.

## Sub-group analysis and other configurative approaches in statistical reviews

The process of conducting a meta-analysis is rarely simply a matter of combining effect sizes from all the studies in the review. There are usually some analyses in which sub-sets of studies are analysed separately and compared to one another. This is an extension of the mode of synthesis, moving away from what can be conceptualised as an aggregative logic towards one that involves configuration as well. As discussed earlier, the conceptual framework (Figure 9.4) is an important driver for such analyses, since it provides a theoretical (and ideally an empirical) basis for the investigation of differences between studies. Thus, as well as using sub-group analyses to determine whether studies which were considered to be less strong methodologically have different results from the stronger ones, the results from different sub-sets of studies may be compared with one another according to, for example, different programme theories and specific population groups. The former analysis – examining study quality – is part of *checking the robustness* of the synthesis, whereas the latter – configuring findings according to the review's conceptual framework – can also be thought of as identifying *patterns in the data*.

Simple sub-group analyses, where one group of studies is being compared with another group, are fairly easy to conduct, and can be accomplished using a few formulae in widely-available spreadsheet software (such as Microsoft Excel). For example, such analyses are suitable to compare the results of randomised and non-randomised trials. Figure 9.13 depicts this, showing that the randomised control-led trials had a combined effect size of -0.5 whereas the pooled effect size of the non-randomised trials was +0.56. While these may seem to be quite different results, an examination of the forest plot might suggest the two sets of studies are not really all that different and, indeed, the statistical test actually shows that this difference is not significant ($p = 0.452$) and no heterogeneity (variance) is explained between studies using this particular sub-division. Please see Borenstein et al. (2009) for further detail on these types of analysis.

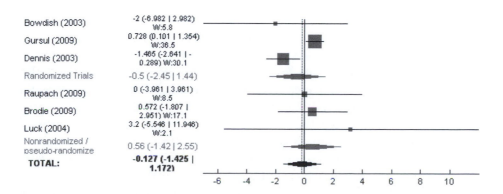

**Figure 9.13**  Sub-group analysis

More advanced analyses that compare multiple sub-groups of studies or assess the impact of one or more moderator variables on effect sizes, such as the theoretical basis for the intervention, can be carried out using meta-regression (Thompson and Sharp 1999), multilevel modelling (Goldstein and Yang 2000; Hox 2010) and Bayesian analysis (Sutton et al. 2000). Software that specifically supports these advanced techniques is needed, such as stata, SPSS, r, MLwiN (for multilevel analyses) or WinBugs (for Bayesian analyses). While conducting an analysis that involves the configuration of statistically pooled results is undoubtedly a demanding undertaking that requires specialist statistical input, it is an extremely powerful research tool. It combines the precision and statistical power that combining many studies can offer with the ability to investigate a multitude of research questions that would be unanswerable using traditional primary research methods (although please see the 'limitations' section below for a cautionary note about these kinds of analysis). Configurative meta-analysis can address both substantive and methodological research questions.

An example of a substantive question that has been addressed using these methods was an investigation into the impact of preventive interventions on inequalities in young people's health (Kavanagh et al. 2009a). While none of the studies in the review specifically addressed the question of whether the interventions had any impact on inequalities, the fact that they had been carried out across different socio-economic groups meant that we were able to categorise the populations of each study and then examine differences in findings between them. Ogilvie et al. 2008 have suggested the *harvest plot* as a way to depict the findings of these sorts of studies graphically.

The harvest plot (Figure 9.14) summarises the strength of evidence in each dimension:

> Each study is represented by a mark in each row for which that study had reported relevant results. Studies with 'hard' behavioural outcome measures are indicated with full-tone (black) bars, and studies with intermediate outcome measures with half-tone (grey) bars. The suitability of study design is indicated by the height of the bar. Each bar is annotated with the number of other methodological criteria (maximum six) met by that study. (Ogilvie et al. 2008)

In the same way, the methodological question of whether randomisation is associated with effect size was investigated in an analysis that compared the results of approximately 200 controlled trials (roughly half of which were randomised) (Oliver et al. 2010). The meta-regression was able to control for many other methodological factors that might confound the results, such as whether the interventions themselves and the circumstances in which they were developed were comparable, enabling the reviewers to determine whether, on average, randomisation is associated with larger, or smaller, effect sizes. (The answer was that 'it depends' and that in some situations randomisation might be associated with larger effect sizes (e.g. tightly controlled experiments) and in other situations with smaller effect sizes (e.g. field trials in some situations). Despite extensive analysis, no consistent explanation for these differences was identified.)

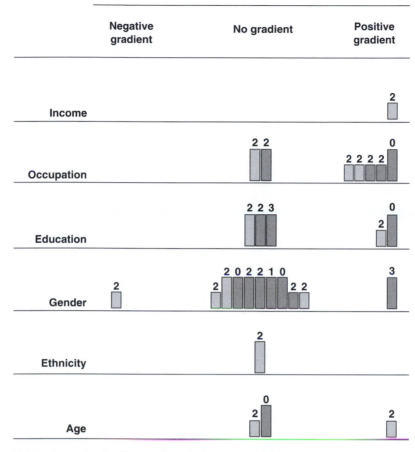

**Figure 9.14** Example of a Harvest Plot (Ogilvie et al. 2008)

The final example of configuration in a meta-analysis is a *cumulative* meta-analysis, showing how results can vary across time. As well as simply demonstrating how researchers may become more confident of the impact of a given intervention (because the estimate becomes more precise as more studies are conducted), these analyses also have the potential to tell us something about how researchers' perception of the phenomena of study changes, sometimes quite dramatically. Nykänen and Koricheva (2004) conducted a cumulative meta-analysis examining how woody plants responded to natural or simulated damage. Some of their results are presented in Figure 9.15, showing how the effects observed changed quite significantly over the years. Rather than concluding that they were observing a real change – that the response of woody plants to damage somehow varies across time – they suggest that their results may reveal paradigm shifts in researchers' theories about how plants respond to damage and/or that differences in research practice also explain the changes observed.

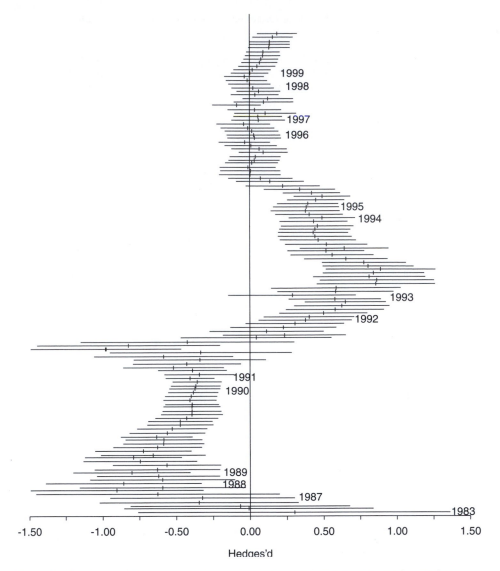

**Figure 9.15**   A cumulative meta-analysis, showing how effect sizes changed over time

## Limitations of configuration in meta-analysis

Sub-group analysis and the other configurative methods described above have one important limitation: they are *observational* in nature. In order to ascertain the impact of, for example, socio-economic status on the effectiveness of a given intervention, the ideal primary study would keep everything constant (outcomes, measurement tools, intervention, etc.) and randomly assign a socio-economic status to different groups. Since this is neither possible nor desirable, in order for a systematic review to answer this question we need to 'observe' the impact of socio-economic status operating across many different interventions in different settings. Even if our analysis is made up of randomised controlled trials, this sub-group analysis is not protected from selection bias by randomisation; it is an observational study, with all the limitations on causality that accompany such studies. This means, of course, that the limitation also applies to the conclusions drawn from the other configurative methods of synthesis – thematic synthesis and meta-ethnography, etc.

This serious limitation notwithstanding, observational studies are the only way of exploring the answers to some questions and these analyses have real value and provide the best evidence we have to answer some important questions. They suggest avenues for future exploration and have more credibility when supported by sound theoretical and empirical evidence.

## Synthesising economics evidence

The economic critique of much systematic review activity has been that systematic reviews of effectiveness are important, but they are also insufficient for policy and practice (Shemilt et al. 2008). Decision-makers do not have unlimited resources, and so require evidence that helps them choose between different 'effective' options. Thus, evidence on the potential costs of different decisions is needed alongside evidence on effectiveness in order that decisions can be taken that will make the most efficient use of the resources available.

The use of economics evidence to inform policy and practice has a long history outside systematic reviewing, employing, for example, cost-effectiveness analyses of interventions and the modelling of possible impacts under a range of assumptions (NICE 2008). Of increasing interest over recent years, however, has been the inclusion of economics evidence within systematic reviews (Lavis et al. 2005) with, for example, the establishment of the Campbell and Cochrane Economics Methods Group (CCEMG), which has a remit to promote and support the consideration of economics issues in systematic reviews.[5]

The optimal economics analysis (known as 'full economic evaluation') combines a consideration of the relative options in terms of outcomes (consequences) with an assessment of the most optimal choices in terms of costs (resources used) (Drummond et al. 2005). Such a goal is often outside the scope of many systematic reviews, both because the data are not available and also because such an analysis requires a full knowledge of the decision that the analysis will inform. For example, the conclusions of a full economic evaluation of the different options to reduce street crime might have very different conclusions in different countries because the contexts, costs and likely options will all vary so much. However, when the problem and context are known, these analyses are performed regularly, for example, informing many of the recommendations from the UK's National Institute for Health and Clinical Excellence (NICE).

---

[5]http://www.c-cemg.org/

Some full economic evaluations need to use a metric that enables them to compare all the costs and benefits of different treatments with one another. (Similar in principle to the way that the standardised mean difference enables meta-analysts to compare outcomes that have used different measurement tools.) The metric often used is the Quality Adjusted Life Year (QALY), which quantifies the potential additional quality and quantity of life to be gained from a specified treatment. The use of these measures can be controversial, as decisions about which treatment to recommend will depend on what can appear to be an arbitrary threshold of around £30,000 per QALY. Treatments with a cost per QALY above this are less likely to be recommended, and the QALY itself has been criticised as lacking an empirical base (Donaldson et al. 2011).

The line taken by the CCEMG is that other types of economic analysis, while not being full economic evaluations, are nevertheless valuable in informing decisions (Shemilt et al. 2008). (Indeed, as the Cochrane Library is aimed at an international audience, it would be impossible to ensure that full economic evaluations were relevant to all potential contexts anyway.) They make the important point that, even if it is unclear as to whether or not an intervention is effective, information about its resource requirements can be extremely useful in helping decision-makers understand the costs of proceeding with the intervention and also to determine whether existing full economic analyses are based on reliable evidence (Shemilt et al. 2008: 4). There is thus a need to carry out economics analyses that do not go as far as full economic evaluation.

There are three broad approaches to synthesising economics evidence: (1) reporting any costs or resources associated with implementing a given intervention; (2) carrying out a systematic review of effectiveness followed by an economic modelling analysis; and (3) systematically reviewing existing economic evaluations (CRD 2008: 201).

The CCEMG is currently promoting the first approach, as currently very few systematic reviews do this (e.g. Shemilt et al. 2006). This is potentially a missed opportunity since information about the resources required by different interventions is often available in reports and papers and it would be possible for reviewers to include this information as part of their routine data extraction (Chapter 7). One of the challenges of comparing the relative resources required by interventions is that studies included in a review will report their costs in a range of currencies and years. Methods for translating such estimates into a common currency and price year are required (Shemilt et al. 2010b).

The second approach involves two stages. First, a standard systematic review of effectiveness is carried out, identifying the balance of benefit or harm attributable to an intervention (or range of interventions). This information is then used to inform a 'decision model' (Briggs et al. 2006) which enables decision-makers to compare the relative costs and benefits of different interventions. Critical to such an analysis is determining the factors that should be included in the model (e.g. outcomes, population groups, etc.), the timeframe that the model will apply to (e.g. 5 or 10 or 50 years) and the viewpoint (or perspective) of the analysis (i.e. identifying the groups of people and organisations who will bear the costs and gain the benefits of intervening or not intervening in specified ways). This model of synthesis amounts to a full economic evaluation and is used by NICE, as mentioned above.

The third approach, while perhaps not as technically challenging as the second, is possibly the most demanding conceptually. While it seems sensible to apply the logic of systematic reviewing to existing economic evaluations (and, indeed, some reviewers have done so successfully), it is often impossible to standardise results across studies because they are so tied to specific contexts. These challenges have led some to conclude that such analyses are 'optimistic and generally futile' (Anderson 2010: 350), though methods to conduct such analyses are available, should the problem of extreme heterogeneity be surmountable in specific situations (CRD 2008).

A good place to start reading more on the issues and methods for synthesising economic evidence is *Evidence-based Decisions and Economics* (Shemilt et al. 2010a).

## Interpreting results

The final stage of a meta-analysis is understanding the meaning of the pooled effect size that is considered to be internally valid, that is, while we are left with a statistic that summarises, for example, the extent of benefit and harm that can be attributed to a given intervention according to a given outcome, what does this statistic mean to the potential user of the review? The problem of determining how results should be interpreted in order to draw scientifically interesting and reliable conclusions is a key problem in social science. In the context of systematic reviews of research on the effectiveness of interventions, the main concern is how to identify the likely degree of usefulness of a particular intervention, and this often involves transforming the effect size into a form that is more easily interpreted.

### *Transforming the effect size in the meta-analysis*

The translation of the results of individual studies into effect sizes enables a comparison of the results between studies and facilitates the production of a summary pooled estimate in a meta-analysis. However, effect sizes are not intuitive – they are just a number – and will require transformation into a metric or concept that is more easily understood. There are a number of ways that this can be done, depending on the type of effect size that has been produced in the meta-analysis and the intended use and audience for the review findings. Figure 9.16 summarises some of these approaches that we will describe in detail below. Binary effect sizes can be interpreted in the two ways depicted at the bottom right, and there

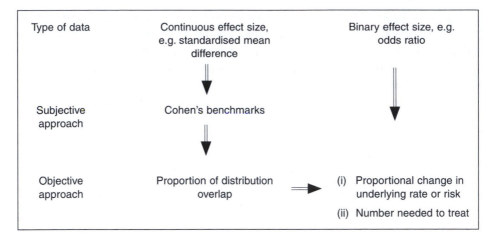

**Figure 9.16** Approaches to interpreting effect sizes

is no 'subjective' interpretation for this family of effect sizes. Continuous effect sizes can be interpreted using Cohen's benchmarks and the 'proportion of distribution overlap' method and can also move from this into the two interpretations available to binary effect sizes.

### From continuous data/standardised mean differences (and correlation effect sizes)

**1. Cohen's benchmarks**   This general approach labels standardised mean difference effect sizes of 0.2 to 0.3 'small', around 0.5 a 'medium' effect, and 0.8 to infinity a 'large' effect (Cohen 1988). (Also, for correlation effect sizes r = 0.1 is small; 0.3 is medium; and > 0.5 is large.) The main drawback of this approach is that it is context free: that is, it takes no account of the importance of the outcome or how many people it is likely to apply to; its likely applicability in the population; or the cost of achieving it.

For example, a comparatively cheap drug that reduces the risk of a very common illness but only by a 'small' amount may still have tremendous value when its effect is multiplied across the whole population at risk. A trial of aspirin was terminated early because it was unethical not to allow people in the control group to benefit – from an effect size of 0.03! (McCartney and Rosenthal 2000).

Because the labels used by Cohen (small, medium, large) inherently contain a value judgement (e.g. large = good), we can refer to this as the 'subjective' approach. Cohen himself said that these were very general guidelines, based on the sort of effect sizes found, on average, across the whole of social science and urged caution in their use in any specific application.

The other approaches outlined below do not contain an inherent value judgement and thus we can refer to these as 'objective' approaches.

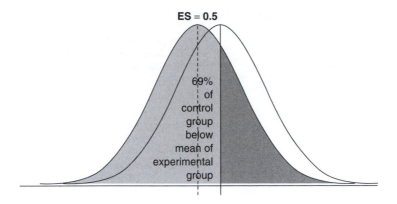

**Figure 9.17**    Interpreting effect sizes from distribution curves

**2. Proportion of difference overlap**    This approach uses the idea of 'standard deviation' to contextualise the difference between the two groups. Provided that the data have, or can be assumed to have, a normal distribution, effect sizes can be readily interpreted in terms of the amount of overlap between the two groups (as shown in Figure 9.17).

In Figure 9.17, the solid curve represents the distribution of test scores in the group that did not receive the intervention; the unshaded curve represents the distribution of test scores in the group that received the intervention. If the difference found between the two groups was a standardised mean difference of $d = 0.5$, the distribution of the two curves would look like Figure 9.17. The lighter shaded portion of the control group distribution curve represents the proportion of control group test scores that would be below the average intervention group test score represented by the solid line. Where there is a normal distribution for an effect size of $d = 0.5$, this will always be 69%. The proportion of the control group who would be below the average person in the experimental group given different standardised mean differences can be simply read from a table, as depicted in Table 9.1 (the higher the score, the better the intervention). This was also proposed by Cohen and he called it $U3$.

**3. Meaningful metric method**    Another approach that can be used where we have some data about the underlying frequency of occurrence of the outcome that has been measured is to apply the effect size (by doing some simple arithmetic) to the figures to estimate how they would change. This can be done using effect sizes calculated from both continuous (following Coe's method outlined above) and binary data.

**From binary data**    When the pooled estimate of effect has been calculated using binary data and there is a measure of an underlying risk base, it is possible to

**Table 9.1**  Conversion of effect sizes to percentiles

| Effect size | Percentage of control group who would be below average person in experimental group |
|---|---|
| 0.0 | 50% |
| 0.1 | 54% |
| 0.2 | 58% |
| 0.3 | 62% |
| 0.4 | 66% |
| 0.5 | 69% |
| 0.6 | 73% |
| 0.7 | 76% |
| 0.8 | 79% |
| 0.9 | 82% |
| 1.0 | 84% |
| 1.2 | 88% |
| 1.4 | 92% |
| 1.6 | 95% |
| 1.8 | 96% |
| 2.0 | 98% |
| 2.5 | 99% |
| 3.0 | 99.9% |

calculate what the change in this base rate would be if the effect size was applied. To do this, the effect size used would need to be a pooled estimate of risk difference. The estimate of risk difference in an individual study is the risk of the undesirable outcome in the intervention group minus the risk of the undesirable outcome in the control group. The resulting 'risk differences' from each of the individual studies are then combined using meta-analysis. Most meta-analysis software that computes effect sizes based on binary data will offer this option.

Here is a worked example:

- The risk of reoffending without any intervention is 24% in any one year (baseline risk).
- An intervention for offenders aimed at reducing reoffending produced a pooled risk difference of 0.129 (or 13%).
- The reduction in the risk of reoffending with the intervention would therefore be 0.24*0.13 = roughly 3%.

So, all other things being equal, the application of this intervention to all offenders would result in the annual rate for reoffending being reduced to roughly 21%.

Another way of expressing this is called the Number Needed to Treat ('treat' because it was first used in health research). This is the reciprocal of the risk difference and can be used to provide the estimate in a different way.

Using the example above:

- 1/Risk difference = 1/13 = 0.07.
- This is interpreted as '7 offenders would need to receive this intervention in order to prevent one offender from re-offending'. (See Shah 1995: 388, for more about this process.)

**From continuous data**   Where the same continuous outcome measure is used in the individual studies and thus in the meta-analysis (such as mmhg in the measurement of blood pressure), then the interpretation of the meta-analysis result is more straightforward provided that the underlying measurement scale is understood. (For example, 'how important is a 40mmhg difference in blood pressure?'). However, as we have noted already, studies do not always use exactly the same outcome measurement tool, or that what appear to be similar outcome measures (e.g. crime rate) are sometimes constructed and measured in different ways. In these circumstances, we use the standardised mean difference to convert our disparate results on to the same scale (discussed earlier). However, this is a non-dimensional measure, meaning that the statistic itself has no easily interpretable meaning.

One way we can interpret a standardised mean difference is by using the 'proportion of difference overlap' method outlined by Coe above, comparing effect sizes with other data that have effect sizes with which we are familiar. The example given by Coe (2002) is the distribution of examination (GCSE) grades in compulsory subjects (Maths and English) in UK secondary schools. These have standard deviations of between 1.5 and 1.8 grades, so an improvement of one GCSE grade represents an effect size of 0.5 – 0.7 (i.e. 1/standard deviation). Therefore, in the context of a UK secondary school, introducing a change in practice whose effect size was known to be 0.6 would be likely to result in an improvement of about one GCSE grade for each pupil in each subject.

## Conclusion

This chapter has detailed methods for configuring and aggregating the results of studies in a synthesis. It has described a range of non-statistical methods that operate along a continuum between many and few pre-specified categories (or themes). The selection of the appropriate model in a statistical meta-analysis depends upon the amount of heterogeneity between included studies. However, moving to a random effects model gives the larger studies relatively less weight, which may not always be desirable. While this chapter has covered a wide area, there is far more material concerned with synthesising research findings than there has been space to encompass. The many references give the reader some essential sources of further reading.

| Box 9.1 |

## The practicalities

- The principles outlined within the *stages of synthesis* should be considered for all types of synthesis.
- Statistical and non-statistical methods of synthesis follow the same principles, being concerned with the systematic aggregation of findings and the exploration and explanation of heterogeneity through configuration.
- There is a range of non-statistical methods for synthesis and the selection of method depends on whether the synthesis is to apply existing categorisations and conceptualisations to the studies or to generate new theory:

  - If you have a well-developed conceptual framework, then following the stages of synthesis and presenting results in a *thematic summary* may be appropriate.
  - If you have a pre-existing framework, but would like the flexibility to adapt it during synthesis, then a *framework synthesis* may suit your needs.
  - If the purpose of your review is to develop new theories and conceptualisations, then a *thematic synthesis* and *meta-ethnography* can offer methods that may be suitable.

- There is a range of statistical methods of synthesis. If it is not possible to carry out a meta-analysis, then care should be taken to avoid some of the common pitfalls in 'vote counting' results.
- As well as effectiveness, decision-makers often need to know the resource implications of different decisions. Collecting such data is practicable and useful in systematic reviews, though synthesising existing economic evaluations can be problematic.
- Once a final pooled effect size has been calculated, there are several ways of presenting this statistic in order to make it more meaningful to review users.

# TEN

## Making a difference with systematic reviews

*Ruth Stewart and Sandy Oliver*

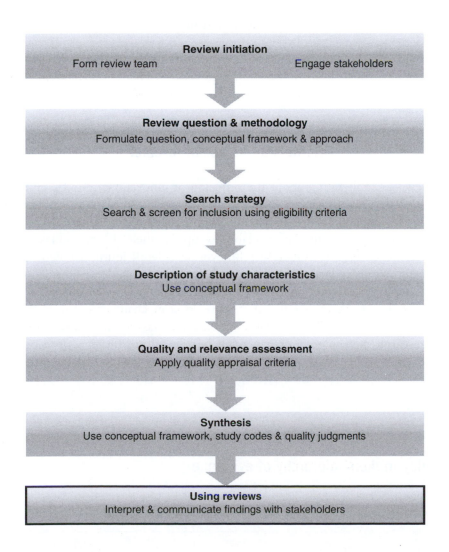

---

### Aims of chapter

This chapter considers three models for understanding how research findings come to be used in wider society by focusing on:

- The role of research for decisions – the instrumental model
- The role of research for understanding – the enlightenment model
- The role of research within a complex system – the interactional model and systems thinking

Finally, it describes institutional efforts to support the use of research and, conversely, provides a reminder of the use of policy and practice for guiding research

---

## Introduction

This chapter is about communicating systematic reviews to those well placed to make use of them. It starts by considering the broader issues of research use before addressing the communication of systematic review findings.

## Barriers to the use of research

A review of the literature about the diffusion of innovations found a myriad of barriers to the use of research (Nutley and Davies 2000). Many researchers lack the skills for communication beyond their immediate sphere and, until recently, there was little time or funding available to support their efforts, and less professional credit for disseminating research beyond academic journals. Potential users of research similarly lack the time to look for research and consider it in their work. There is poor communication of research within organisations; it is often perceived as not timely or relevant, controversial or challenging the status quo, and a threat to 'craft skills' and professional experience. Many organisations fail to value research, or even harbour an actively hostile culture. Other sources of information tend to be valued more, especially by some policy-makers – research attracts relatively little of their attention (see Box 10.1).

---

### Box 10.1

## Policy-makers' hierarchy of evidence

- 'Experts' evidence (including consultants and think tanks)
- Opinion-based evidence (including lobbyists/pressure groups)

- Ideological 'evidence' (party think tanks, manifestos)
- Media evidence
- Internet evidence
- Lay evidence (constituents', citizens' experiences)
- 'Street' evidence (urban myths, conventional wisdom)
- Research evidence

*Source*: Davies (2007)

Although systematic reviewers have made great achievements in scrutinising and summarising mountains of research, review reports still remain firmly in academia unless efforts are made to share their findings with the outside world. Indeed, it takes a combination of issues for policy analysts to consult scientific articles, academic research reports or academic books or chapters (including access to electronic bibliographic databases, appropriate training or continuing professional development and perceived relevance of research evidence), although the most strongly associated factor seems to be personal contact with researchers (Ouimet et al. 2010).

### The role of research for decisions (instrumental model)

The history of events leading up to the lowering of the legal limit of blood alcohol for drivers in the USA demonstrates the use of evidence in a policy decision (see Box 10.2). Initially, when civil servants sought relevant research and reviewed individual studies unsystematically, they concluded that there was no convincing evidence that introducing blood alcohol limits laws would reduce alcohol-related crashes. A subsequent systematic review aggregated the evidence and concluded that introducing legal limits could reduce alcohol-related traffic fatalities by 7%, potentially saving around 500 lives a year. This led to Congress exercising financial levers to encourage states to introduce legal limits.

| **Box 10.2** |

## A timeline of decision-making in the US Congress in the late 1990s

- 'Overall, the evidence does not conclusively establish that [blood alcohol limit] laws, by themselves, result in reductions in the number and severity of alcohol-related crashes' (General Accounting Office 1999).

*(Continued)*

---

*(Continued)*

- Report seen as favouring the alcohol industry.
- A subsequent systematic review (Shults et al. 2001) suggested such laws could be expected to drop alcohol-related traffic fatalities by about 7%, saving about 500 lives a year.
- 'When you looked at all of the data, aggregated into the same table, it became very clear that whatever problems the studies had, they were all coming to roughly the same conclusion' (Randy Elder, scientific director of the Community Guide).
- Findings sent to federal legislators.
- Congress then withheld federal highway construction funds from states that did not pass such laws.

*Source*: Sweet and Moynihan (2007)

---

Although other details are discussed later in the chapter, the brief history of events outlined in Box 10.2 encourages the use of methods to synthesise the full body of evidence; the use of a recognised, credible and impartial process for assessing the evidence; and the development of evidence-based policy recommendations by an independent, impartial body (Mercer et al. 2010).

## The role of research for understanding (enlightenment model)

Research offers policy and practice more than evidence for informing decisions; it offers understanding too. The enlightenment model eschews the notion that research impacts are simple and instrumental in effect. Instead, research is seen to impact through 'the gradual sedimentation of insight, theories, concepts and perspectives' (Davies et al. 2005). Weiss (1991: 313) drew on a series of studies to conclude that 'research as data' has limited influence. Rather, ideas from research will alter how policy-makers perceive problems, permeate their understanding and become absorbed into conventional wisdom.

This is illustrated by a story, which spans 20 years, about a significant change in policy concerning treatment for tuberculosis. Clinical wisdom throughout the twentieth century recommended patients being watched as they took their medicines, as an effective treatment for tuberculosis, either in hospital or in the community. This practice was endorsed by a World Health Organisation (WHO) expert committee in the mid-1970s and short courses of directly observed therapy (DOTS) were hailed by the WHO Director General as the health breakthrough of the late 1990s (Smith 1999). Approaching the millennium, the broader tuberculosis strategy, with five key components (a government commitment to sustained TB control activities; case detection by sputum smear microscopy among symptomatic patients self-reporting to health services; a standardised treatment regime of 6–8 months for all confirmed sputum smear positive cases with directly

observed treatment for at least the initial two months; a regular uninterrupted supply of all essential anti-TB drugs; and a standardised recording and reporting system
that allowed an assessment of the treatment results for each patient and the TB
control programme overall), was branded by part of a single component: DOTS.

Despite doubts about patient respect and effectiveness already being acknowledged, DOTS was seen as central to clinical care: 'writing a prescription for the
best anti-tuberculosis medicines in the world without ensuring that the patient
takes them is pointless and irresponsible' (Smith 1999). The findings of a randomised trial that a direct observation of patients is alienating and authoritarian,
and that self-supervision was as good or better than supervision by health workers,
relatives or neighbours (Zwarenstein et al. 1998), were confidently dismissed as
an example of doing DOTS badly (Smith 1999). However, Zwarenstein's findings
were confirmed by a systematic review in 2001 (Volmink and Garner 2007). A
groundswell of critiques portrayed DOTS as insufficient for addressing a complex
bio-social problem which needed more than just a medical solution and, worse, as
showing a lack of trust towards patients and their families (Harper 2009).

Qualitative studies were being conducted throughout the lifetime of DOTS. These
played a crucial role in influencing policy when two teams conducted separate qualitative reviews and reached the same conclusions. They used different synthesis
approaches as exemplars for the Cochrane Qualitative Methods Group to demonstrate the added value of qualitative evidence syntheses for policy-makers. A meta-
ethnography described how 'four major factors interact to affect adherence to TB
treatment: structural factors, including poverty and gender discrimination; the social
context; health service factors; and personal factors' (Munro et al. 2007: 1230). A
thematic synthesis highlighted the key role of social and economic factors and the
physical side-effects of medication in shaping behaviour in relation to seeking a diagnosis
and adhering to treatment, and concluded that observation within a supportive relationship was more likely to be effective than mere inspection (Noyes and Popay 2007).

The findings were not immediately welcomed by those convinced of the value
of the DOTS component of the global branded policy (Noyes personal communication). It took two decades of debate between clinicians, policy-makers and
researchers, from the time concerns were first expressed about how patients
might perceive directly observed therapy to when this understanding was widely
acknowledged. Guidelines now refer to the qualitative syntheses to justify greater
flexibility and less of an emphasis on health professionals observing patients taking their medicines (Ministerio de Sanidad, Politica Social e Igualdad 2010; WHO
2010a; NICE 2011). Without the qualitative syntheses, the shift in policy presumably
would have taken longer. Since then, the Cochrane Collaboration has been committed to integrating qualitative evidence with selected, relevant Cochrane interventions,
reviews and the *Cochrane Handbook* outlines the principles and processes for doing
so (Noyes et al. 2011). This change has been broadly welcomed by policy-makers
(Noyes personal communication), who have recognised the value of qualitative synthesis, particularly for implementing policy (WHO 2010a). Considerable effort now
focuses not only on what the research is used for, but also on how it is used.

## How research is used: linear, relationship and systems models

A push-pull model describes a simple link between research and decision-making where reliable evidence is either offered by researchers or sought by decision-makers. The classic, knowledge-driven model (push) describes a linear view that research findings may be communicated to impel action. The problem-solving, policy/ practice-driven model (pull) reverses this linear view to begin with the end-users of research and the problems they face, before tracking back in search of useful findings.

It is now increasingly common for researchers to make efforts to reach policy-makers and practitioners, 'pushing' their products across the gap. And some policy-makers and practitioners make complementary efforts to reach research products, 'pulling' them into their own domain. Most commonly, researchers 'push' their research findings by publishing their work, not only in academic journals, but also in practitioner journals and via professional conferences. However, this approach to bridging the gap is limited to the researchers' skills in communicating to non-academic audiences, even assuming that what they have to communicate is of relevance to their audiences, and is accessed and understood by these audiences.

Where policy-makers and practitioners actively seek out relevant evidence – creating 'pull' – the communication of research across the divide may meet their needs. This can be as simple as requests for evidence from academics in the relevant field, or go as far as commissioning specific research projects to answer questions of importance to them. Even then, this pull can still be misunderstood by researchers and the knowledge provided in response may not be timely or fit for purpose, while those making the request may not know what to ask for or how. Policy-makers and practitioners can also 'push' information to the research community by disseminating questions to which they want answers, or communicating their priorities and preferences more generally. This should enable academics to produce research that is more timely, relevant and accessible. Researchers can also seek out this information themselves, 'pulling' knowledge from the policy and practice side of the divide. Thus evidence-based policy and practice is complemented by policy- or practice-informed research.

This model of 'bridging the gap' between research and policy and practice by 'pushing' and 'pulling' information across the divide has a number of limitations, not least the over-simplification of two camps of 'research' and of 'policy and practice', and of their knowledge as 'research evidence' and of 'policy and practice needs'. The reality of complex relationships between many communities of practice engaged in knowledge production and use is glossed over. While the 'push' and 'pull' options allow for both sides to play a role, there is no scope within the model for dialogue or an ongoing relationship. The two sides are seen as different and the gap between them as something which must be overcome. There is no suggestion of narrowing the gap, or of working at the boundaries of the different communities, only of exchanging parcels of knowledge between them.

The emergence of the patients' perspectives on tuberculosis treatment described above also illustrates the idea of a 'knowledge transfer', which goes some way towards overcoming the shortcomings of a linear understanding of bridging the research–policy gap. A 'knowledge transfer' describes the process of information being shared through the interactions between many groups. Originating in the field of organisation learning, this concept focuses on the organisation and distribution of knowledge. It acknowledges that information can be both explicit and tacit, and that it is often held by individuals, not just groups. It focuses on the principle that tacit knowledge is only accessible within communities and needs to be identified and made explicit in order to be shared.[1] As such, it is used to describe the process by which people are able to transfer knowledge to one another. Opinion leaders can be effective in promoting the use of evidence within their own networks (Flodgren et al. 2007). Networks may be particularly successful because they allow the sharing of tacit knowledge – informal, context-specific know-how – as well as explicit knowledge. Even an informal email network can help bridge the gap between research and practice. The CHAIN (Contact, Help, Advice and Information Network) network for Effective Health Care served as 'a rich source of information, providing access to members' experiences, suggestions, and ideas, and facilitating cross-boundary collaboration so that *ad hoc* groupings and communities of practice emerged spontaneously as members discovered common areas of interest' (Russell et al. 2004).

However, this knowledge transfer does not explicitly recognise that knowledge is itself complex and evolving and changes further when it is shared between individuals. Knowledge transforms as it passes between people; that new knowledge is formulated through dialogue is acknowledged in the theory of 'knowledge translation' (Straus et al. 2009). This idea builds on the concepts of 'bridging the gap' and of a 'knowledge transfer' within the literature. Knowledge translation is a more dynamic process and individuals within the process are attributed with accumulating, developing and implementing ideas (Graham et al. 2006). A more recent concept of 'knowledge intermediation' goes one step further, acknowledging that there is an ongoing and interactive relationship between different knowledge as it is communicated, interpreted and applied, allowing scope for the complexities of the process (Davies et al. 2008).

Levin (2004) summarises these theories of knowledge translation in terms of the context of research production, the context of research use, and the connections and interactions between them and suggests there are a number of factors which will mediate between these, enabling, or preventing, effective communication and use of knowledge. These factors include the media as well as bodies committed to debating, summarising and publishing knowledge.

While definitions and terminology vary across the literature, with additional terms such as 'knowledge brokerage', 'knowledge mobilisation', 'mediation' and 'knowledge into action', and a range of overlapping frameworks (Wilson et al. 2010), these different theories build on one another to describe sharing, creating and applying knowledge across communities (Graham et al. 2006).

Alongside developing ideas about the transfer, translation and intermediation of knowledge, a new professional role is beginning to gain recognition: one of knowledge translators, knowledge brokers, boundary spanners or change facilitators. Despite the

---

[1]Government of Alberta www.chr.alberta.ca/

array of terminology, these are individuals who have within their remit the facilitation of knowledge sharing and creation across traditional boundaries. Examples include researchers recruited to work within policy contexts to develop evidence-informed practice, and public involvement managers whose role it is to ensure research reflects the priorities and experiences of the public. Increasingly, secondments facilitate opportunities to work the other side of the policy–research interface.

Returning to the story of the blood limit alcohol limit, a detailed retrospective investigation found more complex interactions than might be apparent from the formal records alone (Mercer et al. 2010). Evidence was readily translated into policy because the issue was important to policy-makers and they could easily understand the intervention (the blood alcohol limit), and see the link between the problem, the intervention and the health outcomes. The evidence was offered to the policy-makers in a particularly timely manner: before their vote, but with little time to cast doubt on the findings or recommendations. Key partners and intended users were engaged throughout the process. The evidence was presented concisely, with a clear graphic, and delivered in person. Multiple stakeholders were engaged in an ongoing campaign, prompting a systematic review and use of the findings.

Knowledge moving across boundaries through individual careers, working relationships and formal structures was also a feature of the journey of DOTS: from the nineteenth-century hospitalisation of patients, doctors adopting it in their primary care practice (but not their private practice) across developed and developing countries, to trialists, public health officers, qualitative researchers, and national and international guidelines developers.

This degree of complexity, where circumstances, events and individuals are interrelated in so many ways that any change can have far-reaching consequences, is captured well by 'systems thinking'. This degree of interactivity between individuals, organisations and time, when applied to knowledge translation, recognises dynamic, interdependent and adaptive systems (such as individuals, organisations and communities), where understanding the roles and interactions of key stakeholders and how they respond to the system is crucial to understanding change (Best and Holmes 2010). Understanding of the system from any particular perspective is limited, which is why systems methods for developing and evaluating interventions start with convening a group of relevant stakeholders (de Savigny and Adam 2009).

---

| Box 10.3 |

## Turning knowledge into action

### 'Linear', push–pull models

- 'Knowledge is seen as a product' to be offered or sought
- 'Effective communication' is essential

Helpful for planning or understanding change when:

- requirements for the easy diffusion of innovations are met ('high relative advantage, low complexity, low risks and costs, and easily trialled');
- supported by 'strong institutional structures and resources', a 'supportive culture and incentives' for changing behaviour.

### Relationship models

- Close collaboration between generating and using knowledge
- Shared ideas and mutual learning are central

Helpful for planning or understanding change when:

- local context and knowledge are seen as legitimate for influencing evidence-informed decisions;
- the 'organisational culture favours evidence informed … decision-making';
- complex problems require changes in systems to support the change of individuals;
- support is available for 'two-way communication and close collaboration'.

### Systems models

- Complex, adaptive systems nested within other interdependent systems
- Change effected through interrelated stakeholders with various roles

Helpful for planning or understanding change when:

- all the key stakeholders can play a role in understanding problems and seeking solutions;
- organisations invest time and resources;
- knowledge translation activities are seen as important and are merged with organisational change strategies.

(Adapted from Best and Holmes 2010)

## Organisational support for knowledge systems

Evidence-informed policy-making is so established that national and international organisations provide support for different elements of the system. Support for the generation of evidence in collaboration with stakeholders exists nationally and internationally (see Chapter 2). The Cochrane Collaboration advocates involving health service providers, practitioners and patients in the conduct of systematic reviews. Similarly, the Campbell Collaboration encourages review authors to seek and incorporate the views of policy-makers, practitioners and users of public services.

Appropriate use of reviews requires accurate reporting that reflects on the findings in light of the related literature, current trends and relevant theories. Formal guidelines exist for reporting specific types of research. Advice on the initial reporting of research is available from the EQUATOR network (Enhancing the QUAlity and Transparency

**Table 10.1** Sources of systematic reviews

| Source | Scope of reviews |
|---|---|
| The Campbell Library[1] The Cochrane Library[2] (requires a subscription) | www.campbellcollaboration.org/library.php Health care interventions Health technology assessments Economic evaluations |
| CASE database of research on culture and sport engagement[3] | Engagement in culture and sport: studies since 1997, systematic reviews keyworded |
| Centre for Reviews and Dissemination Databases[4] | Health care interventions Economic evaluations Health technology assessments |
| EPPI-Centre: DoPHER[5] | Effects of promoting health |
| Health Systems Evidence[6] | Governance, financial and delivery arrangements within health systems, and about implementation strategies that can support change in health systems |
| JBI COnNECT+[7] | Clinical Online Network of Evidence for Care and Therapeutics |
| UK Education Evidence Portal[8] | Education |

1   www.campbellcollaboration.org/library.php

2   www.thecochranelibrary.com (requires a subscription)

3   http://eppi.ioe.ac.uk/webdatabases/Intro.aspx?ID=19

4   www.crd.york.ac.uk/crdweb/

5   http://eppi.ioe.ac.uk/webdatabases/Intro.aspx?ID=2

6   www.healthsystemsevidence.org/

7   http://connect.jbiconnectplus.org/ (requires a subscription)

8   www.eep.ac.uk/dnn2/Home/tabid/36/Default.aspx

Of health Research).[2] It includes reporting tools for quantitative and qualitative primary research, and for aggregative systematic reviews of interventions.[3] Although there is less agreement about how to report qualitative information, research shows that people perceive risk reductions to be larger and more persuasive when the effects are presented as a proportion rather than as a simple difference (Akl et al. 2011). Care in presenting findings, and ensuring that the conclusions accurately reflect those findings, is particularly important as professionals can struggle to generate appropriate conclusions from systematic reviews, even following training (Lai et al. 2011).

The second step is making the reports publicly accessible. Increasingly detailed reports can be found on the World Wide Web, either as grey literature or in Open Access journals. Finding these is made easier by organisations that appraise the quality of reviews and make them available through publicly accessible databases or search engines (see Table 10.1).

A valuable route for searching several high-quality health and social care sources simultaneously, whatever model of research use is being employed, is NHS

[2]www.equator-network.org

[3]www.prisma-statement.org

Evidence.[4] This aims to provide access to the 'best clinical and non-clinical information and best practice, both what high quality care looks like and how to deliver it'.[5]

Systematic research syntheses provide a shortcut to the evidence, but they are
not the whole answer and they need to be combined with different types of
knowledge when being applied to problems. There are initiatives which seek to
formalise procedures for identifying and making use of different types of knowledge in guiding decisions. A systematic search and analysis of the literature, supported by fieldwork seminars and interviews (together presented as a systematic
'knowledge review') characterised three broad approaches (Walter et al. 2004):

1  The evidence-based practitioner model, in which individual practitioners are trained to
   access and appraise evidence to inform their practice. The Critical Appraisal Skills
   Programme (CASP) provides training to individuals to help develop 'evidence-based
   practitioners'.[6]
2  The embedded model, when policy-makers take responsibility for incorporating research
   evidence into organisational processes and procedures. The National Institute for Health
   and Clinical Excellence (NICE) employs an embedded model, convening multi disciplinary
   groups to collect and review a wide range of evidence, including systematic reviews. These
   groups develop the national guidelines which drive standards across the UK's National
   Health Service (NHS). At an international level, as part of the SUPPORT project (SUPporting
   POlicy-relevant Reviews and Trials), researchers have worked with key policy-makers in low
   and middle income countries to develop tools to support processes that ensure relevant
   research is identified, appraised and used appropriately to inform health policy-making.[7]
3  The organisational excellence model, where evidence is used to inform decisions at a local
   organisational level. A multi-agency, research-based key worker service for families with
   disabled children within two local authority (Sloper et al. 1999) was recognised as an
   example of organisational excellence with its planning and implementation supported by
   a research team, opportunities for shared learning, time for reflection, managerial commitment and good co-ordination (Walter et al. 2004).

The embedded model and the organisational excellence model both involve
multidisciplinary, participatory and problem-based approaches to facilitate the
use of research knowledge in decision-making, with all stakeholders engaged and
enabled to contribute to the process (Stewart 2007).

Although systematic reviews are sometimes portrayed as a time-saver (because
they require less time to read than the relevant individual studies), in reality
the time allocated by practitioners or policy-makers is unlikely to be changed. The
benefit is not time-saving, but drawing on a broader research base within the
same time. Systematic reviews are also portrayed as a time-saver because they

[4]www.evidence.nhs.uk

[5]http://collectionseuroparchive.org

[6]www.phru.nhs.uk/casp/casp.htm

[7]www.support-collaboration.org/

are quicker (and cheaper) to do than a new primary study. In reality, whilst they are sometimes quicker and cheaper than some primary studies, the benefit of systematic reviews is in avoiding primary studies that are unnecessary or fail to build on current knowledge. Some of the cost saving comes from relying on a multitude of volunteers who, with relatively little institutional support, produce thousands of systematic reviews for the Cochrane Collaboration (although volunteers are rarely quick with their work). Urgency is a feature of many policy decisions. Partial solutions have been found with commissioning reviews from experienced teams to inform specific policy decisions. Another solution is systematic reviews of systematic reviews, but this clearly only works in research areas already well reviewed. Lastly, 'rapid evidence assessments' (see Chapter 3), where methods take systematic shortcuts, appeal to the policy-makers' timetable, but less to their wish for a sound evidence base. One government department encouraged 'rapid evidence assessments' with methods that showed few, if any, shortcuts, while another government department expected results within six months but avoided the label 'rapid evidence assessments'. Whatever the timescale, the close involvement of stakeholders helps the review team engage with their specific issues, and allows those same stakeholders to act on the emerging findings before they are published.

---

### Box 10.4

## Negotiating the challenge of time for policy-relevant reviews

1  A rapid systematic review of systematic reviews (Caird et al. 2010) completed within three months informed the work of the Prime Minister's Commission on the Future of Nursing and Midwifery.
2  Emerging findings from an equity analysis of a Cochrane systematic review (72 RCTs) of smoking cessation in pregnancy informed the NICE Guidance on quitting smoking in pregnancy and following childbirth before the work was completed.
3  Three months was sufficient for a 'what works?' review narrowly-focused with concepts about mental health and employment that resonated with the stakeholders and had a strong research tradition, which made identifying relevant studies easier and quicker. The funders facilitated the access to electronic publications and data extraction was very concise (Underwood et al. 2007).
4  A five-month review on the impact of microfinance on the poor in sub-Saharan Africa has contributed to policy debates at a crucial time of crisis in the industry (Stewart et al. 2010a).

---

All the examples of institutional support detailed in Box 10.4 contribute to an international system for the production and use of research. This is illustrated in Figure 10.1 as an extension of Levin's (2004) model, and chimes with the systems thinking of Best and Holmes (2010) to include the breadth of stakeholder engagement, the system level, and the study of evidence production and use (Gough et al. 2011).

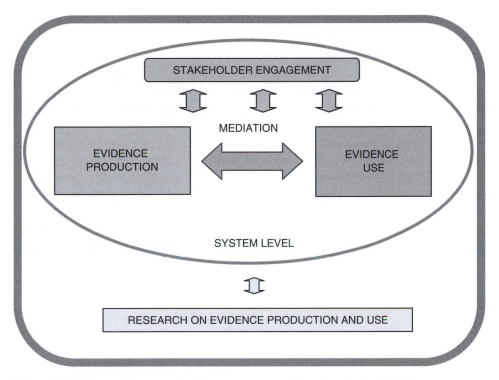

**Figure 10.1** The evidence production to use system (from Gough et al., 2011)

At an international level, a systems approach to supporting the generation and use of evidence is taken by the Alliance for Health Policy and Systems Research (de Savigny and Adam 2009). An example of institutional support for such a system was the commissioning of the UK Newborn Screening Programme Centre. This employed a participative model of public and practitioner involvement in evidence-informed policy to create a collaborative network for the development of a national newborn blood spot screening policy in the United Kingdom (Stewart et al. 2011).

The final element of this system is research about the production and use of evidence. This chapter has already drawn on the outputs of the Research Unit for Research Utilisation,[8] which facilitates research and hosts a research database about the interactions between research and the policy process, service organisations and professional practice (for a recent review, see Nutley et al. 2010). A similar centre at the University of Toronto, 'Research Supporting Practice in Education', is about knowledge mobilisation in education to bring about improved educational experiences for educators and students across Canada.[9] The Evidence-based Health Policy Project at the University of Wisconsin works much more

---

[8]www.ruru.ac.uk/

[9]www.oise.utoronto.ca/rspe/

closely with politicians to enable the 'pull' of research to inform policy.[10] The Canadian Health Services Research Foundation[11] has a broader strategy that engages citizens in the design, delivery, evaluation and quality improvement of health services; accelerates evidence-informed change; and promotes policy dialogue. Guidelines are also available for researchers (Ward et al. 2010). The Evidence Informed Policy and Practice Initiative[12] is reaching across Europe to bring together examples of the range of activities for linking research results with education policy-making – and mapping the relevant European research – before recommending next steps for developing research to policy links and research on this topic across Europe. Working in the same sector is the Coalition for Evidence-Based Education (CEBE), an alliance of researchers, policy-makers and practitioners who are interested in improving the way research evidence is used, and exchanged, across the sector.[13] Their recent systematic review concludes that there is strong evidence of links between teacher engagement in and with research and significant changes in practice, with a positive impact on student outcomes (Bell et al. 2011).

## The practicalities of communicating research

Essential for any system linking policy and research is clear communication between the different stakeholders, whether it is communicating the findings of research, or preparing materials to support research use. A writing team benefits from having members who are familiar with the information to be communicated and having members familiar with groups of people to be reached. Together they can make decisions about the content, style and medium of communication for reaching people who may be interested in different aspects of the research.

However, it is important that the style and medium do not allow for misinterpretation or misunderstanding. In keeping with the principles of systematic research synthesis of transparency and completeness, any summaries of research should signpost where the full report can be found. Increasingly popular in policy circles is the 1-3-25 approach to getting a message across. This includes three formats of 1 page, 3 pages and 25 pages for readers looking for different degrees of detail. However, following feedback to the EPPI-Centre suggesting that there was insufficient difference between 1 and 3 pages, we amended our communication policy to a summary of 1–3 pages (a quick introduction and clear set of key messages); a report of about 20 pages (to consider the issues in depth, and discuss the evidence, its strength, limitations and implications); a full technical report or appendix which may reach about 100 pages (which is a 'reference book' containing

---

[10]www.evidencebasedhealthpolicy.org/

[11]www.chsrf.ca/)

[12]www.eipee.eu/

[13]www.cebenetwork.org/

all the details necessary for ensuring transparency and updating); and the coded studies publicly accessible in searchable databases on the World Wide Web (providing details of studies that differ in their precise focus and context).

The audience determines not only the content and detail of information, but also where the information is to be presented. While researchers are rewarded for publications in academic journals, other outlets may be more influential for policy and practice. This might include professional publications, academic journals, magazines or discussion forums. Such outlets will have their own preferences for style, language and length. The alternative of publishing 'in-house' requires professional design and type-setting skills to ensure the publication is sufficiently attractive to readers, and the resources to support paper or electronic publishing.

Hard-copy publications have the advantage of literally being in someone's hands or on their desk. It is also common for reports to be published in hard copy for a specific circulation (often on completion of a project) and then made available in the longer term online. Online publication is particularly useful when publishing a large volume of work, or for reaching a wide audience. Online publication avoids large print-runs and can be reached throughout the world by anyone with internet access. Reducing the download time where possible is particularly important for reaching audiences in developing countries or individual readers in their homes who may not have access to high-speed internet connections. This publishing route is becoming a common medium for publishing full technical reports for reasons of transparency.

Online publication can also be more than merely a report for downloading. There are opportunities for networking, through discussion boards and new technologies such as email discussion lists, *Facebook*, *Twitter*, *LinkedIn* and blogs. These media can be used for engaging with others, whether fellow academics, policy communities or non-governmental organisations, or the wider society, telling them about research or for hearing about new publications. These sites not only provide up-to-date news of recent publications, but can also give insight into current debates and can be used to invite comments on work in progress as well as disseminating outputs. Indeed, as the manuscript for this chapter was being finalised, a tweet arrived with news of a manual, Impact 2.0 iGuide, offering guidance on how researchers can make use of Web 2.0 tools to link their research to policy and advocacy.[14]

While the relationship between science and mass media has not always been smooth, journalists can be valuable partners for communicating research, engaging a wide and potentially critical audience. Press releases inform the media of research and invite them to take part in communicating it. University Press Offices offer support and training in working with the media. Specialist science writers can also play an important role, as do organisations such as the Science Media Centre, which works independently to support an understanding of science in the media.[15] Further detailed guidance is available from the European Commission (2004) and from the SUPPORT project (see Box 10.5).

---

[14]http://iguides.comunica.org

[15](www.sciencemediacentre.org)

---

| Box 10.5 |

## Tips for working with the media

- Use 'structured press releases' to provide journalists with accurate, balanced information.
- Include 'fact boxes' to illustrate your messages.
- Arrange 'press conferences' with the general or specialist press.
- Provide stories to personalise your message.
- Avoid 'jargon' by writing in plain language and putting technical language in brackets for clear communication.
- Provide journalists with access to experts for interviews.
- Prepare 'tip sheets' for them on what to ask the experts.
- Provide training for the media to help them for understand research.

(Adapted from Oxman et al. 2009)

---

Working more directly, universities can build on theories of knowledge transfer and exchange to provide enhanced access to research and mobilise knowledge among local research users (Phipps and Shapson 2009).

Last but not least, presenting research in person provides opportunities for communication, discussion and networking. This might include presentations at conferences, in meetings, through emails and in informal discussions. Both internal communication to colleagues within an organisation and external communication can be important. Particularly when communicated externally, presentations need to be tailored to the audience. Good communication in person enables relationships to build and arguably shifts the emphasis from research communication to engagement, in which researcher and audience are together engaged in seeking solutions to problems. Debating science outside the usual academic forums is a way for researchers to test their ideas with a wider public and make science more accountable.[16]

Practical guidance on how to build a functional communications interface between researchers and policy-makers that encompasses building relationships and various media has been developed by the European Commission (2010).

## Conclusion

Communication about research in general, and systematic reviews in particular, occurs in a multitude of ways. Figure 10.2 shows the potential role for different types of systematic review.

The linear model of moving knowledge between different bodies of people is sufficient for effecting change when innovations appear particularly beneficial and are low risk, low cost and easily attempted, and with the support of strong institutional structures and

---

[16]For instance, Cafe Scientifique, see www.cafescientifique.org

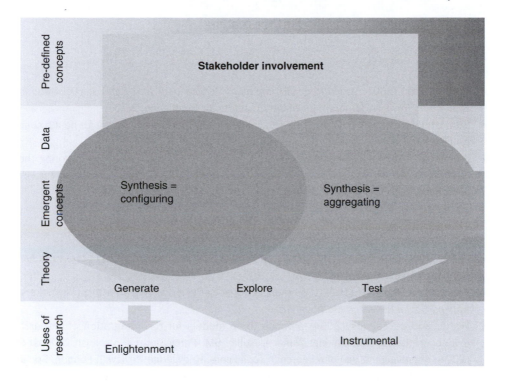

**Figure 10.2**   The different potential purposes of systematic reviews

resources, a supportive culture and incentives for change. This model is most likely to suit aggregative reviews providing evidence about simple interventions as they can be either sought by evidence-inclined practitioners or readily incorporated into guidelines.

Where change depends on new understandings – the enlightenment model – relationships, shared ideas and mutual learning are crucial. Although configurative systematic reviews offer novel ideas, there is as yet too little experience to know whether configurative reviews, without relationships, can lead to new ways of thinking beyond the research community. A systems approach to getting research and policy is advocated for complex circumstances involving many related stakeholders. It relies on key stakeholders each bringing their perspectives to seek solutions, and thus requires time, resources and commitment. Conversely, getting policy into research, by inviting key stakeholders to guide a research team in order to ensure the research is relevant, is already happening with systematic reviews. Chapter 4 described how stakeholders can contribute to the conceptual framework of aggregative and mixed methods reviews. Not only does this approach ensure that the systematic review is relevant to the information needs of stakeholders, it also places stakeholders alongside the research team to interpret the findings as they emerge and consider their implications for policy and practice, and provides an opportunity for stakeholders to contribute to the communication strategy and act as an entry point into their formal and informal networks for sharing the findings.

# Further reading

## Examples of research use:

- Coren E (ed.) (2007) *Collection of Examples of Service User and Carer Participation in Systematic Reviews*. London: Social Care Institute for Excellence, 35-57.
- Stewart R, Hargreaves K, Oliver S (2005) Evidence informed policy making for health communication. *Health Education Journal*, 64(2): 120–128.
- Stewart R, Wiggins M, Thomas J, Oliver S, Brunton G, Ellison G (2005) Exploring the evidence–practice gap: A workshop report on mixed and participatory training for HIV prevention in Southern Africa. *Education for Health,* 18(2): 224–235.

## More on using research:

- Nutley S, Walter I, Davies HTO (2007) *Using Evidence: How Research Can Inform Public Services*. Bristol: The Policy Press.
- Vaughan RJ, Buss TF (1998) Communicating social science research to policymakers. *Applied Social Research Methods*, 48.
- Walter and colleagues (2004) propose three models for the integration of research evidence into decision-making: Walter I, Nutley SM, Percy-Smith J, McNeish D, Frost S (2004) Improving the use of research in social care. Knowledge Review 7. London. Social Care Institute for Excellence and Policy Press. Available at: www.scie.org.uk/publications/knowledgereviews/kr07.pdf

## Examples of sources for enhancing access to research:

- DARE helps to facilitate the interpretation of reviews by publishing abstracts of over 5,000 quality assessed and critically appraised systematic review syntheses, with a focus on the effects of interventions used in health and social care (www.crd.york.ac.uk/).
- The EPPI-Centre provides a searchable online library of systematic research syntheses conducted by the Centre and its external review groups, including syntheses in the fields of education, social care, health and health promotion (http://eppi.ioe.ac.uk/), as well as helping to facilitate related portals such as the UK Educational Evidence Portal (www.eep.ac.uk/).

## Resources about writing in plain English to consider:

- The Academic Writing Centre offers web-based resources and advice on academic writing. Available at: http://writingcentre.ioe.ac.uk/
- DISCERN – a brief questionnaire which provides users with a valid and reliable way of assessing the quality of written information on treatment choices for a health problem. DISCERN can also be used by authors and publishers of information on treatment choices as a guide to the standard which users are entitled to expect (www.discern.org.uk/).
- The Plain English Campaign – www.plainenglish.co.uk/

# ELEVEN

## Moving forward

### David Gough, Sandy Oliver and James Thomas

| Aims of chapter |
| --- |

This chapter considers:

- The importance of systematic reviews
- Their position within empirical enquiry
- Their role within a changing research community
- Methodological challenges
- Capacity building
- Evidence for all

## Introduction

This book has provided an introduction to the logic of systematic reviews and to the range of current and developing methods for reviewing. This final chapter raises some broader issues about where systematic reviews fit within research more generally and their role in assisting policy, practice and personal decision-making, and highlights new areas for, or in, development.

Systematic reviews have increasingly become a focus of both academic and public debate. This book presents examples across policy sectors by drawing on the social sciences: health, education, social welfare, international development and environmental science. But systematic reviews also have a role in the physical sciences (Herring 1968) and the biological sciences (Pullin and Stewart 2006), from astronomy to zoology (Petticrew 2001), and no doubt more. Perhaps because of the increasing profile of reviews addressing public policy, more thought is being given to choosing which questions to address with reviews. The growing number of systematic reviews, and their exacting standards for appraising primary research, has implications for choosing which questions to address with primary research, and how. The question-driven, participative approach to reviewing described in this book has implications for the research community in working across disciplines, across policy sectors and across cultures. It creates challenges yet also opportunities for creative development of research methods. All these advances require: individuals to acquire new skills in doing and using reviews; organisations to develop their resources to support their people; and investments in knowledge management systems.

## The importance of review questions

Chapter 10 described a variety of ways of making the findings of reviews accessible, and how systematic reviews of different kinds are influencing national and international policy. In offering quality appraised answers to research questions, systematic reviews do far more than provide a shortcut to research; they allow for greater 'leverage' by surfacing the evidence from multiple studies, sometimes with different contexts, for open debate. That open debate is happening, for example, as part of Guideline Development Groups internationally, where health clinicians and service-users consider review findings. It is encouraged within UK local authorities who are offered training in understanding systematic reviews. A Canadian exemplar is the Ontario Education Research Panel,[1] which was established to facilitate discussions about research priorities for education, the state of knowledge in specific areas, opportunities for and impediments to the advancement of research, and the potential for future partnerships. Collaborative discussions engage Ontario's school boards, faculties of education, researchers, professional organisations, community agencies and government ministries. Open debate about evidence is also embraced by service-user organisations that wish to add weight to their arguments; see, for instance, breast cancer advocates (Dickersin et al. 2001). Mass media and electronic media can bring the evidence to the wider public and help to challenge evidence that is partial and not contextualised (more on this in the last section of this chapter).

The more that different sections of society have an understanding of the nature of research through reviews that clarify what is known and not known, as seen from different perspectives, the more research can be part of a political dialogue. The opportunity to have access to and engage with research evidence is essentially a democratic issue (Gough and Elbourne 2002). Involving different sections of society in choosing the direction for research throughout its development has fundamental implications for changing the nature of the evidence available for open debate. Teachers, for example, who do not normally have the training or the time to be researchers, may welcome the opportunity to be involved in the occasional research project, to influence the framing and interpretation of a systematic review, share decisions about future research agendas, or make use of research findings or encourage others to do so. The teachers' lack of time is not the only obstacle to

---

[1] www.edu.gov.on.ca/eng/research/

their influence. Crucially, funding for public policy research flows predominantly from government and charitable foundations to academics. Any of these groups can take responsibility for inviting other important sectors of society. Where research funders or researchers themselves take the initiative to invite broader input, systematic reviews provide a forum for discussions where influence may reach beyond a single research project, to a whole body of literature or an agenda for future research, and subsequent changes in public services. In the health sector, patients may draw on the evidence of reviews when sharing decisions with clinicians about their personal care, or they may share their experience and debate the evidence with clinicians and managers in order to improve the health system (Hill 2011). For instance, a systematic review team sought the views of women about their care during childbirth, and the outcomes of care that were important to women were incorporated into the review (Kettle et al. 2007). The review findings were subsequently used by a midwife to change care in her hospital and her description of this work won her the Cochrane Library prize. School teachers, not traditionally research active, are also becoming more engaged with research (Bell et al. 2010) and many attempts are being made to develop the infrastructure to support them, such as the Electronic Education Portal,[2] the Coalition for Evidence Based Education[3] and European networks for evidence-informed policy and practice in education.[4] Similar opportunities could be made for the providers and users of other public services and for minority and disadvantaged communities where broad political debates could be informed by research (Bannister et al. 2011).

As the political debate focuses more on research findings, the questions that lead to the findings become more important. Even deciding which questions to address with research is becoming more systematic. This book has already described how reviewers will invite stakeholders to refine the questions for individual reviews; this often involves discussing a map of the broader research initially identified for a review (see Chapters 2, 3 and 7). A similar approach on an international scale is being undertaken by the Global Evidence Mapping initiative, which considers clinician, patient, carer and policy-maker perspectives when identifying and prioritising questions across a broad clinical area of interest and then maps the matching evidence (Bragge et al. 2011). How to choose the most relevant and useful research questions is also attracting considerable methodological attention. Formal processes in the UK began with the launch of the NHS Research and Development Strategy two decades ago, and continue with The James Lind Alliance,[5] a non-profit making initiative established in 2004 to bring patients, carers and clinicians together to identify and prioritise uncertainties, or 'unanswered questions', about the effects of treatments that they agree are most

---

[2]www.eep.ac.uk/

[3]www.cebenetwork.org/

[4]www.eippee.eu/

[5]www.lindalliance.org/

important. Now there is a growing literature of priority-setting studies (Stewart et al. 2010b), and recognised standards which call for stakeholder engagement, explicit processes, sound information management, consideration of values and reasons, and a revision or appeal mechanism (Sibbald et al. 2009). A World Health Organisation checklist is available based on a literature review of good practice for research priority setting (Viergever et al. 2010). In health research, priority-setting methods are also being applied to the choice of 'core outcome sets' to be applied in controlled trials and systematic reviews, to ensure fairer comparisons between different interventions for the same conditions (Clarke 2007). The principle of adopting formal, inclusive and transparent methods for choosing research questions is appropriate across the whole of the public sector in democratic societies.

## The position of reviews within empirical enquiry

Systematic reviews have not only provided reliable answers to important questions of policy and practice, they have also provided an opportunity to study research activity as a whole and forced us to think differently about the nature of empirical enquiry. As the mapping of evidence reveals the gaps in primary research and thereby sets a research agenda, similarly, reviewing the methods of primary studies reveals persistent flaws and sets a methodological agenda (Oakley et al. 2005). The increasing profile of systematic reviews is a driver for reporting research sufficiently clearly so that it is accessible to reviewers and included in reviews. Reviews require the studies that they include to be fit for purpose in terms of their methodological quality and in terms of contributing findings to the review. As reviews require explicit methods, they require primary research that explains clearly what was done and why. Anyone who has undertaken systematic reviews knows that deficiencies in the reporting of primary research are a major obstacle to reviewing (and to the use of research in general) and so call into question the current editorial practices. Chapter 10 describes the development of standards and tools for the clear reporting of many types of study under the umbrella of the Equator Network, many of whose members come from the systematic review community.

A broad-based user-driven approach to reviewing challenges traditional boundaries within the academic literature. The research literature is often organised along disciplinary and cultural lines. The topic areas proscribed by people outside the academy, however, are not necessarily defined by academic sub-disciplines. If questions cut across disciplinary areas and sub-areas, then a review will include relevant research from all those areas. What is known and not known from the review can then drive further research and understanding in this new cross-cutting area. The potential is for a new 'geography' or landscape for research defined by a plurality of different perspectives and questions. The resultant plurality of reviews expands rather than limits what there is to know from research, as will be illustrated in the last section of this chapter.

Much discussion of reviews and reporting of individual reviews considers them as isolated products rather than being a component in a strategic programme of primary research and reviews and part of the wider research enterprise. Reviews are well positioned to identify gaps in research knowledge and understanding, and thereby justify new empirical enquiry. In describing and synthesising a research field, reviews can present what would be fit-for-purpose methods for such new enquiry. If the significance of individual studies is seen in terms of how they advance the collective understanding and knowledge of prior studies rather than in terms of their individual findings, then the starting point for research changes. For example, the power (or size) required of an impact study can be calculated not in terms of being able to demonstrate an impact, but in terms of the power required to change the impact measured by an existing meta-analysis (Goudie et al. 2010). In some cases a proposed new study may have relatively low power for examining the efficacy of an intervention, yet the power may be sufficient to influence the findings of a meta-analysis by, for example, enabling the meta-analysis to achieve statistical significance. Alternatively, the power required to change statistically significant findings may be so great that it calls into question the value – and ethics – of mounting a new study at all.

Systematic reviews can also make data nested at different levels available for further empirical enquiry. Fine-grained data include observations or views of individual study participants (for instance, individual measures in aggregative reviews, or first-order interpretations in configurative reviews). These are synthesised in the findings of systematic reviews which can be contextualised by broader systematic literature maps. The larger-scale picture is provided by meta-reviews (maps or reviews of reviews). This creates at least five levels of study:

- **Individual primary study data**: data on individual study participants that are increasingly available in data repositories or publicly available cohort studies.
- **Primary research**: new conceptual and empirical work, the methods and findings of which are available in research reports.
- **Syntheses**: findings from research questions being addressed by studying many prior studies (which may include primary study data in aggregative reviews, or themes or first-order interpretations in configurative reviews, extracted from primary studies by reviewers).
- **Maps**: analysis of the research field relevant to a review question.
- **Meta reviews**: reviews of the data or findings from other reviews.

The 'work done' by a piece of research at any of these levels can vary. Reviews expand the extent and complexity of the work done by including many studies, sub-reviews, and several levels of analysis, as in a mixed knowledge reviews (see Chapter 3). In addition, there is the dimension of time and phases of research. Reviews can be part of a sequence with other reviews and primary research. These levels of analysis and phases of research engage with the geography of different questions and perspectives already mentioned to produce very rich, complex and powerful fields of research enquiry. Critiques of systematic reviews may argue that they over-simplify the nature of research production and use. In our view, they help reveal the complexity.

At present, these multiple levels rarely create a coherent body of literature. Some areas are particularly well served by syntheses, and in some of these, meta-reviews are able to compare treatments that have not been addressed in the same primary studies (Caldwell et al. 2010). Others are populated by isolated primary studies; a coherent picture here awaits systematic maps or syntheses. In some fields, systematic reviews are so well established that funders require research proposals to refer to systematic reviews and justify what a new study would add.

## Systematic reviews and research communities

As well as influencing how knowledge advances, systematic reviews influence how researchers (and others) relate to research and to each other. User-driven reviews, as mentioned above, often cut across traditional boundaries. Here we consider first the consequences of crossing traditional boundaries sequentially, and then the consequences of crossing traditional boundaries simultaneously.

Evidence-informed decision-making and systematic review methodology have successively crossed disciplinary boundaries, public sector boundaries and international boundaries. This has enabled the methodology of reviews and research communities themselves to evolve. Evidence-informed decision-making grew with systematic reviews of randomised controlled trials in medicine in the 1980s, thereby challenging the authority of clinical opinion. The response was a more explicit emphasis being placed on the judicious balance of evidence and experience in using systematic reviews (Sackett et al. 1996). The introduction of evidence-based decision-making and systematic reviews into nursing in the 1990s challenged the balance of technical and tender loving care. It inspired an interest in qualitative research as a route to developing knowledge for evidence-based nursing practice (Ploeg 1999).

When moving into health promotion, a systematic review methodology was resisted by those who emphasised the complexity of intervening in people's lives and the need to take into account social behaviour (Speller et al. 1997). This inspired the emergence of reviews that included process evaluations and, at the turn of the millennium, reviews that included studies of people's views of aspects of their lives, not just interventions (Oakley et al. 2005). It saw mixed knowledge reviews in social care that included primary research surveys of professional practice or what professionals considered to be best practice (Chapter 3). In public health, reviews began with a socio-biological agenda, looking at vaccines. Moving into the broader public health arena focused attention on broad social determinants of health, and methods were developed for analysing equity within systematic reviews (Kavanagh et al. 2009a; Oliver et al. 2008a).

Systematic reviews have recently appeared for international development. Here, delineating a theory of change (Weiss 1995) is advocated for addressing complexity, to explain how and why an intervention works (or does not work). It links together the inputs (or resources), activities, outcomes, impacts and contexts of an intervention (see also Chapter 4.) Change processes are typically depicted graphically in the form of causal pathways or programme theories (Jones 2011;

Rogers 2008). Such theory-based impact evaluations contrast with 'black box' approaches to impact evaluation in which impact is simply reported, rather than explained (White 2009). A causal pathway approach is seen as particularly helpful for shedding light on the question of why things work (or do not work), and not just if they work, thereby enhancing policy relevance (Pawson 2006a; White 2011).

Each new boundary brings new challenges, new debates and new opportunities. What we know about the transformation of ideas as they are shared among different groups of people (Chapter 10) can be applied to ideas about methods for doing research as well as ideas about methods for using research (Taylor and Coffey 2008). Systematic review methodology has spread through networks between people who have some common interest, benefits have been seen and the methodology can be adapted to suit new areas.

As user-driven systematic review questions are often not defined by disciplinary boundaries, a systematic review methodology crosses multiple boundaries simultaneously: disciplinary boundaries, public sector boundaries, cultural boundaries, and lay-professional boundaries. Either side of the boundaries there are challenges and contributions to be made as the methodology evolves. Reviews addressing problems in agriculture and environmental conservation span natural and social sciences (Masset et al. 2011; Pullin et al. 2009); they need to call on expertise from all sides. For instance, a review of agricultural interventions for children's nutrition needed to take into account biochemistry (for assessing absorption of micro-nutrients), human physiology (for assessing children's growth), socio-economics (for assessing household income and expenditure), participatory research (for mounting farmer schools) and behavioural science (for assessing participation) (Masset et al. 2011).

The creativity arising from research that spans disciplinary boundaries has been acknowledged in transdisciplinary research (Flinterman et al. 2001) and by reflections on the role of innovation in social research and methodological practice (Taylor and Coffey 2008). Multidisciplinary research draws on the methodologies and assumptions of different disciplines. Further innovation, through integrating these methodologies and assumptions, creates the more holistic approach of transdisciplinary research to address contemporary problems such as climate change or technological advances such as nanotechnology. The broad, problem-based, inclusive approach to systematic reviewing described in this book shares many of the characteristics of transdisciplinary research (Flinterman et al. 2001): a holistic approach; oriented towards public perspectives and problem solving; acknowledging complexity of context and diversity of actors; and integrating knowledge from various scientific and non-scientific sources. The procedures for transdisciplinary research (defining a field, identifying relevant actors, in-depth discussions, repeated feedback and developing shared constructions) correspond closely with the procedures that we have described for systematic reviewing.

The value of transdisciplinary research is its contribution to the quality, relevance and impact of research, resulting in new research directions. Similarly, systematic reviews grounded in real-world problems provide the conditions required to support innovation and capacity-building in research methods (Taylor and Coffey 2008): a culture in which experimentation and creativity are both welcomed and critically appraised; opportunities for working at and across conventional disciplinary boundaries; the development of frameworks and protocols to facilitate methodological transparency; accumulating and disseminating a critical mass of exemplary work; collaboration with research users and service-users; and opportunities for gaining, absorbing and exploiting new methodological practices and knowledge.

Despite the scope of individual systematic reviews spanning disciplinary boundaries, systematic reviewers typically operate within a sub-set of approaches to systematic reviewing, rarely accruing personal experience of working across the complete spectrum of aggregative and configurative reviews. The consequence of this is an expanding menu of systematic reviews without a common language to describe the work (Gough et al. in press). Many descriptors of review methods are not linked to underlying conceptual distinctions. The terms provide ways of identifying well-known approaches to reviewing rather than a classification that reveals the ways in which reviews differ, hence our attempt at describing some of the many dimensions of difference in reviews in Chapter 3.

Understanding the range of available methods is made more difficult by the way that some terms are used to mean different things by different authors and some terms that actually refer to overarching approaches to reviewing being used interchangeably with those that refer to specific methods and tools of synthesis. The term 'narrative review', for example, is used in at least three different ways to describe: (i) traditional non-systematic literature reviews without explicit methods; (ii) systematic or non-systematic reviews that synthesise words (text) rather than numbers as, for example, in a statistical meta-analysis; and (iii) a specific use of narrative explanation to tell a story about what is known from research (Popay et al. 2006). These complications are compounded by the branding of new types of review methods and the ways that discussions of reviews are caught up in paradigm wars between advocates of different primary research methodologies. With reviewers coming from such a range of disciplines, both clarity about terminology and the transparent reporting of methods need to include the ideological and theoretical assumptions, and the stakeholder involvement, influencing a review. By making these assumptions more explicit, the findings from reviews can be understood better. Without this in an increasingly rich and complex web of research reviews, it would be easy for decision-making to be driven by individual research studies or non-explicit summaries of studies, with their implicit assumptions, perspectives and agendas hidden from view. This would be contrary to the hopes we have for reviews to facilitate a more enlightened discussion of what we know and how we know it from different perspectives.

These issues involve, yet go beyond, systematic reviews of research, and reviews need to build on the development of language to describe the generation and use of evidence in general. This book has tried to unpack many of the ways that reviews differ from one another to enable a clearer differentiation between them and, hopefully, move us towards a more integrated language of reviewing as well as, consequentially, a consolidated array of secondary research methods to complement the rich choice of methods available for primary research further methods development. In addition to a new language for reviewing, clearer language is needed for stakeholder involvement, research engagement, review interpretation and review application in decision-making. But that is for another book.

## Methodological challenges

Transdisciplinary approaches to systematic reviewing provide hope for meeting important methodological challenges, including the current particular challenge for aggregative systematic reviews of how to study and understand complexity. The rich diversity of research paradigms and methods for understanding the world provides us with many perspectives and techniques, including mixed methods primary research and reviews to address complexity at different levels of analysis and phases of research. There is a danger that using one method exclusively may lead us to ignore important facets of a phenomenon. This is a current challenge for aggregative reviews assessing the efficacy of an intervention. The aggregative methodology requires homogeneity to fulfil the statistical assumptions and to provide a robust probabilistic estimate of the strength of an effect. This is powerful in understanding the overall effect of an intervention on an average human being but not for predicting the effect on an individual or groups of human beings.

Although methods of experimental evaluation and the statistical meta-analysis of their findings are in many ways highly advanced, current techniques offer limited help in assessing the effect of an intervention in another setting. The reasons for this are that within any single study there are numerous variables that may be interacting to influence the impact of the intervention, such as sample characteristics, the implementation of the intervention, or aspects of the study design. Statistical techniques such as meta-regression can potentially be used to 'control' for these confounding effects, but many of the moderator variables may themselves also be confounded by variations in the study design and with one another (Lipsey 2003). While providing an opportunity for exploration, systematic reviewers often see such potential confounders as problematic and aim to minimise these with an homogeneity of data and methods of analysis to limit the effects of any remaining heterogeneity. This makes for a tighter review (with possibly a simpler answer), but limits its ability to generalise to different contexts.

Equity is a good example of the challenge involved in identifying differential effects in different populations using current statistical methods. In a paper entitled "Damned if you do, damned if you don't: Subgroup analysis and equity', Petticrew and colleagues (2012) discuss the dilemma facing reviewers who are interested in identifying the impact of interventions on equity. Statistical meta-analysis in health care examines gross effects and is concerned about the analysis of sub-groups in the population for two reasons. First, any such analysis should be pre-specified, otherwise it could be seen as fishing for sub-group differences which might be due to random error or a combination of unknown factors – or both. Second, even if the analyses are pre-specified, the sub-groups have to contain sufficient data points for the statistical analysis to be robust. However, a lack of focus on sub-groups can mean that important differences between different types of people are not examined and the needs (and in this case health outcomes) of some are compromised (Petticrew et al. 2012). The effectiveness of interventions for some groups of people may be indistinguishable within an average 'ineffective' result across the whole sample in the study.

Generalisability is an interesting methodological aspect of complexity as most aggregative methods of review push for homogeneity rather than heterogeneity. It has become an issue because the questions that are being asked of research are increasingly about understanding and valuing difference and equity. Again, it is user participation driving the methodological developments. As discussed in Chapter 9, generalisability also relates to how systematic reviews can consider resource use and costs of services. It is possible to count up the resources used in an intervention and to make assumptions to create models to estimate its cost effectiveness, but to compare its benefits in relation to costs with alternative courses of action requires a better understanding of the factors that affect the generalisability of evidence on resource use, costs and relative efficiency from one setting, context or time to another. As research and policy debates become more international, variations in economic contexts become increasingly important.

## Capacity building

Systematic reviewing is a fast-growing activity and a fast-developing activity. Methodological developments and increasing interest rely on individuals developing new skills in doing and using reviews. Twenty years ago systematic reviews were not seen as 'real research'. They were not usually accredited in metrics-based systems to assess individual or institutional academic performance. Systematic reviewers were often clinicians committed to their clinical specialties rather than academics committed to accumulating knowledge. If these individuals are to be able to employ their new skills, they need support from institutions that recognise systematic reviews as legitimate research activities, and from practitioners and policy-makers willing to invest their craft and organisational knowledge in advising review teams on how to design reviews that will provide useful findings. They need infrastructures for sharing knowledge: research organisations with libraries staffed by information scientists; policy organisations with libraries staffed by information scientists; and university curricula that include systematic review methodologies alongside primary research methodologies. They also need school systems that perceive discussion of the role of research as part of education for citizenship.

At a systems level, infrastructures are being established for systematic reviewing, although these are much leaner than infrastructures for primary research, being built more slowly in developing countries – the majority of the world's population who face the majority of the world's social and environmental problems. Fragile internet connections and electricity supplies have a direct negative impact on the ability to generate and use evidence in those countries in most need.

Currently, there is energy to develop the capacity in systems and structures for health and welfare research. There has been a growth in registers of primary research studies and reviews, quality standards for reporting primary research and undertaking and reporting reviews (and reviews of reviews), and appraisals of evidence and recommendations (see Chapter 6). There are also moves to structure databases of evidence according to the needs of policy and practitioner users of that evidence. What is missing is the development of similar structures in areas of social policy beyond health and welfare. This is why the internet provides a vital resource as it allows reviewers to do their work, it supplies a platform for the new structures and processes being developed, and enables other users to access information, and engage with and influence these processes.

In addition to building this capacity for research is a need to build the capacity for working across boundaries, whether these are disciplinary, professional or policy sector boundaries. Again, capacity is required in terms of individual skills and inclinations, an organisational recognition of the value of cross-boundary working and national and international communication and mutual learning.

## Evidence for all

Capacity is particularly driven by a pressure on universities to be useful in the world and to show practical achievements for the large investment in higher education by many governments. This was originally focused on making best use of the potential commercial exploitation of university-based research but this has now broadened to include government interest in universities showing societal impact. Some governments now actively fund impact activities and financially reward institutions that achieve impact. This interest in making a difference with knowledge transfer (see Chapter 10) is to be welcomed, but such initiatives do not always consider the quality of the knowledge that is being transferred. The pressure on academics used only to be 'publish or be damned', now it is also to 'KT or be damned', resulting in a plethora of primary studies, rather than systematic reviews, being reported in the media. This is problematic of course because individual studies may be atypical and subject to random error. Ideally, the media would give far more prominence to systematic reviews.

The media are, of course, a crucial part of the move to raise the level of debate about research. They are one of the main means by which ideas are shared and discussed in society. Being so powerful, they can be a hindrance in communicating unfounded or uncontextualised research findings, yet also a powerful asset to communicating and debating evidence-informed ideas. Unfortunately, the mass media are only just beginning to draw on reports of systematic reviews when writing about advances in science. One way forward is for academic researchers to be more concerned about communicating the complexity of research and the assumptions that lie behind it. A complementary approach is for journalists to do so. Many mass media stories are of dramatic 'breakthroughs' that raise hopes rather than progress knowledge in the time-honoured incremental fashion of real science. The exceptions are the growing reports of systematic review findings. Surprisingly compelling reading was a journalist's comparative account of two meta-analyses testing the effects of treating a varicocele (varicosed vein draining the testicles) (Rumbelow 2011). A painstaking disentangling of the different signs and symptoms in the populations eligible for two systematic reviews with apparently contradictory findings explained why a simple treatment for male infertility is available in the USA but not in the UK. This is an emotive example of heterogeneity where the apparent effectiveness of a treatment for one group of men cannot be seen if tested with a broader population. The angst of childlessness, public concern for a well-performing national health service and the high profile of the UK National Institute for Health and Clinical Excellence (NICE) gave the statistics an emotive appeal and earned the journalist a double-page spread.

The public debate about microfinance is similarly focusing on complexity and heterogeneity on an international scale. Microfinance, introduced in Chapter 4, includes savings, credit and insurance services offered to low-income clients with the intention of helping them lift themselves out of poverty. This is another area of public and private concern where individual stories show either remarkable successes or tragic consequences, highlighting the need for a systematic review and reliable primary research. The enthusiasm for microfinance was encouraged by the promising findings of small-scale, uncontrolled evaluations. The first very recent randomised controlled trials (Banarjee et al. 2009; Karlan and Zinman 2010) found limited evidence in support of micro-credit, fuelling the controversy. In response, a number of systematic reviews have been commissioned (Copestake et al. 2010; Ezedunukwe and Okwundu 2010; Stewart et al. 2010a; Vaessen et al. 2010). So far only one of these has published its findings (Stewart et al. 2010a): that micro-credit and micro-savings make some people poorer, not richer; clients save more, but also spend more; health generally increases; education has limited gains, with some clients' children missing out; micro-credit may empower some women, while both micro-credit and micro-savings improve clients' housing; and there is little evidence about the impact on job creation or social cohesion. This complexity is attracting the attention of thousands of readers through electronic media where academic and industry blogs[6] are scrutinising the evidence for both the average effects of microfinance and its impact on particular groups in particular circumstances. These discussions have included a wide range of stakeholders, including industry providers, microfinance researchers, and those interested in evidence and its use.

These two examples illustrate how advances in systematic review methodology meet systems that support broad public debate. This is the goal of inclusive approaches to systematic reviewing: rigorous science that is more often at the centre of public debates because it resonates with public and private lives.

---

[6]www.developmenthorizons.com/2011/06/microfinance-angel-or-devil.html; http://blogs.cgdev.org/open book/2011/02/literature-review-on-microfinance-impacts-in-africa.php; www.microcapital.org/microfinance-paper-wrap-up-what-is-the-impact-of-microfinance-on-poor-people-a-systematic-review-of-evidence-from-sub-saharan-africa-by-ruth-stewart-carina-van-rooyen-kelly-dickson-mabolaeng-maj/

# Glossary

**Accountable:** answerable and responsible and justified.

**Aggregative reviews:** reviews where the synthesis is predominantly aggregating (adding up) data to answer the review question. Aggregative reviews commonly use quantitative data but qualitative data can also be aggregated.

**Bayesian analysis:** a statistical approach that allows for prior assumptions to be included in the assessment of probabilities that something will happen (or not). It allows for subjective knowledge to be included in statistical estimates.

**Bibliographic database:** an organised database of bibliographic records of publications. The databases are often on particular topic areas, indexed by sub-topic, and include titles and abstracts and sometimes full copies of publications.

**Causal pathways** link a series of events that result in effects some time or distance later; they may be hypothetical (particularly before a piece of review) or supported by evidence. Other similar but different terms include programme theories, logic frameworks and theories of change.

**Coding:** any keywording, data extraction or other collection of information or annotation of studies in order to conduct a systematic review.

**Collaboration:** an on-going partnership to work together and share decisions.

**Communicative competence:** the ability to exchange ideas with other people.

**Conceptual:** a set of ideas or principles and their relation to each other.

**Conceptual framework:** ideological and theoretical assumptions that underlie a review question and may be implicit or explicit.

**Confidence interval:** a statistical estimate of the probability that a particular measure (such as a measure of effect in an experimental trial) reflects a true estimate (such as of the hypothesised effect in a trial).

**Configurative reviews:** reviews where the synthesis is predominantly configuring (organising) data from the included studies to answer the review question. Configurative reviews commonly use qualitative data but quantitative data can also be configured.

**Consultation:** seeking others' opinions, but not necessarily acting upon them.

**Controlled trial:** an experiment where two groups are compared, an experimental group who receives an experimental intervention and a control group that does not receive the intervention. A randomised controlled trial aims to avoid hidden bias by randomising all other variables that might create a differential outcome between the groups apart from the effect of the experimental intervention.

**Critical Interpretive Synthesis:** a method of synthesis that generates a coherent and illuminating theory of a body of evidence that is based on a detailed critical study of the theoretical contribution of that evidence (Dixon-Woods et al. 2006).

**Data collection or data extraction:** a term often used for a form of detailed coding (Op. Cit) of information of studies to inform synthesis.

**Diagnostic test:** any kind of test performed to aid in the detection or assessment (diagnosis) of a problem.

**Empirical:** based on observation and experiment rather than theory or logic.

**Epistemology:** assumptions about the nature of knowledge.

**Exhaustive search:** the aspiration in a search strategy to identify all the publications that meet a review's inclusion criteria and thus achieve unbiased aggregation (see Publication bias).

**Extent of review:** the degree that a review engages with a research issue (dependent on the breadth, depth, and rigour of a review).

**Forest plot:** a graphical display that illustrates the relative strength of treatment effects in a number of different quantitative scientific studies in, for example, a statistical meta analysis of controlled trials.

**Framework synthesis:** uses structured text and matrices to display data according to a tentative framework of themes or concepts identified in advance, with the framework being open to amendment with concepts and themes that emerge during the qualitative analysis of the data.

**Full text screening:** assessing whether a study meets the review question's inclusion criteria by inspecting the full paper rather than, for example, only the abstract.

**Funnel plot:** a graphical representation of the effects of an intervention (in a number of controlled trials) against a measure of study size. It is used to identify heterogeneity of studies in a statistical meta analysis.

**Generalisability:** the extent that a research finding is applicable to different individuals and groups.

**Heterogeneity statistic:** a statistical measure of heterogeneity in the distributions of results of controlled trials in statistical meta analysis; for example a funnel plot.

**Inclusion criteria:** criteria that specify the nature of studies to be included in a review.

**Key wording:** a term often used for a form of coding (Op.Cit.) where studies are described in terms of their bibliographic details, focus of interest and study design.

**Knowledge translation:** the process of movement between knowledge production and knowledge use. A number of similar terms with different meanings have also been developed such as knowledge transfer, knowledge mobilisation, knowledge exchange and knowledge to action.

**Logic framework:** see Causal pathways.

**Map (systematic):** a systematic description and analysis of the research field defined by a review question. It may be a review product on its own or a stage on the way to synthesis.

**Meta epidemiology:** the analysis of a series of reviews to address questions about the nature of the research field.

**Meta ethnography:** a method for reviewing ethnographic (and other qualitative) studies using methods similar to the ethnographic analysis of primary research data, extracts, concepts, metaphors and themes arising from different studies, then interpreting and synthesising these into a 'line or argument' (Noblitt and Hare 1988).

**Meta evaluation:** the evaluation of evaluations (systematic reviews of evaluations are one type of meta evaluation).

**Meta narrative:** a method of synthesis that undertakes a critical analysis of research studies to examine the relationship between studies and their research paradigms (Greenhalgh et al. 2005a and 2005b).

**Meta review:** a review 'of' or 'about' other reviews (such as reviews of reviews and meta epidemiology).

**Mixed methods synthesis:** a synthesis that includes diverse forms of evidence; this may be mixed types of studies and/or mixed methods of synthesis.

**Multi level analysis:** statistical methods that enable the study of interactions of effects across different levels of analysis; for example, correlations (a lack of statistical independence) between data from pupils in a class, classes in a school, and schools in a geographical area.

**Narrative review:** term used in three different ways to describe (i) traditional non systematic literature; (ii) reviews that synthesise words (text) rather than numbers; (iii) a specific approach of narrative explanation in research synthesis (Popay 2006).

**Participatory research:** undertaking research together in order to generate knowledge and act on that knowledge.

**Programme theories:** see Causal pathways.

**Protocol:** a statement of the approach and methods to be used in a review made prior to the review being undertaken.

**Publication bias:** bias in the results of a review due to some research studies being more likely to be published, and thus identified in a review search, than others.

**Qualitative research:** in-depth enquiry in order to understand the meaning of phenomena and their relationships.

**Quality assessment tool:** a scale or other method to assist with an assessment of the quality and relevance of a study in a review.

**Quantitative research:** the systematic empirical investigation of quantitative properties of phenomena and their relationships. Quantitative research often involves measurement of some kind.

**Realist synthesis:** a method of synthesis that seeks evidence to populate an explicit programme theory to provide an explanatory analysis aimed at discerning what works for whom, in what circumstances, in what respects and how (Pawson 2006).

**Reference management software:** software to manage bibliographic information about a research publication such as the authors, title and other publication information.

**Review:** a critical appraisal and analysis of the literature.

**Review of reviews:** a systematic review where the data are from other reviews.

**Saturation:** when a configurative review has reached a stage where further studies identified in the search do not contribute any new concepts to the synthesis even though they are otherwise relevant to the review.

**Scoping:** preliminary examination of a field of research.

**Search strategy:** a structured plan for searching.

**Sensitivity analysis:** a statistical method for examining the effect of changing a variable in an analysis; for example, the effect of withdrawing poor quality studies from a statistical meta analysis.

**Stakeholders:** people having some self-interest in a piece of work, either because they might use the findings, or because decisions made by others in light of the findings might have an impact on them.

**Standard error:** a statistical measure which is the standard deviation of the means of different samples taken from a population; for example, if you undertook a controlled trial many times, the mean (average) effect in each trial would be different: the standard error is a measure of that variation.

**Statistical meta analysis:** the use of statistical techniques to aggregate the results of included studies. It is often used as method of synthesis of effect sizes from experimental trials in reviews of the effectiveness of interventions.

**Synthesis:** creating something new from separate elements (a synthesis of findings from studies to answer a review question).

**Systematic:** undertaken according to a fixed plan or system or method.

**Systematic review:** a review of the research literature using systematic and explicit accountable methods.

**Systematic review software:** specialist software to assist with the processes involved in undertaking, managing and updating a systematic review.

**Text mining:** an automated process that can assist with the identification and structuring of patterns in the text of individual documents and across multiple documents. This can be useful in several stages of a review, particularly in automating aspects of the searching and screening of studies.

**Thematic synthesis:** a method of synthesis that uses the coding of text 'line-by-line'; the development of 'descriptive themes'; and the generation of 'analytical themes' (Thomas and Harden 2008).

**Theoretical lens** focuses a review on a particular way of analysing the evidence, such as an 'equity lens' focusing a review on unjust differences between groups of people, or an 'advocacy lens' with a goal of social change.

**Theories of change:** see Causal pathways.

**Traditional literature review:** a review of research literature where there was not an expectation of detailed explicit accountable methods (as expected in a systematic review).

**Transdisciplinary research:** research that integrates methodologies and assumptions from different disciplines.

**Transformative reviews** are designed with the perspectives of marginalised or disadvantaged people in mind, with the intention of synthesising evidence to improve their situation.

**Unbiased aggregation:** aggregating the findings of studies in a review without introducing any hidden biases by, for example, not searching thoroughly or systematically.

**Views synthesis:** a systematic review that synthesises studies on the views of participants in order to answer a review question.

**Weight of evidence:** a framework for appraising the generic and review specific quality and relevance of the findings of a study for synthesis.

# References

Abraham N, Moayyedi P, Daniels B, Veldhuyzen Van Santen S (2004) The methodological quality of trials affects estimates of treatment efficacy in functional (non-ulcer) dyspepsia. *Alimentary Pharmacology and Therapeutics*, 19: 631–641.

Abrami PC, Borokhovski E, Bernard RM, Wade CA, Tamim R, Persson T, Surkes MA (2010) Issues in conducting and disseminating brief reviews of evidence. *Evidence & Policy*, 6(3): 371–389.

Akl EA, Oxman AD, Herrin J, Vist GE, Terrenato I, Sperati F, Costiniuk C, Blank D, Schünemann H (2011) Using alternative statistical formats for presenting risks and risk reductions. *Cochrane Database of Systematic Reviews*, Issue 3. Art. No.: CD006776. DOI: 10.1002/14651858.CD006776.pub2.

Alderson P, Green S (eds) (2002) *Cochrane Collaboration Open Learning Material for Reviewers: Cochrane Collaboration,* www.cochrane-net.org/openlearning/PDF/Openlearning-full.pdf (accessed 7 February 2011).

Ananiadou S, McNaught J (eds) (2006) *Text Mining for Biology and Biomedicine*. Boston and London: Artech House.

Ananiadou S, Okazaki N, Procter R, Rea B, Sasaki Y, Thomas J (2009) Supporting systematic reviews using text mining (Special issue on E-Social Science). *Social Science Computer Review,* 27: 4.

Anderson R (2010) Systematic reviews of economic evaluations: utility or futility? *Health Economics*, 19: 350–364.

Andrews, R (ed.) (2004) *The Impact of ICT on Literacy Education*. London: Routledge Falmer.

Andrews R, Burn A, Leach J, Locke T, Low G, Torgerson C (2002) *A Systematic Review of the Impact of Networked ICT on 5–16 Year Olds' Literacy in English (EPPI-Centre Review, version 1.1\*)*. London: EPPI-Centre, Social Science Research Unit, Institute of Education, University of London.

Anzures-Cabrera J, Higgins JPT (2010) Graphical displays for meta-analysis: an overview with suggestions for practice. *Research Synthesis Methods,* 1: 66–80.

Arksey H, O'Malley L (2005) Scoping studies: towards a methodological framework. *International Journal of Social Research Methodology,* 8(1): 19–32.

Arnstein S (1969) A ladder of citizen participation. *Journal of American Institute of Planners*, 35: 216–224.

Attree P, Milton B (2006) Critically appraising qualitative research for systematic reviews: defusing the methodological cluster bombs. *Evidence and Policy,* 2(1): 109–126.

Banarjee AV, Duflo E, Glennerster R, Kinnan C (2009) *The Miracle of Microfinance? Evidence from a Randomized Evaluation*. Washington, DC: CGAP.

Bannister EM, Leadbeater BJ, Marshall EA (2011) *Knowledge Translation in Context: Indigenous, Policy and Community Settings.* Toronto: University of Toronto Press.

Barnett-Page E, Thomas J (2009) Methods for the synthesis of qualitative research: A critical review. *BMC Medical Research Methodology*, 9: 59. DOI: 10.1186/1471-2288-9-59.

Bastian H (1994) *The Power of Sharing Knowledge: Consumer Participation in the Cochrane Collaboration*. Oxford: UK Cochrane Centre.

Beck CT (2002) A meta-synthesis of qualitative research. *The American Journal of Maternal/Child Nursing,* 27(4): 214–221.

Becker H (1970) *Sociological Work: Method and Substance*. Chicago, IL: Aldine.

Begg CB, Mazumdar M (1994) Operating characteristics of a rank correlation test for publication bias. *Biometrics*, 50: 1088–1101.

Bell M, Cordingley P, Isham C, Davis R (2010) *Report of Professional Practitioner Use of Research Review: Practitioner Engagement in and/or with Research*. Coventry: CUREE, GTCE, LSIS and NTRP. Available at: www.curee paccts.com/node/2303.

Berthoud R, Ermisch J, Francesconi M, Liao T, Pevalin D, Robson K (2004) Long-Term Consequences of Teenage Births for Parents and their Children: final report to the Department of Health. London UK: Department of Health/Teenage Pregnancy Unit.

Best A, Holmes B (2010) Systems thinking, knowledge and action: towards better models and methods. *Evidence and Policy*, 6(2): 145–159.

Blackmore P (1999) Mapping professional expertise: old tensions revisited. *Teacher Development*, 3(1): 19–38.

Bohlin I (In press) Formalising syntheses of medical knowledge: The rise of meta-analysis and systematic reviews. *Perspectives on Science*.

Borenstein, M, Hedges L, Higgins J, Rothstein H (2009) *Introduction to Meta-analysis*. Oxford: Wiley and Sons.

Boyatzis RE (1998) *Transforming Qualitative Information*. Cleveland: Sage.

Bragge P, Clavisi O, Turner T, Tavender E, Collie A, Gruen RL (2011) The global evidence mapping initiative: scoping research in broad topic areas. *BMC Medical Research Methodology,* 11: 92.

Brannen J (2005) Mixing methods: the entry of qualitative and quantitative approaches into the research process. *International Journal of Social Research Methodology*, 8(3): 173–184.

Briggs A, Sculpher M, Claxton K (2006) *Decision Modelling for Health Economic Evaluation*. Oxford: Oxford University Press.

Britten N, Campbell R, Pope C, Donovan J, Morgan M, Pill R (2002) Using meta ethnography to synthesise qualitative research: a worked example. *Journal of Health Services Research and Policy,* 7(4): 209–215.

Brittton A, McPherson K, McKee M, Sanderson C, Black N, Bain C (1998) Choosing between randomised and non-randomised studies: a systematic review. *Health Technology Assessment,* 2(13).

Brouwers M, Kho ME, Browman GP, Burgers JS, Cluzeau F, Feder G, Fervers B, Graham ID, Grimshaw J, Hanna S, Littlejohns P, Makarski J, Zitzelsberger L for the AGREE Next Steps Consortium. AGREE II: Advancing guideline development, reporting and evaluation in healthcare. *Can Med Assoc J. 2010*. The Agreee II Guidlines are available at http://www.agreetrust.org/ (accessed 20th February 2012)

Brunton G, Oliver S, Oliver K, Lorenc T (2006) *A Synthesis of Research Addressing Children's, Young People's and Parents' Views of Walking and Cycling for Transport*. London: EPPI-Centre, Social Science Research Unit, Institute of Education, University of London.

Brunton G, Wiggins M, Oakley A (2010) *Becoming a Mother: A Research Synthesis of Women's Experiences of First-time Motherhood*. London: EPPI-Centre, Social Science Research Unit, Institute of Education, University of London, pp. 1–55.

Bryanton J, Beck CT (2010) Postnatal parental education for optimizing infant general health and parent–infant relationships. *Cochrane Database of Systematic Reviews*, Issue 1. Art. No.: CD004068. DOI: 10.1002/14651858.CD004068.pub3.

Bryman A (1998) *Quantity and Quality in Social Research*. London: Unwin.

Buetow S, Adair V, Coster G, Hight M, Gribben B, Mitchell E (2003) GP care for moderate to severe asthma in children: what do infrequently attending mothers disagree with and why? *Family Practice*, 20: 155–161.

Burls A (2009) *What is Critical Appraisal?* (2nd edition). Newmarket: Hayward Medical Communications. (Full text available at: www.medicine.ox.ac.uk/bandolier/painres/download/whatis/What_is_critical_appraisal.pdf)

Burn A, Leach J (2004) A systematic review of the impact of ICT on the learning of literacies associated with moving image texts in English, 5-16. In: *Research Evidence in Education Library*. London: EPPI-Centre, Social Science Research Unit, Institute of Education, University of London.

Caird J, Rees R, Kavanagh J, Sutcliffe K, Oliver K, Dickson K, Woodman J, Barnett-Page E, Thomas J (2010) *The Socioeconomic Value of Nursing and Midwifery: A Rapid Systematic Review of Reviews*. London: EPPI-Centre, Social Science Research Unit, Institute of Education, University of London.

Caldwell DM, Welton NJ, Ades AE (2010) Mixed treatment comparison analysis provides internally coherent treatment effect estimates based on overviews of reviews and can reveal inconsistency. *Journal of Clinical Epidemiology,* 63(8): 875–882.

Campbell R, Pound P, Pope C, Britten N, Pill R, Morgan M, Donovan J (2003) Evaluating meta-ethnography: a synthesis of qualitative research on lay experiences of diabetes and diabetes care. *Social Science and Medicine,* 56: 671–684.

Carroll C, Booth A, Cooper K (2011) A worked example of 'best fit' framework synthesis: a systematic review of views concerning the taking of some potential chemopreventive agents. *BMC Medical Research Methodology,* 11: 29. DOI: 10.1186/1471-2288-11-29.

Cartwright J, Crowe S (2011) *Patient and Public Involvement Toolkit*. London: John Wiley and Sons.

Cesario S, Morin K, Santa-Donato A (2002) Evaluating the level of evidence of qualitative research. *Journal of Obstetric, Gynecologic, and Neonatal Nursing,* 31(6): 708–714.

Chalmers I (1995) What do I want from health research and researchers when I am a patient? *British Medical Journal,* 310: 1315.

Chalmers I (2001) Invalid health information is potentially lethal. *British Medical Journal,* 322: 998.

Chalmers I (2003) Trying to do more good than harm in policy and practice: the role of rigorous, transparent, up-to-date evaluations. *Annals of the American Academy of Political and Social Science*, 589(1): 22–40.

Chalmers I, Hedges L, Cooper H (2002) A brief history of research synthesis. *Evaluation and the Health Professions,* 25: 12–37.

Chalmers TC, Smith H Jr, Blackburn B, Silverman B, Schroeder B, Reitman D, Ambroz A (1981) A method for assessing the quality of a randomized control trial. *Controlled Clinical Trials,* 2: 31–49.

Chen HT (1994) *Theory Driven Evaluations*. Newbury Park, CA: Sage.

Clarke M (2007) Standardising outcomes for clinical trials and systematic reviews. *Trails,* 8.

Cochrane AL (1972/1989) *Effectiveness and Efficiency: Random Reflections on Health Services* (2nd edition). London: Nuffield Provincial Hospitals Trust.

Coe R (2002) It's the effect size, stupid: what effect size is and why it is important. Paper presented at the British Educational Research Association annual conference, Exeter, September.

Cohen J (1988) *Statistical Power Analysis for the Behavioral Sciences* (2nd edition). Englewood Cliffs, NJ: Lawrence Erlbaum Associates.

Cooper HM (1982) Scientific guidelines for conducting integrative research reviews. *Review of Educational Research*, 52: 291.

Cooper HM, Rosenthal R (1980) Statistical versus traditional procedures for summarizing research findings. *Psychological Bulletin,* 87: 442–449.

Copestake J, Duvendack M, Hooper L, Loke Y, Palmer-Jones R, Rao N (2010) *What is the Evidence of the Impact of Micro-Credit on the Incomes of Poor People? DFID Systematic Review Protocol*. London: Department for International Development.

Corbin J, Strauss A. (1990) Grounded theory research: procedures, canons, and evaluative criteria. *Qualitative Sociology*,13: 3–23.

Coren E, Hutchfield J, Thomae M, Gustafsson C. (2010) Parent training support for intellectually disabled parents. *Cochrane Database of Systematic Reviews,* Issue 6.

Cornwall A (1995) Towards participatory practice: PRA and the participatory process. In: deKoning K (ed.), *Participation and Health*. London:

CRD (2009) *Systematic Reviews: CRD's Guidance for Undertaking Reviews in Health Care*. York: Centre for Reviews and Dissemination, University of York.

Cresswell J (2003) *Research Design: Qualitative, Quantitative and Mixed Methods Approaches*. (2nd edition). London: Sage.

Critical Appraisal Skills Programme (CASP) (2002) *Ten Questions to Help You Make Sense of Qualitative Research*. Milton Keynes: Milton Keynes Primary Care Trust.

Crotty M (1998) *The Foundations of Social Research: Meaning and Perspective in the Research Process*. London: Sage.

Davies H, Nutley S, Walter I (2008) Why knowledge transfer is misconceived for applied social research. *Journal of Health Services Research and Policy,* 13: 3.

Dahlgren G, Whitehead M (1991) *Policies and Strategies to Promote Social Equality in Health*. Stockholm: Institute of Future Studies.

Davies H, Nutley S, Walter I (2005) *Assessing the Impact of Social Science Research: Conceptual, Methodological and Practical Issues: A Background Discussion Paper*. St Andrews: Research Unit for Research Utilization, School of Management, University of St Andrews.

Davies P (2007) Types of knowledge for evidence-based policy. Presentation to NORFACE Seminar on Evidence and Policy, University of Edinburgh, 26 November.

de Savigny D, Adam T (2009) *Systems Thinking for Health Systems Strengthening*. Geneva: World Health Organisation Alliance for Health Policy and Systems Research.

Deeks DD, Higgins JPT (2007) *Statistical Algorithms in Review Manager* (Vol 5). Place: The Cochrane Collaboration.

DeLuca JB, Mullins MM, Lyles CM, et al. (2008) Developing a comprehensive search strategy for evidence based systematic reviews. *Evidence Based Library and Information Practice.* 3(1): 3–32.

Dickersin K (2005) Publication bias: recognizing the problem, understanding its origins and scope, and preventing harm. In: H Rothstein, A Sutton, M Borenstein (eds), *Publication Bias in Meta-Analysis: Prevention, Assessment, and Adjustments*. London: John Wiley, pp. 11–33.

Dickersin K, Braun L, Mead M, Millikan R, Wu AM, Pietenpol J, Troyan S, Anderson B, Visco F (2001) Development and implementation of a science training course for breast cancer activists: Project LEAD (leadership, education and advocacy development). *Health Expectations,* 4: 213–220.

Dickson K, Gough D (2008) *Supporting People in Accessing Meaningful Work: Recovery Approaches in Community-Based Adult Mental Health Services*. SCIE Knowledge Review 21. London: Social Care Institute of Excellence.

Dickson K, Sutcliffe K, Gough D (2010) *The Experiences, Views and Preferences of Looked after Children and Young People and Their Families and Carers about the Care System*. London: EPPI-Centre, Social Science Research Unit, Institute of Education, University of London.

Dixon-Woods M, Agarwal S, Jones D, Young B, Sutton A (2005) Synthesising qualitative and quantitative evidence: a review of possible methods. *Journal of Health Services Research and Policy,* 10(1): 45–53.

Dixon-Woods M, Bonas S, Booth A, Jones DR, Miller T, Shaw RL, Smith J, Sutton A, Young B (2006a) How can systematic reviews incorporate qualitative research? A critical perspective. *Qualitative Research,* 6: 27–44.

Dixon-Woods M, Cavers D, Agarwal S, Annandale E, Arthur A, Harvey J, Hsu R, Katbamna S, Olsen R, Smith L, Riley R, Sutton AJ (2006b) Conducting a critical interpretive synthesis of the literature on access to healthcare by vulnerable groups. *BMC Medical Research Methodology,* 6(35).

Dixon-Woods M, Shaw R, Agarwal S, Smith J (2004) The problem of appraising qualitative research. *Quality and Safety in Health Care,* 13: 223–225.

Doak C, Heitmann, B, Summerbell C, Lissner L (2009) Prevention of childhood obesity: what type of evidence should we consider relevant? *Obesity Reviews,* 10(3): 350–356.

Doak CM, Visscher TL, Renders CM, Seidell JC (2006) The prevention of overweight and obesity in children and adolescents: a review of interventions and programmes. *Obesity Reviews,* 7(1): 111–136.

Donaldson C, Baker R, Mason H, Jones-Lee MW, Lancsar E, Wildman J, Bateman I, Loomes G, Robinson A, Sugden RC, Prades JLP, Ryan M, Shackley P, Smith R (2011) The social value of a QALY: Raising the bar or barring the raise? *BMC Health Services Research,* 11(8).

Drummond MF, Sculpher MJ, Torrance GW, O'Brien BJ, Stoddart GL (2005) *Methods for the Economic Evaluation of Health Care Programmes* (3rd edition). Oxford: Oxford University Press.

Duval S, Tweedie R (2000a) A non-parametric 'trim and fill' method of accounting for publication bias in meta-analysis. *Journal of the American Statistical Association,* 95: 89–98.

Duval S, Tweedie R (2000b) Trim and fill: a simple funnel-plot-based method of testing and adjusting for publication bias in meta-analysis. *Biometrics,* 56: 455–463.

Egger M, Juni P, Bartlett C, Holenstein F, Sterne J (2003) How important are comprehensive literature searches and the assessment of trial quality in systematic reviews? Empirical study. *Health Technology Assessment,* 7: 1–76.

Egger M, Smith GD, Schneider M, Minder C (1997) Bias in meta-analysis detected by a simple graphical test. *British Medical Journal,* 315: 629–634.

Elmir R, Schmied V, Wilkes L, Jackson D (2010) Women's perceptions and experiences of a traumatic birth: a meta-ethnography. *Journal of Advanced Nursing,* 66(10): 2142–2153.

Entwistle VA, Renfrew MJ, Yearley S, Forrester J, Lamont T (1998) Lay perspectives: advantages for health research. *British Medical Journal,* 316: 463.

Ernø-Kjølhede E (2000) *Project Management Theory and the Management of Research Projects.* Working Paper No. 3. Copenhagen: Department of Management, Politics and Philosophy Copenhagen Business School.

European Commission (2010) *Communicating Research for Evidence-based Policymaking: A Practical Guide for Researchers in Socio-economic Sciences and Humanities.* Luxembourg: Publications Office of the European Union.

European Commission (2004) *European Research: A Guide to Successful Communication.* Luxembourg: Office for Official Publications of the European Communities.

Evans J, Harden A, Thomas J, Benefield P (2003) *Support for Pupils with Emotional and Behavioural Difficulties (EBD) in Mainstream Primary Classrooms: A Systematic Review of the Effectiveness of Interventions.* London: EPPI-Centre, Social Science Research Unit, Institute of Education, University of London.

Evans T, Brown H (2003) Road traffic crashes: Operationalizing equity in the context of health sector reform. *Injury Control & Safety Promotion,* 10(1–2): 11–12.

Ezedunukwe I, Okwundu CI (2010) Economic interventions for prevention of HIV risk and HIV infection (Protocol). *Cochrane Database of Systematic Reviews,* Issue 1. Art. No.: CD008330. DOI: 10.1002/14651858.CD008330.

Flinterman JF, Teclemariam-Mesbah R, Broerse JEW, Bunders JFG (2001) *Bulletin of Science, Technology and Society,* 21(4): 253–266.

Flodgren G, Parmelli E, Doumit G, Gattellari M, O'Brien MA, Grimshaw J, Eccles MP (2007) Local opinion leaders: Effects on professional practice and health care outcomes. *Cochrane Database of Systematic Reviews,* Issue 1. Art. No.: CD000125. DOI: 10.1002/14651858. CD000125.pub3.

Forsberg M (2007) *Sexual Health in Young People: International Research Summaries and Swedish Experiences of Preventive Work.* Stockholm: Socialstyrelsen.

Frantzi K, Ananiadou S, Mima H (2000) Automatic recognition of multi-word terms: the C-value/NC-value method. *International Journal on Digital Libraries,* 3(2): 115–130.

Furlong J, Oancea A (2005) *Assessing Quality in Applied and Practice-based Educational Research: A Framework for Discussion.* Oxford: Oxford University, Department of Educational Studies.

Garcia J, Sinclair J, Dickson K, Thomas J, Brunton J, Tidd M, the PSHE Review Group (2006) *Conflict Resolution, Peer Mediation and Young People's Relationships: Technical Report.* London: EPPI-Centre, Social Science Research Unit, Institute of Education, University of London.

Gardner B, Whittington C, McAteer J, Eccles MP, Michie S. (2010) Using theory to synthesise evidence from behaviour change interventions: the example of audit and feedback. *Social Science and Medicine*, 70: 1618–1625.

Garrett D, Hodkinson P (1998) Can there be criteria for selecting research criteria? A hermeneutical analysis of an inescapable dilemma. *Qualitative Inquiry*, 4: 515–539.

General Accounting Office (1999) *Highway Safety: Effectiveness of State .08 Blood Alcohol Laws.* Report to Congressional Committees. Washington, DC: General Accounting Office (GAO). Available at: www. gao.gov/archive/1999/rc99179.pdf (accessed 24 December 2009).

Giacomini M (2009) Theory-based medicine and the role of evidence: why the emperor needs new clothes, again perspectives. *Biology and Medicine,* 52(2): 234–251.

Giacomini MK, Cook DJ. (2000) A user's guide to qualitative research in health care: Part I. Are the results of the study valid? *JAMA* 284: 357–62.

Glaser BG, Strauss A (1967) *Discovery of Grounded Theory: Strategies for Qualitative Research*. Chicago, IL: Aldine.

Glass G (1976) Primary, secondary and meta-analysis of research. *Educational Researcher,* 5: 3–8.

Glass G (2000) Meta-Analysis at 25. Available at: www.gvglass.info/papers/meta25.html (accessed 17 July 2011).

Glass GV, McGaw B, Smith ML (1981) *Meta-analysis in Social Research*. Newbury Park, CA: Sage.

Gleser LJ, Olkin I (2010) Stochastically dependent effect sizes. In: H Cooper, LV Hedges, JC Valentine (eds), *The Handbook of Research Synthesis and Meta-Analysis (*2nd edition). New York: Russell Sage Foundation, pp. 357–376.

Goldring, E. (1990) Assessing the status of information about classroom organizational frameworks for gifted education students. *Journal of Educational Research*, 83: 313–326.

Goldstein H, Yang M (2000) Meta-analysis using multilevel models with an application to the study of class size effects. *Applied Statistics*, 49(3): 399–412.

Gomersall A, Cooper C (2010) Database selection bias and its affect on systematic reviews: a United Kingdom perspective. Workshop presented at the Joint Colloquium of the Cochrane and Campbell Collaborations, Keystone, Colorado, USA, 18–22 October.

Goudie AC, Sutton AJ, Jones DR, Donald A (2010) Empirical assessment suggests existing evidence could be used more fully in designing randomised controlled trials *Journal of Clinical Epidemiology,* 63(9): 983–991.

Gough D (2007a) Giving voice: evidence-informed policy and practice as a democratizing process. In: M Reiss, R DePalma, E Atkinson (eds), *Marginality and Difference in Education and Beyond.* London: Trentham Books.

Gough D (2007b) Dimensions of difference in evidence reviews (Overview; I. Questions, evidence and methods; II. Breadth and depth; III. Methodological approaches; IV. Quality and relevance appraisal; V. Communication, interpretation and application). Series of six posters presented at National Centre for Research Methods meeting, Manchester, January. London: EPPI-Centre, Social Science research Unit, Institute of Education, University of London.

Gough D (2007c) Weight of evidence: a framework for the appraisal of the quality and relevance of evidence. In: J Furlong, A Oancea (eds), *Applied and Practice-based Research* (Special edition of research papers in education).

Gough D (2011) User-led Reviews of Research Knowledge: Enhancing Relevance and Reception. In Banister E et al *Knowledge Translation in Context: University-Community, Policy and Indigenous Approaches*. Toronto: University of Toronto Press.

Gough D et al. (in preparation) *Meta Evaluation*.

Gough D, Thomas J, Oliver S (In press) Clarifying differences between review designs and methods. *Systematic Reviews Journal.*

Gough DA, Elbourne D (2002) Systematic research synthesis to inform policy, practice, and democratic debate. *Social Policy and Society,* 1(3): 225–236.

Gough DA, Kiwan D, Sutcliffe K, Simpson D, Houghton N (2003) *A Systematic Map and Synthesis Review of the Effectiveness of Personal Development Planning for Improving*

*Student Learning.* London: EPPI-Centre, Social Science Research Unit, Institute of Education, University of London.

Gough DA, Oliver S, Brunton G, Selai C, Schaumberg H (2001) *The Effect of Travel Modes on Children's Mental Health, Cognitive and Social Development: A Systematic Review.* London: EPPI-Centre, Social Science Research Unit, Institute of Education, University of London.

Gough DA, Oliver S, Newman M, Bird K (2009) Transparency in planning, warranting and interpreting research. *Teaching and Learning Research Briefing 78.* London: Teaching and Learning Research Programme.

Gough, DA, Tripney J, Kenny C (2011) *Evidence Informed Policy in Education In Europe. Final Report of the EIPEE Project.* London: EPPI-Centre, Social Science Research Unit, Institute of Education, University of London.

GRADE Working Group (2004) Education and debate: grading quality of evidence and strength of recommendations. *British Medical Journal,* 328: 1490.

Graham ID, Logan J, Harrison MB, Straus SE, Tetroe J, Caswell W, Robinson N (2006) Lost in knowledge translation: time for a map? *The Journal of Continuing Education in the Health Professions,* 26: 13–24.

Greenhalgh T, Taylor R (1997) How to read a paper: papers that go beyond numbers (qualitative research). *British Medical Journal,* 315, 740–743.

Greenhalgh T, Robert G, Bate P, Macfarlane F, Kyriakidou O (2005a) *Diffusion of Innovations in Health Service Organisations: A Systematic Literature Review.* Oxford: Blackwells.

Greenhalgh T, Robert G, Macfarlane F, Bate P, Kyriakidou O (2004) Diffusion of innovations in service organizations: systematic review and recommendations. *Millbank Quarterly,* 82(4): 581–624.

Greenhalgh T, Robert G, Macfarlane F, Bate P, Kyriakidou O, Peacock R (2005b) Storylines of research in diffusion of innovation: a meta-narrative approach to systematic review. *Social Science and Medicine,* 61: 417–430.

Greenwald, AG (1975) Consequences of prejudice against the null hypothesis. *Psychological Bulletin,* 82(1): 1–20.

Guyatt G, DiCenso A, Farewell V, Willan A, Griffith L (2000) Randomized trials versus observational studies in adolescent pregnancy prevention. *Journal of Clinical Epidemiology,* 53: 167–174.

Guyatt GH, Oxman AD, Schunemann HJ, Tugwell P, Krottneruse G (2011) GRADE guidelines: a new series of articles. *Journal of Clinical Epidemiology,* 64(4): 380–382.

Guyatt GH, Oxman AD, Vist GE, Kunz R, Falck-Ytter Y, Alonso-Coello P, et al. (2008) GRADE: an emerging consensus on rating quality of evidence and strength of recommendations. *British Medical Journal,* 336: 924–926.

Habermas J (1970) Towards a theory of communicative competence. In: HP Dreitzel (ed.), *Recent Sociology 2: Patterns of Communicative Behaviour.* New York: Macmillan, pp. 114–148.

Hammerstrøm K, Wade A, Jørgensen A (2010) Searching for Studies: *A Guide to Information Retrieval for Campbell Systematic Reviews* 2010: *Supplement 1.* Oslo: The Campbell Collaboration Collaboration.

Hanley B, Bradburn J, Gorin S, Barnes M, Evans C, Goodare H, Kelson M, Kent A, Oliver S, Wallcraft J (2000) *Involving Consumers in Research and Development in the NHS: Briefing Notes for Researchers.* Winchester: Consumers in NHS Research Support Unit.

Harden A (2007) The quality of qualitative evidence: A review of assessment tools. Paper presented at the Seventh Annual International Campbell Colloquium, 14–16 May, London.

Harden A, Brunton G, Fletcher A, Oakley A (2009) Teenage pregnancy and social disadvantage: A systematic review integrating trials and qualitative studies. *British Medical Journal,* 339. Available at: www.bmj.com/cgi/content/full/bmj.b4254 (accessed 15 February 2012).

Harden A, Brunton G, Fletcher A, Oakley A, Burchett H, Backhans M (2006) *Young People, Pregnancy and Social Exclusion: A Systematic Synthesis of Research Evidence to Identify*

*Effective, Appropriate and Promising Approaches for Prevention and Support.* London: EPPI-Centre, Social Science Research Unit, Institute of Education, University of London.

Harden A, Oakley A, Oliver S (2001) Peer-delivered health promotion for young people: A systematic review of different study designs. *Health Education Journal,* 60(4): 339–353.

Harden A, Thomas J (2005) Methodological issues in combining diverse study types in systematic reviews. *International Journal of Social Research Methodology,* 8(3): 257–271.

Harden A, Thomas J (2010) Mixed methods and systematic reviews: Examples and emerging issues. In: A Tashakkori, C Teddlie (eds) *SAGE Handbook of Mixed Methods in Social and Behavioral Research.* London: Sage, pp. 749–774.

Harden A, Weston R, Oakley A (1999) *A Review of the Effectiveness and Appropriateness of Peer-delivered Health Promotion Interventions for Young People.* London: EPPI-Centre, Social Science Research Unit, Institute of Education, University of London.

Hargreaves DH (1996) Teaching as a research-based profession: Possibilities and prospects. Teacher Training Agency Annual Lecture 1996. London: Teacher Training Agency. Available on the EPPI-Centre website.

Harper I (2009) Tuberculosis control in Nepal and India are national programmes using correct treatment regimens? *Journal of Health Studies,* 2: 51–67.

Hedges LV, Vevea JL (1998) Fixed-and random-effects models in meta-analysis. *Psychological Methods,* 3: 486–504.

Herring C (1968) Distil or drown: The need for reviews. *Physics Today,* 21: 27–33.

Higgins JPT, Green S (eds) (2009a) *Cochrane Handbook for Systematic Reviews of Interventions.* Version 5.0.2. London: The Cochrane Collaboration. Available at: www.cochrane-handbook. org (accessed 17 November 2010).

Higgins JPT, Green S (editors) *Cochrane Handbook for Systematic Reviews of Interventions* Version 5.1.0 [updated March 2011]. The Cochrane Collaboration, 2011. Available from www.cochrane-handbook.org.

Higgins JPT, Thompson SG, Deeks JJ, Altman DG (2003) Measuring inconsistency in meta-analyses. *British Medical Journal,* 327: 557–560 (6 September).

Hill A, Spittlehouse C (2003) What is critical appraisal? *Evidence Based Medicine,* 3(2): 1–8.

Hill S (2011) *The Knowledgeable Patient: Communication and Participation in Health.* A Cochrane handbook. London: Wiley-Blackwell.

Hodnett ED, Gates S, Hofmeyr GJ, Sakala C, Weston J (2011) Continuous support for women during childbirth. *Cochrane Database of Systematic Reviews,* Issue 2. Art. No.: CD003766. DOI: 10.1002/14651858.CD003766.pub3.

Hox JJ (2010) *Multilevel Analysis: Techniques and Applications* (2nd edition). New York: Routledge.

InterTASC Information Specialists' Sub-Group (ISSG) (2010) *Search Filter Resource.* Available at: www.york.ac.uk/inst/crd/intertasc/index.htm (accessed 15 February 2012).

Ioannidis JP (2009) Integration of evidence from multiple meta-analyses: A primer on umbrella reviews, treatment networks and multiple treatments meta-analyses. *Canadian Medical Association Journal,* 181(8): 488–493.

Irwin A (2001) Constructing the scientific citizen: Science and democracy in the biosciences. *Public Understanding of Science,* 10: 1.

Jackson N, Waters E, Guidelines for Systematic Reviews of Health Promotion and Public Health Interventions Taskforce (eds) (2005) *Guidelines for Systematic Reviews of Health Promotion and Public Health Interventions.* Version 1.2. Melbourne, Vic.: Deakin University.

Johnson R, Onwuegbuzie A (2004) Mixed methods research: A research paradigm whose time has come? *Educational Researcher,* 33: 14–26.

Jones H (2011) *A Guide to Monitoring and Evaluating Policy Influence.* Background note. London: Overseas Development Institute.

Juni P, Altman D, Egger M (2001) Assessing the quality of controlled clinical trials. *British Medical Journal,* 323: 42–46.

Juni P, Witschi A, Bloch R, Egger M (1999) The hazards of scoring the quality of clinical trials for meta-analysis. *Journal of the American Medical Association,* 282: 1054–1060.

Kalaian HA, Raudenbush SW (1996) A multivariate mixed-effects linear model for meta-analysis. *Psychological Methods*, 1: 227–235.

Kalaian SA, Kasim RM (2008a) Applications of multilevel models for meta-analysis. In: AA O'Connell, DB McCoach (eds), *Multilevel Analysis of Educational Data*. Greenwich, CT: Information Age Publishing.

Kalaian SA, Kasim RM (2008b) Why multivariate meta-analysis methods for studies with multivariate outcomes? Paper presented at the MWERA Annual Meeting, Westin Great Southern Hotel, Columbus, Ohio.

Karlan D, Zinman J (2010) Expanding credit access: Using randomised supply decisions to estimate the impacts. *Review of Financial Studies,* 23(1): 433–464.

Kastner M, Straus S, Goldsmith CH (2007) Estimating the horizon of articles to decide when to stop searching in systematic reviews: An example using a systematic review of RCTs evaluating osteoporosis clinical decision support tools. *American Medical Informatics Association Annual Symposium Proceedings Archive*. Place: Pub, pp. 389–393. Available at: www.ncbi.nlm.nih.gov/pmc/articles/PMC2655834/ (accessed 30 November 2010).

Katrak P, Bialocerkowski AE, Massy-Westropp N, Kumar VSS, Grimmer KA (2004) A systematic review of the content of critical appraisal tools. *BMC Medical Research Methodology,* 4: 22.

Kavanagh J, Oakley A, Harden A, Trouton A, Powell C (2010) Are incentive schemes effective in changing young people's behaviour? A systematic review. *Health Education Journal,* 70(2): 192–205.

Kavanagh J, Oliver S, Lorenc T (2008) Reflections in developing and using PROGRESS-Plus. *Equity Update,* 2: 1–3.

Kavanagh J, Oliver S, Lorenc T, Caird J, Tucker H, Harden A, Greaves A, Thomas J, Oakley A (2009a) School-based cognitive-behavioural interventions: A systematic review of effects and inequalities. *Health Sociology Review*, 18(1): 61–78.

Kavanagh J, Oakley A, Harden A, Trouton A, Powell C (2011) Are incentive schemes effective in changing young people's behaviour? A systematic review. *Health Education Journal,* 70(2): 192–205.

Kavanagh J, Stansfield C, Thomas J (2009b) *Incentives to Improve Smoking, Physical Activity, Dietary and Weight Management Behaviours: A Scoping Review of the Research Evidence*. London: EPPI-Centre, Social Science Research Unit, Institute of Education, University of London.

Kavanagh J, Trouton A, Oakley A, Powell C (2006) *A Systematic Review of the Evidence for Incentive Schemes to Encourage Positive Health and other Social Behaviours in Young People*. London: EPPI-Centre, Social Science Research Unit, Institute of Education, University of London.

Kettle C, Hills RK, Ismail KMK (2007) Continuous versus interrupted sutures for repair of episiotomy or second degree tears. *Cochrane Database of Systematic Reviews*, Issue 4. Art. No.: CD000947. DOI: 10.1002/14651858.CD000947.pub2.

Koehlmoos T, Gazi R, Hossain S, Rashid M (2011) *Social Franchising Evaluations: A Scoping Review*. London: EPPI-Centre, Social Science Research Unit, Institute of Education, University of London.

Koehlmoos TP, Gazi R, Hossain SS, Zaman K (2009) The effect of social franchising on access to and quality of health services in low- and middle-income countries. *Cochrane Database of Systematic Reviews*, Issue 1. Art. No.: CD007136. DOI: 10.1002/14651858. CD007136.pub2.

Krieger N (1999) Embodying inequality: A review of concepts, measures, and methods for studying health consequences of discrimination. *International Journal of Health Services,* 29(2): 295–352.

Kuhn TS (1962) *The Structure of Scientific Revolutions*. Chicago: University of Chicago Press.

Kunz R, Oxman A (1998) The unpredictability paradox: Review of empirical comparisons of randomised and non-randomised clinical trials. *British Medical Journal,* 317: 1185–1190.

Kuzel A, Engel J (2001) Some pragmatic thought on evaluating qualitative health research. In J Morse, J Swanson, A Kuzel (eds), *The Nature of Qualitative Evidence* (pp. 114–138). Thousand Oaks, CA: Sage.

Lai NM, Teng CL, Lee ML (2011) Interpreting systematic reviews: Are we ready to make our own conclusions? A cross-sectional study. *BMC Medicine,* 9: 30. DOI: 10.1186/1741-7015-9-30.

Lavis J, Davies H, Oxman A, Denis JL, Golden-Biddle K, Ferlie E (2005) Towards systematic reviews that inform health care management and policy-making. *Journal of Health Services Research and Policy*, 10(1): 35–48.

Lawlor DA, Shaw M (2002) Too much too young? Teenage pregnancy is not a public health problem. *International Journal of Epidemiology* 31: 552–3.

Lefebvre C, Manheimer E, Glanville J (2010) Searching for studies. In: J Higgins, S Green (eds), *Cochrane Handbook for Systematic Reviews of Interventions.* Version 5.0.2 (updated September 2009). Place: The Cochrane Collaboration.

Levin, B (2004) Making research matter more. *Education Policy Analysis Archives,* 12(56). Available at: http://epaa.asu.edu/epaa/v12n56/ (accessed 16 December 2010).

Lewin S, Lavis J, Fretheim A (in press) SUPPORT Tools for evidence-informed health policymaking (STP) 19: Involving the public. *Health Research Policy and Systems,* 7(I): S15. DOI: 10.1186/1478-4505-7-S1-S15.

Liabo and Gray (2008): Liabo K, Gray K (2008) Working together to produce a systematic review. INVOLVE conference newsletter p8–9

Liabo K, Mulcahy D, Gray K. (in press) A systematic review of interventions to support looked after children in school. *Child & Family Social Work.*

Lipsey M (2003) Those confounded moderators in meta-analysis: Good, bad, and ugly. *The Annals of the American Academy of Political and Social Science,* 587: 69–81.

Lipsey MW, Wilson DB (2001) *Practical Meta-analysis.* Applied Social Research Methods Series Vol. 49. Thousand Oaks, CA: Sage.

Locke T, Andrews R (2004) *A Systematic Review of the Impact of ICT on Literature-related Literacies in English 5–16.* London: EPPI-Centre, Social Science Research Unit, Institute of Education, University of London.

Lorenc T, Brunton G, Oliver S, Oliver K, Oakley A (2008) Attitudes to walking and cycling among children, young people and parents: a systematic review. *Journal of Epidemiology and Community Health,* 62: 852–857. DOI: 10.1136/jech.2007.070250.

Low G, Beverton S (2004) *A Systematic Review of the Impact of ICT on Literacy Learning in English of Learners between 5 and 16, for whom English is a Second or Additional Language.* London: EPPI-Centre, Social Science Research Unit, Institute of Education, University of London.

MacLehose R, Reeves B, Harvey I, Sheldon T, Russell, I, Black A (2000) A systematic review of comparisons of effect sizes derived from randomised and non-randomised studies. *Health Technology Assessment Reports,* 4: 1–154.

Masset E, Haddad L, Cornelius A, Isaza-Castro J (2011) *A Systematic Review of Agricultural Interventions that Aim to Improve Nutritional Status of Children.* London: EPPI-Centre, Social Science Research Unit, Institute of Education, University of London.

Mays N, Pope C (1995) Qualitative Research: Rigour and Qualitative Research. *British Medical Journal*, 311(6997): 109–112.

McCartney K, Rosenthal R (2000) Effect size, practical importance, and social policy for children. *Child Development,* 71(1): 173–180.

Mercer SL, Sleet DA, Elder RW, Hopkins Cole K, Shults RA, Nichols JL (2010) translating evidence into policy: lessons learned from the case of lowering the legal blood alcohol limit for drivers. *Annals of Epidemiology,* 20(6): 412–420.

Meremikwu MM, Oyo-Ita A (2002) Paracetamol versus placebo or physical methods for treating fever in children. *Cochrane Database of Systematic Reviews* Issue 2. Art. No.: CD003676. DOI: 10.1002/14651858.CD003676.

Mertens, DM (2003) Mixed methods and the politics of human research: The transformative-emancipatory perspective. In: A Tashakkori, C Teddlie (eds), *Handbook of Mixed Methods in Social and Behavioral Research*. Thousand Oaks, CA: Sage, pp. 135–164.

Miles MB, Huberman MA (1994) *Qualitative Data Analysis: An Expanded Sourcebook* (2nd edition). Beverley Hills, CA: Sage.

Ministerio de Sanidad, Politica Social e Igualdad (2010) *Guía de Práctica Clínica sobre el Diagnóstico, el Tratamiento y la Prevención de la Tuberculosis*. Versión complete. Guisias de Practica Clinica EN EL SNS.

Moher D, Jadad AR, Nichol G, Penman M, Tugwell P, Walsh S (1995) Assessing the quality of randomized controlled trials: an annotated bibliography of scales and checklists.*Controlled Clin Trials*, 16: 62–73.

Moher D, Cook S, Eastwood S, Olkin S, Rennie S, Stroup S (2000) Improving the quality of reports of meta-analyses of randomised controlled trials: The QUOROM statement. *The Lancet*, 354(9193): 1896–1900.

Moher D, Liberati A, Tetzlaff J, Altman DG, The PRISMA Group (2009) Preferred reporting items for systematic reviews and meta-analyses: The PRISMA statement. *PLoS Med*, 6(6): e1000097. DOI: 10.1371/journal.pmed1000097.

Moher D, Pham B, Jones A, Cook DJ, Jadad AR, Moher M, Tugwell P, Klassen TP (1998) Does quality of reports of randomised trials effect estimates of intervention efficacy reported in meta-analyses? *Lancet,* 352: 609–613.

Moher D, Pham B, Lawson ML, Klassen TP (2003) The inclusion of reports of randomised trials published in languages other than English in systematic reviews. *Health Technology Assessment,* 7: 1–90.

Morgan DL (2007) Paradigms lost and pragmatism regained: Methodological implications of combining qualitative and quantitative methods. *Journal of Mixed Methods Research*, 1(1): 48–76.

Munro SA, Lewin SA, Smith HJ, Engel ME, Fretheim A, Volmink J (2007) Patient adherence to tuberculosis treatment: A systematic review of qualitative research. *PLoS Med,* 4(7): e238. DOI:10.1371/journal.pmed.0040238.

National Collaborating Centre for Chronic Conditions and the Centre for Clinical Practice at NICE (2011) Tuberculosis: Clinical diagnosis and management of tuberculosis, and measures for its prevention and control. *NICE Clinical Guideline,* 117.

NICE (National Institute for Health and Clinical Excellence) (2007) One-to-one interventions to reduce the transmission of sexually transmitted infections (STIs) including HIV, and to reduce the rate of under 18 conceptions, especially among vulnerable and at risk groups. *NICE Public Health Intervention Guidance,* 3. London: NICE.

NICE (2008) *Guide to the Methods of Technology Appraisal*. London: National Institute for Health and Clinical Excellence.

Noblit G, Hare RD (1988) *Meta-ethnography: Synthesizing Qualitative Studies*. Newbury Park, CA: Sage.

Noyes J (2010) Never mind the qualitative, feel the depth! The evolving role of qualitative research in Cochrane intervention reviews. *Journal of Research in Nursing*, 15(6): 525–534.

Noyes J, Popay J (2007) Directly observed therapy and tuberculosis: How can a systematic review of qualitative research contribute to improving services? A qualitative meta-synthesis. *Journal of Advanced Nursing,* 57(3):227–243.

Noyes J, Popay J, Pearson A, Hannes K, Booth A (2011) Qualitative research and Cochrane reviews. In: JPT Higgins, S Green (eds), *Cochrane Handbook for Systematic Reviews of Interventions*.Version 5.1.0 (updated March 2011). Place: The Cochrane Collaboration. Available at: www.cochrane-handbook.org. (accessed 15 February 2012).

Nutley SM, Davies HTO (2000) Making a reality of evidence-based practice: Some lessons from the diffusion of innovations. *Public Money and Management,* 20(4): 35–42.

Nutley SM, Morton S, Jung T, Boaz A (2010) Evidence and policy in six European countries: Diverse approaches and common challenges. *Evidence & Policy: A Journal of Research, Debate and Practice,* 6(2): 131–144.

Nykänen H, Koricheva J (2004) Damage-induced changes in woody plants and their effects on insect herbivore performance: A meta-analysis. *Oikos*, 104: 247–268.

O'Blenis P (2004) *The Electronic Systematic Review Handbook*. Place: Trialstat Corporation.

Oakley A (1998) Experimentation in social science: The case of health promotion. *Social Sciences in Health*, 4: 73–89.

Oakley A (2000a) Paradigm wars: Some thoughts on a personal and public trajectory. *International Journal of Social Research Methodology*, 2(3): 247–254.

Oakley A (2000b) *Experiments in Knowing: Gender and Method in the Social Sciences*. Cambridge: Polity Press.

Oakley A (2002) Social science and evidence-based everything: The case of education. *Educational Review*, 54(3): 277–286.

Oakley A (2003) Research evidence, knowledge management and educational practice: Early lessons from a systematic approach. *London Review of Education*, 1(1): 21–33.

Oakley A (2011) *A Critical Woman: Barbara Wootton, Social Science and Public Policy in the Twentieth Century*. London: Bloomsbury Academic.

Oakley A, Gough D, Oliver S, Thomas J (2005) The politics of evidence and methodology: Lessons from the EPPI-Centre. *Evidence and Policy*, 1(1): 5–31.

Oakley L, Hollowell J, Kavanagh J, Barnett-Page E, Vigurs C, Oliver S (in preparation) Increasing the early initiation of antenatal care by disadvantaged women in the United Kingdom: a systematic review and mixed methods synthesis of women's views and the literature on intervention effectiveness. Oxford: National Perinatal Epidemiology Unit.

Oancea A. and Furlong, J. (2007) Expressions of excellence and the assessment of applied and practice-based research. *Research Papers in Education*, 22(2), pp. 119–137.

Ogilvie D, Fayter D, Petticrew M, Sowden A, Thomas S, Whitehead M, Worthy G (2008) The harvest plot: A method for synthesising evidence about the differential effects of interventions. *BMC Medical Research Methodology*, 8(8).

Oliver S (1997) Exploring lay perspectives on questions of effectiveness. In: A Maynard, I Chalmers (eds), *Non-random Reflections on Health Services Research*. London: BMJ Publishing Group.

Oliver S, Bagnall AM, Thomas J, Shepherd J, Sowden A, White I, Dinnes J, Rees R, Colquitt J, Oliver K, Garrett Z. (2010) RCTs for policy interventions: A review of reviews and meta-regression. *Health Technology Assessment*, 14(16).

Oliver S, Clarke-Jones L, Rees R, Buchanan P, Gabbay J, Gyte G, Milne R, Oakley A, Stein K (2004) Involving consumers in research and development agenda setting for the NHS: Developing an evidence-based approach. *Health Technology Assessment*, 8(15).

Oliver S, Kavanagh J, Caird J, Lorenc T, Oliver K, Harden A, Thomas J, Greaves A, Oakley A (2008a) *Health Promotion, Inequalities and Young People's Health: A Systematic Review of Research*. London: EPPI-Centre, Social Science Research Unit, Institute of Education, University of London.

Oliver S, Milne R, Bradburn J, Buchanan P, Kerridge L, Walley T, Gabbay J (2001a) Investigating consumer perspectives on evaluating health technologies. *Evaluation*, 7(4): 468–486.

Oliver S, Oakley L, Lumley J, Waters E (2001b) Smoking cessation programmes in pregnancy: Systematically addressing development, implementation, women's concerns and effectiveness. *Health Education Journal* 60(4): 362–370.

Oliver S, Peersman G, Harden A, Oakley A (1999) Discrepancies in findings from effectiveness reviews: The case of health promotion for older people in accident and injury prevention. *Health Education Journal*, 58(1): 66–77.

Oliver S, Rees RW, Clarke-Jones L, Milne R, Oakley AR, Gabbay J, Stein K, Buchanan P, Gyte G (2008b) A multidimensional conceptual framework for analyzing public involvement in health services research. *Health Expectations*, 11(1): 72–84.

Orwin RG (1994) Evaluating coding decisions. In: H Cooper, LV Hedges (eds), *The Handbook of Research Synthesis*. New York: Russell Sage Foundation.

Ouimet M, Bédard P, Turgeon J, Lavis JN, Gélineau F, Gagnon F, Dallaire C (2010) Correlates of consulting research evidence among policy analysts in government ministries: a cross-sectional survey. *Evidence & Policy: A Journal of Research, Debate and Practice*, 6(4): 433–460.

Overton RC (1998) A comparison of fixed effects and mixed (random-effects) models for meta-analysis test of moderator effects. *Psychological Methods,* 3: 354–379.

Oxman AD, Lewin S, Lavis JN, Fretheim A (2009) SUPPORT Tools for evidence-informed health Policymaking (STP) 15: Engaging the public in evidence-informed policymaking. *Health Research Policy and Systems,* 7(1): S15. DOI: 10.1186/1478-4505-7-S1-S15.

Patterson BL, Thorne SE, Canam C, Jillings C (2001) *Meta-Study of Qualitative Health Research: A Practical Guide to Meta-analysis and Meta-synthesis.* Newbury Park, CA: Sage.

Patton MQ (1990) *Qualitative Evaluation and Research Methods* (2nd edition). Newbury Park, CA: Sage.

Pawson R (2002) Evidence-based policy: In search of a method. *Evaluation,* 8: 157–181.

Pawson R (2006a) *Evidenced-based Policy: A Realist Perspective.* London: Sage.

Pawson R (2006b) Digging for nuggets: how 'bad' research can yield 'good' evidence. *International Journal of Social Research Methodology,* 9: 127–142.

Pawson R, Boaz A, Grayson L, Long A, Barnes C (2003) *Types and Quality of Knowledge in Social Care.* London: Social Care Institute for Excellence.

Pawson R, Greenhalgh T, Harvey G, Walshe K (2004) Realist synthesis: An introduction. *RMP Methods Paper 2/2004.* Manchester: ESRC Research Methods Programme.

Peersman G (1996) *A Descriptive Mapping of Health Promotion Studies in Young People.* EPPI Research Report. London: EPPI-Centre, Social Science Research Unit, Institute of Education, University of London.

Peersman G, Oliver S (1997) EPI-Centre Keywording Strategy. Data Collection for the BiblioMap Database. London EPI-Centre, Social Science Research Unit.

Peersman G, Harden A, Oliver S (1999) *Effectiveness Reviews in Health Promotion.* London: EPPI-Centre, Social Science Research Unit, Institute of Education, University of London.

Petrosino A, Turpin-Petrosino C, Buehler J (2002) 'Scared Straight' and other juvenile awareness programs for preventing juvenile delinquency. *Cochrane Database of Systematic Reviews,* Art.No.: Issue 2.

Petticrew M (2001) Systematic reviews from astronomy to zoology: myths and misconceptions. *British Medical Journal,* 322: 98. DOI: 10.1136/bmj.322.7278.98.

Petticrew M, Roberts H (2006) *Systematic Reviews in the Social Sciences: A Practical Guide.* Oxford: Blackwell.

Petticrew M, Tugwell P, Kristjansson E, Oliver S, Ueffing E, Welch V. (2012) Damned if you do, damned if you don't: subgroup analysis and equity. *J Epidemiol Community Health* 66: 95–98.

Petticrew M, Anderson L, Elder R, Grimshaw JM, Hopkins D, Hahn R, Krause L, Kristjansson E, Mercer S, Sipe T, Tugwell P, Ueffing E, Waters E, Welch V. (In Press). Complex interventions and their implications for systematic reviews: a pragmatic approach. BMJ.

Phillips R (2003) *Stakeholder Theory and Organizational Ethics.* San Francisco: Berrett-Koehler.

Phipps DJ, Shapson S (2009) Knowledge mobilisation builds local research collaborations for social innovation. *Evidence & Policy,* 5(3): 211–227.

Ploeg J (1999) Identifying the best research design to fit the question. Part 2: Qualitative designs. *Evidence Based Nursing,* 2: 36–37. DOI:10.1136/ebn.2.2.36.

Popay J, Arai L, Roberts H, Roen K (2003) *Preventing Accidents in Children – How Can We Improve Our Understanding of What Really Works?* London: Health Development Agency.

Popay J, Roberts H, Sowden A, Petticrew M, Arai L, Rodgers M, Britten N, Roen K, Duffy S (2006) *Guidance on the Conduct of Narrative Synthesis in Systematic Reviews: A Product from the ESRC Methods Programme.* Lancaster: Institute for Health Research, Lancaster University. Available at: www.lancs.ac.uk/shm/research/.../NS_Synthesis_Guidance_v1.pdf (accessed 2 April 2011).

Pope C, Mays N, Popay J (2007) *Synthesizing Qualitative and Quantitative Health Evidence: A Guide to Methods.* Milton Keynes: Open University Press.

Pope C, Ziebland S, Mays N. (2000) Qualitative research in health care: Analysing qualitative data. *British Medical Journal,* 320: 114–116.

Prictor M, Hill S, Car J, Chan S-P, Edwards A, Glenton C, Horey D, Kis-Rigo J, Lewin S, McKenzie J, McKinstry B, Oliver S, Ryan R, Santesso N, Stewart R (2010) *Cochrane Consumers and Communication Group: About The Cochrane Collaboration (Cochrane Review Groups (CRGs).* Issue 1. Art. No.: COMMUN.

Pullin AS, Knight TM, Watkinson AR (2009) Linking reductionist science and holistic policy using systematic reviews: Unpacking environmental policy questions to construct an evidence-based framework. *Journal of Applied Ecology,* 46: 970–975. DOI: 10.1111/j.1365-2664.2009.01704.x.

Pullin, AS, Stewart GB (2006) Guidelines for systematic review in conservation and environmental management. *Conservation Biology,* 20: 1647–1656.

Rees R (2008) *The Theory and Principles of Searching in Systematic Reviews: A Paper Produced for the Online Module 'Research Synthesis for Policy and Practice'.* London: EPPI-Centre, Social Science Research Unit, Institute of Education, University of London.

Rees R, Garcia J, Oakley A (2007) Consent in school-based research involving children and young people: A survey of research from systematic reviews. *Research Ethics Review,* 3(2): 35–39.

Rees R, Kavanagh J, Burchett H, Shepherd J, Brunton G, Harden A, Thomas J, Oliver S, Oakley A (2004) *HIV Health Promotion and Men Who Have Sex with Men (MSM): A Systematic Review of Research Relevant to the Development and Implementation of Effective and Appropriate Interventions.* London: EPPI-Centre, Social Science Research Unit, Institute of Education, University of London.

Rees R, Caird J, Stansfield C, Dickson K, Kavanagh J, Thomas J (2010) *Young people's views relating to obesity and body size, shape and weight: protocol for a systematic review.* London: EPPI-Centre, Social Science Research Unit, Institute of Education, University of London.

Rees R, Oliver S (2007) User involvement in systematic reviews: An example from health promotion. In: E Coren (ed.), *Collection of Examples of Service User and Carer Participation in Systematic Reviews.* London. Social Care Institute for Excellence. Available at: www.scie.org.uk/publications/details.asp?pubID=125 (accessed 6 September 2007).

Rees R, Oliver K, Woodman J, Thomas J (2009) Children's Views about Obesity, Body Size, Shape and Weight: A Systematic Review. London: EPPI Centre, Social Science Research Unit, Institute of Education, University of London.

Rees R, Woodman J, Kavanagh J, Harden A, Stansfield C, Lorenc T, Thomas J, Roberts H, Oakley A (2008) *Children's Views Relating to Obesity and Body Size, Shape and Weight: Protocol for a Systematic Review.* London: EPPI-Centre, Social Science Research Unit, Institute of Education, University of London.

Ring N, Ritchie K, Mandava L, Jepson R (2010) *A Guide to Synthesising Qualitative Research for Researchers Undertaking Health Technology Assessments and Systematic Reviews.* NHS Quality Improvement Scotland. Available at: www.healthcareimprovementscotland.org/programmes/clinical__cost_effectiveness/programme_resources/synth_qualitative_research.aspx (accessed 15 February 2012).

Ritchie, J. and Spencer, L. (1994) 'Qualitative data analysis for applied policy research' in Bryman, A. And Burgess, R.G. (eds) Analyzing Qualitative Data, London: Routledge.

Rogers PJ (2008) Using programme theory for complicated and complex programmes. *Evaluation: The International Journal of Theory, Research and Practice,* 14(1): 29–48.

Rosenthal R, Rubin DB (1986) Meta-analytic procedures for combining studies with multiple effect sizes. *Psychological Bulletin,* 99: 400–406.

Rumbelow H (2011) Has the NHS lost a piece of the fertility puzzle? *The Times,* section 2, Tuesday 21 June: 6–7.

Russell J, Greenhalgh T, Boynton P, Rigby M (2004) Soft networks for bridging the gap between research and practice: Illuminative evaluation of CHAIN. *British Medical Journal,* 328(7449): 1174.

Ryan R, Hill S, Lowe D, Allen K, Taylor M, Mead C (2011) Notification and support for people exposed to the risk of Creutzfeldt-Jakob disease (CJD) (or other prion diseases) through medical treatment (iatrogenically). *Cochrane Database of Systematic Reviews*. Issue?. Art No.: CD007578. Available at: http://onlinelibrary.wiley.com/o/cochrane/clsysrev/articles/CD007578/frame.html (accessed 15 February 2012).

Sackett DL, Rosenberg WM, Gray JA, Haynes RB, Richardson WS (1996) Evidence based medicine: What it is and what it isn't. *British Medical Journal*, 312(7023): 71–72.

Sakala C, Mayberry L (2006) Vaginal or Caesarean birth? Application of an advocacy organization-driven research translation model. *Nursing Research*, 55(2S): S68–74.

Sandelowski M (2008) Reading, writing and systematic review. *Journal of Advanced Nursing*, 64(1): 104–110.

Sandelowski M, Barroso J (2002) Reading qualitative studies. *International Journal of Qualitative Methods*, 1: 1–47.

Sandelowski M, Barroso J (2007) *Handbook for Synthesizing Qualitative Research*. New York: Springer.

Sandelowski M, Docherty S, Emden C (1997) Qualitative metasynthesis: issues and techniques. *Research in Nursing and Health*, 20, 365–371.

Sandelowski M. Voils CJ, Leeman J, Crandlee JL (2011) Mapping the Mixed Methods–Mixed Research Synthesis Terrain. *Journal of Mixed Methods Research 1558689811427913*, first published on December 28, 2011 doi:10.1177/1558689811427913

Sandelowski M, Voils C, Barroso J (2006) Comparability work and the management of difference in research synthesis studies. *Social Science & Medicine*, 64(1): 236–247.

Savović J, Harris RJ, Wood L, Beynon R, Altman D, Als-Nielsen B, Balk EM, Deeks J, Gluud LL, Gluud C, Ioannidis JPA, Jüni P, Moher D, Pildal J, Schulz KF, Sterne JA (2010) Development of a combined database for meta-epidemiological research. *Research Synthesis Methods*, 1 (3–4): 212–225.

Schulz K, Chalmers I, Hayes R, Altman D (1995) Empirical evidence of bias: Dimensions of methodological quality associated with estimates of treatment effects in controlled trials. *Journal of the American Medical Association*, 273: 408–412.

Schutz A (1971) *Collected Papers* (Vol. 1). The Hague: Martinus Nijhoff, p. 361.

Shah E (1995) Numbers needed to treat derived from meta-analyses: Pitfalls and cautions. In: M Egger, G Davey-Smith, DG Altman(eds), *Systematic Reviews in Health Care: Meta-analysis in Context*. London: BMJ Books, pp. 386–399.

Shea BJ, Grimshaw JM, Wells GA, Boers M, Andersson N, Hamel C, Porter AC, Tugwell P, Moher D, Bouter LM (2007) Development of AMSTAR: A measurement tool to assess the methodological quality of systematic reviews. *BMC Medical Research Methodology*, 2288-7-10

Shemilt I, Mugford M, Byford S, Drummond M, Eisenstein E, Knapp M, Mallender J, McDaid D, Vale L, Walker D (2008) Incorporating economics evidence. In: JPT Higgins, S Green (eds), *Cochrane Handbook for Systematic Reviews of Interventions*. Version 5.0.1 (updated September 2008). Place: The Cochrane Collaboration.

Shemilt I, Mugford M, Drummond M, Eisenstein E, Mallender J, McDaid D, Vale L, Walker D, The Campbell, Cochrane Economics Methods Group (CCEMG) (2006) Economics methods in Cochrane systematic reviews of health promotion and public health related interventions. *BMC Medical Research Methodology*, 6(55).

Shemilt I, Mugford M, Vale L, Marsh K, Donaldson C (2010a) *Evidence-based Decisions and Economics: Health Care, Social Welfare, Education and Criminal Justice*. Chichester: Wiley-Blackwell.

Shemilt I, Thomas J, Morciano M (2010b) A web-based tool for adjusting costs to a specific target currency and price year. *Evidence and Policy*, 6(1): 51–59.

Shepherd J, Kavanagh J, Picot J, Cooper K, Harden A, Barnett-Page E, Jones J, Clegg A, Hartwell D, Frampton GK, Price A (2010) The effectiveness and cost-effectiveness of behavioural interventions for the prevention of sexually transmitted infections in young people aged 13–19: A systematic review and economic evaluation. *Health Technology Assessment,* 14(7).

Sheppard S., Lewin S., Straus S., Clarke M., Eccles M.P., Fitzpatrick R., Wong G., Sheikh A. (2009). Can we systematically review studies that evaluate complex interventions? *PLoS Medicine,* 6(8).

Shepperd S, McClaran J, Phillips CO, Lannin NA, Clemson LM, McCluskey A, Cameron ID, Barras SL (2010) Discharge planning from hospital to home. *Cochrane Database of Systematic Reviews,* Issue 1. Art. No.: CD000313. DOI: 10.1002/14651858.CD000313.pub3.

Shults RA, Elder RW, Sleet DA, Nichols JL, Alao MO, Carande-Kulis VG, Zaza S, Sosin DM, Thompson RS, and the Task Force on Community Preventive Services (2001) Reviews of evidence regarding interventions to reduce alcohol-impaired driving. *American Journal of Preventive Medicine, Prev Med* 21(4S).

Sibbald SL, Singer PA, Upshur R and Martin DK (2009) Priority setting: What constitutes success? A conceptual framework for successful priority setting. *BMC Health Services Research,* 9: 43. DOI:10.1186/1472-6963-9-43.

Sloper P, Mukherjee S, Beresford B, Lightfoot J, Norris P (1999) *Real Change Not Rhetoric: Putting Research into Practice in Multi-agency Services.* Bristol/York: The Policy Press/ Joseph Rowntree Foundation.

Smith I (1999) Stop TB: Is DOTS the answer? *Indian Journal of Tuberculosis,* 46: 81–90.

Smith V, Devane D, Begley CM, Clarke M (2011) Methodology in conducting a systematic review of systematic reviews of healthcare interventions. *BMC Medical Research Methodology,* 11(15).

Smyth R (2004) Exploring the usefulness of a conceptual framework as a research tool: A researcher's reflections. *Educational Research,* 14: 167–180.

Song F, Parekh S, Hooper L, Loke YK, Ryder J, Sutton AJ, Hing C, Kwok CS, Pang C, Harvey I (2010) Dissemination and publication of research findings: An updated review of related biases. *Health Technology Assessment,* 14(8).

Speller V, Learmonth A, Harrison D (1997) The search for evidence of effective health promotion. *British Medical Journal,* 315: 361.

Spencer L, Ritchie J, Lewis J, Dillon L (2003) *Quality in Qualitative Evaluation: A Framework for Assessing Research Evidence.* Government Chief Social Researcher's Office. London: Cabinet Office.

Staley K, Hanley B (2008) *Scoping Research Priority Setting (and the Presence of PPI in Priority Setting) with UK Clinical Research Organisations and Funders.* Oxford: James Lind Alliance.

Stansfield C, Kavanagh J, Brunton G, Rees R, Thomas J (2010) Search wide and dig deep: Identifying 'views' research for systematic reviews. Paper presented at the Joint Colloquium of the Cochrane and Campbell Collaborations, Keystone, Colorado, USA, 18–22 October.

Stewart R (2007) Expertise and multi-disciplinary training for evidence-informed decision making. PhD thesis. Institute of Education, University of London.

Stewart R, Oliver S, Coppinger C, Cavanagh C (2011) Participative research and policy. *International Public Health Journal,* 3(2): 145–149.

Stewart R, van Rooyen C, Dickson K, Majoro M, de Wet T (2010a) *What is the Impact of Microfinance on Poor People? A Systematic Review of Evidence from sub-Saharan Africa (Technical Report).* London: EPPI-Centre, Social Science Research Unit, University of London.

Stewart RJ, Caird J, Oliver K, Oliver S. (2010b) Patients' and clinicians' research priorities. *Health Expectations.* First published online: 22 December 2010. DOI: 10.1111/j.1369-7625.2010.00648.x.

Straus S, Tetroe J, Graham ID (eds) (2009) *Knowledge Translation in Health Care: Moving from Evidence to Practice.* Chichester: Wiley-Blackwell.

Strike K, Posner G (1983) Types of synthesis and their criteria. In *Knowledge Structure and Use: Implications for synthesis and interpretation.* Edited by: Ward S, Reed L. Philadelphia: Temple University Press.

Summerbell CD, Waters E, Edmunds LD, Kelly S, Brown T, Campbell KJ (2005) Interventions for preventing obesity in children. *Cochrane Database of Systematic Reviews*. Issue 3. Art. No.: CD001871.

Sutcliffe K (2010) Shared decision-making: An evidence-based approach for supporting children, parents and practitioners to manage chronic conditions. Unpublished doctoral thesis, Institute of Education, University of London.

Sutcliffe K, Brunton G, Twamley K , Hinds K, O'Mara-Eves AJ, Thomas J (2011) Young people's access to tobacco: a mixed-method systematic review. London: EPPI-Centre, Social Science Research Unit, Institute of Education, University of London.

Sutcliffe, K, Brunton G, Twamley K, Hinds K, Caird, J, Stansfield C, Rees, R, Dickson K, Thomas J (2011) *Young People's Access to Tobacco: A Mixed-method Systematic Review: Draft Protocol.* London: EPPI-Centre, Social Science Research Unit, Institute of Education, University of London.

Sutton AJ, Jones DR, Abrams KR, Sheldon TA, Song F (2000) *Methods for Meta-analysis in Medical Research.* London: John Wiley.

Sweet M, Moynihan R (2007) *Improving Population Health: The Uses of Systematic Reviews.* Milbank Memorial Fund and Centers for Disease Control. Available at: www.milbank.org/reports/0712populationhealth/0712populationhealth.html (accessed 9 August 2011).

Tashakkori A, Teddlie C (2010) *SAGE Handbook of Mixed Methods in Social and Behavioral Research.* London: Sage.

Taylor C, Coffey A (2008) Innovation in qualitative research methods: Possibilities and challenges. *Cardiff School of Social Sciences Paper*, 121. Cardiff: Cardiff University.

Taylor BJ, Dempster M, Donnelly M (2003) Hidden gems: systematically searching electronic databases for research publications for social work and social care. *British Journal of Social Work*; 33(4): 423–439.

Thomas G (2004) What is evidence? In: G Pring, G Thomas (eds), *Evidence-based Practice in Education.* Maidenhead: Open University Press.

Thomas J, Brunton J, Graziosi S (2010) *EPPI-Reviewer 4.0:Software for Research Synthesis. EPPI-Centre Software.* London: EPPI-Center, Social Science Research Unit, Institute of Education, University of London.

Thomas J, Harden A (2008) Methods for the thematic synthesis of qualitative research in systematic reviews. *BMC Medical Research Methodology*, 8(45).

Thomas J, Harden A, Oakley A, Oliver S, Sutcliffe K, Rees R, Brunton G, Kavanagh J (2004) Integrating qualitative research with trials in systematic reviews: An example from public health. *British Medical Journal,* 328: 1010–1012.

Thomas J, McNaught J, Ananiadou S (2011) Applications of text mining within systematic reviews. *Research Synthesis Methods,* 2(1): 1–14.

Thomas J, Sutcliffe K, Harden A, Oakley A, Oliver S, Rees R, Brunton V, Kavanagh J (2003) *Children and Healthy Eating: A Systematic Review of Barriers and Facilitators.* London: EPPI-Centre, Social Science Research Unit, Institute of Education, University of London.

Thompson SG, Sharp SG (1999) Explaining heterogeneity in meta-analysis: A comparison of methods. *Statistics in Medicine,* 18: 2693–708.

Thomson D, Russell K, Becker L, Klassen T, Hartling L (2011) The evolution of a new publication type: Steps and challenges of producing overviews of reviews. *Research Synthesis Methods,* 1 (3–4): 198–211.

Thorne S, Jensen L, Kearney MH, Noblit N, Sandelowski M (2004) Qualitative metasynthesis: Reflections on methodological orientation and ideological agenda. *Qualitative Health Research,* 14(10): 1342–1365.

Torgerson C, Zhu D (2003) *A Systematic Review and Meta-analysis of the Effectiveness of ICT on Literacy Learning in English, 5–16.* London: EPPI-Centre, Social Science Research Unit, Institute of Education, University of London.

Torgerson CJ, Gorard S, Low G, Ainsworth H, See BH, Wright K (2008) *What are the Factors that Promote High Post-16 Participation of Many Minority Ethnic Groups? A Focused Review of the UK-based Aspirations Literature.* London: EPPI-Centre, Social Science Research Unit, Institute of Education, University of London.

Tripney J (2010) Use of IT strategies to facilitate policy relevant systematic reviews. Paper presented at the Joint Colloquium of the Cochrane and Campbell Collaborations, Keystone, Colorado, USA, 18–22 October.

Underwood L, Thomas J, Williams T, Thieba A (2007) The effectiveness of interventions for people with common mental health problems on employment outcomes: A systematic rapid evidence assessment. In: *Research Evidence in Education Library*. London: EPPI-Centre, Social Science Research Unit, Institute of Education, University of London.

UNICEF (2010) UN Convention. Available at: www.unicef.org.uk/UNICEFs-Work/Our-mission/UN-Convention/ (accessed 24 November 2010).

Vaessen J, Bastiaesen J, Bonilla S, Holvoet N, Leeuw F, Lukach R, Rivas A (2010) The effects of microcredit on women's control over household spending in developing countries. *3ie Synthetic Reviews* – SR003-1

Valentine JC, Cooper HM (2008) A systematic and transparent approach for assessing the methodological quality of intervention effectiveness research: The Study Design and Implementation Assessment Device (Study DIAD). *Psychological Method, 13:* 130–149.

van Zwanenberg P, Millstone E (2005) *BSE:Risk, Science and Governance.* Published to Oxford Scholarship Online: September 2009. DOI:10.1093/acprof:oso/9780198525813.001.0001.

Viergever RF, Olifson S, Ghaffar A, Terry RF (2010) A checklist for health research priority setting: Nine common themes of good practice. *Health Research Policy and Systems*, 8: 36. Available at: www.health-policy-systems.com/content/8/1/36.

Voils CI, Sandelowski M, Barroso J, Hasselblad V (2008) Making sense of qualitative and quantitative findings in mixed research synthesis studies. *Field Methods, 20:* 3–25.

Volmink J, Garner P (2007) Directly observed therapy for treating tuberculosis. *Cochrane Database of Systematic Reviews*, Issue 4. Art. No.: CD003343. DOI: 10.1002/14651858. CD003343.pub3.

Waddington H, Snilstveit B, White H, Fewtrell L (2009) Water, sanitation and hygiene interventions to combat childhood diarrhoea in developing countries. Synthetic Review, no. 001. New Delhi: International Initiative for Impact Evaluation (3ie).

Wallace BC, Small K, Brodley CE, Trikalinos TA (2010a) Active learning for biomedical citation screening. Paper presented at the ACM SIGKDD Conference on Knowledge Discovery and Data Mining, Washington, DC, xx Month.

Wallace BC, Trikalinos TA, Lau J, Brodley C, Schmid CH (2010b) Semi-automated screening of biomedical citations for systematic reviews. *BMC Bioinformatics*, 11(55).

Walter I, Nutley SM, Percy-Smith J, McNeish D, Frost S. (2004) *Improving the Use of Research in Social Care. Knowledge Review* 7. London: Social Care Institute for Excellence and Policy Press. Available at: www.scie.org.uk/publications/knowledgereviews/kr07.pdf (accessed 15 February 2012).

Walters DJ (1996) Powerful politics at the XI International Conference on AIDS. *Canadian Medical Association Journal*, 155(6): 712–713.

Walters DJ (2006) Powerful politics at the XI International Conference on AIDS. *Canadian Medical Association Journal*, 155(6): 712–713.

Ward V, Smith S, Foy R, House A, Hammer S (2010) Planning for knowledge translation: A researcher's guide. *Evidence & Policy,* 6(4): 527–541.

Webler T (1995). Right discourse in citizen participation: An evaluative yardstick. In: O Renn, T Webler, P Wiedelmann (eds), *Fairness and Competence in Citizen Participation: Evaluating Models for Environmental Discourse*. Boston, MA: Kluwer Academic Press.

Weiss C (1991) Policy research: Data, ideas, or arguments. In: P Wagner, CH Weiss, B Wittrock, H Wollmann (eds), *Social Sciences and Modern States: National Experiences and Theoretical Crossroads.*. Cambridge: Cambridge University Press, pp. 307–332.

Weiss CH (1995) Nothing as practical as good theory: Exploring theory-based evaluation for comprehensive community initiatives for children and families. In: J Connell, A Kubisch, L Schorr, C Weiss (eds), *New Approaches to Evaluating Community Initiatives: Concepts, Methods, and Contexts*. Washington, DC: Aspen Institute.

Weiss CH (1997) *Theory Based Evaluation*. San Francisco, CA: Jossey-Bass.

White IR, Thomas J (2005) Standardized mean differences in individually-randomized and cluster-randomized trials, with applications to meta-analysis. *Clinical Trials*, 2: 141–151.

White H (2009) Theory-based impact evaluation: Principles and practice. *3ie Working Paper* No. 3. New Delhi: International Initiative for Impact Evaluation (3ie).

White H (2011) An introduction to the use of randomised control trials to evaluate development interventions. *3ie Working Paper* No. 9. New Delhi: 3ie.

Whiting P, Rutjes AWS, Reitsma JB, Bossuyt PMM, Kleijnen J (2003) The development of QUADAS: A tool for the quality assessment of studies of diagnostic accuracy included in systematic reviews. *BMC Medical Research Methodology*, 2288-3-25.

Wilson PM, Petticrew M, Calnan MW, Nazareth I (2010) Disseminating research findings: What should researchers do? A systematic scoping review of conceptual frameworks. *Implementation Science*. 5(91). DOI:10.1186/1748-5908-5-91. Available at: www.implementationscience.com/content/5/1/91 (accessed 15 February 2012).

Wong G, Greenhalgh T, Pawson R (2010) Internet-based medical education: A realist review of what works, for whom and in what circumstances. *BMC Medical Education*, 10: 12. DOI:10.1186/1472-6920-10-12. Available at: www.biomedcentral.com/1472-6920/10/12 (accessed 12 December 2010).

Wootton B (1959) *Social Science and Social Pathology*. London: George Allen & Unwin.

World Health Organisation (1978) *Declaration of Alma Ata: Report of the International Conference on Primary Health Care*. Geneva: WHO.

World Health Organisation, USAID. Public policy and franchising reproductive health: current evidence and future directions. Guidance from a technical consultation meeting (unpublished) 2007.

World Health Organisation (2010a) *Treatment of Tuberculosis Guidelines* (4th edition). Geneva: WHO.

World Health Organisation (2010b) *Call for Letters of Intent for Evidence Synthesis on Strategies for Implementing Interventions for Achieving MDGs 4, 5 or 6 as Part of the 2010–2011 Implementation Research Platform*. Geneva: WHO.

Zwarenstein M, Schoeman JH, Vundule C, Lombard CJ, Tatley M (1998) Randomised controlled trial of self-supervised and directly observed treatment of tuberculosis. *Lancet*, 352: 1340.

# Index